A KIN

The

H.R.H.
the Duke of Windsor
K.G.

*With a new Introduction
by Philip Ziegler*

First published in Great Britain in 1951

This edition published in 1998 by
Prion Books Limited
32-34 Gordon House Road,
London NW5 1LP

Introduction © Philip Ziegler 1998

ISBN 1-85375-303-3

Cover design by Bob Eames

Front cover image courtesy of Hulton Getty Picture Library
Back cover image courtesy of The Illustrated London News

Picture Plate Credits
Associated Press 4
Hulton Getty 6 (bottom), 9 (top), 11, 13 (top), 14, 15, 16
Illustrated London News 1, 7 (all), 8 (top), 10, 12 (bottom),
        13 (bottom)
Popperfoto 2, 3, 5, 6 (top), 8 (bottom), 9 (bottom), 12 (top)

Printed and bound in Great Britain
by Creative Print & Design, Wales

TO WALLIS

INTRODUCTION

Early in 1947 the Duke of Windsor contracted with Henry Luce, owner of *Time Life*, for a series of articles about his childhood and life up to the outbreak of the First World War. He was pleased to provide himself with an interesting and not too demanding occupation. Though he did not admit it publicly, he also saw the enterprise as a sighting shot for a far more ambitious and controversial undertaking, a full-scale autobiography that would run up to and encompass the abdication.

Predictably, the news that the Duke was thus occupied did not go down too well in the Palace. Alan Lascelles, King George VI's private secretary, who had once revered and now despised the Duke, considered that publication of the articles would be at the best degrading, at the worst positively dangerous. The only way to stop them, he told the King, would be 'by appealing to the Duke's better nature; but I am sorry to say that long experience has convinced me that he has no such feelings when the interests of the Monarchy or the Royal Family conflict with what he imagines to be the interests of himself and the Duchess'.

In the event, no such appeal was made. The articles duly appeared, and proved to be good-tempered and colourful pieces which reflected nothing but credit on the British royal family. Even Lascelles admitted that they were innocuous. But their success, and the pleasure the Duke had derived from digging into the past, whetted his appetite for the next stage. Though he at first hinted that he might end the narrative in 1935, there does not seem to be any real doubt that he always meant *A King's Story* (a working title which in time became accepted as the final version) to be what the name suggested – the history of a reign and of its ending.

To help the Duke write the articles about his childhood, Luce had provided him with the services of Charles Murphy, a journalist of considerable charm and experience. The partnership proved fruitful. The Duke did not need a 'ghost' in the sense that he found it hard to write; on the contrary, he had covered so many thousands of pages over the years with his clear, rather childish script that it sometimes seemed his problem was knowing when to stop. What he lacked was the experience or the inclination to undertake the necessary research, or to organise huge blocks of material into a lucid and readable narrative. This Murphy provided.

While preparing the earlier articles the relationship had been notably harmonious; as work progressed on *A King's Story* strains became apparent. There was a fundamental conflict of interest: Murphy wanted to make the book as sensational as possible; the Duke, who had still not despaired of a *rapprochement* with the Palace which would lead to a job being found for him and the acceptance of his wife as a member of the royal family, was anxious to spare people's feelings and avoid scandal. But there was more to it than that: the Duke began to complain that Murphy was arrogant and tactless; Murphy, with somewhat better reason, accused the Duke of being feckless, idle and irresponsible. In the end the work got done, but Murphy never forgave his employer and had the last laugh when, in collaboration with another of the Duke's bookwrights, J Bryan, he wrote a highly successful and notably indiscreet double biography, *The Windsor Story*.

'My book is not a novel,' the Duke would have explained if he had ever delivered the speech prepared for the annual dinner of the BPRA – the association of British publishers' commercial travellers, 'but it is a romance, and all I can say is that I hope it can end like most fairy tales – "and they lived happily ever after"'. It was the personal elements in the story which particularly offended the starchier members of the establishment in London. 'It is obscene to write gainfully about one's own love affairs', ruled Lascelles indignantly. An autobiography of the Duke of Windsor which dealt with the abdication and yet made no mention of the love affair that led up to it would have made curious reading. In fact he handled his relationship with Mrs Simpson movingly yet with discretion. Lascelles might have had grounds for complaint if the author had indulged in the mawkish and hot-house sentiment which figures so prominently in the correspondence between the Duke and Duchess; the book, however, while leaving no doubt about the strength of the Duke's passion, was dignified and restrained in its telling.

Dignity and restraint were indeed evident throughout the book. His family and their attitude during the abdication crisis were described with sympathy and even approval; the worst he said of them was that 'the iron grip of Royal convention would not release them'. There was no trace of the fearful bitterness which was already apparent in his letters and was to become so marked in the coming years. When his mother died her eldest son described her to his wife as 'hard and cruel... I'm afraid the fluids in her veins have always been as icy cold as they now are in death'. In *A King's Story* he did no more than comment sadly that she 'had been schooled to put duty, in the stoic Victorian sense, before everything else in life'.

The book was deservedly well-received. Though the author eschewed sensationalism he had an intensely dramatic story to tell and a vast supply of material unknown to the reader. He was commendably fair to almost all the parties involved, though his dislike of the Archbishop of Canterbury, Cosmo Lang, was hardly concealed: 'for a prelate he was almost too polished, too worldly. He seemed to me... more interested in the pursuit of prestige and power than the abstractions of the human soul.' The other principal villian in his story was the Prime Minister, Stanley Baldwin – not that the Duke charged him with villiany, only with cunning and a chilling indifference to any sort of human instinct. 'My recollection,' he wrote, 'is not so much that of a generous Prime Minister trying to help his sovereign through a personal situation of almost indescribable complexity as that of a political Procrustes determined to fit his regal victim into the bed of convention.'

It could have been a great deal worse. 'Most dignified, objective and historically valuable', wrote the *Economist*; 'marked throughout by firmness and generosity', judged the *Manchester Guardian*. In spite of Murphy's ministrations, the

Duke's own voice spoke loud throughout. It was his own book, wrote the *Times Literary Supplement*, 'and he has worked with care over every page; even if he has needed help to put his thoughts into words, his own personality, his likes and strong dislikes, spring to life as well as his keen sense of humour.'

'So far as I was concerned,' the Duke concluded his memoirs, 'love had triumphed over the exigencies of politics.' The book is half over before he even meets Mrs Simpson, but without that meeting there would have been no book. There is a sense of marking time before he reaches that fateful encounter early in 1931; the fact that there is not a single mention of Freda Dudley Ward – by far the most important woman in his life between 1918 and 1930 and recipient of some three thousand of his letters – shows how far the story was tailored to suit its resounding climax.

Was it indeed, as some would have one believe, the romance of the century, the story of the king who gave up his throne for love and never doubted that he had made the right decision? Whatever one's view of his decision to abdicate, the reality of the Duke's love is incontestable. Never did he waver in his belief that she was the most wonderful of women, never did he cease to be besotted by her; until the day he died his eyes would follow her around the room, he would fret uneasily and make some excuse to follow if she slipped away.

There is no satisfying answer to the question so many people have asked themselves: 'What did he see in her?' What there is, told in a way which is the more impressive because its author is largely unconscious of what he is revealing, is the explanation of why he needed her; why, when he had found her, it was inevitable that he would put his love before his country. This is not only an important piece of history, it is a fascinating and poignant human document. The Duke called it *A King's Story*; a subtitle might have been: 'The man who was born but not cut out to be King.'

Philip Ziegler
1998.

AUTHOR'S NOTE

The rule of reticence that binds Kings and Princes in a constitutional society is not lightly put aside. It was therefore with some hesitation that I approached the task of writing this book.

However, after the passage of a decade and a half the political passions aroused by the most historically controversial aspect of my career, the Abdication, have long since cooled, and a just perspective of my life and reign should by now be possible. As the years have gone by, error and supposition have persisted; and it has become more and more plain to me that it is my duty to tell the facts as I know them before time and unchallenged repetition have given their sanction to misconceptions. Furthermore, in writing my memoirs at this time I have had the advantage, while they are still alive and their memories unclouded, of being able to draw upon the recollections of many who were close to me in those days.

Mine is the story of the life of a man brought up in a special way, as a Prince trained in the manners and maxims of the nineteenth century for a life that had all but disappeared by the end of his youth. And in retracing the fraying, half-forgotten shreds of memory into the past, I have been astonished by the velocity of change that has characterized the times in which I was destined to live. At fifty-six a man is not inclined to consider himself old. Yet, to a generation that takes for granted nuclear fission, radar, television, psychiatry, and God knows what else, somebody who was dandled on Queen Victoria's knee must appear as an old fogy, a relic to be classed with square-rigged ships, kerosene lamps, and the Prince Albert coat. Indeed, when I add up all that has overtaken mankind since my birth, I feel as if I have been travelling through history in a time machine. And this sense does not depend alone upon my having witnessed the convulsions of two world wars, or upon the social upheavals that have in consequence rent the fabric of Western civilization. Rather it derives from the fact that people born, as I was, on the threshold of the twentieth century grew up among those who could look back along the calmer vistas of the nineteenth, when the tempo of change was much slower.

In the late 1890's men who had fought in the Crimea or who had survived the Indian Mutiny were still in their sixties; the great Liberal leader, Mr. William Ewart Gladstone, who gave up office as Prime Minister to retire from public life the year I was born, had heard the guns saluting the Duke of Wellington's victory over Napoleon at Waterloo. And it is strange to reflect that in the year of my birth twenty monarchs ruled on the Continent of Europe; to-day only six of these empires and kingdoms survive. I was eight years old before I switched on an electric light, had my first ride in a horseless carriage, or listened with mystification to a phonograph. I was a fifteen-year-old naval cadet before I saw an aeroplane in flight, and almost thirty before I heard a spoken message broadcast by radio.

I make no claim to being a man of letters or a social historian. I have attempted to tell here only about the things that affected my life as a Prince, as a King, and as a human being.

No more than any other author, making his first serious foray into writing, could I have completed this work alone.

I wish first of all to express my appreciation to those who have given me their time and valuable information: Lord Beaverbrook, Sir Walter Monckton, Mr. A. George Allen, Sir Duff Cooper, Sir Godfrey Thomas, Sir Ulick Alexander, Sir Owen Morshead, Mr. Herman L. Rogers, Sir John Aird, the Earl of Dudley, Major E. D. Metcalfe, Captain Michael Wardell, Sir Clive Burn, Mr. Theodore Goddard, Commander J. B. Adams, R.N., and Mr. Frederick Finch.

I am especially grateful to Lord Beaverbrook, Sir Walter Monckton, Mr. A. George Allen, Sir Duff Cooper, Mr. Henry J. Taylor, and Mr. Henry G. Walter, Jr., for having read the manuscript and provided constructive criticism; and to Mr. Kennett L. Rawson for his expert assistance in the final editing.

I appreciate the untiring services of Mrs. Elsa Blaisdell, Miss Hilary Gray, Miss Anne Seagrim, Miss Edith Sweeney, Miss Helen Ferrigan, Mrs. Lelia B. Ryan, Miss Betty Barras, Mr. Wendel A. Roos, and Mr. Reynard Biemiller in the physical preparation of the manuscript.

For research and for keeping me straight on innumerable factual details I am indebted to Mr. Victor A. Waddilove, Mr. A. A. Prior, Mr. F. H. Evans, the British Information Services, New York, and especially to Mrs. Monica Wyatt Burnham and Mrs. Hildegard Meili Maynard.

For their advice and co-operation in connection with the articles from which the work grew I wish to thank Mr. Henry R. Luce, Mr. John Shaw Billings, Mr. Daniel Longwell, and the editors of *Life*.

And, above all, I want to acknowledge my great debt to Mr. Charles J. V. Murphy, who has worked with me from the inception of this book.

CHAPTER I

THE LITTLE PRINCE

In Richmond Park there stands a fine, commodious Georgian house called White Lodge. Towards the end of the century this house was the home of my maternal grandparents, the Duke and Duchess of Teck. One summer's evening in 1894, a future King of England, the then Duke of York, was in the library reading, or attempting to read, *Pilgrim's Progress*, while waiting for his first child to be born. It is doubtful whether this ponderous classic could have provided my father with a satisfactory distraction from his anxiety. Nevertheless, he persevered, and all in the proper time the news for which he longed came. In the diary in which were confided the hopes and trials of a lifetime he wrote: "WHITE LODGE, 23rd June—At 10.0 a sweet little boy was born and weighed 8 lb. .... Mr. Asquith [Home Secretary] came to see him."

Somehow I imagine this was the last time my father was ever inspired to apply to me that precise appellation. But in any case, since the star of Mr. Herbert Henry Asquith's political fortunes was in the ascendant, circumstances favoured that my first visitor should be a future Prime Minister of England. It was Ascot Week, and on the night I was born my grandfather, Albert Edward, then Prince of Wales, was host at a ball in the Fishing Temple at Virginia Water, in Windsor Great Park. The news of my advent into the world appears to have caused a slight stir in that gay concourse. Stopping the orchestra, my grandfather announced: "It is with pleasure that I am able to inform you of the birth of a son to the Duke and Duchess of York. I propose a toast to the young Prince." The dance, I like to think, went on.

However, in the midst of the polite rejoicing over my birth, at least one grumpy voice made itself heard. The ageing Scottish Radical, Keir Hardie, rose in the House of Commons to say:

"The assumption is that the newly-born child will be called upon, some day, to reign over this great Empire. But, up to the present, we certainly have no means of knowing his qualifications or fitness for the position. From his childhood this boy will be surrounded by sycophants and flatterers by the score, and will be taught to believe himself as of a superior creation. A line will be drawn between him and the people he might be called to rule over. In due course, following the precedent which has already been set, he will be sent on a tour round the world, and probably rumours of a morganatic marriage will follow, and the end of it will be that the country will be called upon to pay the bill."

The impress of Mr. Keir Hardie's doctrines now lies heavily on Socialist Britain, and even as a prophet of Royal destiny he has proved uncannily clairvoyant. If my life hasn't turned out quite as he predicted, he was certainly right about my being something of a traveller.

Although I have only recently begun to appreciate the fact, it was, at least for people in my stratum of life, a wonderful time to be born. My great-grandmother, Queen Victoria, was in the fifty-seventh year of her glorious reign, having been on the Throne as long as most Britons could remember. At the time of her accession the population of the United Kingdom was only about 25,500,000. The British nation, under the gathering momentum of the Industrial Revolution, had long since recovered from the loss of the American colonies and had largely thrown off the enormous burden of debt left by the Napoleonic Wars. Now, in 1894, aged seventy-five, Queen Victoria looked out over a world not riven and shattered, but prosperous and teeming. Her children and grandchildren ruled the Courts of Europe. The Dowager German Empress Victoria was her eldest daughter "Vicky"; Kaiser Wilhelm II, who only four years before had summarily dismissed the Iron Chancellor Bismarck, was her grandson "William." And the Czar of all the Russias, Nicholas II, was her grandson by marriage—"Nicky." The Empire over which Queen Victoria herself ruled was the most powerful in the world, embracing a quarter of the earth's surface and nearly a quarter of its population. British sea power and financial and commercial influence were nearly everywhere supreme. Ships built on Clydeside carried the hardware of Birmingham, the steel of Sheffield, the cotton of Manchester and Paisley, and the textiles of Bradford and Leeds, into every corner of the world. British capital, its home market saturated, was building the railroads of Argentina and Japan, was opening up the Middle East, and turning to the raw materials of undeveloped Africa. Income tax was measured in the pence on pound sterling. Socialism was scarcely more than a theory.

My christening took place when I was nearly a month old; my great-grandmother drove over from Windsor Castle to preside at the ceremony. In this Royal Family gathering was included the Prime Minister, Lord Rosebery, who, apart from his political leadership of the nation, was a close friend of my grandfather. My twelve god-parents, all related to me in varying degrees, included Queen Victoria herself, my grandparents the Prince and Princess of Wales, my great-uncle the Duke of Cambridge, the Czarevich, soon to become Czar, my maternal grandparents the Duke and Duchess of Teck, and, by proxy, my great-grandparents the King and Queen of Denmark, the Queen of the Hellenes, King William of Württemberg, and the Duke of Saxe-Coburg-Gotha. Of the occasion, Queen Victoria wrote:

"The dear fine baby, wearing the Honiton lace robe (made for Vicky's christening, worn by all our children and my English grand-children) was brought in . . . and handed to me. I then gave him to the Archbishop and received him back. . . . The child was very good. There was an absence of all music, which I thought was a pity. When the service was over I went with Mary to the Long Gallery, where in '61 I used to sit with Dearest Albert and look through dear Mama's letters. Had tea with Mary, and afterwards we were photographed, I, holding the Baby on my lap, Bertie and Georgie standing behind me, thus making the four generations."

I was christened Edward Albert Christian George Andrew Patrick David. The name Edward had already been borne by six English Kings. The inclusion of Albert was in deference to Queen Victoria's desire that all her descendants should bear the name of her beloved husband, Albert of Saxe-Coburg and Gotha, the Prince Consort. I was named Christian after King Christian IX of Denmark, the father of my grandmother Alexandra. The last four names are those of the patron saints of England, Scotland, Ireland and Wales respectively. My family have always called me David.

My grandfather was fifty-two and my father twenty-nine when I was born. I was, moreover, third in the direct line of succession to the Throne; and could I but be conducted safely through the diseases which made the actuarial incidences of a Victorian childhood a good deal more ominous than they are to-day, my parents could reasonably count upon my one day becoming King. I owed this noble yet sombre prospect to the untimely death, only two years before, of an unknown uncle, Albert Victor, Duke of Clarence, who was my father's elder brother, and to whom we referred as Uncle Eddy.

In January 1892, at the age of twenty-eight, Uncle Eddy fell ill and died suddenly at Sandringham of pneumonia. In consequence of this tragedy, my father's life was to be profoundly influenced.

At the time of Uncle Eddy's death, my father was an officer on the active list of the Royal Navy. Indeed, until then he had envisaged an uninterrupted Naval career. Instead of going to Eton or Harrow or Winchester to learn the classics, he had been sent, when only twelve, in company with his brother, to the Cadet Training Ship *Britannia*. This old wooden "ship of the line," broad of beam and painted black and white as were all the ships of Nelson's day, was moored in the River Dart, and had long served as a school for British Naval officers. Two years later, having passed out of the *Britannia*, the two brothers joined their first ship, H.M.S. *Bacchante*, a newly-commissioned fully-rigged cruiser corvette, aboard which they made a cruise to the West Indies. The *Bacchante* was then attached, with four other men-of-war, to what my father always proudly referred to as "the flying squadron"—crack ships chosen to "show the flag" in foreign waters. This mission lasted two years and took the two boys round the world. Thereafter they separated. Uncle Eddy left the Navy and went to Cambridge to broaden the education of a presumed Heir Apparent. He was subsequently gazetted to the 10th Hussars. My father, despite a proneness to seasickness that made hideous for him rough days at sea, carried on in the Navy, serving in various ships on the North America and West Indies station

4

and in the Mediterranean. At twenty-four my father commanded his first ship, Torpedo Boat No. 79, which took part in Naval exercises off Spithead in honour of the visit of his first cousin Kaiser Wilhelm II of Germany. In 1890 he took the gunboat *Thrush* across the Atlantic to Halifax, where he remained a year on the North America and West Indies station. His professional qualifications having been amply demonstrated, he was promoted Commander upon his return, and could look forward to the eventual attainment of Flag rank through all the successive stages. Then Uncle Eddy's death in 1892 changed everything.

My uncle was then engaged to be married to my mother, Princess Victoria Mary of Teck, the eldest child and only daughter of Francis and Mary Adelaide, Duke and Duchess of Teck. "Grandpapa Teck" was born in Vienna in 1837. His father was Alexander, Duke of Württemberg, his mother was Claudine, Countess Rhedey, who was descended from the illustrious Hungarian house of Arpad, which traces its history back to the year 1001. He passed his youth in Austria, entering the service of Kaiser Francis Joseph as an officer in the 7th Imperial Hussars. Like most Viennese, Grandpapa Teck had a flair for music and the arts, and was something of an amateur gardener. Though not yet thirty when he visited Great Britain, his soldierly bearing and artistic accomplishments attracted the favourable notice of Queen Victoria's Court. There he met Princess Mary of Cambridge, daughter of Adolphus, Duke of Cambridge, the son of George III. After a brief courtship they were married, and Queen Victoria gave them apartments at Kensington Palace, where my mother was born in May 1867.

As a young girl my mother saw a good deal of my father and Uncle Eddy, her second cousins. They called her May. Because of her direct line of descent from her great-grandfather, King George III, she was the most eligible Princess of British birth, and Queen Victoria had already singled her out to be a future Queen of England. She and Uncle Eddy were to have been married in February, but he died a month before. My father was very fond of his brother, to whom he had always been close. However, when the first sorrow of his loss had abated Queen Victoria encouraged him to speak up for himself. He proposed to my mother and was accepted. The wedding took place in July 1893, in the Chapel Royal, St. James's Palace, while my great-grand-mother looked on approvingly.

Although my father had commanded *Melampus* the year before, and had been promoted Post Captain on the Active List on his marriage, he now found the path of his hopes for a Naval career increasingly blocked by the demands and responsibilities of his new position. In 1898, as Captain of the *Crescent*, he carried out a last routine cruise in home waters. The entry in my father's diary in which he recorded the breaking of his ties with the Navy, after fifteen years' service, was matter of fact and unemotional. Yet the abrupt and irreversible closing of the door upon a life in which his ambitions and aspirations had been focused since boyhood, no doubt affected him deeply. If the curse of seasick-ness had kept him from ever loving the sea, he did love the Navy. The associations that he had formed in the Service ripened into friendships that lasted all his life; and long after he had taken up his work ashore, the habits and outlook he had formed in the Navy continued to regulate his daily routine. He retained a gruff, blue-water approach to all human situations, a loud voice, and also that affliction so common to Navy men, a damaged ear-drum. From his years at sea he retained a fund of stories and reminiscences, in which he delighted to indulge whenever he had as guest a contemporary who had shared the same experiences. And finally, he never lost the nautical habit of consulting the barometer the first thing every morning and the last thing at night. No matter where he was, on his way to breakfast or to bed, he would make a beeline for this instrument. He would peer at the glass, tap the case sharply to make sure that the needle was not stuck, and set it again.

Tantalizingly dim are the recollections of my childhood. My parents first materialize on the threshold of memory as Olympian figures who would enter the nursery briefly to note, with gravely hopeful interest, the progress of their first-born. For better or for worse, Royalty is excluded from the more settled forms of domes-ticity. While affection was certainly not lacking in my upbring-ing, the mere circumstances of my father's position interposed an impalpable barrier that inhibited the closer continuing inti-macy of conventional family life. Apart from the public and social duties that kept my parents constantly occupied, the fact that they had in their own home so many people to do things for them tended to restrict their association with their children to a fixed and regulated pattern. My first years, therefore, were spent almost entirely under the care of nurses; and one appears to have been to blame for an early unfavourable impression that I made upon my parents. They liked to have the children brought downstairs to be with them at tea-time. I was, after all, their first child, and my father no doubt looked forward to this interlude at the end of the day as an occasion of possible mutual pleasure and understanding. But it seldom turned out that way. Before carrying me into the drawing-room, this dreadful "Nanny" would pinch and twist my arm—why, no one knew, unless it was to demonstrate, according to some perverse reasoning, that her power over me was greater than that of my parents. The sobbing and bawling this treatment invariably evoked understandably puzzled, worried, and finally annoyed them. It would result in my being peremptorily removed from the room before further embarrassment was inflicted upon them and the other witnesses of this pathetic scene. Eventually, my mother realized what was wrong, and the nurse was dismissed.

During their first years of married life, when my parents were Duke and Duchess of York, their London residence was York House, which forms part of that ancient heterogeneous collection of connected buildings known as St. James's Palace. But in those early days we children saw but little of London. Home for us meant Sandringham, my grandfather's property in Norfolk near the south shore of the Wash. There I passed most of my childhood. When the Prince Consort purchased this 700-acre estate for my grandfather more than thirty years before, it was rundown and untended. Over a period of many years the place was gradually cleared and developed; under my grandfather's painstaking supervision houses were built, gardens laid out, and trees planted in profusion until there was eventually created a model property which, like Balmoral, has come to be associated with the relaxations of the British Sovereigns.

Sandringham is a hundred and twenty miles from London. Before the age of automobiles, the slow railway journey across the flat, featureless, fen country of East Anglia took three hours. At the end there was a three-mile drive in a horse-drawn carriage

7

from the station in the little village of Wolferton. Imposing wrought-iron gates—a gift from the people of Norwich—framed the main entrance into the grounds, from which a straight, broad, gravel drive led to Sandringham House, an impressive red-brick structure with a grey slate roof. The front of the "Big House," as we used to call it, looked out over a wide expanse of lawn; on the west side was a terrace, descending to a formal sunk garden. Some have linked the architectural style hopefully with the Elizabethan, but the family never took this theory seriously. It was always our understanding that the secret of the original inspiration had vanished unmourned with the passing of the Victorian architects who designed it.

From the Big House paths wound through the landscaped grounds, where fine trees, standing gracefully in the well-tended lawns, and two ornamental ponds added to the sense of spaciousness. Within the grounds, enclosed by a high stone wall, were large stables for the horses and carriages, and kennels housing an assortment of some fifty dogs. Outside the wall were a pheasantry where thousands of game birds were raised annually, and a vast kitchen garden with glass-houses to supply the voracious demands of the Big House for flowers, fruit, and vegetables. Adjoining the gardens was a dairy farm with a herd of pure-bred milking cows, barns, and a model dairy. Farther on was the stud-farm, with paddocks and loose-boxes for the brood mares from which my grandfather bred his race-horses.

On the west side of the property, separated from the formal grounds by a high wire fence, was a 200-acre park in which stood, only a few hundred yards from the Big House, a small stone church with a clock tower. Here the family worshipped every Sunday. The park eventually lost itself imperceptibly in the great woods that in fact surrounded Sandringham on all sides. There, among the oaks, yews, and the stands of pine, was wonderful cover for game, which extended almost uninterruptedly for some miles through broad rides and bracken clearings down to the tidal margins of the property, where the fens and marshes abounded with wild fowl.

A quarter of a mile from the Big House, on the banks of the lower pond, was a comparatively small house. Known originally as the Bachelors' Cottage, it had been built by my grandfather to accommodate the overflow of guests from his large house-parties. He had given it to my father as a wedding present, and it had been renamed York Cottage for him. For the next thirty-three years it was my parents' favourite residence. My sister and four brothers were all born there—Bertie in 1895, Mary in 1897, Harry in 1900, George in 1902, and John in 1905. And in the process of making room for the successive additions to the family, "The Cottage" had suffered the indignity of improvised enlargements. Downstairs were a small entrance hall, "The Library" (my father's study), two drawing-rooms, a dining-room, and of course, as in all nineteenth-century houses, a spacious billiard-room. Upstairs were first of all my parents' dressing- and bed-rooms, and several other rooms for members of the household. Farther down the passage, with a swinging door in between, were two small, simply-furnished rooms set apart for the children. In these two rooms my conscious memories began. One was called the "Day Nursery." There we had our meals; there I learned to walk, and was taught the alphabet and how to count. The other, and larger of the two rooms, was called the "Night Nursery." In the late 1890's, when there were only three of us children, Bertie, Mary, and myself, we all slept in this one room with a nurse. There we were bathed in round tin tubs filled from cans of hot water, brought upstairs by servants from a distant part of the house. Our windows looked out over the pond, and the quacking of the wild duck that lived there supplied a pleasant pastoral note at dawn and dusk. Across the pond was the park, where small, web-antlered Japanese deer roamed and grazed peacefully.

When very small, I was taken by my parents to visit Queen Victoria at the three places where she spent the greater part of her long life: Windsor, whose historic castle dates from Norman times, and whence my family and my dukedom take their name; and the two houses which she and the Prince Consort had built for themselves, Balmoral, the granite castle in the Highlands, and Osborne, that utterly un-English house in imitation of an Italian villa, near Cowes. Such was the majesty that surrounded Queen Victoria, that she was regarded almost as a divinity of whom even her own family stood in awe. However, to us children she was "Gangan," a childish interpretation of "great-grandmama."

She wore a white tulle cap, black satin dress and shiny black boots with elastic sides. What fascinated me most about "Gangan" was her habit of taking breakfast in little revolving huts mounted on turn-tables, so that they could be faced away from the wind. If the weather was fine, a small low-slung carriage, drawn by a pony led by a kilted attendant, would be at the front door. In this, with a relation or a lady-in-waiting walking alongside, she would ride slowly to one or another of the shelters, where her "Kitmutgars" —Indian servants wearing turbans and gold-braided native livery —would be waiting with her wheel-chair. They would serve her breakfast, which always began with a bowl of steaming hot porridge. Later she would call for her Private Secretary and begin the business of the day.

My great-grandmother always seemed to be surrounded by members of her immense family. She had nine children, forty grandchildren, numerous great-grandchildren, and countless nephews, nieces, and cousins by marriage. In addition to our own Princes and Princesses, there were Hohenzollerns, Hesses, Romanoffs, Coburgs, and Battenbergs; not to mention her collateral relatives in the Royal Houses of Belgium, Holland, Scandinavia, and the Balkan countries. This galaxy of Emperors, Kings, Princes, Grand Dukes, Dukes, and their wives was constantly reappearing over here for family occasions and reunions, or to stay with the great Queen herself, who ruled the Courts of Europe like a matriarch. This somewhat overwhelming collection of foreign relations rotated around her as she moved with the seasons from Windsor to Osborne and from Osborne to Balmoral. From the time I learned to walk, one of my strongest recollections of these visits to "Gangan" was of my being pushed forward to say "how do you do" to Uncle Ernie or Aunt Louisechen. Their greeting would be affectionate, but more often than not the words, though in fluent English, would be pronounced in the guttural accents of their mother tongue.

My first experience of foreign travel came at the age of four when, in 1898, my parents took me to Denmark to visit my father's maternal grandparents, King Christian and Queen Louise. The old King, who was my godfather, was then eighty years old, but still sprightly and active. However, I remember little of that trip save a hazy mental picture of the ferry-boats that carried us back and forth across the Baltic, and of large ornate rooms full of elderly ladies and bearded gentlemen in frock-coats and high stiff collars. In truth, the recollections of my childhood did not really come into focus until a year later, with the outbreak of the Boer War, in the autumn of 1899. In after-years I was to be persuaded by friends of a more Liberal cast that the war in South Africa was an imperialistic one, waged for ends somewhat less noble than were asserted at the time. Be that as it may, the emotion generated by the war registered itself powerfully upon my consciousness. In my family little else was talked about; my three Teck uncles, my mother's brothers, were all away on active service with their regiments. Their letters from the front were read aloud to us, and in the more sensational newspapers favoured by the nurses I would pore over artists' sketches of battles depicting Highlanders dying on the barbed wire in front of Magersfontein or the capture of Royal Horse Artillery guns at Colenso. The shock of the early humiliating reverses suffered by the British regulars in Natal brought home to the public the realization that the existing standing Army, which had hitherto been able to cope successfully with uprisings of Maoris, Zulus, Afridis, and other unruly subjects of the great Queen, could not win the war alone. A call went up for volunteers, and the response was given with a patriotic fervour that permeated every British home.

The normal excitement of coming to London was heightened for us children by the expectation of witnessing some of the martial scenes that had become an everyday occurrence in the great metropolis. When we were taken for a walk in Hyde Park, we would stop to watch the troops drilling on the grass, and a drive through the streets seldom failed to bring us within view of columns of khaki-clad troops with wide-brimmed hats on their way to the front, swinging along behind brass bands banging out the popular tunes of the hour—"Soldiers of the Queen," "Tommy Atkins," and other jingoistic airs. And one spring evening at Balmoral a great bonfire was lit by Queen Victoria's Highland retainers, on top of the hill above the Castle, in celebration of the relief of Ladysmith or Mafeking or some other victory, I do not remember exactly which.

So deeply had the power of Queen Victoria's personality

pervaded the existence of her family that I can no longer differentiate with certainty between what I actually saw of her with my own eyes and what I afterwards heard of her from my parents, or the courtiers who had served her, or what I learned from books. After the death of the Prince Consort, in 1861, the Queen withdrew into widowed seclusion. She went rarely to London, and until her first Jubilee, in 1887, appeared seldom in public. State business she conducted mainly by remote control from Windsor, Balmoral, or Osborne, as she moved from one to the other. Whenever she had to hold a Privy Council, or her Ministers desired an audience, they would be summoned from London. Going to Windsor involved no particular inconvenience; it was only half an hour by train from Paddington. But Balmoral meant an all-night train journey; and while the distance to Osborne was not so great, the prospect of the crossing from Portsmouth in a small naval despatch boat was enough to make many a Minister quail. If the sea was rough, the statesmen would arrive at Osborne for their audiences in a woebegone condition. Still dizzy from seasickness they would be summoned into my great-grandmother's presence, and as often as not their greeting would be a queenly reprimand for having initiated some legislation displeasing to her. It was an impressive demonstration of the power of the Sovereign, never again exercised in quite the same way, which in later years my father liked to describe.

Queen Victoria reigned on for nearly seven years after my birth, long enough to welcome into this world my brother Bertie, now King George VI; my sister Mary, the Princess Royal; and my brother Henry, the Duke of Gloucester. In January 1901, we four children were at York Cottage, quarantined in the nursery for German measles. My parents had gone to London for a great reception given for Lord Roberts, Commander-in-Chief of the British Forces in South Africa, in recognition of his victory over the Boers. While there they were informed by my grandfather that the Queen had had a slight stroke at Osborne, but as her condition was not then considered dangerous, my parents returned to Sandringham for the last days of the shooting season. But because of our quarantine, we were not allowed to see them. A day or two later we were told that they had left hurriedly for Osborne and that "Gangan" was dying.

On January 22 she passed away. The next thing we heard was that my father was ill at Osborne, having broken out with German measles, which he had caught from us. He was therefore unable to accompany the great funeral cortège when it left Osborne for London and Windsor; my mother, who had remained behind to nurse him, asked my grandmother to arrange for us three elder children to see the funeral service in St. George's Chapel at Windsor, and her final interment beside the Prince Consort in the private mausoleum at Frogmore near by.

The occasion was mournful beyond description, and no doubt the elderly and the sage who witnessed it must have shared a sense of the passing of a great era of peace and security, and a foreboding of the inevitable changes that would profoundly affect their own lives while altering Britain's destiny. But at seven one's sense of destiny is limited, and one's appetite for historical pathos even more so. I remember now only the piercing cold, the interminable waits, and of feeling very lost among scores of sorrowing grown-up relatives—solemn Princes in varied uniforms and Princesses sobbing behind heavy crêpe veils.

Less than two months later, my parents, who had meanwhile become the Duke and Duchess of Cornwall, left Great Britain for a tour of the British Empire in the *Ophir*, an Orient liner chartered by the Admiralty. They were away nearly eight months, and during their absence we children were left with my grandparents, the new King and Queen. As their Court moved from Marlborough House to Sandringham, we trailed after it with our governess and nurses. With the coming of summer, we went with the Court to Osborne and later to Balmoral. Although I had been to both places in Queen Victoria's time, I was too young and the visits too short for their unusual characteristics to impress themselves upon me. That year, however, I had a better chance to explore them. Osborne is on the north shore of the Isle of Wight and overlooks Spithead. There my great-grandmother had sought to reproduce the exotic atmosphere of the Italian Riviera. Even as a child I was struck by the ugliness of the house, which has been described as "a family necropolis." The floors of the corridors and passages were inlaid with mosaic; let into the walls were numerous alcoves each displaying in life size a white marble statue of a dead or living

member of "Gangan's" large family. It had long been Queen
Victoria's ardent wish that her eldest son would make it his home.
But by this time my grandfather's affections had been too long
rooted in Sandringham. He had long since made up his mind to
get rid of Osborne when it fell to him; and shortly, in spite of
the mild protestations of some of his sisters, he handed the property over to the State as a convalescent home for disabled officers
of the Boer War.

At Balmoral, Queen Victoria and the Prince Consort had taken
up Scottish Gothic architecture as enthusiastically as they had
embraced the Italian at Osborne. From plans drawn up by my
German great-grandfather they had erected a large turreted
granite castle with a hundred-foot tower. Inside, the carpets,
curtains, and even the chair covers were made of material imitating
the variations of the Stuart tartan. In the Royal Stuart, red is predominant; in the Hunting Stuart, green. There were even a
white "Victoria" and a grey and red "Balmoral" tartan, both
adapted by the Prince Consort. But even here, as at Osborne, my
great-grandmother, in her craving to immortalize her own private
memories and ward off the encroachments of time, had surrounded herself with countless monuments commemorating her
past associations. The hills and crags above the River Dee lent
themselves to a profuse display of these tangible signs proclaiming
her dedication to the dead. On the summit of nearly every hilltop
within sight of the Castle was a granite memorial cairn; and as one
walked around the grounds, every turn of the paths brought one
face to face with a statue erect or recumbent, an inscribed granite
drinking-fountain, or a granite seat dedicated to the memory of
a relation or a faithful retainer or even a pet dog. It was the
same at Windsor and at Frogmore, where the grounds were
similarly bestrewn with bronze and marble tokens of remem-
brance. And commemorative statuettes, miniatures, gold lockets
containing strands of hair, and letter-weights of bronze human
hands modelled after death, crowded the rooms in which she
lived.

If the superimposition of four noisy children upon the Royal
Household during my parents' absence was ever a nuisance, my
grandparents never let us know it. On the contrary, they encouraged our innate boisterousness to such an extent that the

quiet routine of York Cottage suffered a brief but harmless set-back. For a little less than a year our lessons had been in the charge of an Alsatian lady, Mlle Helen Bricka, who had taught my mother as a girl. By now plump and elderly, Mlle Bricka had undoubtedly been an ideal governess for a girl of finishing-school age, but she was to find that the teaching of small and restless boys presented problems outside her previous experience. Nor were her conscientious efforts furthered by the fact that I had passed temporarily under the sunny auspices of a grandfather who remembered how dull his own lessons had been, and of a grandmother who believed that lessons were less important to children than their happiness. If my grandparents were not entertaining distinguished company at lunch, they liked to have us romping around in the dining-room. In this congenial atmosphere it was easy to forget that Mlle Bricka was waiting for us upstairs with her French and German primers. If we were too long in going, she would enter the dining-room timidly to warn us that we were already late for our afternoon lesson. Usually my grandmother would wave her away, and my grandfather, puffing at his cigar, might add reassuringly to the governess, "It's all right. Let the children stay with us a little longer. We shall send them upstairs presently." So unconcerned were my grandparents over the lapses from the schoolroom routine that on taking us to Sandringham for a two-weeks' stay, they left poor Mlle Bricka behind in London lest she should spoil the fun.

CHAPTER II

EDWARDIAN SCHOOLROOM

My parents returned to Great Britain from their Empire tour in the autumn of 1901. King Edward and Queen Alexandra took us children to Portsmouth to greet them. There we embarked in the Royal Yacht *Victoria and Albert* and steamed out to meet the *Ophir* at sea off the Isle of Wight. When the two ships were close enough, we all got into a steam barge from which we were to have boarded the liner. However, it was blowing hard, and my disquiet had meanwhile been somewhat intensified by my grandfather's grave warning that we had better prepare ourselves for a shock. Our parents, he reminded us, had been exposed a long time to the fierce tropical sun and in all probability their skins had turned black. Needless to say, I was horrified, and the pleasure at the prospect of being reunited with my mother and father was overlaid with apprehension concerning the drastically altered state in which I would doubtless find them. Because of the choppy sea, it was impossible to board the *Ophir*. However, a fleeting glimpse of my parents as they waved down to us from the top of the ladder had revealed to my immense relief that their complexions were still as naturally white as I had remembered them.

At Sandringham, at a family reunion for his birthday on November 9, King Edward created my father Prince of Wales. During that winter as he took up his new duties as Heir Apparent he must have given thought to my immediate future, for in the spring a major upheaval occurred in the nursery.

The feminine suzerainty that had ruled there was suddenly terminated when one evening Bertie and I were told that a man named Frederick Finch would wake us up next morning and thenceforth we should be under his care.

16

Frederick Finch, or Finch as we called him, was no stranger to us. He had entered my father's service three years before as nursery footman, which is to say that he brought us our meals, carried the bath water, and performed all the other heavy chores of the nursery. He was then about thirty, handsome, stalwart, and muscular, naturally respectful but without a trace of servility.

In the hierarchy of those who wait upon others, Finch was something of a personality. As a young man his father had been a retainer in the service of the first Duke of Wellington when he died at Walmer Castle in 1852. And, beyond the old-fashioned pride that servants of that generation had in their calling, Finch was a resourceful character armed with convictions no less determined than those of his young Royal charges. In the beginning he was a sort of nanny, who shined my shoes, nursed me when I was sick, made me scrub my hands and face, and knelt beside me in the evening when I said my prayers. After I grew up, Finch became my valet who travelled with me, concocted the pitiless remedy for my first hang-over, and never hesitated to address unsolicited advice when, in his opinion, the developing interests of his young master required it. Still later he became my butler. Now retired and in the eighth decade of his life, he lives in a small cottage in Berkshire with perhaps more than his share of memories.

Not long ago Finch told a friend of mine that as a boy I had been a handful—"or, if I might use the word, a 'stubborn' character." He went on to describe an occasion when he played the rôle of "rod in pickle" to me. Evidently, one afternoon when my sister was supposed to be taking a nap, I had invaded the nursery and on one pretext or another had kicked up a fuss. My father was out shooting, and no one dared disturb my mother. My sister's harassed nurse, "Lala" Bill, stormed into Finch's room crying, "That boy is impossible. If you don't give him a thrashing, I will." Finch marched me off to the bedroom, laid me face down on the bed, and while I kicked and yelled, applied a large hand to that part of the anatomy nature has conveniently provided for the chastisement of small boys. I yelled more out of hurt pride than pain; and, as Finch was leaving the room with the air of a man who had performed a distasteful but inescapable duty, I shouted after his receding back that I would get even with him. "You just wait!" I cried. "I will tell Papa what you have done." Later that evening my mother heard the whole story from the nurse. I was summoned to her room; but instead of my being embraced and mollified I was admonished first for my bad behaviour in the nursery and next for my mistaken judgment that a servant had no right to punish me. I was sent back to Finch's room to apologize for having been such a nuisance. That, at any rate, is Finch's story; for myself I can only say that I have no recollection of the incident and may have rubbed from my memory a scene that I did not choose to remember. Finch is a man of probity; let his testimony stand.

My removal from the nursery to Finch's charge was swiftly followed by another important event in my life. I was then nearing eight, an age at which the sons of upper-class families are usually deposited in a private boarding school to be ruled by the master's rod and the older boys. But my father, who had set ideas about education, had long before decided that Bertie and I should be raised along precisely the same lines that had been laid down some thirty years earlier for himself and Uncle Eddy: we should be taught at home by tutors until we were old enough to join the Royal Navy as cadets.

One morning at York House in the spring of 1902 Bertie and I heard my father stamping up the stairs. He had a noticeably heavy footfall, but on that particular morning it sounded more ominous than ever. Besides, it was not his habit to come often to our room. In some apprehension we watched the door. When it opened, it revealed next to my father a tall, gaunt, solemn stranger with a large moustache.

"This is Mr. Hansell," my father said coldly, "your new tutor," and with that he walked out of the room, leaving us alone with Mr. Hansell, who was no doubt as embarrassed as we were. Hoping to put us at our ease and at the same time to enable himself to gauge where to begin his tutoring, he asked us a few questions as to what we had studied with Mlle Bricka. Our timid answers could hardly have encouraged him.

Of good Norfolk stock, Henry Peter Hansell was born in 1863 and was therefore two years older than my father. He had been educated at Malvern, and at Magdalen College, Oxford, where he had taken Second Class Honours in history. He was a typical English schoolmaster of a period in British life that demanded of its pedagogues not only a broad command of the classics and a sure grounding in Protestant doctrine but also proficiency in several forms of athletics as well. He had played football at Oxford, was a six-handicap golfer, and a crack rifle shot. He thus combined a mild scholarship with a muscular Christianity, accentuated by tweeds and an ever-present pipe. Needless to say, he was a bachelor. While he presided over our table at breakfast and lunch, he dined with my parents and the members of their Household. We called him "Mider," a familiar nickname inspired by our mispronunciation of our formal way of addressing him as "Mister."

Guided in the distance by my parents, these two men, Mr. Hansell and Finch, brought up my three brothers and me until one by one we went off to school. They made a good team, and of the two I sometimes think that the servant had a stronger influence, possessing a livelier comprehension of a small boy's secret interests and ambitions as well as of his inhibitions.

With Mr. Hansell's arrival, our lives took on a more purposeful air. Our lessons, which had previously been more or less spasmodic, were now organized into a methodical routine.

That spring we were mostly in London, bustling with preparations for my grandfather's Coronation, which was to take place at the end of June. Our tutor took advantage of the approach of this great event to teach us history in a lively and practical way. Having attempted to explain to us the symbolism of the Coronation service and the meaning of the pageantry, he often took us around London and showed us round Westminster Abbey, the Houses of Parliament, St. Paul's Cathedral, and other famous landmarks of the metropolis. It was all very exciting. And, if Mr. Hansell's painstaking expositions concerning the significance of the Coronation were somewhat above our young heads, the erection of the great stands in the streets, gaily decorated with scarlet bunting and emblems, and the large encampments of troops in the parks registered themselves most vividly upon my mind.

However, only three days before the Coronation was to take place my grandfather was suddenly seized with an attack of what is now called appendicitis. The operation that was immediately performed upon him was probably one of the first of its kind. And my father liked to tell how he found King Edward next day sitting up in bed at Buckingham Palace enjoying a long cigar. My grandfather's illness, which remained a matter of grave concern for some days, necessitated a postponement of the Coronation. However, in several weeks' time his health had sufficiently improved for the date to be set for August 9. This time there was no hitch. Bertie and I, dressed, I remember, in kilts, and I believe Mary, too, watched the service in Westminster Abbey from a box reserved for the Princesses of the Blood Royal.

The scene inside the Abbey was magnificent, but after a lapse of nearly half a century it is hardly surprising that I have no recollection of seeing the crown actually put on my grandfather's head. But I do remember a story that was afterwards circulated to the effect that the octogenarian Archbishop of Canterbury, Dr. Frederick Temple, stumbled as he mounted the steps of the throne and might have fallen with the crown had my grandfather not reached out and caught him.

Now that my father had become Prince of Wales and next in the line of succession, our family régime began to change in many ways, reflecting his new importance. Two additional residences were handed over to him by the King for his personal use. One was Frogmore, a Georgian house in the Home Park, Windsor; the other was Abergeldie, an old Scottish castle three miles down the River Dee from Balmoral.

We stopped at Frogmore for the first time in the spring of 1902 in the midst of the preparations for the Coronation. It lies about half a mile below the Castle to the south-east, enclosed within its own cosy grounds. The house was almost totally lacking in modern conveniences; there was neither electric light nor central heating. But we children came to love the place, since Windsor opened up new fields for our playtime. There was the seemingly limitless expanse of the Great Park to ride in; and exploring the vast roof of the Castle itself offered endless enjoyment, which was all the more desirable because it was forbidden ground. And finally there was the River, which at Windsor makes a sleepy loop around the slopes below the Castle walls. Either that year or the next my parents acquired a roomy electric launch with a white tasselled awning. In this trim, silent craft my mother took us on many happy voyages on those upper reaches of the Thames past Eton to Maidenhead and down past Magna Charta Island as far as Staines, where luscious green meadows rise gently from the willow-bordered banks.

Like Osborne, Frogmore was a veritable family necropolis. Not only were the grounds studded with family monuments, but the inside of the house was cluttered with enough marble busts and life-size statues to fill a small museum. In this overpowering array was one of Queen Victoria's father, Edward, Duke of Kent, which soon caught our eye. It bore a striking resemblance to one of my parents' footmen, a jovial, rotund man named Smithson. The likeness became irresistible after the head of the bust had been further ornamented with a cloth check cap that Smithson wore off duty. So pleased were we with the effect that we invited my mother to survey the product of our improvisation. She was greatly amused but lectured us gently on the impropriety of making fun of our great-great-grandfather, and also of holding up a servitor to ridicule. Yet the temptation to test the likeness on Smithson himself was too great to be put so lightly aside. One day when my mother had gone out, the cloth cap was restored to the marble Hanoverian head, and the genial footman was called in to have a look at himself. His reaction was not as my mother had led us to expect. He was not offended in the least. Beaming with pleasure, he exclaimed, "The likeness I must say is striking, especially the nose." That the footman was gratified by the discovery of his close facial resemblance to the Royal Duke was evidenced when he was observed not long afterwards standing admiringly before the bust.

A vague disappointment is associated with my memory of that first spring at Frogmore. The ancient game of golf, which had until then been largely confined to Scotland, had at about this time begun to gain popularity among the Sassenachs. Having taken up the game to the extent that his age and corpulence allowed, King Edward had caused a nine-hole course to be laid out at Windsor in the grounds below the East Terrace. My father had also become interested in the game; and at the suggestion of one of his friends, the Duke of Roxburghe, who was his guest for Ascot Week, the famous North Berwick professional, Ben Sayers, was sent for. The three of them used to play on the Castle course late each afternoon after the races, and often my father pressed me into service as his caddy for a shilling a round. One day, seeing me staggering under my load, Ben Sayers suggested mildly to my father that it might be a good thing for Bertie and me to start learning to play golf under him. Disregarding the fact that a good iron shot cannot be played without taking a divot, my father brushed off the suggestion: "If we let those boys on the fairway, they will only hack it up." Although my father relented to the extent of letting us play on the course in the park at Sandringham, he saw little purpose in our having professional instruction, perhaps because he had already decided that a game that could make a man so unaccountably mad at himself ought not to be encouraged. In consequence, I have never quite overcome the faulty swing I developed in the absence of expert correction.

That same summer in August, directly after the Coronation ceremony, our parents took us to Scotland, where we moved into Abergeldie Castle. In the matter of creature comforts it was no improvement on Frogmore. Its ancient granite walls were covered with a gritty white stucco that could be ripped off with one's fingernails. Its most conspicuous architectural feature was a tall stone tower surmounted by a wooden cupola infested with bats and haunted, we were led to believe, by the ghost of Kittie Rankie, an unfortunate creature who had been burned at the stake as a witch on the hilltop overlooking the Castle. The wild Highland scenery of Deeside was in sharp contrast to the noble, well-tended beauty of Windsor and the wooded tranquillity of Sandringham; and the gurgling of the swift-running river splashing over the granite boulders scattered along the length of its shallow bed filled the rooms of the old house with a sound I loved to hear.

But the attraction of Abergeldie for my father was the grouse-shooting and the deer-stalking. He was considered one of the best game shots in the country; during the six weeks that we were in the Highlands he spent every day but Sunday banging away with shotgun and rifle. It was some years before Bertie and I were judged old or strong enough to endure these long days on the grouse moors or the deer forest. My mother, who was left behind, filled many of her days taking us children for carriage rides along the forest roads with a picnic tea that we brought in a basket and spread out on the heather in some picturesque spot. Otherwise, when we could escape from Mr. Hansell, we were left pretty much to our own devices. Spanning the Dee near the Castle was a foot suspension bridge that swayed on windy days; we liked to race across it at such times, relishing the sense of danger imparted by the motion. We also carried to the centre of the bridge the largest stones we could lift, which we would drop into the rapids for the splash they would make.

Eventually that exciting summer came to an end. We children were sent back to York Cottage to settle down for the autumn and winter to our first serious work with Mr. Hansell. However, the quietude of Sandringham was soon to be interrupted by an imperial descent of the Kaiser, for the sixty-first birthday of the King, his uncle. His hostile attitude towards the British during the Boer War had made for coldness in the family, which did not relish the prospect of being nice to "William," as might otherwise have been the case. There was a great influx of important guests to the Big House for the birthday party and the daily shoots, but we children were kept in the background. However, I do remember my father's remarking with the appreciation of an expert how well the Kaiser shot in spite of the handicap of a left arm that had been withered from birth.

Meanwhile Mr. Hansell had had a chance to size up the difficult educational problem with which my father had confronted him. It had been all very well for my father to rule that Bertie and I should be educated exactly as he and his elder brother had been. But as a schoolmaster by profession Mr. Hansell realized that since the 1870's ideas had changed as to the best way of preparing boys for life. From the outset it was his personal conviction that the proper place for us was a preparatory school, where we would have been projected into the normal, rigorous, and competitive world of other boys of our age. As this was not to be, he set himself with uncommon tact and resourcefulness to the task of reproducing at York Cottage in a school for two as much of the atmosphere and discipline of a boarding school as he could devise.

Mr. Hansell organized a schoolroom on the second floor. He imported two standard school desks with hinged lids and attached chairs, with hard wooden seats and straight backs. A blackboard, a set of wall maps, and, of course, an ample stock of arithmetic and history books, grammars, and copy books with lined pages completed the equipment.

Next he drew up a daily time-table of work designed to make us follow the regime of the ordinary schoolboy. Finch woke us at seven and saw to it that we were dressed and at our desks half an hour later for three-quarters of an hour's "preparation"—homework—before breakfast. In the winter it would still be dark, and I dreaded entering that cold room to grapple with some unfamiliar problem on an empty stomach. At 8.15 Mr. Hansell would appear to take us downstairs to breakfast, and by nine we were back at our desks to study until lunch, with an hour's break in the forenoon for play. After lunch he would take us out, perhaps for a walk in the woods or to kick a football on the lawn. Then we would go back to our lessons for another hour, always stopping at tea-time for muffins, jam, and milk—our last meal of the day.

If my parents were at the Cottage, they would be having their tea at the same time in the drawing-room, with whichever members of the Household were "in waiting." Freshly scrubbed and with hair combed, we would be summoned downstairs. My father never lingered long over his tea. He would stride off alone to the Library, where he would remain occupied—perhaps with his stamp collection, already becoming famous, or his correspondence, or writing up his game book, or reading *The Times*—until dinner. Sometimes my mother, with the lady-in-waiting at the piano, taught us folk-songs from the *Scottish Song Book*. The ones I remember best, strangely enough, are "Old Black Joe," "Suwannee River," "The Camptown Races," " Oh, My Darling Clementine," "Funiculi, Funicula."

It was my mother's habit to rest in her boudoir before dinner, and this hour she saved for us. At 6.30 we were called in from the schoolroom. She would be in negligée resting on the sofa; and, when we were gathered around her on little chairs, she would read and talk to us. Looking back upon this scene, I am sure that my cultural interests began at my mother's knee. The years that she had lived abroad as a young girl had mellowed her outlook; and reading and observation had equipped her with a prodigious knowledge of Royal history. Her soft voice, her cultivated mind, the cosy room overflowing with personal treasures were all inseparable ingredients of the happiness associated with this last hour of a child's day.

Being also practical by nature, my mother utilized the time to teach us how to make woollen comforters for one of her many charities. She supplied each of us with a wooden ring into which were fitted upright brass pegs. While she read, we busily looped the wool yarn around each peg, thus forming, by means of a succession of crochet stitches, a comforter five feet in length.

As a small boy I enjoyed making these things more than did my sister or my brothers. Many years later, during an enforced period in bed while recovering from a riding accident, I became quite proficient with a crochet-hook. When at the beginning of the last war I was attached to a British mission with the French Army and was obliged to make long motor trips through the zone of operations, I returned once again to my gentle diversion, as a means of killing time. This was during the period of the so-called "phony war," and I was understandably discreet about my hobby at first. It would hardly have done for the story to get around that a major-general in the British Army had been seen bowling along the roads behind the Maginot Line crocheting. Nevertheless, crocheting did for me what detective novels do for statesmen. It relaxed my mind and, incidentally, provided a number of anonymous but not unworthy samples for a charity that my wife had organized for the French Army.

Such was my mother's pride in her children that everything that happened to each one was of the utmost importance to her. With the birth of each new child, Mama started an album in which she painstakingly recorded each progressive stage of our childhood—the dates upon which "Baby cut his [or her] first tooth," or took "his [or her] first step," with a lock of hair inserted on the day of the first haircut.

My boyhood was a strict one because my father was strict in his own life and habits. He was a perfect expression of the Victorian and Edwardian eras, those closely joined epochs to which his immediate forbears had lent their names. He had the Victorian's sense of probity, moral responsibility, and love of domesticity. He believed in God, in the invincibility of the Royal Navy, and the essential rightness of whatever was British. At the same time, he had the Edwardian flair for clothes and fondness for sport—from partridge- to tiger-shooting, from deer-stalking to fishing. He was, as I have already implied, a fine shot; and there were few men in the country who could teach him anything about sailing a boat.

Yet, through everything cut the sharp concept of duty summed up for him in the precept that, copied in his round hand, he kept on his writing-desk: "I shall pass through this world but once. Any good thing, therefore, that I can do or any kindness that I can show any human being, let me do it now. Let me not defer nor neglect it, for I shall not pass this way again." These lines are attributed to an American Quaker of the early nineteenth century, Stephen Grellet. I was made while very young to memorize them, and they were often to influence my actions in later life. If through my family's position my childhood was spared the mundane struggle that is the common lot, I nevertheless had my full share of discipline. For the concept of duty was drilled into me, and I never had the sense that the days belonged to me alone.

Combined with his stern sense of duty was an almost fanatical sense of punctuality. Only through rare accidents was he ever known to be late. His days were organized with railway precision—even to the habit of a post-luncheon nap, a carry-over from his watchkeeping days in the Navy. Such was the power of my father's will that he could fall asleep instantly and wake up exactly fifteen minutes later, just as if an alarm-clock had gone off inside his head.

I have often felt that despite his undoubted affection for all of us, my father preferred children in the abstract, and that his notion of a small boy's place in a grown-up world was summed up in the phrase, "Children should be seen, not heard."

It was once said of him that his naval training had caused him to look upon his own children much as he regarded noisy midshipmen when he was captain of a cruiser—as young nuisances in constant need of correction. No words that I was ever to hear could be so disconcerting to the spirit as the summons, usually delivered by a footman, that "His Royal Highness wishes to see you in the Library." My father's study was in a sense his "Captain's Cabin," and one never knew on being summoned there what one might be in for. He might wish to show some new stamps he had just acquired or to give me some knick-knack he had brought back from his travels. But more often we would be called to account for some alleged act of misbehaviour. Bertie and I—and mostly I—came in for a good deal of scolding for being late or dirty, for making a noise on some solemn occasion, or for wriggling and scratching in church. And inevitably, just as my mother's room came to represent a kind of sanctuary at the end of the day, so the Library became for us the seat of parental authority, the place of admonition and reproof.

It was a small and cheerless room with two windows opening upon the drive. Its furnishings consisted of a large desk and a well-worn leather sofa, where he used to sit and read. Although the room was called the Library, the most conspicuous item was a closet with a glass door in which were racked his treasured shotguns. The walls were covered with a red fabric, the identical material that was used in the distinctive trousers worn by the French Army of that period. Some of the last surviving samples may still be seen in the Musée des Invalides in Paris. My mother never knew where my father got the idea that this army-trousers material would make an original kind of wall-covering nor whether his intent was to evoke a mildly martial atmosphere or merely to warm up a room with a northern aspect. But my father loved this red cloth; and when, one summer, the moths reduced it to shreds, he was heartbroken over having to remove the remnants.

Yet, often as I dreaded these summonses to the Library, I have reason to be grateful to my father. One theme that he inculcated into us from the start was that we must never get the idea that we were different from, or better than, other people. To be sure by *other people* he meant the children of the well-born. In any case he was determined that whatever else might come of us we should not be prigs or snobs. And he literally pounded good manners into us, hammering home the old-fashioned, and I regret to observe, fast-vanishing rules of courtesy. We were made to get up whenever ladies or older people entered the room and not allowed to sit down until they had first done so. And, whenever we walked with him about Sandringham or Balmoral or Windsor, he insisted on our being punctilious in returning the salutations of the estate employees. The laws of behaviour as revealed to a small boy tended to be ruled by a vast preponderance of "don'ts." But with Mama life was less severe. Although she backed up my father in all matters of discipline, she never failed to take our side whenever in her judgment he was being too harsh with us.

In the spring of 1903 my family changed its London residence. My grandparents having moved into Buckingham Palace, Marlborough House became vacant and was available for my father. Designed by Christopher Wren for the famous Sarah, Duchess of Marlborough, it stands in a spacious garden surrounded by a wall. On one side it is separated from St. James's Palace by a narrow street; on another it faces the Mall. My grandparents had lived there, when in London, ever since their marriage forty years before. During that period, as Queen Victoria had deliberately isolated herself from the life of the metropolis, leaving the Palace empty, Marlborough House had become the focal-point of diplomatic and political circles and the glittering society that rotated around Albert Edward and Alexandra, Prince and Princess of Wales.

We moved there from York House that April. While my mother, who loves London, was delighted with her new and grander surroundings, I accepted the change with mixed emotions. Even at that early age, I had begun to dislike the noise and restriction of the streets; and, for all the space that the garden provided as a playground, I never ceased to long for the greater freedom and liberty of our country homes. That preference for the country has remained with me throughout my life, and it has been my good fortune to possess the means to indulge it.

At Marlborough House we children lived on the third floor. From Bertie's room and mine one could see Buckingham Palace beyond the Green Park; and we could also hear across St. James's Park, if the wind was right, the boom of Big Ben striking the hours. It was then and yet remains one of the finest houses in London, and its spacious drawing-rooms lent themselves to sumptuous entertainment. But what impressed me most about the interior decoration were the La Guerre mural paintings on the walls of the great saloon and the two main staircases, depicting the great Duke of Marlborough's victories. These fascinated me, for around the heroic and commanding figures of the Duke and his generals lay the debris of battle: dead and dying soldiers and horses and shattered cannon. The agonized expression of some of the wounded redcoats, painted with fine realism, haunted my boyhood dreams of a warrior's life; and the pathetic glint in the eye of a maimed animal is still imprinted on my memory.

I was now almost nine years old; and my mother, thinking the time had come for us three older children to polish the somewhat rustic ways of Sandringham, decided that a good beginning would be to learn the first simple steps of dancing. After discussing the matter with friends who had children of the same age, she formed a class of twenty to thirty girls and boys; and the doyenne of the Victorian dancing mistresses, Miss Walsh, was engaged to teach us. The class met twice a week, sometimes in the dining-room of Marlborough House, or else at one or another of the great houses of London. The little girls all had long hair, and their short dresses were pulled tight at the waist with silk sashes tied with a bow at the back; all the little boys wore Eton suits—surely one of the most uncomfortable rigs ever invented to confine the restless energy of boys. A lady at the piano provided the music; Miss Walsh, whom I remember as being decidedly stout yet surprisingly light and quick on her feet, showed us the intricate steps of the polka, the waltz, and the Highland schottische. These afternoons with Miss Walsh could hardly be described as a leap into gregariousness; even in their most abandoned moments they never approached the spontaneous fun of a children's party. But at the same time those dancing classes meant something to the three of us: they lifted us out, if only briefly, from our walled-in life in London and brought us together with other children of our own age.

Casting about for some additional way of filling our free hours in London, Mr. Hansell tried at this time to interest us in a mild form of cricket. A long, green fibre mat was acquired, which, whenever we played, was unrolled and laid on the lawn to protect the grass. We played with a soft ball; and a net screen was rigged behind the wicket to catch the balls missed by the batsmen, which otherwise might have been lost in the soot-begrimed shrubbery. Like most schoolmasters of that era, Mr. Hansell knew all about cricket and was imbued with the hallowed tradition of the game. Sometimes Finch would be called in to bowl to us; and my father, if in the mood, would take his turn at the wicket. To be sure we watched his determined efforts with full respect, but Bertie and I were never too sure that he was much more successful at the game than we were. While my father, the tutor, and the valet could have a good time playing together, Bertie and I, owing to our inexperience and even more to the wide discrepancy in age between us and them, always felt at a disadvantage; and on that account I, for one, was never able to work up much enthusiasm for the Marlborough House version of the game. In the hope of stimulating our flagging zest, Mr. Hansell took us to Lord's and the Oval to watch important matches. I recall being introduced somewhat later to Dr. W. G. Grace, one of the immortals of the sport, a bearded giant of a man who practised occasional medicine as an avocation. But cricket must be put down as one of Mr. Hansell's failures, though through no fault of his own. Whatever interest for it he might have inspired in us was undone later, at least for me, at school, where interminably long, dull afternoons were by tradition given over to a game I found too slow for my temperament.

Another thing that I remember about our move to Marlborough House was the entrance into my father's service of two Scots—Henry Forsyth and Findlay Cameron. Kilted retainers had been a Household tradition in the Royal Family ever since Queen Victoria's and the Prince Consort's first joyous discovery of the Highlands. My grandfather had had a kilted valet as well as a piper who awakened him in the morning with the skirl of the pipes and who sometimes, if there were guests, marched around the table playing Highland tunes. Now that my father had in his turn become Prince of Wales he carried on this tradition by engaging two veterans of the Boer War recently discharged from the Army.

Forsyth had been a pipe major in the Scots Guards, which is to say that he had risen to warrant rank and become the senior piper in one of the battalions. He had been born in Edinburgh in humble circumstances, and I recall my surprise when he told me one day that when he was my age he had never worn shoes even in winter. Every morning just before eight, carrying his pipes, the kilted Forsyth appeared in the garden under my father's window. On the stroke of the hour the morning silence would be rent by the skirl of a Scottish march while the piper strode back and forth playing under my father's window. My father took this reveille for granted, but I always thought that it was a trial to my mother, who no doubt felt that there were gentler ways of being roused to the day's obligations.

Cameron was a different sort. He came, I believe, from Inverness-shire, the home of the clan whose name he bore; and he had seen twenty-one years' service appropriately enough with that famous regiment, the 79th Queen's Own Cameron Highlanders. He had fought in the Sudan and South Africa and was reputed to possess more medals than any other British soldier of his day. Robust and erect of figure, with a ruddy complexion and an imposing handle-bar moustache, he became a footman; and, when dressed in his kilted livery with his row of medals banked on his left chest, he seemed in our youthful eyes the undoubted hero of many wars. This awed impression was one that Cameron himself never attempted to minimize. He had an endless fund of hair-raising stories about his personal exploits; his accounts of hand-to-hand fights with Fuzzy-Wuzzies or of desperate last stands when he shot it out with the Boers were masterpieces of self-glorification. In time my mother was to suspect that Cameron carried the Scotsman's well-known preference for whisky to a point that made him a dubious example for impressionable young Princes. Understandably, he never became altogether the model footman. I well recall an occasion when, either through inattention or else as a result of having perhaps imbibed a trifle more than the usual customary nip of his favourite restorative, he tripped as he entered the dining-room, catapulting across the room a large ham that missed one of the guests by inches.

Happily we children were oblivious of the minor blemishes that may have marred Cameron as a servant. To Bertie and me he and Forsyth personified all that was exciting and stimulating in the world outside the quiet purlieus of Sandringham and the walled garden of Marlborough House.

When we were in London, nothing open to Bertie and me could equal the thrill of watching with Forsyth and Cameron the Changing of the Guard. If the King was not in residence at Buckingham Palace, the ceremony always took place in Friary Court, St. James's Palace, across the street from Marlborough House. About 10.30 in the morning while we were doing our lessons with Mr. Hansell, the sound of the band leading the new guard through Marlborough Gate would reach the schoolroom.

Our tutor was understanding; with a smile he would release us to dash out across the garden and up a flight of steps to the top of the wall facing Friary Court, in time to see the new guard in "guard order"—red tunics; pipe-clayed, buff belts and equipment; and bearskin caps—arrive to relieve the old. The two old soldiers, having been charged with keeping an eye on us, were usually there waiting. Forsyth taught us to salute the Colour as it was carried by. The picturesque ceremony filled us with admiration; and on observing our intense interest in the precision of the drill and the flawless handling of arms, Cameron was inspired to organize Mary, Bertie, and me into a squad. Armed with wooden guns, we paraded every morning with Cameron in the rôle of drill sergeant and Forsyth marching ahead playing his pipes. It was great fun, especially at Sandringham, where the King walked down sometimes from the Big House to inspect us.

That summer of 1903 my parents gave a great ball for the King and Queen. For days ahead the normal routine of the household was upset by the preparations. Then one day a small army of workmen invaded the garden to erect two large tents on the lawns, one for a temporary ballroom and one for refreshments. Our first distress over the violation of our playground was soon succeeded by an absorbing interest in the method and speed with which the work was completed. We made friends with the carpenters, who let us help them with small chores, no doubt in the hope of getting us out of the way.

Although to us "home" always meant Sandringham, it thereafter became with Marlborough House, Frogmore, and Abergeldie but one of the four residences between which my family migrated with the seasons like a flock of birds. From that time on, my father, a man of fixed habits, settled into an annual routine that became as regular, as unchanging, as permanent, it seemed, as the revolution of a planet in its orbit.

January would always find our family at York Cottage for the last weeks of the pheasant shooting. Then in February, my parents, leaving us behind with Mr. Hansell, would go to London, where my father would be occupied until the end of March with the innumerable and varied duties that are the business of the Heir Apparent—attendance at levees, civic and charitable banquets, the chairmanship of hospitals, the State visits of foreign rulers, and the entertainment of Dominion and Colonial visitors. We all came together for Easter. Either my parents returned to York Cottage or we would join them at Frogmore for the first weeks of the English spring. Throughout May and June we were always in London for the Season; the succession of balls, garden parties, presentations at Court, being interrupted only by a ten-day visit to Frogmore in June for Ascot.

My mother, who was a poor sailor, disliked yachting and had more than her fill of shooting parties at Sandringham. So, when my father departed on his round of summer sport, she would repair to Frogmore with us children for a quiet rest. Although we missed my father, his absence proclaimed somewhat of a let-up in the strict régime he enforced when at home. First we would hear of him at Goodwood House, stopping with the Duke of Richmond for the races; and next from Cowes, yachting with the King. From August 12—"the Glorious Twelfth"—onward we would hear from him as he visited the private grouse moors of his friends—perhaps at Abbeystead in Lancashire with Lord Sefton, or with the Duke of Devonshire at Bolton Abbey, or at Studley Royal with Lord Ripon, and then at Moy Hall in Inverness-shire, the ancestral estate of the Mackintosh of Mackintosh. We always had a happy time with my mother at Frogmore; and, although we liked Scotland, it was with some regret that we would board the train for Abergeldie to join my father at the end of August.

By early September, the best of the grouse shooting being over, my father would spend most of his days "on the hill" deer-stalking. By that time the weather would have turned colder, and the first snow would have whitened the hilltops before we returned to London during the second week of October. With Mr. Hansell, Finch, and the nurses we children would continue on to the Cottage, while my parents stayed at Marlborough House. However, first the partridge and then the early pheasant shoots would bring them to Sandringham at intervals. And Christmas always found the whole family reunited there, with my grandparents at the Big House, and the whole estate wearing a festive air.

CHAPTER III

THE SQUIRE OF SANDRINGHAM

ALL this moving about was not without its compensation. Our recreational hours in Scotland, for example, were naturally spent in surroundings and with people different from those with which we were familiar at Windsor or at Sandringham, and so in a superficial way we began to have a wider understanding of our country than was the lot of most children. London, of course, offered the most spectacular contrast of all. During our sojourns there Mr. Hansell made a practice of varying our lessons by taking us on educational visits to the famous historical buildings and cultural institutions of the great city: the Houses of Parliament, the Tower of London, the British Museum, the Natural History Museum, and the Imperial Institute. When I reflect to-day upon the publicity that in my later years attached to my every movement, I recall with wonder and appreciation the ease with which we were able to move about in public places. The thought occurs to me that one of the most inconvenient developments since the days of my boyhood has been the disappearance of privacy. I grew up before the age of the flash camera, when newspapers still employed large staffs of artists to depict the daily events with pen sketches. This artistic form of illustration seldom achieved the harsh or cruel accuracy of the camera lens, nor could it match the volume and mobility of the present-day photographer dogging his often unsuspecting victim or waiting in ambush for a candid shot. Because our likenesses seldom appeared in the Press, we were not often recognized on the street; when we were, the salutation would be a friendly wave of the hand or, in the case of a courtier or family friend, a polite lifting of the hat.

Although this sight-seeing was sometimes hard on our feet and

harder still upon the resources of our curiosity, Bertie and I nevertheless preferred it to the immobile instruction of the schoolroom.
However, we began to notice that the places we were taken to
visit included a high preponderance of churches. This observation
led presently to the surprising discovery that our tutor had a
secret hobby: he loved churches, not so much as a worshipper,
but rather as a connoisseur of ecclesiastical architecture. He loved
to wander around the famous cathedrals studying with a knowing
eye the Norman arches, flying buttresses, or the design of the
nave and quality of the stained-glass windows. But far from being
alone in this unique speciality, he was, we observed with still greater
surprise, a member of what appeared to be a club of cathedral
lovers. Every Easter he would leave us to join his friends in a pilgrimage to some cathedral town. We children considered this a
strange and almost morbid diversion; yet, we were obliged to
be passive and reluctant participants, inasmuch as Mr. Hansell,
whenever he took us on a day's outing, would sooner or later
head with a collector's zeal for a church possessing some architectural detail that he wished to examine. As we patiently followed
his eager, retreating figure through a succession of vast, dank,
eerie naves and cavelike crypts, I more than once found myself
longing for the warm sunshine outside.

Yet, for all his fascination with cathedrals and churches themselves, Mr. Hansell did not seem to be so interested about what
went on inside them. My grounding in religious matters was
therefore confided, for the most part, to my father's old tutor,
Canon John Neale Dalton of St. George's Chapel, Windsor.
This formidable cleric was then sixty-four years old; and his
stooped, bony frame might have been quarried from the same
old grey stone as the Castle itself. Some thirty years before,
while a young curate at Whippingham, near Osborne, he had
been selected by Queen Victoria herself to tutor my father and
his elder brother before they joined the training ship *Britannia*.
He was their companion and guide on the round-the-world
cruise in H.M.S. *Bacchante*, the narrative of which he faithfully
set forth in a two-volume 1,400-page work that even my father
conceded must certainly be one of the dullest books ever written.

It is an interesting commentary upon the flexibility of British
society that this man who played so influential a part in moulding

the conservative character of my father should himself have produced under the shadows of Windsor Castle a son, Hugh Dalton, who became Chancellor of the Exchequer in a Socialist Government. However, Canon Dalton could not be held responsible for his son's espousal of the doctrine of public ownership of the means of production, distribution, and exchange any more than he could be blamed for my failure to become deeply versed in the intellectual bases of my Protestant faith, of which, by virtue of my birth, I was destined one day to be the "Defender." Dogma and theological questions never held my interest for long. In that respect I resembled my father, who, while he liked to read the Bible from time to time and never missed going to church every Sunday— because it was the right thing to do—and loved the old, familiar psalms and hymns, nevertheless used to say that much in religious doctrine was over his head. For myself I accepted humbly the Articles of Religion of the Church of England and memorized the Ten Commandments (although they appeared to have little relevance to my young, sheltered life); and even if my childish mental image of God was vaguely identified with the sun and the giving off of light, that does not mean that my mind was insensitive to deeper meanings.

I no longer remember just when Mlle Bricka faded out of the picture. She lingered on, I think, for a little while after Mr. Hansell's arrival, to continue the French lessons. About this time Mary was old enough to leave the nursery, and her life underwent a transition similar to ours. A "Finch" was provided for her in the person of a German maid, Else Korsukawitz, a buxom and kindly woman who soon became a great favourite in the family. And the "Mr. Hansell" in whose care Mary was placed was a young French governess, Mlle José Dussau, who like her masculine counterpart was unmarried and a Protestant. Mlle Dussau had a sharp and agile tongue, and Bertie and I were soon to suspect that she had but little use for small boys. No doubt it was only a coincidence, but the fact was soon ruefully noted by Bertie and me that her entry into the family had been followed by more frequent falls from our parents' graces. Minor infractions that previously had passed off without detection now became known with an accuracy bordering on the clairvoyant; and the summonses to the Library came more often.

The explanation for our plight was soon forthcoming. Mlle Dussau was a far stricter disciplinarian than either Mr. Hansell or Finch, who were more inclined to take a tolerant view of our pranks. She must have told Mary that the discipline in our school-room left much to be desired. Mary adored her new governess and, no doubt wishing to please her, began to our surprise to fall in with this prudish attitude; her threat, "I'll tell Mama," although seldom carried out, had a powerfully subduing effect upon us. In this manner Bertie and I discovered for the first time the power that little girls the world over are able to exert over their brothers. The realization that we were at her mercy awoke in us a strong aversion for the foreign interloper who had thus disrupted a previously happy alliance, and our aversion turned into hostility when Mlle Dussau undertook to make French the compulsory language whenever she was present at our meals. Mary, who was rapidly mastering the language under the daily instruction of her exacting teacher, was able to join to some extent in the exchanges between Mlle Dussau and Mr. Hansell, who, to our intense disappointment, welcomed the opportunity, so he said, to brush up his "rusty" French. For my brother and me, these meals were humiliating ordeals. Far from firing us with enthusiasm for Mlle Dussau's native language, they produced a completely opposite effect on us. And rather than lend ourselves to an experiment that, if successful, would only enhance Mlle Dussau's position, we resolved to try to defeat it by limiting our conversation to simple monosyllabic responses.

However, one unexpected consequence of our cold war against Mlle Dussau was the decision by my father to call in from semi-retirement another of the former teachers of his naval cadet days —a venerable Anglicized Frenchman with a black beard, a bald head, and the improbable name of Gabriel Hua. M. Hua could hardly have looked upon my father as one of his most successful pupils, as my father, who no doubt considered French a somewhat effeminate language, would deliberately mispronounce French words whenever they appeared on the menu. Nevertheless, the former pupil held his old tutor in high regard. M. Hua was an erudite man, a famous and revered master at Eton with a host of friends. My father appointed him his librarian, a post that entitled him as a member of my father's Household to wear at official dinners the special, blue, Household evening coat with black velvet collar and flat, gilt buttons bearing the Prince of Wales's feathers, a distinction not conferred upon Mr. Hansell for some years. However, even with these high attributes, combined with a generous and jovial nature, he could not escape being an occasional victim of the crude practical jokes schoolboys from time immemorial have played on their French masters.

One day at lunch when we were at Frogmore, M. Hua digressed from a learned exposition of the subjunctive to praise the excellence of the French cuisine, dwelling at some length on the merit of frogs' legs. As we children had no idea that frogs were in any way edible, our immediate conclusion was that M. Hua had made up a good story. But, as he talked on, his earnestness impressed us; and we finally realized with amazement that not only did M. Hua make a practice of eating the legs of frogs but he considered them one of the most succulent delicacies.

I think it was Mary who first had the idea of exploiting M. Hua's eccentricity, but my mother was in on it, too. Armed with a fine-mesh net and bucket, we sallied forth to the lake in search of frogs. But, as it was the spawning season, we had to content ourselves with a catch of tadpoles. These we carried triumphantly to the kitchen and instructed the cook to broil and serve them on toast that evening as a special savoury dish for the French tutor. M. Hua was, of course, ignorant of the plot; and, when the time came for the savoury and the footman passed the dish to him, I saw out of the corner of my eye that all the conspirators wore an expression of pleasurable anticipation.

Of course it had not been our intention to carry the joke to the point of allowing the French tutor actually to eat the tadpoles; but, before my mother could utter a warning, he had hungrily attacked the toast with his knife and fork and conveyed a large piece to his mouth. Mama cried, "No, no! That special savoury is not meant to be eaten at all." But it was too late.

Horror gripped the whole table. We all expected M. Hua to be seized at once by a dreadful convulsion. Realizing that something was amiss, he asked in alarm what was wrong. It was Mary, as I remember it, who finally stammered out in a stricken voice the awful truth.

My impression is that M. Hua gallantly swallowed what was

already in his mouth, but wounded pride was in the glance with which he swept the table. With a curt bow to my mother, he strode from the dining-room, his beard bristling with suppressed agitation. Mama's eyes twinkled. "I am afraid," she said, smiling, "that between *grenouilles* and *têtards* a French gourmet draws a fine line." She directed me to seek out M. Hua in his room, to make my apology on the family's behalf for having taken such liberties, and to bring him back, mollified, to the dinner-table.

The other important language of those days was German, the *Muttersprache* of many of our relations. I had picked it up simultaneously with English; for, ever since I could remember, we had had a German nursemaid who made me repeat solemnly before and after every meal in the nursery the following grace:

> *Dem Herrn sei Dank*
> *Für Speis und Trank. Amen.*

To increase this rudimentary knowledge my father now imported another elderly master, Professor Eugen Oswald, a wizened old man with a tobacco-stained beard and a strong guttural accent. My impression is that he had taught my father briefly at Heidelberg when he had been sent there in 1892 to learn German, which, incidentally, he never mastered. Thereafter, whenever we were in London, Professor Oswald came to Marlborough House almost every morning to conduct us laboriously through the head-splittingly complicated declensions. I liked German and studied diligently and profited from the hours I passed with the Professor. However, Bertie did not share the same partiality and treated these *Stunden* lightly. In one of the Professor's weekly reports to my father on our separate progress, he once wrote under Bertie's column "Inattentive and playful." The next time Professor Oswald returned to Marlborough House my father sent for him to ask precisely what he meant. The Professor, embarrassed, finally explained, "Your Royal Highness, it isn't only that Prince Albert is inattentive; but, when I scold him, he just pulls my beard."

While these foreign-language lessons were undoubtedly beneficial, they had, so far as we children were concerned, an unfortunate by-product. Birthdays were important events in the family calendar. While we naturally looked forward to our own with eager anticipation, those of our parents and grandparents invariably confronted us with an agonizing problem, for the reason that we were expected according to family custom to render happy birthday greetings with a poem we had each committed to memory. Even in English this obligation was difficult enough at best. Under Mr. Hansell we had to memorize and practise reciting excerpts from Shakespeare or Tennyson until word perfect. But, as we progressed in French and German, more was expected of us. And with a view to displaying our newly acquired virtuosity our foreign tutors were ambitious enough to have us attempt similar performances in their languages. I remember the labour of memorizing some of La Fontaine's fables—"La Cigale et la Fourmi," "Le Corbeau et le Renard," "La Laitière et le Pot au Lait"—and later the complicated verses of Uhland's "Das Schwert," and Goethe's stirring ballads "Der Sänger" and "Der Erl König."

Not only were we required to memorize such pieces but we were further obliged to copy them out with painful care on long sheets of white paper, which were then tied together with bright-coloured ribbons. Directly after breakfast on these birthdays we would bear the compositions to the person celebrating. Mary, Bertie, and I would advance in turn, each nervously recite his or her poem, and then, with a bow, present the copy. If it was the birthday of my father or my mother, these prodigies of memory were mercifully performed in private. But at Sandringham my grandparents liked to invite their guests to listen. My grandfather always applauded indulgently, but no more so than my grandmother, who was very deaf; hence I was never quite sure how much pleasure either derived from these performances. In any case, for us children the whole business was a nightmare.

This ordeal apart, family birthdays were festive occasions, and the ritual was always the same. Those of both my grandparents fell in the late autumn, at Sandringham; my mother's in May, and my father's in June, when we were at Marlborough House. On June 23, my birthday, the family was usually at Frogmore for the Ascot Races, and those of Mary and my brothers were celebrated at whichever of the houses our seasonal wanderings might have taken us to.

Our presents were always displayed on a square table covered with a white tablecloth, from which hung the initial, delineated in wired flowers, of the birthday child. Dominating the grouped gifts—some of them surprises, some things we had asked for, or sometimes a piece of silver for a tea and coffee service that my parents had started for us—was a tiered birthday cake decorated with candles. For my seventh birthday my grandfather gave me my first bicycle; on another, a leather sporran with silver-ball tassels, which I still wear with kilts. And once his gift was a tie-pin: Persimmon, his Derby winner, in diamonds complete with jockey. One of my father's gifts to me was a silver watch and chain; from my mother came a Prayer Book. Our humble offerings took the form of pathetic daubs of unrecognizable flowers done in water-colours, or perhaps a mat of misshapen design worked in coloured wools on coarse canvas.

The birthdays of my aunts, my father's sisters, were also remembered. One of them had an unfortunate knack for picking useless gifts, and these were usually relegated to a special drawer. Whenever we were at a loss for a present for anybody, we had only to dip into this drawer to avoid the accusation of callous forgetfulness. However, this practice once had an embarrassing result. On being reminded by Mary that this aunt's birthday was imminent, I rummaged in the drawer and selected a silver pencil, which I wrapped and sent to her with love and good wishes. The thank-you letter that followed stunned me. "I don't mind so much your returning the pencil which I gave you for Christmas," she wrote, "but what makes me sad is that you didn't like it."

Another unusual aspect of my growing up was the fact that we were never "alone" with our parents at any one of our houses. There were always a lady-in-waiting and an equerry in attendance, who slept in the house and sat at their table. Yet, at the same time we were lonely in a curious way, partly because of the isolation imposed upon us by virtue of my father's position and even more because of the absence of close association with children of our own age. Except when we were taken to parties for the children of our parents' friends, or the members of the Household brought their sons and daughters to one of the Royal estates, we almost never saw our contemporaries.

If we were thus deprived of the company of other children,

there was at least compensation in that no intruders appeared to contest our possessions or interfere with the fun we evolved for ourselves. In the country, and especially at Sandringham, Mary, Bertie, and I were never at a loss for something to do. The happiest hours were those in which we three were left to our own resources. Mary was our close companion in many of our activities. Loving horses, she rode better than either Bertie or I; her yellow curls concealed a fearlessness that commanded our respect. Mary could at times be quite a "tomboy"; but at others, supported by her formidable "Mademoiselle," she wielded a sweet tyranny over our lives. It will in no way detract, I am sure, from the prestige of my brother, the King, when I say that when we were young I could always manage him. That is, after all, the established prerogative of older brothers. Moreover, through long observation and experiment, we knew exactly how to make each other angry.

For us children the best part of Sandringham was that there at least we could roam to the limits of our physical capacity. Our free hours were spent mostly on our bicycles. The woodland trails of that great estate became for two boys and their sister on rubber tires an enchanted forest in which almost anything might happen, although it never did. Sometimes we would bicycle to the neighbouring villages of West Newton or Castle Rising or to Dersingham to buy sweets at Parker's store. Or we might pedal down to the station at Wolferton to watch the train come in. The most exciting part of the ride there was down a steep hill with cross roads at the bottom. Arriving at the crest, I would crouch down over the handle-bars as racing cyclists do; then, pedalling as hard as I could, I would race downhill, with Mary and Bertie tearing along behind and Finch bringing up the rear, shouting hoarse warnings that I could not hear. That flying descent was exhilarating beyond description, and I was sure that I was breaking all speed records.

The lake in front of York Cottage, so tranquil in appearance, was in our imaginations infested with pirates. It could in a flash become for us the scene of sanguinary encounters as we made valiant landings on the little island from a flat-bottomed boat. The lake also teemed with roach; Finch taught us to catch them by the score with worms impaled on bent pins. And close by were tall fir-trees, so easy to climb that I established in one of the stout branches a secret cache—a wooden box for my treasures.

Sandringham had its personalities; and the one we came to know best was the village schoolmaster, Mr. Walter Jones. A Yorkshireman, he had in the early 1880's taken over the school at West Newton, a tiny village of perhaps a score of houses near the Big House. There he taught the children of the estate employees. But like many country teachers he was something of a philosopher and sage. He was a self-taught naturalist with an unsurpassed knowledge of the botany and animal lore of Norfolk. There was scarcely a square foot of woodland or fen that he had not tramped seeking out the nesting-places of birds. My father, who shared the same love of nature, was naturally drawn to him. Their association probably began during my father's leaves at Sandringham from the Navy; and, from happy and unsullied days in the field, slowly there ripened a companionship that lasted to the end of their lives. When my father went on his Empire tour in 1901, he took Mr. Jones with him. Inevitably the village schoolmaster came to occupy an important if unobtrusive place in the closed world of Sandringham. Among other things he kept, in a fine Spencerian hand, the famous game book in which was recorded the bag of each day's shooting.

It was only natural, therefore, that my father should call in Mr. Jones to preside over the schoolroom at York Cottage whenever Mr. Hansell went on holiday. He spoke with a Yorkshire burr and had a rich laugh; his lean frame and weatherbeaten countenance evidenced his remarkable powers of physical endurance. What we learned from Mr. Jones in that cramped schoolroom on the second floor was not half so interesting as the new perspectives of nature he opened to us in the course of long tramps about the estate. Mr. Jones was never tired; as we made our way home through the bracken, legs aching and not too sure of making it, our guide would be striding ahead chiding Bertie and me for not being quite the big, strong boys he thought we were. And there was another thing about him: on that vast preserve, abounding with game and renowned for its prodigious bags, Mr. Jones never to my knowledge fired a shot.

We children were singularly fortunate in that the ample acreage of Sandringham offered scope for many kinds of sport. As I have said, we were all taught to ride at an early age; and, as soon as we could jump fences without falling off, my father sent us out with the West Norfolk Hounds. Later on he taught me how to handle a shotgun; and, while he himself looked on, I shot my first rabbit. Bertie and I were given some old golf clubs with which we used to practise on the rough, nine-hole course in the park. Mr. Hansell, Mr. Jones, Finch, and Mr. Sayward, the stationmaster at Wolferton, had their own foursome; if one or another were absent, we might be invited to tag around after them, struggling to keep up with their long drives.

However, our opportunity to play group games was handicapped by our separation from other children. But Mr. Jones, having observed the ineffectual efforts of Bertie and me to play football with Mary, persuaded my father to let us play with the boys of his school. These boys were the sons of the coachmen, gamekeepers, and other employees of the estate. Bertie and I entered eagerly into their games, and for some time were both under the exciting illusion, despite our having been immediately elected captains of the opposing teams, that we were accepted as one of them, that no quarter having been asked none was being given. However, one can be naïve about such things. It has been my experience that the pleased incredulity with which the public reacts to the elementary demonstrations on the part of Royalty that they are, after all, like other people is matched by the public's firm refusal to accept them as such. No doubt Mr. Jones's whistle served to restrain the natural exuberance of the other boys. And candour forces me to admit that we were spared the bloody noses, barked shins, black eyes, and other usual bumps and bruises of strenuous youth. Happily for all of us, Mr. Jones understood boys, and this mixing-up process was only intermittently pursued, to the inner relief, I am sure, of the other boys, whose football games might otherwise have been turned into tame affairs.

Although Sandringham may not have been the best place in which to prepare a boy for the world's harsh realities, it nevertheless possessed most of the ingredients for a boyhood idyll. And because it was there, rather than in the more solemn precincts of palaces, that I saw the most of my grandparents, I propose to interrupt the recital of the simple facts of my own upbringing, in order to describe, in such detail as I can remember, the kind of life they had created for themselves at Sandringham, the fine times they shared there with their family and their friends, and the excitement their comings and goings brought to us children. There were older and lovelier places in the country, but for my grandfather it summed up his idea of the good life. And in another sense it exemplified a uniquely English way of life centred around the great estates: an elegant, undoubtedly paternalistic, and self-contained existence that a quarter of a century of progressive taxation has virtually destroyed.

In my gallery of childhood memories, the portrait of my grandfather seems bathed in perpetual sunlight. He was in his sixties, in the twilight of his life, when his personality began to mean something to me. Few men could match his vitality, his sheer *joie de vivre*. The Parisian term, *un bon boulevardier*, might have been invented for him. And while I can remember him, of course, as the regal figure of solemn ceremonies, I like best to recall him presiding over a well-laden table or making gallant gestures towards beautiful women.

Queen Victoria, as I have already suggested, stood not only as a symbol of Monarchy but as a way of life. Piety and respectability had provided the moral pillars of her Court. Yet, at the same time, her prolonged, widowed seclusion, which had evoked certain republican rumblings, had left a vacuum in State ceremonial and the leadership of society that my grandfather, out of the vitality of his spirit, had gradually come to fill. Sandringham, like Marlborough House, had become the meeting-place not only of statesmen and diplomats, but also of politicians, industrialists, bankers, artists, and their patrons—the new society of Europe and America. After Queen Victoria's passing it was only natural that the gay little Court of Marlborough House and Sandringham should have moved tumultuously into Buckingham Palace, Windsor, and Balmoral, where during my great-grandmother's reign only Cabinet Ministers, clerics, aristocrats, and courtiers of more austere interests had been admitted. Light opera, cards, and a keen interest in the Turf replaced polite conversation and amateur theatricals as acceptable Royal pursuits. The Edwardian Era had arrived in the genial shape of my grandfather; and the effect upon the remnants of the Victorians was, I was given to understand, much as if a Viennese hussar had suddenly burst into an English vicarage.

My grandparents' migrations took them even farther afield than did ours. Their yearly round of London, Windsor, and Balmoral was extended in March by cruises in the Mediterranean in the Royal Yacht, or a sojourn at Biarritz in April. After Cowes Week they would separate as my mother and father did. Queen Alexandra would join her sister, the dowager Czarina Dagmar of Russia, at the seaside cottage they had jointly acquired in their native Denmark. King Edward would meanwhile repair to his favourite watering-place, Marienbad, in Bohemia, for his annual cure. There in the company of friends he would submit to a Spartan régime: drinking the waters, eating only boiled food, and walking off the effects of a year's fine living. Much reduced in girth, he would rejoin my grandmother at Balmoral, where, succumbing to the irresistible genius of his French chef, he would in about two weeks undo all the drastic and beneficial effects of the cure.

My grandparents were always back at Sandringham for November 9, my grandfather's birthday. Some days in advance the Big House would bestir itself like a giant from his slumbers and bustle with activity: a small army of servants would arrive; plants from the greenhouses would be carried into the drawing-rooms; fires would be lighted; and then, without a word of warning, the clocks on the estate would all with mysterious unanimity be put half an hour ahead. My grandfather, wishing to make the most of the short winter day for the shooting, was a pioneer in the use of daylight saving. This same practice had earlier been introduced with marked success at Holkham Hall, the near-by estate of the famous Norfolk family of Coke. The family, the Household, and old friends were, of course, accustomed to this half-hour difference between Sandringham and Greenwich time; but it could confuse new guests who would arrive half an hour late. These occasional embarrassments caused my grandfather's Keeper of the Privy Purse, the venerable Sir Dighton Probyn, V.C., to protest that there were two kinds of time in the world, God's and heathen—meaning Greenwich and Sandringham time.

Be that as it may, the putting ahead of the clocks was for us children a signal for festival. That same evening, the great house on the hill would itself spring to life, with a bonfire blaze of lights; and the crunch of gravel and the clatter of horses' hoofs on the drive would herald the arrival of my grandparents, with twenty or thirty guests, every gentleman with his valet, every lady with her personal maid.

Meanwhile, at the Cottage our immediate family would be forgathered, together with a lady-in-waiting for Mama and an equerry for Papa, a governess for Mary, and one or two tutors for my brothers and me. The little house would be full almost to bursting, so much so that when someone asked where the servants slept, my father answered that he really didn't know, but supposed it was in the trees.

Then for a week the fields and coverts of the estate resounded all day long to the fusillades of my grandfather and his guests, as they proceeded with a methodical decimation of the clouds of pheasants that had been raised the previous summer. There would be a pause for lunch in the field—but a lunch that was a veritable feast and was served in a tent. After the shooters, with their ladies, had dealt with this splendid repast, the company would group itself, with the morning's bag laid out before them, for one of those panoramic poses in which Edwardians loved to arrange themselves. Sometimes Bertie and I were allowed to watch the afternoon shooting. That was an era when monarchs and princes, noblemen and tycoons, vied with each other for the honour of bringing down the largest number of birds. When dusk in its slow descent brought an end to the shooting, the day's kill might total nearly 2,000 pheasants.

If Bertie and I had our homework in hand, we were allowed after tea to run up the hill to the Big House to say good night to our grandparents. It was like being given an open-sesame to a totally different world, and excitement never failed to possess me as the gaily-lighted house materialized out of the dusk. The huge hall, known to the family as the Saloon, and upholstered in the red, blue, and gold of the Royal racing colours, would then be filled with handsome people and humming with conversation. In the adjoining drawing-room others would be playing bridge. And there was always music, provided by Gottlieb's famous German orchestra from London, which, established inconspicuously on a balustraded balcony at one end of the Saloon, would run through a light repertoire of selections from Strauss operettas to sooth the tired sportsmen or to dispel the shock of a bad bridge hand.

Fascinating as was all this, we children were never altogether at our ease. My father had laid down a rule that we must be back at the Cottage by seven o'clock. But, although we kept an anxious eye on the ornate clock on the mantelpiece of the Saloon, my grandparents seemed to delight in conspiring to defeat that particular point of parental discipline. So all too often these good-night excursions, which began so happily, would end in the Library with my father upbraiding us for being late.

Then, as suddenly as it had begun, the fun would stop. In carriages and *fourgons* piled high with baggage, the King and Queen and their guests would clatter down the drive on their way to the station, bound for London. Silence descended over the woods and coverts; the clocks were put back; and the Big House relapsed into darkness. Then, shortly before my grandmother's birthday on December 1, the same imposing charge through the Norwich Gates would be repeated; and my grandparents would return with a different group of guests. Another week of birthday festivities and shooting then followed; to end with the same whirling departure for London.

This brilliantly varied company—statesmen, diplomats, bankers, luminaries of the arts and international society, *bons vivants* —gave me my first tantalizing glimpse of another life. Although I was too young to realize it, I was seeing the birth of a new era and the ascendancy at Court of other kinds of people. Their advent marked a breach in the old hierarchical framework of British life. The outward forms might still be observed unchanged, but the inner spirit was different. High office or ancient lineage were no longer the sole criteria of status. Beauty, wit, wealth, sophistication—these had now become valid passports to the Sovereign's intimate circle.

Yet, for all the outward show of luxury, Sandringham was a happy place because of the kindness and human understanding that my grandfather exuded. There he relaxed, and the country squire took precedence over the Monarch. And the squire was most expansively in evidence on Sundays. The Sabbath was always scrupulously observed. Gottlieb's orchestra would have returned to London, and black clothes and top-hats would replace the shooting tweeds and caps of my grandfather and his male guests for the ritual of going to church. The morning service was at 11.30. Ten minutes before, the bell of the little church in the park would start to ring. That would be the signal for my father to set out from York Cottage, and we would follow him up the path past the lake. At the church gate we met Queen Alexandra and my mother, who would have preceded us with the other ladies in their carriages. On each side of the altar, in the place ordinarily occupied by the choir, were two pews facing each other: the one on the right was for the Royal Family, the other for the ladies. With my grandmother in the lead, the party now made its entrance into the church through a side door, taking its places in the two pews. By that time the body of the church would have filled with retainers and villagers and their families. The King and all the men guests were still conspicuously absent. Nevertheless, the door would close softly and the prayers would begin. Half an hour later, on the stroke of noon, the church bell tolled again. Then there would come the sound of steps on the path outside the church, and a moment later the side door would open to admit my grandfather, looking as if he had been detained by matters of great moment, followed by a dozen or so men guests. Our pew would creak as the King settled himself into the place left vacant for him nearest the altar, while the other late arrivals made their way past us towards the empty pews reserved for them in front of the congregation. Whenever my grandfather was at Sandringham, the sermons, which on other Sundays would be painfully long-winded, never exceeded ten minutes. It was our understanding that the rector had been advised that the King considered that quite long enough. By 12.30 the service was over; and we children, meditating on my grandfather's lateness for church, once figured out ruefully that he actually spent there only half as much time as we did.

The other unchanging event that marked a Sandringham Sunday was my grandfather's conducted tour of the principal establishments on the estate. The tour always began exactly at three o'clock, after a sumptuous lunch; and with the punctuality of figures issuing from a Swiss clock the King and Queen, with the members of the Household, would lead the guests into the garden, where the tour began. Meanwhile, my parents' contingent, which included us older children, would have sallied forth from the Cottage to meet the procession at its first stop, the stables. Thence the group moved on at a stately pace to the kennels, continuing to the gardens and my grandmother's model farm. The promenade always culminated at the stud farm. Here, in commodious loose-boxes, were King Edward's stallions and mares; and while my grandfather discoursed in detail on the pedigrees and performances of each one, Queen Alexandra dispensed carrots to the thoroughbreds from a basket.

There was a special building for the two stallions of the stud that had won the Derby. One large box was for the great Persimmon, a fine bay foaled at Sandringham, with which my grandfather, as Prince of Wales, had won the classic in 1896, two years after I was born. Across the yard in a similar box was Diamond Jubilee, which had repeated the feat four years later. In contrast with the docile Persimmon, Diamond Jubilee was notorious for a mean temper. While my grandfather, standing outside the box, held forth on the temperamental shortcomings of his fine horse, Diamond Jubilee as if in protest would interrupt with noisy neighing and pawing of the ground. The horse was eventually sold to a wealthy breeder in Argentina. As a racehorse owner, my grandfather established two notable and still unbeaten records; for in 1900, the year in which he won the Derby with Diamond Jubilee, he also won the Grand National with Ambush II, thus becoming the first and only owner ever to win both great races and in the same year.

So ended the formal tour. But the foot-weary guests were not yet allowed to return to the Big House. Near the stud farm was a technical school instituted by my grandmother for the training of local boys in arts and crafts. Here were displayed the simple objects of their industry, chiefly carved, wooden furniture. With my grandmother lauding the beauty and usefulness of the individual wares, it was difficult for the guests to leave the showroom without making a purchase.

While these promenades were always diverting to us children, they could be trying for those who were not interested in either the Turf or farming. Moreover, since they were necessarily conducted at a slow, measured pace and entailed a good deal of standing about in the cold, the older and feebler guests were subjected to considerable strain. Among my grandfather's less robust friends, an invitation to Sandringham was regarded as an almost sure invitation to the grippe.

Christmas at Sandringham was Dickens in a Cartier setting. It was more of a family gathering, and my grandparents always came back for that. Since serious purpose was usually injected even into our pleasures, Mr. Hansell, working to instil in us a knowledge of the ancient meanings of this Christmas fête, would attempt to explain to us the religious meaning of the Nativity. He also read to us Dickens's well-known Christmas story; and Mama, with her lady-in-waiting at the piano, taught us the Christmas carols. And to remind us to think of others, my parents always took us on Christmas Eve to the coach-house at the stables to watch the distribution of meat to the employees on the estate. When, from these days of rationing and controls, I look back upon this simple scene, I appreciate, as I did not then, the bounty thus displayed. Inside the coach-house, on long tables covered with white tablecloths were laid scores of bloody joints of beef, one for each family, and each tagged with the name of the recipient. Outside in the stable yard, waiting their turn, were the gamekeepers, gardeners, foresters, and stable hands, or their wives —in all some three hundred people. My grandparents with their family sat just inside near the door of the coach-house; and, as the employees walked out with their meat, the men touching their caps and the women making a quick bob of a curtsy, the King wished each a Happy Christmas.

In my family the display of the Christmas tree and the exchange of gifts always took place on Christmas Eve. After tea we all piled into my father's omnibus, ordinarily used for transporting the servants, and rode up to the Big House, where my grand-parents would be waiting in the Saloon with some of the older members of the Household, who usually spent Christmas with them. It would not be long before the loud banging of a gong heralded the approach of Santa Claus himself. An instant later there would appear in our midst the real thing: a tall, hooded figure in full regalia, a flowing white beard, red coat, black patent-leather boots, and over his shoulder a bulging bag. The fact that we knew this resplendent impersonator to be one of the upper servants in no way diminished our joy over his arrival. After bowing to the King and Queen, who would greet him jovially, Santa Claus led the company out of the Saloon towards the Ballroom. The double doors flew open before his advance, revealing in the centre of the room a fir-tree from the woods, tall enough to touch the ceiling, festooned with tinsel, tinted glass balls, patches of cotton-wool in imitation of snow, and ablaze with candles. But, as with everything else at Sandringham, even the business of Christmas proceeded along prescribed lines. Around the Ballroom were tables heaped with presents, with an ample section marked off for each person, the first for the King and the Queen, the next for my mother and father, and the rest more or less according to precedence.

The children's tables were in a far corner, segregated from the rest. This precaution was no doubt intended to safeguard a precious Fabergé jade masterpiece or a bejewelled clock on my grandmother's table from becoming the casualty of a wild shot from a toy gun or a misdirected football issuing from our direction. We children were always shown our presents last, and the suspense was agonizing. And when finally our turn came, the Ballroom floor was rapidly inundated with a sea of wrapping-paper, through which we pedalled and honked in toy motors.

On the way home we might pass the village choir with its winking lanterns on its way to sing Christmas carols to the King and Queen.

CHAPTER IV

"THE NAVY WILL TEACH DAVID"

Like the Parliamentary system, the constitutional Monarch who stands aloof from and above politics is a British invention. As a device for preserving the Crown as a symbol of national unity while divesting it from abhorrent forms of absolutism it is a remarkable example of the British genius for accommodation. But one effect of this system, which is perhaps not so well understood by the public, is the handicap imposed upon a Prince, who, while obliged to live and work within one of the most intensely political societies on the earth, is expected to remain not merely above party and faction, but a-political.

Some Princes bend their characters more easily than others to this rule. It was to be my fate to find it at times irksome because I had been endowed with a questioning, independent mind; and I found it difficult ever to take anything for granted, even my own position. And, since this general restraint upon my curiosity was to follow me through my public life, I shall now describe how I first became aware of it.

It was during the general election of 1906. My grandfather had inherited a Conservative Government headed by Lord Salisbury. However, the continuing repercussions of the Boer War ushering in heavier taxation and giving rise to increasing social clamour of the masses had already begun to shake the political structure. The Tory leadership, which had meanwhile passed to Mr. Arthur James Balfour, Lord Salisbury's nephew, was further menaced by the spectacular proposals of Mr. Joseph Chamberlain, the Birmingham politician and Colonial Secretary, that the Conservative Party should abandon the traditional policy of Free Trade in favour of an Imperial preferential tariff. The Tory Party was riven; Mr. Balfour's Government was eventually obliged to resign; and the King turned to the Liberal leader, Sir Henry Campbell-Bannerman, to form a new Government. Sir Henry, a Scotsman, genial and witty, also led the left-wing faction of his Party, which included such rising figures as Mr. David Lloyd George, the Welsh radical, and the young and brilliant Mr. Winston Churchill, who had only recently deserted the Tory Party of which his father had been so conspicuous an ornament. Seeking a mandate from the country, the new Liberal Prime Minister called for a general election early in 1906; and British politics was thrown into turmoil.

Meanwhile, in the autumn of 1905 my parents had gone to India on an official visit and were away until the spring. We children were left at York Cottage in the charge of our tutors and the governess. Even at our remote retreat in Norfolk we became conscious of the rising excitement over the elections. Naturally, the great issues were above Bertie's head and my own; but all the talk around us aroused our curiosity; and we began to ask questions of Mr. Hansell, who discovered in a London newspaper a graphic and noncommittal means of satisfying our curiosity.

To enable its readers to follow the fortunes of the opposing Parties, this newspaper had published a supplementary page upon which were shown figures of the opposing leaders together with sections of two tall ladders. The readers were instructed to cut out the silhouettes of the two ladders and the two Party leaders, who were portrayed in the posture of climbers. Each rung of the ladders represented a Parliamentary constituency, and the idea was to move the figures up the rungs according to how they separately fared in the voting. Mr. Hansell made us follow these instructions; first we cut out the ladders, which we tacked to the schoolroom door. Next we cut out the figures, which we pinned each with a foot on the bottom rungs. Thus my first impression of British politics was of a game in which two lively politicians raced each other up ladders. As the election returns were published, Bertie and I advanced each figure. Despite the neutrality Mr. Hansell had enjoined upon us as Princes, I found myself pulling for Sir Henry Campbell-Bannerman—no doubt because he led from the start—while Bertie, for lack of another candidate, championed Mr. Balfour.

From Mr. Hansell's connexions I have no doubt that he was a

Tory, and his sentiments, therefore, were wholly allied to Mr. Balfour. Nevertheless, his countenance betrayed no sign of disappointment when Sir Henry Campbell-Bannerman scampered triumphantly to victory. As he removed the dirty, torn pieces of paper from the schoolroom door, he remarked philosophically that, while some people would no doubt regard the results as disastrous, he was confident that the good sense of the British nation would in the end prevail against the wild policies of such extremists as Mr. Lloyd George. With the disappearance of the figures from the door, politics vanished from our field of interest. I ceased to be a little Liberal and Bertie a little Tory.

Experience had taught Bertie and me to associate my father's return home with a tightening of the screw of our schoolroom discipline. Nor was his arrival back from India in the spring of 1906 to prove any exception. Since his heart was set on our entering the Navy and as mathematics was of course one of the principal bases of naval education, he inquired into my progress in arithmetic with particular attention. The results in my case and Bertie's had been hardly what he had hoped for; and, concluding that mathematics was not Mr. Hansell's forte, he decided to test our knowledge in the subject by presenting us with practical problems of his own devising. For example, the number of stags, with their weights, he had shot at Balmoral the previous stalking season was carefully recorded in his game book. One morning at Abergeldie he handed us a copy of this record, commanding us to strike the average weight of the stags he had killed over this period. The problem was more complicated than it sounds; for the reason that our system of weights and measures includes the stone of fourteen pounds. My father maintained that *anybody* over ten years old should be able to solve so simple a problem; but on returning to the schoolroom Bertie and I found that we had been given a task of brain-racking complexity. The day was spent at our desks, adding and dividing, while Mr. Hansell, who had been instructed not to help us, paced about the room or stood at the window, staring meditatively out across the Dee. Unhappily for Bertie and me, the results of these agonized calculations, influenced less by logic than by desperate hope, failed by a wide margin to tally with those my father had independently arrived at.

He promptly engaged a special tutor to teach us only mathematics—Mr. Martin S. David, a master at Tonbridge School. During his own holidays, Mr. David, a Welshman with a taste for Craven A tobacco, joined us after New Year at York Cottage, and interminable hours were devoted exclusively to algebra and geometry. These gallant efforts were not wholly unrewarded.

The average age in those days for entering the Royal Navy as a cadet was thirteen years. I was therefore due to take the entrance examination in February, 1907. My prospects of passing were scarcely encouraging. Our apparent lack of progress under Mr. Hansell used to worry my mother; she blamed him for not arousing in us the spark of ambition to learn, which she was sure lay dormant in Bertie's character and mine. My father, however, took the opposite view. Defending Mr. Hansell's methods, he maintained with disheartening candour that the fault lay in my dumbness. Yet, quite apart from the question of whether I ever possessed the intellectual equipment, the circumstances of my birth tended to dilute and slow down my preparation for the outer world.

I had, after all, grown up in isolation and detachment; and, approaching thirteen, I had yet to know the spur of competition that is the common lot. While its absence undoubtedly made my childhood easier, those formative years were devoid of the sudden creative bursts and ranging interests that are normally inspired by the competitive association of young boys. Then, too, the fact that I had been destined from birth for the Navy operated to throw an iron ring around my education. Indeed, about the only condition enjoined on my tutors by my father was that I should be able to pass into the Royal Navy. Because Latin or Greek were not required at sea, my father saw no sense in my learning them.

Yet, in justice to Mr. Hansell, it must be said that no one was more conscious than he of the shortcomings of his tutoring. Possibly at the risk of losing his job, he had repeatedly warned my father that if I were ever to hold my own with my contemporaries at the Naval College and in whatever other educational institution I might thereafter attend, I should be sent to a good preparatory school. Knowing what my future would be, Mr. Hansell was not worried over whether or not I should ever attain a sure grasp of book knowledge; that achievement was not indispensable in a Prince. What I suspect he most feared for me was that, in consequence of my being deprived of the communal habits of thought and code of behaviour that are absorbed at an early age in a private school, I was bound at first to feel lonely and insecure when brought into close association with my contemporaries. But my father would not hear of it, saying, "My brother and I never went to a preparatory school; the Navy will teach David all that he needs to know."

I do not wish to be critical of Mr. Hansell; but, on looking back over those five curiously ineffectual years under him, I am appalled to discover how little I really learned. He could scarcely be said to have possessed a positive personality. If he harboured strong views about anything, he was careful to conceal them. Although I was in his care on and off for more than twelve years, I am to-day unable to recall anything brilliant or original that he ever said.

No doubt, in view of the restraints laid upon the Monarchy, this was all for the best. To have put a Prince in the direct line of succession under the tutelage of a bold and opinionated teacher might well have led to the one conflict with which the constitutional system cannot cope.

I used to wonder whether Mr. Hansell did not have a secret yearning for some other kind of life and whether he ever regretted having dedicated himself to the care and education of unwilling and ungrateful little boys. I rather suspect that this was so. His was an unrelieved responsibility, and it is possible that his position in our closely-knit household developed in him a form of mental claustrophobia from which he tried to escape. Close to York Cottage on the way to the kennels there was a slight rise of ground. Every morning after breakfast Mr. Hansell would disappear in that direction, to be gone fifteen minutes. From the top of the rise one had a view over the open plough-land. There Mr. Hansell used to stand, smoking his pipe, meditating, and looking abstractedly into space. This habit puzzled Bertie and me. We finally decided that Mr. Hansell liked to be alone, but in later years I was to think that these brief withdrawals of my tutor had a deeper meaning. Once when he took us there I asked him what he found to look at in so dull a view. He looked at me in surprise. "I don't think you will understand," he said, "but for me it is freedom." Thereafter that spot became known to us as "Freedom," and in my own time I was to realize to the full exactly what Mr. Hansell meant.

The year 1907 marked the end of my cloistered boyhood and the start of the career my father had decided upon for me. I was twelve and a half, old enough for the competitive examination for naval cadetships.

The first ordeal was an oral interview by a committee of stern admirals and schoolmasters. One of the questions fired at me was whether I was scared of the dark, and barely had I answered a quavering "no" when I was asked to name my favourite author.

A few days later I was notified that I had been selected to compete in the written examination. Here was the test of what I had been able to learn from Mr. Hansell. I crammed far into the night. Two weeks later, along with some one hundred boys from all manner of schools here and from the Dominions, I sat at a desk in a public examination hall in London, and for three days struggled with papers. There were only sixty-seven places open, and I left the hall praying that I would not fail.

After days of suspense my father told me that my prayer had been answered: I had passed into the Navy and in May would enter the Royal Naval College at Osborne. On February 18, 1907, my father wrote in his diary—"David went up before a Committee and was examined to see if the Admiralty would give him a nomination for the Navy. I am glad to say that he did remarkably well, they said he is the best boy they had examined, which is very gratifying." I rather doubt whether my father took the Committee's unexpectedly favourable judgment so literally, but all the same my first success pleased him and the rest of the family.

A man from Gieves, the naval outfitters, came to measure me for my uniform, the trying on of which my father personally supervised. I was proud of the blue, round jacket with its brass buttons and cadet's white collar tab and of my naval cap, and paraded in them before my sister and brothers.

Then the fateful day of leaving arrived, and my father took me away to Osborne. Despite my most determined efforts to uphold what I guessed must be the traditions of the British Navy, I left Marlborough House with tears drenching my new blue uniform.

In the train to Portsmouth my father calmed me with stories of his early naval life. Steaming down Spithead to Cowes he fell silent. Then, just before the Admiralty yacht touched the dock, he said, "Now that you are leaving home, David, and going out into the world, always remember that I am your best friend."

The education of a naval cadet at that time required four years' training ashore, the first two of which were spent at Osborne. The Naval College consisted of a collection of buildings grouped around Queen Victoria's old Osborne House stables. This large, one-story structure had been converted into a mess hall and classrooms opening into the stable yard. Osborne College had the reputation of being unhealthy, for which its location on the site of the old stables was rightly or wrongly blamed. In any case, the structure of the dormitories in which we slept had already deteriorated so much by the time I joined that we could kick holes in the outer walls without hurting our feet.

The central and largest building of the College was a vast hall called "Nelson," which served all manner of purposes—parades, physical training, and church, or divine service, on Sunday. At the end of each term "Nelson" would be decorated with bunting and used for prize-giving and theatricals. On the great oak crossbeam supporting the organ gallery at one end of this barn-like structure was spelled in large, polished, brass, block letters Lord Nelson's famous motto, "There is nothing the Navy cannot do."

By custom the new termers always arrived two days before the rest of the College returned from leave, which gave me time to shake down before the seniors appeared. It was customary for each boy of the new term to be scrutinized for peculiarities in his appearance and to be asked all manner of personal questions— his name, who his father was, where he lived. Manifestly all the answers that I mustered could not have been more damning; for, quite apart from my Royal parentage and homes, the fact that I had never been to school before caused me to be regarded as a freak.

The seclusion of my previous existence was rolled up like a curtain. Within a day or two of their return several sixth, or senior, termers decided that Cadet Prince Edward would look much better with his fair hair dyed red. So one evening, before "quarters" (evening parade), I was cornered by my betters and made to stand at attention while one of them poured a bottle of red ink over my head. The ink dropped down my neck, ruining one of the few white shirts I possessed; a moment later the bugle sounded for quarters, and the sixth termers dashed away to fall in their ranks, leaving me in a terrifying dilemma for which nothing that I had ever learned under Mr. Hansell seemed to supply a solution.

I couldn't go to quarters dripping red ink—that would have been telling on the seniors—but if I missed quarters I was for the Commander's Report in the morning. The only sound course open to me, therefore, was to sacrifice my good record in favour of the seniors, knowing that my punishment at the hands of the Commander would be nothing to the tanning I should get if I tattled. So I slunk away under the cover of darkness to get a clean shirt out of my sea chest and await the discovery of my absence and the entering of my name on the Defaulters' List. The punishment was not unduly severe, coming under the category of "Three days I.A.," which sentenced me to spending my leisure hours for the next three days alternately going round the stable yard at the double carrying a rod across the back of my shoulders, and facing the paint work for an hour at a time in the seamanship room.

Another form of hazing that caused me no little discomfiture was a mock ceremony performed, if I can rightly recall, by the same persecutors. An empty classroom window was raised far enough to push my head through and then banged down on my neck, a crude reminder of the sad fate of Charles I and the English method of dealing with Royalty who displeased. Quite a while after the sound of the seniors' retreating footsteps had died away, my cries attracted a sympathetic passer-by who released me, fortunately with my head intact.

Yet, apart from these relatively mild republican correctives, my life at Osborne was no different from that of any other British naval cadet, which, by contrast with the pampering that goes on in some schools to-day in the name of progressive education, was a fairly Spartan business. Each term was divided into two watches: starboard for the top, or brainy, half; port for the dumb-bells. Two of the twelve dormitories, each named after a famous admiral, were allotted to each term—mine bore the name of Exmouth. Where I stood as a naval cadet may be judged by the fact that I began my College career in the port watch.

At first it seemed especially hard, because I was caught up, without the previous experience of school, in the unfamiliar community life of small boys, with all its fierce and subtle relationships. Formerly I had had Finch to take care of my clothes and pick up after me; I now had to look out for myself. And from the comfortable rooms of our different homes I found myself thrust, in company with some thirty other boys, into a long, bare dormitory. The orbit of my living shrank to a hard, iron bed and a black-and-white sea chest with three compartments in which to keep my clothes, a tray, and a private till.

The head of the Naval College at Osborne was a post-captain, R.N., who, assisted by a staff of twenty-seven officers, enforced the discipline and ran the administration. Separate and subordinate was a professorial staff with a headmaster and thirty-two masters, responsible only for the studies of the cadets.

I was fortunate in having two fine captains to command the College while I was there. A rugged, sandy-haired Scot from Caithness, Edwyn S. Alexander-Sinclair, who was known to his friends as "Ginger," was in command when I joined. He had a son called Mervyn in my term. Mervyn was so often in the report for petty misdemeanours that his father had eventually to sentence him to "six official cuts" with a bamboo rod. This extreme and rare punishment was carried out in "Nelson" in the presence of the cadets, fallen in in two ranks. With a naval doctor in attendance, the boy was strapped to a gymnasium "horse," and the cuts were administered by a sturdy, physical-training petty officer. What lasting benefits such harsh physical correction ever bestowed on boys was doubtful.

Captain Alexander-Sinclair was relieved by Captain Arthur H. Christian, an old term-mate of my father's in the *Britannia* and a less severe character. He impressed me very favourably from the start, for early in his command I wrote home: ". . . What a nice man Captain Christian is!! He has got a few fields for partridge shooting here & he very kindly took me & a few other cadets out shooting with him the other day. He & the 1st Lieutenant shot while the cadets beat. We only got 3 head but it made a good walk. . . ." And again I wrote home: ". . . Captain Christian asked me out to tea last Sunday and he showed me a lot of photos of you in the Bechante."

The routine of each dormitory was regulated by two cadet captains—the Navy counterpart of monitors. There were twenty-four of them, selected from the three senior terms as possessing potential qualities of leadership. The cadet captains, who wore distinctive gold-lace badges on the right sleeves of their jackets, wielded considerable unofficial power. The summary justice they meted out to the cadets in their charge was often more effective than the official punishments.

Reveille at six o'clock in summer and 6.30 in winter was pro-claimed on a blaring bugle that made me yearn for Forsyth's bag-pipes. A moment later the cadet captain, with one peremptory pull of the gong above his bunk, would rout us out of bed, and in a convulsive motion we would all kneel down and say our prayers. After the minimum time that in the cadet captain's judgment was required for the Lord to hear us, he would yank the gong twice; and, still half asleep, we would jerk to our feet and in a communal motion start brushing our teeth.

Then the gong would sound three times, the signal for the plunge into the arctic pool at the end of the dormitory. To-day I have only to close my eyes to see again that pathetic crowd of naked, shivering little boys, myself among them, being herded reluctantly towards that green-tiled pool in the first morning light.

Throughout our naval training it was continuously hammered into our young minds that there were only two ways of doing things—the Navy way and other ways—and all the other ways were wrong. With so dogmatic a principle dominating our life it is small wonder that our characters and outlook tended to develop along narrower, more prescribed, and more stereotyped lines than those of our contemporaries at public schools. Besides, we were, to all intents and purposes, committed to a career at a much earlier age than other boys.

Furthermore, the Admiralty, which prescribed our studies, admitted no divergence from the specialized curriculum it had drawn up. Priority was not unnaturally given to mathematics, navigation, science, and engineering. Instead of Latin and Greek we learned to tie knots and splice rope, sail a cutter, read and make signals, box the compass, and master all the intricacies of seamanship. Unfortunately for me, relatively little time was given to the other subjects taught in schools—geography, history, modern languages—for which I had more aptitude.

Mr. Hansell's earlier misgivings about my ability to hold my own in the classroom were all too convincingly borne out at the end of my first term. There were examinations at the finish of every term, and marks were posted on a bulletin board for the cadets to see where they stood "in the order." However, according to a peculiar Osborne custom, all cadets, when going on leave, were required to carry home a confidential report in a sealed envelope, which was to be handed to parents or guardian upon arrival. Mine showed all too plainly that I was not far from the bottom of the term.

However, since my father had not complained about the first report, I bore the second home to York Cottage in December, 1907, without misgivings. While I had not distinguished myself in any subject, I was not conscious of having failed in any. As soon as the affectionate homecoming salutations were disposed of, I handed the fateful envelope to my father, who, evincing no immediate interest in its contents, put it casually in his pocket.

As there was no mention of the report that evening at dinner, I said to myself, This is fine. However, the next morning Finch appeared with a long face and a chilling summons to the Library; and a minute later those red, cloth-covered walls witnessed a painful scene. My father looked me in the eye. "David," he said, "I am sorry to have to tell you that you have a bad report. Read it."

It was a curt, cruel document that bore no relation whatever to my own appraisal of my efforts. The sad fact was that mathematics, that spectre of Mr. David's tutoring, had in all its hideous aspects pursued me to Osborne. My father's remedy for this crisis was to engage a master from Osborne; and, as soon as the Christmas festivities were over, I buckled down to work, forgoing in the interest of my survival a great part of my leave.

When that spring I took home the third-term report, so overpowering was the sense of failure that on being summoned into the Library, and without waiting for my father to speak, I burst into tears. "Come, David," he said with unexpected kindness, "this is no way for a naval cadet to act. Besides, you have quite a good report this time; and I am pleased with the progress you have made."

Still, I never really felt secure in my standing; and in reporting to my father on my position in the order, I was careful to put any adverse change in the best possible light when writing home: "I was 46th, last order, which is not so bad on the whole. . . ." Another time when my place took a dip I put a brave face on a situation that I knew would displease my father: "I [am] 32nd, which is quite good for me, although I went down a few places. . . ."

On the other hand, my father was not entirely lacking in understanding of my difficulties, as the following excerpt from one of his letters to me shows: "I am sorry that . . . you . . . lost several places in the last order, that is a pity & I am afraid you didn't pay as much attention as you ought to have done, but perhaps the questions were harder. . . ."

Every Saturday at noon we would file past the paymaster to receive our weekly pocket-money. As soon as the shilling had been placed in our hands, we would run off to the canteen, a small, inadequate structure in the centre of the playing-fields. There an old naval pensioner sold us fruit, ice-cream, stuffed dates, and sweets. A shilling went a long way in 1907, and three pennyworth of these delicacies filled a good-sized paper bag. But by the middle of the week the shilling had been spent, and we had nothing to supplement the unappetizing fare of the mess hall. One afternoon, feeling miserably hungry, I thought up a way to relieve my distress. During a brief spell in the sick bay a few weeks before I had made friends with the matron. Feigning sickness, I reported to her quarters. She soon realized that I was malingering and was about to send me away when I burst into tears and confessed that all I wanted was something good to eat. While admonishing me never to try this form of deception again, she took me into her kitchen and with true Irish sympathy prepared for me a sumptuous tea of buttered eggs, fresh bread, and jam.

We all had to play outdoor games, and the cadets were classified according to their proficiency. In this way boys like me, who possessed less aptitude for athletics, could play football, cricket, and hockey without self-consciousness. There were boxing competitions and track meets and regattas on the Medina. In the summer we marched down through the terraced grounds to Osborne Bay, to swim in the Solent. Although I did not excel at games, I believe that, except for cricket, my fondness for exercise caused me to enjoy them more than most of the other boys.

The only time we could really call our own was Sunday afternoon. Even then the scope of our wandering was confined to the College grounds. The world beyond was "out of bounds" for cadets unless in the company of an officer or a master, parents or friends of parents. What we most looked forward to, therefore, was being taken out for lunch or for a walk and tea; these excursions were our only release from the dull, monotonous routine that was our master.

During my last term, my brother Bertie joined the College. Since the school's rigid caste system did not permit a senior to be seen in the company of a first termer, I could not re-establish there the close companionship we had always known. However, he was soon beset by the same new-boy difficulties that had nearly overpowered me; and by prearrangement we used to go for walks beyond the playing-fields. Bertie would tell me his troubles, and I would try to advise him on the basis of my own experience.

In May, 1909, I was transferred to Dartmouth to complete my last two years' naval training ashore. In contrast to Osborne's collection of prefabricated bungalows at ground level, the imposing stone and red-brick College stood halfway up a hill overlooking the Dart. As a reminder of past naval glories, there lay the hulk of the *Britannia*, from which two or three generations of naval officers had graduated.

The great College buildings provided more comfortable accommodation than Osborne, with spacious halls, dormitories, gun-rooms, classrooms, and a chapel, also a Captain's House and officers' quarters. At the back of these buildings, higher up the hill, was a gymnasium and a swimming-pool; at the bottom of many flights of steps leading down to the Dart nestled the engineering workshops at Sandquay.

There were only local variations in the life and routine at the senior College. Our studies were more advanced, and we were allowed a little more liberty. On Sundays we could go farther afield and roam the undulating countryside or explore the wooded creeks of the Dart in "Blue Boats." There was some improvement in the food. A generous old lady had thoughtfully left a legacy to provide the cadets with Devonshire cream for their Sunday tea. On Saturday evenings there was dancing to the College band on the "Quarter Deck," or central hall, and the wives of the officers and masters were, notwithstanding their age, in great demand.

While the move to Dartmouth was quite a step up the ladder in our naval career, it was not promotion. On the contrary, from our proud position as sixth termers at Osborne, the seniors, whom we had not seen for almost two years, quickly reminded us of the lowly status we had resumed. The hazing and persecutions they devised were all the worse for the extra years of practice they had had.

The cadet captains especially took advantage of their authority to invent mean ways of tormenting us. One evening while we were undressing in our dormitory, the cadet captain rang the gong for silence. He told us that we were an idle, lazy bunch of "warts" and that we needed a good shake-up. He went on to announce that henceforth the time allowed for undressing and putting on our pyjamas before running down to the washhouse would be reduced from one minute to thirty seconds. Although we were used to doing everything "at the double" and obeying orders unquestioningly, this order was the last straw. The inevitable result was a series of summonses to the washhouse after "lights out" and a harsh application of the gong rope to any boy who had failed to meet the deadline.

In order to comply with this tyrannical order, we had to use our wits; and we resorted to the expedient of removing all clothing that did not show before we fell in for prayers on the "Quarter Deck." No one watching us marching out of there erect and with arms swinging could have guessed the ordeal ahead. For, as soon as we were through the big doors, a stampede began. We tripped in the passage and fell up the stairs in our frantic struggles to reach the dormitory and get undressed and pass the cadet captain, standing by, watch in hand, under the gun. Every evening produced a few minor casualties; and we fell into bed panting and scared, waiting for the delinquents to be called for punishment.

I had not dared to complain to my parents. All I had written was: "There is an awful rush here, and everything has to be done so quickly." But even this cautious report caused my mother some concern:

> . . . I am very glad to hear you like Dartmouth & I hope that in time you will get accustomed to the rush which I believe is rather trying. . . . Do tell me whether you have time to clean yr. teeth at night for Langhurst always says this is so important & I want to know. Don't forget to answer this question. . . .

It was two or three weeks—all too long, we thought—before our Term Lieutenant, a pleasant but casual young officer, discovered the unnecessary hardship to which we were being subjected and told the cadet captain to rescind the order.

I liked Dartmouth better than Osborne. For one thing I was beginning to grow up and to make some real friends among the boys of my term. Even my father seemed to have more confidence in me, and during the holidays I was treated less like a child. My father had taught me to shoot two years before, and now he let me join him on his rambles through the coverts of Sandringham to bag stray cock pheasants at the end of the season. Instead of being sent to bed at the same time as Mary and my younger brothers, I was allowed to dine downstairs with my parents. I was taken to the theatre, a ride in a motor-car was no longer an exciting novelty, and I was kept less in the background.

A highlight of 1909 was the one and only time I ever saw Czar Nicholas II of Russia, on the occasion of a semi-official visit to my grandfather. Because of the recurrent assassination plots revolving around the person of the Czar, the Imperial Government would not consider risking their Little Father's life in a great metropolis. Therefore, the meeting was set for Cowes, which could be sealed off almost completely from anyone whose business was even remotely suspicious. Uncle Nicky came for the Regatta with his Empress and their numerous children in the Imperial Russian yacht *Standart*. I do not recall him as a man of marked personality; but I do remember being astonished at the elaborate police guard thrown around his every movement when I showed him through Osborne. This certainly made me glad I was not a Russian prince. The first week of May, 1910, found Bertie and me at Marlborough House, preparing to return to Osborne and Dartmouth after an Easter leave at Frogmore unmarred by a single melancholy note. My grandfather had returned to London from his annual holiday at Biarritz and had taken us with my father to hear Tetrazzini sing in *Rigoletto* at Covent Garden. Over the next week-end he had gone to Sandringham, where he had contracted a bad cold. Back in London, this developed into bronchitis; and his family and the doctors became very concerned. As the King grew progressively worse, official bulletins were posted on the Palace gates to inform the public of the seriousness of his condition. Our father sent for us the day before we were due to go back and said, "I have wired your Captains that I want you both to remain with me here. Your grandpapa is very ill, and the end may not be far off."

CHAPTER V

I BECOME PRINCE OF WALES

MY grandfather died at Buckingham Palace a few minutes
before midnight on May 6, 1910. That afternoon one of
his fillies, Witch of the Air, won her race at Kempton
Park; and I remember the sad pleasure with which my father
walked over from Marlborough House to convey this information
to his dying father.

Next morning I was awakened by a cry from my brother
Bertie. From the window of our room he cried, "Look, the
Royal Standard is at half-mast!" I jumped out of bed to see for
myself. Across the Mall, Buckingham Palace stood grey and
silent, and on the roof in the bright morning sunlight the Standard
hung limply on the mast. And then I knew for myself that King
Edward VII had died, aged sixty-nine, after a reign of nine years.

As I look back, it seems to me that it was my grandfather's fate
that his lighter side should have obscured the fact that he had both
insight and influence. There was plenty of trouble brewing towards the end of his reign, and he was well aware of it. The rise of
Germany's power on the Continent, which my grandfather had
countered by fostering the famous alliance with France, was
clearly and ominously visible. At home the ebb and flow of party
politics and the social and economic forces that were undermining
the Edwardian world were constantly making themselves felt.
But in a small boy's view, as distinct from the impersonal
biographer's, he loomed as one of the most contented of men.

That morning, while Bertie and I were dressing, Finch appeared with word that my father wished to see us both downstairs. My father's face was grey with fatigue, and he cried as he
told us that Grandpapa was dead. I answered sadly that we had
already seen the Royal Standard at half-mast. My father seemed

not to hear as he went on to describe in exact detail the scene around the deathbed. Then he asked sharply, " What did you say about the Standard?"

"It is flying at half-mast over the Palace," I answered.

My father frowned and muttered, "But that's all wrong," and repeating as if to himself the old but pregnant saying, "The King is dead. Long live the King!" he sent for his equerry, and in a peremptory naval manner ordered that a mast be rigged at once on the roof of Marlborough House. An hour later the Royal Standard was broken and flying "close up" over the house, as it was to do wherever my father resided during the twenty-five years of his reign.

The strain thrown upon him by his father's death was tremendous, for across his grief thrust the urgent demands of the constitutional crisis, centring about the Liberal Government's efforts to break the veto power of the House of Lords and culminating in the passage of the Parliament Bill. The only way the Tory majority in the House of Lords could be made to bow to the will of the country was through the King's consenting to create if necessary enough new peers to outvote the diehards.

This political episode was indicative of the social evolution that was to gain momentum during my father's reign. Here was the first decisive challenge by the Liberals, spearheading the forces of change, since the landslide of 1906, which the cautious Mr. Hansell had recorded for us with the outline figures climbing the ladders.

But at the time the preparations for the funeral overshadowed all else. In order to give the rulers and representatives of distant nations and possessions time to reach London, the ceremony did not take place until two weeks later. During that prolonged wait, while the dead King lay unburied, Marlborough House became a vortex of activity with the comings and goings of Court officials. We children were pushed into the background, emerging only for melancholy afternoon calls upon our bereaved grandmother, Queen Alexandra.

My grandfather's body lay in the Throne Room of Buckingham Palace, with the massive bejewelled crown upon the coffin. Four tall Grenadier Guardsmen of the King's Company stood rigidly at each corner, resting on their arms reversed, their bearskin-capped heads inclined in respect. My grandmother could not stay out of the Throne Room; she returned there constantly to rearrange the flowers or to show a foreign relative or old friend the scene. After ten days the coffin was removed from Buckingham Palace to Westminster Hall, where it lay in State for three days to give the public an opportunity to pay its last homage to the dead King. Hundreds of thousands of people from all parts of the country and every walk of life filed past the bier, at which officers of the Corps of Gentlemen-at-Arms and of the Household Troops kept a continuous vigil.

The funeral took place on May 20, a hot and sultry day. Nine monarchs on horseback, led by my father, rode in the funeral procession from Westminster Hall to Paddington Station. Kaiser Wilhelm II, in the uniform of a British field-marshal, rode a white charger. Flanking him rode the Duke of Connaught, my grandfather's only surviving brother; and then followed the Kings of Spain, Portugal, Denmark, Greece, Norway, Belgium, and Czar Ferdinand of Bulgaria. Emperor Francis Joseph of Austria was represented by the Archduke Franz Ferdinand, Czar Nicholas II of Russia by his brother the Grand Duke Michael Alexandrovitch, and the King of Italy by the Duke of Aosta.

Not long ago I happened to turn up an old photograph showing these nine sovereigns together in the funeral procession, and I could not but reflect on how swiftly for most of them time ran out. Within three years the King of Denmark died; and his brother, the King of the Hellenes, fell before an assassin's bullet at Salonika. The young King of Portugal was soon an exile in England, and four years later the Archduke Franz Ferdinand and his wife were the victims of a double political murder at Sarajevo. Before the convulsions unloosed by that insane act subsided, three great Empires lay shattered; eight and a half million men were dead; and the principal architect of Europe's tragedy, the German Emperor, had become the lonely wood-chopper of Doorn.

But all this was far in the future as Mary and I rode with my mother in one of the State coaches. A hush lay over the dense, perspiring, and fainting crowds in the London streets, broken only by the sounds of the horses' hoofs and the mournful funeral marches of the massed military bands. A half-hour train journey brought us to Windsor. The coffin was placed on a waiting gun-carriage. Bluejackets dragged it slowly up the hill to St. George's Chapel; the long funeral procession followed on foot. Bertie and I in our naval-cadet uniforms marched behind my father.

It was all rather overpowering for us grandchildren, even a little eerie; and it was not until all this impressive funeral pomp was over that the full meaning of our grandfather's death registered itself on our young minds. That our parents had become King and Queen of England we took for granted; it was our new position, and especially mine, that was harder to figure out. For now, as Heir Apparent, nothing save death itself was at all likely to prevent me from one day becoming "by the Grace of God, of Great Britain, Ireland, and the British Dominions beyond the Seas, King, Defender of the Faith, Emperor of India."

In the first place, I had a new name—by the law of succession I had become Duke of Cornwall. This title conferred immediate practical advantages. Created six centuries ago for the Black Prince, the Duchy of Cornwall is the personal estate of the King's eldest son, the income of which serves to make him financially independent. Its holdings include valuable London property and thousands of acres in the West Country. The greater part of the not inconsiderable revenue is reinvested in the estate, and the rest passes to the Duke of Cornwall, as his age and responsibilities warrant, for the maintenance of his household and establishment. For the first time I now had my own independent income, the first I had ever received, except for the weekly shilling of pocket-money doled out at the Naval Colleges. Still I do not recall that this new wealth gave rise to any particular satisfaction at that time.

Anxious for me to continue my naval education, my father sent me back to Dartmouth as soon as the funeral ceremonies were over. By then I had lost three weeks of the summer term, and my one thought was to resume as quickly as possible my ordered cadet life. My term mates welcomed me back with appropriate condolences; yet, in a way difficult to express, there had grown up unconsciously among them a subtle respect for my new position. Although the cadets continued to call me Prince Edward, on parade and in the classroom I was the Duke of Cornwall and Heir Apparent.

However, there was still another interruption for me that

summer term. In June I was summoned to Windsor to spend my sixteenth birthday with my family. In a conversation lasting but a minute, my father informed me that he had decided to create me Prince of Wales, which he did that day. Contrary to popular belief, the King's eldest son does not by right become Prince of Wales. If the King should decide that his first son was unfit to bear the title, he could withhold it.

Next day I was confirmed by Dr. Randall Davidson, Archbishop of Canterbury, in the private chapel of Windsor Castle. In the presence of my parents, my grandmother, and other relatives, the Primate reminded me that: "Here in Windsor, if anywhere, must the memory live and glow of the high ideals of Christian manhood that were set and followed in the centuries that are gone."

Before I went back to Dartmouth, my father told me that, since the time had come for me to learn something about politics, he had arranged for the study of civics to be substituted for some of the engineering classes. Mr. Hansell, who had stayed on with the family to teach my younger brothers, Harry, George, and John, felt that my progress in this new field would be furthered if I were to read more serious newspapers than the cheaper dailies, which I, in common with the other cadets, devoured from cover to cover. Accordingly he consulted one of the Dartmouth masters, Mr. George H. F. Cookson. Deciding that *The Times* might be too stiff reading for me at that age and for my taste, they worked out a daily reading plan, of which I in all innocence hastened to apprise my father:

November 15, 1910.

Dear Papa,

. . . I take in the Morning Post and the Westminster Gazette, as both Mr. Cookson & Mr. Hansell came to the conclusion that those were the best two for me to take in. By this means, I have both a Conservative & a Liberal paper to read. . . . It is ever so much more interesting for me to follow the political proceedings now, that I have been taught something of the country's constitution. . . .

But for a Prince even the most cautious foray into contemporary politics was not simple, as shown by my next letter to my father:

November 23, 1910.

Dear Papa,

. . . I have changed the papers as you wished, & Mr. Cookson quite agreed, & said that he thought The Times put everything clearer & more to the point. So now I take in The Times. . . .

Our family life changed appreciably after the death of my grandfather. By December my grandmother's possessions had been moved from Buckingham Palace to Marlborough House to make room for us. The simple comforts of Frogmore were replaced by the grand and spacious accommodation of the Royal apartments at Windsor Castle. And, instead of occupying Abergeldie for the grouse shooting and deer-stalking that summer of 1910, we lived in the Castle at Balmoral.

Only at Sandringham did we retain our familiar surroundings, for we continued to live on in York Cottage, leaving my grandmother in possession of the Big House. This was a real inconvenience to my parents; for there was no room in our already overcrowded establishment for the extra staff that, in the discharge of his Royal duties, my father required. Yet, he could not bring himself to ask Queen Alexandra to move. His attitude caused my mother to point out that, as a practical matter, it was rather ridiculous for one old lady to reside in grandeur in that vast mansion, while the King and Queen lacked room in their congested Cottage for a single guest. But my father always insisted, "It is my mother's home. My father built it for her." So Queen Alexandra remained at the Big House until her death in 1925. She closed off my grandfather's room, leaving everything in place, exactly as if he were still alive. No one ever slept there again as long as she lived. Whenever I went to the Big House, even when I lived there briefly as King, the very air still seemed to be alive with the throb of my grandparents' personalities.

My last term at Dartmouth passed swiftly—too swiftly. I wrote home: ". . . It is very nice for me being 6th term here now, & I gain many priviledges. . . ." My brother Bertie had meanwhile been transferred from Osborne, and I assumed an elder brother's responsibility for him. Halfway through the term both he and I fell victim for the second time in our lives to a severe epidemic of mumps and measles, which laid low two-thirds of the cadets at one time. Mr. Hansell came down from London and took us away to convalesce at Newquay on the rugged Cornish coast. There we were joined by the Secretary of the Duchy of Cornwall, Mr. Walter Peacock, who, with a view to stimulating my interest in my affairs, conducted me in my ducal capacity around some of the estates.

It was while I was at Newquay that my first serious ambition was thwarted. The goal of my cadet life had been the final training cruise and graduation that would qualify me for the dirk and white patch of a midshipman. No cadet yearned for this proof of success more than I. Now, without warning came a letter from my father explaining that, since I would naturally be obliged to play a prominent rôle in his Coronation in June, I would have to forgo the training cruise in North American waters upon which my hopes were set.

So it was with a heavy heart that I returned to Dartmouth to say good-bye to the officers and masters and the cadets of my term. It was a severe wrench to part company with sixty-odd boys with whom I had shared all the fun and all the setbacks of school days. For four impressionable years we had grown up together with one common goal—to go to sea. Now that that goal was within our grasp, it was my fate to have it snatched away. So we parted; and, thinking back, I am surprised to find how few have been my associations with any of my term since then.

Looking through the most recent Navy List, I find that as I write the names of only four are recorded in its pages: one Admiral of the Fleet (myself); one Admiral, Sir Philip Vian; and two Vice-Admirals, Sir Charles Daniel and Sir Reginald Portal. More surprising still, out of the 759 cadets whose time at Osborne overlapped any of the six terms I spent there, only twenty-seven are still on active duty. They are all flag officers. One of them is my brother Bertie, who, like me, assumed the rank of Admiral of the Fleet on becoming King.

My naval farewells were interrupted by my having to take part in my first official function. A silver oar, symbol of the ancient rights of the Duke of Cornwall over the water of Dartmouth, had long been deposited in the Duchy office in London. It was Mr. Peacock's idea that it would be a generous gesture if I, as Duke, should give it back to the town. It was a simple ceremony as I subsequently described it in my diary entry of March 29, 1911:

. . . At 5.00 I left . . . in a steam boat for the Dartmouth pontoon, to present the silver oar. On arriving there I shook hands with the Mayor & others, inspected the guard and proceeded by carriage to the Subscription Rooms. There I said a few words to the Mayor & gave the oar. . . . This was my first function, & I think it went off very well. . . .

I then went to London and joined my family at Buckingham Palace, to which we had moved in December. My room was on the third floor, overlooking the Mall. The Palace seemed enormous, with its stately rooms and endless corridors and passages. It was something of a walk merely to reach my mother's room; we used to say we visited her only by appointment. And the vast building seemed pervaded by a curious, musty smell that still assails me whenever I enter its portals. I was never happy there.

The morning after I arrived, there was the usual post-breakfast summons relayed by Finch. My father took me for a walk in the Palace gardens and warned me that the happy obscurity of the naval cadet was over. He never wasted words, saying only, "You are now old enough to take part in the forthcoming State ceremonies, when many eyes will be upon you. Remember to conduct yourself at all times with dignity and set a good example to others. You must be obedient and respectful and kind to everyone."

Then, as was our habit in the spring, we moved to Windsor. I have long supposed this was a period of sadness for me. My Exmouth term mates had sailed off in the cruiser *Cornwall*, and fragments of their voyage to North America came back to me in their letters. Yet, for all the remembered disappointment, I find to-day that my diary during that period at Windsor was actually full of sunny and intimate details: ". . . The trees are just coming out & the place looks lovely. . . . Rode before breakfast with Major Wigram, Bertie & Harry. . . . I helped Mary fly a patent kite. . . ." I was happy when my father said that he would soon give me the cherished insignia of a midshipman. But I sensed that, henceforth, my life was going to be different; within those ancient, grey, Castle walls, quite without realizing how, I arrived at the end of my boyhood.

By June the elaborate preparations for my father's Coronation had reached their final stage. As Prince of Wales I took precedence over the peers of the realm and would normally have worn a peer's robes. But this was not possible; I was not of age—and too young to take my seat in the House of Lords. To get over this difficulty, which was a very real one, my father decided to invest me with the Order of the Garter a short time before he was crowned. In the Garter Room at Windsor Castle, with the portraits of ancestors in their Garter robes looking down from the panelled walls, I was admitted into one of the most ancient orders of chivalry. I wore a cloth-of-silver costume, white stockings, and white satin slippers with red heels; and a sword in a red velvet scabbard hung at my side:

> June 10, 1911.
> ... After Papa & Mama had gone into the Garter Room, I waited outside in the Rubens Room till Uncle Arthur [Duke of Connaught] & Cousin Arthur had come for me. Then I fell in between the two & we walked in & up the room, bowing three times, Then Papa put the garter, riband & george, & star on me, & then I went round the table shaking hands with each knight in turn. I kissed both Papa & Mama's hands. ...

There is no occasion that rivals the solemn magnificence of a Coronation, when Church and State unite in the glorification of the majesty of kingship. My father's Coronation took place in Westminster Abbey on June 22. The simple entry in my diary for that auspicious day hardly does justice to the impressive, colourful scene:

> Buckingham Palace, London
> June 22, 1911.
> Papa and Mama's Coronation Day. Papa rated me a Midshipman—I breakfasted early & saw Mama & Papa at 9.00 & then dressed in my Garter clothes and robe, & left in a state carriage at 10.00 with Mary & the brothers. We arrived in the Abby at 10.30 & then walked up the Nave & Choir to my seat in front of the peers. All the relatives & people were most civil & bowed to me as they passed. Then Mama & Papa came in & the ceremony commenced. There was the recognition, the annointing and then the crowning of Papa, and then I put on my coronet with the peers. Then I had to go & do hommage to Papa at his throne, & I was very nervous. ...

Kneeling at my father's feet, I swore: "I, Edward, Prince of Wales, do become your liege man of life and limb, and of earthly worship; and faith and truth I will bear unto you, to live and die, against all manner of folks. So help me God." When my father kissed my cheeks, his emotion was great, as was mine.

My diary entry concludes: "Then Mama was crowned. . . . We got into our cariage & had a long drive back. My coronet felt very heavy, as we had to bow to the people as we went along. . . ."

Those weeks of Coronation festivities were very exciting to Mary and me, who had never seen such splendid ceremonies at close range before. We were fascinated by the magnificence of it all—the foreign representatives in their elaborate uniforms, the beflagged streets lined with red-coated troops, the naval reviews, the full-dress military parades, the gilt coaches, the glittering escorts.

Early in July, by which time the enthusiastic crowds in London had become exhausted, these scenes of pageantry shifted to Ireland, Wales, and Scotland. Mary and I accompanied our parents on these State visits. For me the climax was reached in Wales with my investiture as Prince of Wales at Caernarvon.

This ceremony had been allowed to lapse for centuries. But surprisingly enough the Welsh radical, Mr. David Lloyd George, who only a few years before had shocked my family with his famous Limehouse speech attacking inherited privilege, decided that its revival would appeal to the national pride of his people. With an eye to what would please his constituents, "L. G." proposed that the ceremony be transformed into a spectacular Welsh pageant. My father agreed.

Mr. Lloyd George became my coach in the Welsh language, and I still have, written in his own hand, some of the Welsh sentences he taught me to speak at the investiture. One was "Mor o gan yw Cymru i gyd," meaning, "All Wales is a sea of song." Mr. Lloyd George made me repeat it over and over again, saying with a twinkle, "All Welshmen will love you for that." Out of these meetings, despite the difference in our years—and I might add, in politics—grew a friendship that lasted until his death.

But that was not all. The ceremony I had to go through with, the speech I had to make, and the Welsh I had to speak were, I thought, a sufficient ordeal for anyone. But when a tailor appeared to measure me for a fantastic costume designed for the occasion, consisting of white satin breeches and a mantle and surcoat of purple velvet edged with ermine, I decided things had gone too far. I had already submitted to the Garter dress and robe, for which there existed a condoning historical precedent; but what would my Navy friends say if they saw me in this preposterous rig? There was a family blow-up that night; but in the end my mother, as always, smoothed things over. "You mustn't take a mere ceremony so seriously," she said. "Your friends will understand that as a Prince you are obliged to do certain things that may seem a little silly. It will be only for this once." I also got the impression, although the thought was never actually put into words, that, if I did what was asked of me, it would help Papa in his dealings with the difficult Mr. Lloyd George.

So on a sweltering summer day within the vast ruin of Caernarvon Castle, before some ten thousand people, with Winston Churchill, as Home Secretary, mellifluously proclaiming my titles (he told me afterwards that he rehearsed them on the golf course), my father invested me as Prince of Wales. Upon my head he put a coronet cap as a token of principality, and into my hand the gold verge of government, and on my middle finger the gold ring of responsibility. Then, leading me by the hand through an archway to one of the towers of the battlements, he presented me to the people of Wales. Half fainting with heat and nervousness, I delivered the Welsh sentences that Mr. Lloyd George, standing close by in the ancient garb of Constable, had taught me.

When all this commotion was over, I made a painful discovery about myself. It was that, while I was prepared to fulfil my rôle in all this pomp and ritual, I recoiled from anything that tended to set me up as a person requiring homage. Even if my father was now beginning to remind me of the obligations of my position, had he not been at pains to give me a strict and unaffected upbringing? And if my association with the village boys at Sandringham and the cadets of the Naval Colleges had done anything for me, it was to make me desperately anxious to be treated exactly like any other boy of my age.

My father, happily, sensing what was going on in my mind, arranged for me to go to sea at once as a midshipman. More than that, he personally selected the ship—the coal-burning battleship

Hindustan—commanded by Captain Henry Hervey Campbell, his old friend and shipmate, who often stayed with us. Having known him since childhood, I looked forward to serving in his ship. But I was soon to discover that the Captain Campbell with a deck under his feet was a wholly different man from the genial guest at York Cottage.

I joined the *Hindustan* at Cowes in the early part of August and served three months aboard her as junior midshipman. After putting into a number of South Coast ports, we were ordered to the Firth of Forth, where the Home Fleet was assembled. The Captain worked me very hard. I was under the instruction of the officers, warrant officers, and chief petty officers responsible for every part of the battleship. I kept watch at sea and in harbour; I learned how to run a picket boat; I served in a turret during battle practice, and was taught to read flag signals by the Chief Yeoman. In short, I was expected to know as much about a battleship in three months as it takes the average "snottie" three years to learn.

The truth, of course, was that I did not; but I enjoyed the experience immensely. Though I was the junior midshipman in the gun-room and all the others were senior to me, they and the two sub-lieutenants treated me with more compassion than I had received when I joined Osborne. Tobacco and alcohol are prohibited for midshipmen until they are eighteen. But I was allowed to drink a glass of port on guest nights, and looked forward to the dirty, back-breaking job of coaling ship for the cigarettes I was allowed to smoke on those occasions.

My last days in the *Hindustan* were spent at Portland. She was under orders to sail for Ireland when my father called me to Sandringham. I was genuinely sorry to leave the only warship in which I ever actually served. But he had other plans for me. Soon after I arrived at York Cottage, he called me to the Library. "You must remember, David," he began, "that I too loved the Navy; and I am therefore well aware that what I am about to say will disappoint you." Characteristically, he went to the point. First, I must give up the Navy—"too specialized." Secondly, I was to take educational trips to France and Germany—"very important that you should learn the languages and study their politics." Thirdly, I was to go to Oxford.

It was the Oxford part that took me by surprise. The promise of travel in Europe compensated somewhat for the loss of a naval career. But Oxford was unexpected, for the reason that my father, who had little sympathy for experiences different from his own, had always been suspicious of college dons and professors. In Navy fashion, he regarded them as unpractical, unworldly people whose lives and ways were alien to his own. Wondering, therefore, what lay behind this sudden interest in Oxford, I protested that, as I had neither the mind nor the will for books, my years at a university would be wasted. "If I cannot stay in the Navy, please let me go round the world," I pleaded, "and learn about the different countries and their peoples at first hand."

But my father was insistent, and eventually it emerged that Mr. Hansell was the villain of the Oxford plot. "It was Hansell's idea," said my father, "and you are to go to his old college, Magdalen." What I had to say to the poor man after I left the Library was—to use a highly satisfactory American phrase—nobody's business.

One amusing entry in my diary about this time was on the subject of clothes. It seemed that my father thought it was time for me to have a suit of tails and dress clothes. My comment after going to my tailor's was: "I shall look an ass." Whether I did or not is beside the point; but this entry does illustrate my early dislike for formal clothes, which I have never lost.

While I am speaking of clothes I might add that to the end of his life my father upheld his own ideas of fashion against the inroads of modern informality. He always kept a frock coat in his audience room at Buckingham Palace, which he would hastily slip on whenever an official visitor was announced. And he had never yielded to the new style in men's trousers, which introduced what in England were called "turn-ups" and in America "cuffs." His aversion to this innovation was impressed upon me with almost shattering finality about this time. It happened this way: when I came in to breakfast one morning, dressed in a brand-new suit of which I was rather proud, instead of complimenting me on my taste, my father looked at me in a curious way and suddenly asked, with magnificent irrelevance, "Is it raining in *here?*" For a second I was speechless; but, when my father repeated the question, with his eyes focused in obvious repugnance on my feet, I realized what he meant: Why turn up one's trousers in such an absurd manner except to cross puddles? Thereafter, just as my father kept a frock coat handy against the arrival of unexpected visitors, I always kept a pair of old trousers without turn-ups, which I could slip on before I went to see him.

On November 11 my father and mother sailed for India with a large suite in H.M.S. *Medina*. I went to Portsmouth to see them off, and this was another disappointment, for I had hoped they would take me with them to be a witness of the Oriental splendour of the Coronation Durbar at Delhi. But my father prescribed that I should stay at home to work up the new subjects I would have to take at Oxford.

In spite of all my disappointments I spent a pleasant enough autumn and winter at Sandringham. Mary and my two youngest brothers were with me at York Cottage, and we enjoyed this period of freedom from parental restraint. Although we were in the charge of Mlle Dussau and Mr. Hansell, the four years I had been away in the Naval Colleges and my time at sea had given me a certain independence of tutorial discipline. I no longer stood for being ordered about in quite the same way as before. For the first time in my life I felt more or less on my own.

During this interlude at home between the Navy and my new life of study abroad and at Oxford, my constant companion was my brother George, the youngest but one of the family. My other brothers, Bertie and Harry, were both away at school and came back only for the holidays. Although George was eight and a half years my junior, I found in his character qualities that were akin to my own; we laughed at the same things. That winter we became more than brothers—we became close friends.

My grandmother, Queen Alexandra, was as usual at the Big House. I used to go to see her nearly every day, walking over in the evening to chat or play patience or do jigsaw puzzles with her. Although she was quite an old lady by then, she still retained much of the beauty of the lovely young woman who had come from Denmark almost fifty years before to marry my grandfather. With her delicately-chiselled features, her high coiffure, and the grace of her manner, she was still greatly admired. Her charm was irresistible and overcame such disabilities as a stiff leg,

acute deafness, and rebellious unpunctuality in a family determined to be run by clockwork. She was late for everything—
meals, church, trains, and, worst of all, big ceremonies. The story
is told that she was even late for her Coronation and that my
grandfather, exasperated, burst into her room, watch in hand,
remonstrating, "My dear Alix, if you don't come immediately
you won't be crowned Queen."

With all her queenly dignity my grandmother had a wonderful
way with people. The warmth and understanding of her approach to human problems left no doubt as to the sincerity of her
solicitude. During the First World War, while visiting wounded
soldiers in an orthopædic hospital, she noted the depressed expression on one patient's face. On her inquiring the reason, the
Medical Officer informed her that the man's knee would be permanently stiffened as the result of a gunshot wound. My grandmother went straight to his bed to comfort him. "Never mind if
you have a stiff leg," she reassured him. "I have one, and look
what I can do." Whereupon she swung her bad leg easily over
the seat of an adjacent chair.

Queen Alexandra's interest and care for the workers and
villagers at Sandringham were bountiful. Her generosity was a
source of embarrassment to her financial advisers. Whenever she
received a letter soliciting money, a cheque would be sent by the
next post, regardless of the authenticity of the mendicant and
without having the case investigated. She also loved animals,
especially horses and dogs. A lame horse or one pulling too heavy
a load would cause her to stop in the street or on the road to
upbraid the driver.

The great Sandringham house parties were no more, but one
was always sure to find the same intimate circle around my
grandmother at the Big House—one of my aunts, Princess Victoria, and two or three members of her small Court. "Aunt
Toria" was Queen Alexandra's only unmarried daughter, who
had given up her whole life to her mother, perhaps at the sacrifice
of her own. If she had any regrets, she kept them a secret and
always encouraged our fun.

To the end of her life my grandmother was attended by two
devoted old friends: one was Miss Charlotte Knollys—the sister
of King Edward's private secretary, Lord Knollys—who for half

a century had been my grandmother's inseparable companion. "Miss Charlotte," as she was known in the family, was one of those undefinable characters that earn the sobriquet "an institution." She was a diplomatic pillar of strength in a Royal Household that was not without its jealousies and intrigues. Miss Knollys was in continuous attendance, had never taken a holiday, and dealt in longhand with all my grandmother's personal correspondence.

The other personage I always associate with my grandmother was General Sir Dighton Probyn, V.C., her Comptroller, who had served King Edward VII for many years. To us children Sir Dighton, with his white beard flowing over his chest, had always been a heroic personage who had raised and led a famous Indian cavalry regiment called "Probyn's Horse." Yet, it was a matter of painful knowledge to all that the old general's bravery, which had contributed to numerous dashing cavalry exploits during the Indian Mutiny, in which he was awarded the Victoria Cross, when transferred to the field of finance had the tendency to produce results comparable to the Charge of the Light Brigade. My father watched with unconcealed misgivings while Sir Dighton created at Sandringham costly rock gardens, complete with rustic wooden shelters, all dedicated with respectful adoration to "The Beloved Lady," as he affectionately referred to my grandmother.

The devotion of these two old courtiers was fully appreciated by Queen Alexandra, who would, indeed, have been quite lost without them. Still, constant companionship of this kind can pall; and one day at Marlborough House my grandmother determined to give them the slip. The next morning, taking one of her younger ladies-in-waiting into her confidence, she ordered the motor earlier than usual and set off for Sandringham, leaving Miss Charlotte and Sir Dighton in blissful ignorance of her departure. As the forenoon wore on, without the Queen's bell having rung or any word coming from her, the old couple became anxious. After frantic inquiries the truth was out: "The Beloved Lady" had gone to Sandringham alone. They were not so indispensable after all!

This impish little trick, however, had a happy ending. Shaken but undaunted, Miss Charlotte and Sir Dighton summoned another of the Marlborough House motors, enjoining the driver to cover the one hundred and ten miles to Sandringham in record time. When they reached the Big House, my grandmother was delighted to see them again; and the possessiveness of their position was re-established in full.

By this time shooting had become my chief outdoor interest. And, no doubt wishing to make up to me for the quick succession of blows he had felt it necessary to inflict on my youthful aspirations, my father gave me the run of the shooting at Sandringham during the time he was away in India. As I wrote him:

January 11, 1912.

. . . I love shooting more than anything else, & it was very kind of you to allow me to shoot so much here while you were away. I have had some splendid practise, & feel that my shooting has very much improved. It is the small days that give one far more practise than the big ones. One can take ones time & shoot much better. . . .

More often than not circumstances and environment influence the development of people's tastes. Shooting was certainly one of my father's greatest pleasures in life. For him the magic period from August to January meant glorious days on the moors, or "on the hill" in Scotland, or matching his skill with other famous "guns" during the partridge and pheasant seasons in England. So I grew up in an atmosphere of shooting. Before I went to school I used to hire myself out as a beater and was paid two shillings a day.

But, since my father was almost a fanatic on the subject of the handling of firearms, there could be no question of my using a gun until I had memorized a long piece of doggerel entitled "A Father's Advice," the first and last verses of which went something like this:

If a sportsman true you'd be
Listen carefully to me:
Never, never let your gun
Pointed be at anyone;
That it might unloaded be
Matters not the least to me.

You may hit or you may miss,
But at all times think of this:
All the game birds ever bred
Won't repay for one man dead.

Bad poetry, I agree, but it saved me from ever making a dangerous shot.

I was a guest at several of the great pheasant shoots of the sumptuous era before the First World War. These spectacular affairs were organized on a lavish scale. Fifty to a hundred beaters would drive or flush the birds from coverts towards the guns, ranging from four to eight in number. A good day's bag was a thousand head, but two thousand was not uncommon on the larger estates.

But I shall never forget a certain day two years later at Hall Barn, near Beaconsfield, the home of Lord Burnham, one of the Fleet Street Barons, and then owner of the *Daily Telegraph*. On December 18, 1913, my father and I were invited to shoot there with Lord Charles Fitzmaurice, Mr. Henry Stonor, Lord Ilchester, Lord Dalhousie, and Lord Herbert Vane-Tempest. Lord Burnham had set himself out to show that he could provide the King with the biggest shoot in history. I always suspected that in addition to the birds raised on the place, a good many hundred pheasants were brought in and released for the King's benefit.

We were six hours in the field, and the show of birds was fantastic. My father was deadly that day and used three guns. He had an individual, stylized way of shooting—left arm extended straight along the barrel, both eyes open. An onlooker reported that at one stand he saw my father bring down thirty-nine pheasants before missing one. Young and unused to firing as I was, my left arm ached from lifting my gun, my shoulder from the recoil, and I was deaf and stunned from the banging. Then, about one o'clock, we were conducted to a large tent where waited some twenty distinguished guests whom our host had invited from London to meet the King and partake of a baronial repast of the choicest of victuals and the rarest of wines. A story was later told that one of the guests with simpler tastes floored the harassed major-domo by calling for a glass of iced water, which was the only item the unfortunate man had not provided.

When in the late afternoon the carnage stopped, almost 4,000 pheasants had been killed. The bright, limp carcasses were laid out in rows of 100; the whole place was littered with feathers and spent cartridges. My father had shot over 1,000 birds; I had even passed the 300 mark. He was proud of the way he had shot that day, but I think that the scale of the bag troubled even his conscience; for, as we drove back to London, he remarked, "Perhaps we went a little too far to-day, David."

Actually my father got more enjoyment out of what he used to call "a small day" at Sandringham. That part of Norfolk is the sportsman's paradise, with its coverts and heathland and the marshes. Each spot had its special name, and I can still remember some of them: Whin Hill, Grimston Car, Captain's Close, Cat's Bottom, Folly Hang, and Ugly Dale. My father knew them all; each had its memories of a difficult shot or a right and left at woodcock.

He often took me with him to beat out coverts, to walk up game in the heathland, or to tramp the fens and marshes for wild duck, teal, and snipe. These "small days" were unplanned. We would start off from York Cottage on foot with dogs and keepers to retrieve and carry the game. Mr. Jones would come along if his school was closed for the holidays, and sometimes one of the tenant farmers would be invited to join us—Mr. George Brereton or Mr. Stanton or Mr. Bullard—simple men of fine old yeoman stock who would address my father as "Your Majesty" but who, in the field, were his equals. We would walk all day with only a brief halt for a light lunch. The great thing was to "fill the card"—to try to secure at least one of each of the kind of game listed on the printed game card.

Sometimes it would be dark before the last species had been brought down. Out on these forays my father was in his element. Stimulated by the bracing air and hard exercise and on the alert for a flushed bird, he would put aside the cares of State. He laughed and joked, and these "small days" provided some of my happiest memories of him.

CHAPTER VI

STUDENT PRINCE

THE foreign phase of my education began in the spring of 1912, with a four-month trip to France. Mr. Hansell and Finch accompanied me; and, resorting to the convenient Royal practice of the incognito, I travelled as the "Earl of Chester." This device had its precedent and had been successfully employed by my grandfather when, using the title "Baron Renfrew," he visited the United States in 1860. It had the practical advantage of relieving the French Government of the obligation of rendering the honours due to me as Heir Apparent, and I on my side escaped the ordeal of having to respond to them. There was, however, no such reprieve from the Press; and from Paris, my second night in a foreign land, I wrote to my father:

> . . . There were a great many photographers at the Gare du Nord, & they let off a flash light as I was getting out of the train, which was very disconcerting. They are a great nuisance, & there were about 10 on board the steamer, & they followed one about the whole time. . . . I noticed on the way [from the Station], the chairs & tables in front of the cafés which you told me about. But as it was very cold, the chairs were very deserted. . . .

It must not be supposed from this naïve, uninspired account of my arrival in France that I was not inwardly excited at the prospect of this stay abroad. This was the first time I had been abroad since I had been taken to Denmark when I was four years old. I had always harboured a secret desire to travel; and, even if France was not very far afield, it was at least a beginning.

In Paris I was handed over to the care of the Marquis de Breteuil, who had been a close friend of my grandfather's. An aristocrat of the old school, the Marquis was wealthy, a *bon viveur*, a

dilettante of the arts and of politics, and as much at home shooting
tigers in India as he was in the exclusive salons of Paris. With his
American-born wife and his two sons, François and Jacques, he
lived in a fine house, No. 12, Avenue du Bois de Boulogne, near
the Arc de Triomphe. I had a suite to myself there far superior
to any accommodation I had previously known at home. The
elegant *boiserie* rooms on the second floor exuded the flavour of
le beau monde. And an invitation to one of the de Breteuils'
weekly lunch parties, attended by attractive women and the most
stimulating minds in France—politicians, artists, writers, financiers
—was much sought after socially.

The atmosphere peculiar to all French salons is a pretty heady
mixture. And, while everybody was unfailingly polite to the
young Prince, I am afraid they put me down as just another un-
cultivated Englishman speaking their lovely language with a
barbarous accent. Few wasted more than a word on me. A bow,
a charming phrase, and off they would dart to exercise their powers
of logic and exposition on some gifted compatriot.

Of that brilliant and varied company two figures stand out with
special clarity. One was our Ambassador, Sir Francis Bertie. A
distinguished and portly personage with snow-white hair and
flowing moustache, "Sir Frank" was a typical product of old-
school diplomacy except, perhaps, for his bluntness. In his official
rôle as the King's representative in France it was his duty to keep
a fatherly eye on the young Prince of Wales. If I was not actually
afraid of him, I viewed him with respectful awe.

The other was a venerable Frenchman picturesquely garbed in a
cutaway coat and green tartan trousers. One day I suddenly
realized that I was in the presence of something familiar: the
gentleman was wearing the "trews" of the Black Watch. Fascinated and delighted, I engaged him in conversation, and soon
learned he was the distinguished artist, Édouard Detaille, and a
member of the Académie des Beaux-Arts, whose speciality was
military painting. I finally screwed up my courage to ask him:
"How did you come by those trousers?"

He explained that, having been commissioned by my grandfather to paint some pictures of life in the British Army, he had at
one point been the guest, at Aldershot, of a battalion of the 42nd
Royal Highlanders. "As a result of this pleasant association," he

said, "I was made an honorary member of the officers' mess and presented with these 'trews' from the Quartermaster's stores. To show my appreciation, Sir, I have worn them on special occasions ever since." We became friends; and he invited me to his studio, where he was working on some of the fine military paintings that hang in the Musée des Invalides.

Now there came into my life yet another tutor, M. Maurice Escoffier of the École Libre des Sciences Politiques, who was to teach me not only French grammar but French history and to show me the sights of Paris and other parts of his country. Not the least of his attributes was a flowing beard—a fact that prompts the observation that my early life seems to have progressed through a forest of beards. Every morning he would be ushered into my sitting-room, in tail coat, bowler hat, grey gloves, and with a formidable collection of books under his arm. After I had overcome my initial distaste for the pungent aroma of the French "Caporal" cigarettes to which he was addicted, he and I became good friends.

At first the Professor could hardly speak a word of English; but four months later, out of the sheer necessity of communicating with me, he had gained a far greater mastery of my language than I had of his. Whenever I got too entangled in French grammar he would take me sight-seeing—the Louvre, the Invalides, Notre Dame, the Musée Carnavalet, Versailles, St. Germain, Fontaine-bleau. But there was a drawback to this, too. I had to write an essay in French about each place I visited, which detracted some-what from the pleasure of these otherwise-interesting excursions.

The Marquis de Breteuil saw to it that my social life was broad-ened by taking me to a number of select Parisian gatherings. I was painfully shy in those days, and it was a great ordeal for me to meet numbers of strangers. Nevertheless, I was able to meet many interesting French people.

Fortunately my stay in Paris was not all study and museums, and I was not always with older people. The Marquis's two sons became my companions, especially Jacques, the younger. Through them I got to know many of their young friends, and with this group of boys I saw the lighter side of French life. Although older than I, they let me join them at tennis and in their swimming parties.

We went motoring; and with true French *élan* they soon encouraged me to speed along the *routes nationales* to the terror of M. Escoffier who, beard flying, clung by his fingernails to the back seat. A few of these boys often came to the de Breteuils' house of an evening when the Marquis and Marquise were out for dinner, to talk and play cards. And as a diversion they took me up the Eiffel Tower and riding on the switchback at Luna Park.

A fascinating incident during my visit to France was a cruise I made in May with the French Mediterranean fleet off the Côte d'Azur. An interesting footnote to history was that the Minister of Marine, M. Delcassé, personally arranged this naval interlude for me. It was he who fourteen years before, as Minister of Foreign Affairs, had barely averted an Anglo-French war stemming from Colonel Marchand's hoisting of the tricolour at Fashoda on the banks of the Nile in the Sudan.

After four instructive days aboard the battleship *Danton*, my host, Admiral Boué de Lapeyrère, put me ashore at Villefranche. From there I set out for a motor tour of France with my two tutors and Finch. We stopped at provincial towns, inspected historic châteaux, and as a gesture to Mr. Hansell's unique hobby, wandered through nearly every cathedral on our leisurely way north to Paris. At Lyons the mayor, M. Édouard Herriot, then in the seventh year of his perennial mayoralty, conducted me over his Hôtel de Ville. The Schneider family also were my hosts at their great armament works at Le Creusot.

There were times when I felt that my teachers enjoyed the trip a great deal more than I did. The French all love their food, and they all love their wine. I did not drink, and food as such did not interest me; but M. Escoffier encouraged Mr. Hansell to linger at the restaurant tables over the *plat du jour* and the *vin du pays*.

My stay in France was interrupted that June by an important occasion in my life—my eighteenth birthday—for which my father recalled me for a few days to Windsor. On this day I came of age with regard to the succession to the Throne; from then on, were I to succeed my father, I would have full regal powers and there would no longer be need for a regency. This, however, impressed me less at the time than a tangible and satisfying privilege that this birthday brought me. Now that I was eighteen my

father—a stickler for Navy rules—lifted the ban on my smoking.
Like most boys, I had already secretly sampled the pleasing effects
of nicotine; but the fact that I could now smoke in public gave
me more self-assurance and increased my stature in the eyes of
Mary and my brothers.

July passed pleasantly at the Marquis de Breteuil's charming
château near Chevreuse. It was a welcome change from the
formalities of Paris and provided full scope for the country pursuits I loved. One day at the end of that month I was summoned
by the President of the French Republic to the Palais de l'Élysée.
There M. Fallières decorated me with the Legion of Honour—
"except death," as a cynic once remarked, "the only thing a
Frenchman cannot hope to escape."

With sad farewells to happy memories and my friends, I returned
home, and that was the end of "Lord Chester." If I did not learn
much of the language, France had helped to dilute my sorrow over
having to give up the Navy. But it had also whetted my appetite
for travel; and Oxford in consequence loomed as a dreary chore
to be finished with the least possible effort and as quickly as
possible.

From my point of view, as a human being, the easy conditions
under which I took up residence at Oxford in October, 1912,
were a vast improvement over those laid down by the Prince
Consort for my grandfather some fifty years before. To prevent
young Albert Edward's possible contamination from too intimate
association with the undergraduates of Christ Church, my
grandfather was obliged to live apart in a rented house, with
a large household, and to wear a special gown when he attended
lectures. His classmates had to rise respectfully whenever he
entered "Hall" or a lecture room.

Fortunately for me, all that had passed by the time I went to
Oxford. I took my place freely among the other four thousand
undergraduates—a circumstance that was hailed by the Press as
fresh evidence of the innate democracy of the British Monarchical
system. But the Socialist son of a miner who might sit beside
me at lectures would scarcely have agreed that I entirely shared
the common lot. I had been spared having to pass Responsions,
the University entrance examinations. The rooms assigned to
me at Magdalen in "Cloisters" had been specially redecorated;

and I had a tub—the first private undergraduate bathroom, I believe, to be installed at the College. Also I had with me my personal tutor, Mr. Hansell, who occupied a room directly under mine, and my valet, Finch. And my princely status was further established by my father's appointment of an equerry, Major the Honourable William Cadogan, of the 10th Hussars, to attend me on non-academic occasions. Also, for reasons that soon became apparent, Dr. T. Herbert Warren (later knighted), the President of Magdalen College and a former Vice-Chancellor of the University, took a special interest in me.

Yet all these ostensible advantages could not entirely cure my nostalgia for the Navy. All around me were young men united in friendships formed at Eton, Harrow, Winchester, Charterhouse, and all the other public schools. At first I was acutely lonely, and I was under the added disadvantage of being something of a celebrity.

A crowd of reporters and photographers descended upon Oxford to record for the popular Press the more intimate aspects of my adjustment to university life. Their vivid accounts in turn stimulated a rush of tourists, and for two or three days I hardly dared to venture out of my rooms lest I find myself the object of their concentrated gaze. Nor did I wish to be seen near the College deer park until all the publicity had died down, for the local guides had spread the story that the park had been restocked to enable me to do a little stalking when my studies palled.

All this vulgar commotion within Magdalen's ancient precincts irritated the Fellows, but no more so than the undergraduates, who showed their displeasure by emptying pitchers of water upon the inquisitive sightseers' heads.

The plain fact is, of course, that I was pretty much of a problem to Oxford. To be sure, I could box a compass, read naval signals, run a picket boat, and make cocoa for the officer of the watch. But these accomplishments, which the Navy had been at such pains to teach me, were manifestly without significance to Oxford's learned dons.

To lead me with all possible celerity into the higher fields of learning, Oxford generously gave me access to its best brains. I attended the history lectures of Mr. Charles Grant Robertson, later Vice-Chancellor of the University of Birmingham. The

Rev. Lancelot Ridley Phelps, later Provost of Oriel College, talked to me voluminously on political economy. My study of the French language continued under M. Berthon; and Professor Hermann Fiedler, who later became Taylorian Professor of Modern Languages, was brought in to improve my German.

But of all the erudite men selected as my tutors I especially remember Sir William Anson, a distinguished British jurist and Warden of All Souls College. Every Monday morning the door of his house on High Street was opened to my ring. Sir William would be waiting in his study dressed in a morning coat—his habitual garb. After a brief comment on the weather this brilliant, distinguished, and charming man discoursed in a rare musical voice for an hour on constitutional law and the political problems of the day.

My Thursday morning sessions with Dr. Warren were, I regret, not so rewarding. A burly man with a beard, he undertook as a pundit of English poetry to fire my interest in the humanities. With half a dozen other undergraduates we met weekly in his book-lined study to read aloud for his direct criticism essays on various subjects prepared at his direction. We all dreaded this hour. Our essays were dull and the President's comments uninspiring; but, looking through these compositions to-day, I find they did reflect to some extent my interests at the time. Historical characters appear to have attracted me more than the poets. But, given my choice of subject, which was sometimes the case, I found less difficulty in giving expression to my youthful enthusiasm. I became especially absorbed in the epic of Captain Scott.

The President was a man of learning; it was therefore disillusioning to discover that the thing he appeared to value most in the world was his connexion with a certain baronet, a fact he managed to insert into every conversation. It was generally suspected that he was obsessed with the idea of filling Magdalen with titled undergraduates; hence, whenever he beamed upon me, I was never quite certain whether it was with a teacher's benevolence or from a collector's secret satisfaction with a coveted trophy.

Yet, despite this formidable outlay of intellect, Oxford failed to make me really studious. The old witticism, "only the poor learn at Oxford," had long since ceased to have any meaning. However, even in my time there were still a few men to whom graduation meant little more than the satisfaction of having passed the examinations and was not a prerequisite to the comfortable futures that, barring family financial disasters, they had good reason to look forward to. For relaxation I have always preferred outdoor exercise to reading. And, ever since I can remember, it has been from people rather than from text-books that I have got my education. So it was not only to save his venerable institution from one day being blamed for the absence of intellectual qualities in the Heir Apparent but also as a shrewd judge of character that Dr. Warren published after I had left Oxford a generous but somewhat apologetic report upon my progress: "Bookish he will never be: not a 'Beauclerk,' still less a 'British Solomon,' " he warned, adding, however, ". . . all the time he was learning more and more every day of men, gauging character, watching its play, getting to know what Englishmen are like, both individually and still more in the mass. . . ."

If by "learning . . . of men" Dr. Warren had in mind that along with English literature, modern languages, and constitutional law there was a bright leavening of all forms of amusement, Oxford certainly lived up to its reputation as a teacher. I was initiated into the more sophisticated pleasures of carousing and even indulged in mild games of roulette. The stakes were not high, but the conspiratorial atmosphere in which these games of chance were conducted added to the excitement. In this way I got to know some young men whose upbringing had been a good deal less strict than mine.

There were plenty of excuses for celebration. If the College Eight had "bumped" itself to "head of the river" on the Isis during Eights Week, the feat would be celebrated with a festive "bump supper" in "Hall" that would climax with a bonfire inside the walls, fed with furniture tossed out of the rooms of undergraduates who had incurred their classmates' displeasure.

Twenty-first birthdays by custom called for a party, and, eventually, the carrying out of those who could no longer walk by those who thought they could. And on Sunday evenings after dinner in "Hall" everybody who counted for something repaired to "Gunner's," a musty little taproom at the foot of the stairway leading to the Junior Common Room, where Gunstone, the steward, a plump, red-faced, bald-headed old-timer, dispensed beer and other drinks. There with mounting enjoyment we listened to his rough stories and never left until he had performed his famous banana trick—inserting a banana in the neck of a bottle filled with burning paper and watching the vacuum suck it down with a thud. The only time my father came to Oxford to see me I had Gunner perform this feat for his special benefit. "By God," said the King appreciatively, "that is one of the darnedest tricks I have ever seen."

Whatever the occasion, Magdalen celebrations always ended the same way. Arms linked together, the celebrants would head for the President's house, to stand swaying under his bedroom window, chanting in chorus, "Well rowed, the Pree." Wholly apart from his literary leanings, Dr. Warren's corpulence would have removed him from any conceivable athletic connexion; nevertheless, all through the night little bands of undergraduates would deviate from their way to bed to pay the President this incongruous compliment.

It is characteristic of collegiate memories that in reminiscence the hell-raising side momentarily overshadows the daily plodding drudgery I always associated with study. Oxford is a serious place; and the truth is that my days by and large were sober, tranquil, and studious. In the winter my leisure was given to football, beagling with the New College, Magdalen, and Trinity packs, and riding; in the summer I punted on the Cherwell and went for natural-history walks. At these pursuits and in the company of the small groups who forgathered in mine or other men's rooms when the evening work was over, I formed new friendships that compensated in part for the uprooted attachments of the Navy.

The experiment of sending me to France the year before having apparently had no ill effects, it was my mother's idea that I should go to Germany during the Easter and summer vacations in 1913. The purpose of these two trips was to improve my German and to teach me something about these vigorous people whose blood flows so strongly in my veins. For I was related in one way or another to most of the many Royal houses that reigned in Germany in those days. So I progressed sumptuously from one *königlichen Palast* or *grossherzoglichen Schloss* to another, sampling the lavish, if formal, hospitality my kind relatives had to offer. It is strange, looking back on the life of those German courts of varying size and importance as I knew them, to think how close they were to the end of their stiffly ordered days. With defeat in war, in 1918, the power of those hierarchies—the focal-points of the social pattern of the pre-war Reich—disappeared almost overnight. And, although some of the rulers still retained their castles and their estates and even the respect and affection of their subjects, their courts were relegated to the limbo of Graustark.

About the middle of March of that year I set off for Württemberg with Major Cadogan in place of Mr. Hansell; Dr. Hermann Fiedler, a jovial man of fifty with the moustache of a German burgher, in place of M. Escoffier, and always the faithful Finch. I enjoyed the motor trip up the Rhine and seeing the places of interest on the way to Stuttgart, where I was the guest at the palace of King Wilhelm and Queen Charlotte of Württemberg. For a *Königspaar* Onkel Willie and Tante Charlotte were sympathetic and easygoing. Their ample figures betrayed the justice they did to their four full meals a day. Their pleasures were simple and sedentary. As a diversion from the quiet evenings spent at the palace or in their box at the opera, the King would escape to dine with one of his regiments—*"Den zweiten Uhlanen"* or *"Den gelben Dragonern."*

After an enormous lunch, almost every fine afternoon the King and Queen took a leisurely drive through the suburbs of Stuttgart in an open victoria, and sometimes I was summoned to drive with them. Under the influence of the warm sun and the gentle motion of the carriage, Onkel Willie would quickly fall asleep, only to be constantly aroused by a swift jab of the Queen's elbow to acknowledge the salute of one of his soldiers, the precise salutation of a stolid Württemberger, or to straighten the Homburg hat that kept sliding rakishly to one side of his head. This process had been going on for so many years that, when Onkel Willie got that dig into his well-padded ribs, he was able to straighten his hat in his sleep.

From Stuttgart I paid Count Zeppelin a visit at his airship plant at Friedrichshafen on the Lake of Constance. Then at the ripe age of seventy-five, this vigorous old man showed me the Z4, the latest dirigible he had built, and in the evening entertained me with his reminiscences of the Franco-Prussian War of 1870.

I got a great deal more out of my second trip to Germany. I spoke the language more fluently and had come to know the habits and customs of the country better. With the same companions I set forth by motor from Munich on a comprehensive sightseeing tour, which took us eventually to the sleepy little town of Neustrelitz. Here my host was the genial Adolphus, Grand Duke of Mecklenburg-Strelitz; but the dominating personality at the great *Schloss* was his mother, the old Grand Duchess. Born Princess Augusta Caroline of Cambridge, a granddaughter of George III and my mother's aunt, I had known Aunt Augusta since I was a child, when she lived in widowhood in London. Every day I spent at least an hour with her in her own wing of the *Schloss*, listening to anecdotes of her long life, which for my educational benefit she croaked to me in German. At ninety-one she could hark back to the day in the late 1820's when her uncle, George IV, had patted her on the head.

If the atmosphere of the grand ducal court at Neustrelitz—my seminary for six weeks—was distinctly elderly, I took advantage of its even, unchanging tempo to work hard at my German with Dr. Fiedler. Still, I eagerly seized upon invitations, which were fortunately not wanting, to sample more stimulating company. The first came from Prince Henry of Prussia, the Kaiser's younger brother, who asked me to spend a few days with him and his family at Hemmelmark, Eckernförde, near Kiel. Uncle Henry, a good-looking man with a greying beard, was a senior flag officer in the German Navy. I do not know whether it was his sailor's make-up or his more flexible and sympathetic approach to life, but of all my German relatives he impressed me the most. In the navy yard at Kiel, where he took me aboard some of the latest German warships, there was no mistaking his authority as a *Grossadmiral*. But back at the Herrenhaus, which he had built for himself, he preferred working about his property or in his garage to the more pompous pastimes of those days. Uncle Henry sponsored modern ideas and inventions with vigour and enthusiasm. In fact his great interest in the development of the still comparatively primitive motor-car brought him often to Great Britain, where he competed in automobile endurance tests. He had a great way with people and looked you straight in the eye. His un-questioned popularity and his pro-British leanings brought him, so I was told, into conflict with his Imperial brother, who jealously denied him the top Navy posts, for which he was pre-eminently qualified.

The next invitation came from my second cousin, Charles Edward, Duke of Saxe-Coburg and Gotha. He was posthum-ously born Duke of Albany, but a tortuous set of circumstances had made him ruler of the German Duchy from which had come Albert, the Prince Consort. Queen Victoria was determined that one of her direct descendants should always reign over her be-loved husband's ancestral domain. When in 1900, therefore, the Dukedom fell vacant and only her grandson Charlie would accept the hereditary obligation, she removed him, while a schoolboy at Eton, from his native land to Coburg. Charlie was only ten years older than I, and I had known him in Great Britain, to which he would often escape from his enforced exile in Ger-many. Guessing that I must be longing at Strelitz for company nearer my age, and knowing that I liked sport, he invited me to his Gothic castle at Reinhardsbrunn near Gotha, to shoot deer on his vast wooded estate in the Thuringian Forest.

After these excursions Neustrelitz seemed even more confined; and, as no more invitations were forthcoming, I began to invent plausible excuses for going to Berlin, a gay city in those pre-war days. There I had my first taste of night life. I would somehow manage to park the good Professor Fiedler in the hotel after dinner, while Major Cadogan and I would join a party of friends for a night of dancing not on the Baedeker schedule. The *Kino Königin* was the hit musical show at the Metropole Theatre, and the Palais de Danse one of the more respectable of night clubs.

But there was one obligation that had to be fulfilled before I left Germany: that was to pay a courtesy call on Kaiser Wilhelm II. I knew him distantly, of course, from his spectacular descents upon our little island; but at the *königlichen Schloss*, Unter den Linden, in Berlin, I saw him for the first time in his own environ-ment. Arriving in the late afternoon, I was taken at once to the Emperor's room. He was sitting in uniform behind an extra-ordinarily high desk; and in greeting me he rose in a most curious manner, as if dismounting from a horse. Upon drawing closer I saw to my astonishment that he had risen from a wooden block shaped like a horse's body; to this was girthed a military saddle, complete with stirrups. Noting my startled expression, the Emperor smiled and explained condescendingly that he was so accustomed to sitting on a horse he found a saddle more conducive to clear, concise thinking than a conventional desk chair.

The Kaiser's saddle was only the first of a series of exciting events in store for me. I dined that night with him, the Empress, and several other members of the family. The Kaiser, in a different and more colourful uniform, led the conversation in German to test my fluency. Satisfied that I had not been wasting my time, he relapsed into English, which he spoke well, and asked all sorts of questions about my parents and his English relatives.

Dinner over, he excused himself, only to reappear almost immediately in the most dazzling uniform of all, and whisked me off alone to the opera for a performance of *Aïda*. We swept through the streets in a gleaming limousine; a *Jäger*, in a rich, green uniform, with gilt hunting dagger and plumed hat, rode in front, while distinctive notes on the horn warned the police to hold the traffic for the Emperor.

But for all his striking uniforms and brusque manners, Wilhelm II had undoubted charm, of which I caught the full effect. The next day when I re-entered his study to take my leave, he was again astride that incredible saddle, his face, with upturned moustache, bent over a document. He expressed the hope that I had learned something of the German people from my stay, adding that, despite all the terrible things my country thought about them, he and they really were not so difficult to get along with. And at this impressionable age I believed him. Kaiser Wilhelm played all parts. He was impatient, haughty, equally eager to please, to frighten, or to astonish; paradoxically stubborn-minded and weak-minded, and, above all, truly humourless. He did little in foreign affairs—or in anything else—that he did not shout from the housetops.

Much of what I saw in Germany impressed me. I admired the industry, the perseverance, the discipline, the thoroughness, and the love of the Fatherland so typical of the German people, qualities that were to be found in every calling—in officials and industrialists, in soldiers and workers, in engineers and craftsmen, in the huntsmen who had taken me shooting, and in the waiters who served me steins in the beer halls. Before the madness of its leaders was evident, Germany was a prosperous, industrious, and agreeable country. It echoed with work and song. Although the war clouds were unmistakably gathering, I must confess that I, like most people, saw but few indications of the impending catastrophe. I ended in liking Germany so much that I left planning another trip in 1914, little knowing that it would be more than five years before I would sojourn there again, and then as a guest of an army commander in the victorious American Expeditionary Force.

My second year at Oxford slipped by, outwardly as uneventful as the first. But knowing that the education of Princes goes beyond the confines of dons and books, my father began to select opportunities to induct me into Court ceremonial and diplomatic ways. He had already deputed me to meet the President of the French Republic, Raymond Poincaré, on his arrival at Portsmouth for a visit the previous June. One evening there was a State banquet in the President's honour: ". . . there were 190 people. Papa & the President made speeches & we rose at 9.45 talking to many people till 10.45. I got on well with all the Ambassadors etc. . . ." Two nights later there was a State ball, ". . . which commenced with a 'quadrille d'honneur' & I danced with Aunt Toria." In November my father called me from Oxford to Windsor when the Archduke Franz Ferdinand, Heir Apparent to the Austro-Hungarian Empire, came to England with his wife, the Fürstin Hohenberg, and they were invited to stop at the Castle for two days. For the big dinner in the evening I wore the Windsor uniform and afterward practised the subtle art of talking to the right people about the right things. The next day there was a duck shoot in the Great Park. There I watched the Archduke, who could match my father as a wing shot, pull two hundred and seventy-three birds down out of the sky. No suggestion of tragedy then touched the elegant couple who only seven months later would fall before the assassin's fateful bullets at Sarajevo.

But, while my father was showing me how he entertained foreign Royalty and I was doing my best to play my part at these Court functions with credit, I was beginning to form my own ideas about all this lavish hospitality. Although this State pomp and ceremony had previously seemed exciting and colourful and I had accepted it all without question, my association at Oxford with men far removed from the trappings of Royal life had begun to give me a more sceptical view. When I was once more called from Oxford the following spring for another of these State visits, this time by the King and Queen of Denmark, the comments that I confided to my diary after the formal banquet would have surprised my father: "... I took in Granny. ... Then we stood about in the picture gallery till 11.15 talking to the guests. ... What rot & a waste of time, money, & energy all these State visits are!! This is my only remark on all this unreal show & ceremony!!"

During my last year at Oxford my interests as well as my opinions were changing. Although I had learned to ride as a child, I had been brought up in the atmosphere of game and guns at Sandringham and in Scotland. The manly accomplishment that I coveted above all others, therefore, was to be a good shot rather than a good man to hounds. Then one day, soon after I had been removed from the Navy, my father saw me riding and suddenly discovered that my seat on a horse—an indispensable accomplishment for Princes in those days—left much to be desired.

From then on he was constantly finding fault with me on this score. He even tried to shame me by telling me he had heard how impressed the British Cavalry officers in India had been by the horsemanship of the Crown Prince of Germany. But to no avail; I just did not like riding. However, at Oxford I had to comply—if with bad grace—with his instructions to my equerry, Major Cadogan, that he should make me ride four hours a week. "I motored to Nuneham at 9.15 with Major Cadogan & I went out for an hour's ride in the park there. It is very dull & I only do it because Papa wants me to. ..." But Major Cadogan was both patient and tactful. He taught me to jump fences with confidence, and riding gradually became a pleasant recreation and not a dull chore. Eventually Major Cadogan took me out with the South Oxfordshire Hounds. "Got back at 5.15 after 7 hrs. in the saddle!! So ended my first day's hunting & I enjoyed it. ... I wore a 'topper' & hunting coat, but the hat didn't fit & bothered. However, it was a successful day. . . ." It is not without irony that from so reluctant a beginning riding was later to become my favourite pastime.

By June, 1914, it was agreed that I had had enough of Oxford. Instead of returning to Magdalen for the following Christmas term I had persuaded my parents to let me travel for the balance of the year before I should join the 2nd Battalion of the Grenadier Guards the following January. In fact my Army career had already begun in the Oxford Battalion of the Officers' Training Corps. I had reached the rank of corporal and had to my credit two "summer camps" under canvas near Aldershot. The Adjutant, Captain Henry Maitland Wilson of the Rifle Brigade (now Field-Marshal Lord Wilson of Libya), worked us hard and long on day and night operations in the field. On one occasion we were ordered to Laffan's Plain to see the King's Birthday Parade of the Aldershot garrison. As we watched the troops, in full-dress review order, march past the Commander-in-Chief, Sir Douglas Haig (later Field-Marshal Earl Haig), little did we suspect that within a few months their ranks would be decimated in war. In June, 1914, the atmosphere was still deceptively tranquil.

That O.T.C. training camp ended my connexion with Oxford. During the month of July I was attached to the 1st Life Guards. Although I had already learned to ride quite well enough to enjoy the rough and tumble of the hunting-field, my father thought there was still much that the riding master of the 1st Life Guards could teach me. From nine to eleven each morning I paraded with the recruits in the riding school. We were put through the most bone-jarring exercises—mounted sword drill, riding bareback, jumping fences, and vaulting off and on horses at the canter.

But the riding master did not claim all my time, for this was my first experience of a "London Season," and I entered into it with zest. Until then I had been of a retiring nature. Perhaps it was my strict upbringing; but, looking back on my early years, I can remember being shy and scared of strangers. As recently as March, 1913, my reactions to a party at Buckingham Palace show how little I cared for social functions. ". . . 300 people came for a private dance. . . . I had to dance, a thing I hate. However, I started off with Miss B. & was frightfully nervous . . . the whole thing was a great strain. . . . I was *very* glad when it was over. . . ."

During my last year at Oxford, however, the inhibitions from which I had suffered began to disappear, and I gained confidence in myself. In short, I was growing up. And so that July I began to learn, as my diary attests, about the gayer side of life.

> Tuesday, July 7th, 1914—Buckingham Palace, London. . . . to dine with Ld. & Lady Londesborough. . . . After dinner a lot more people arrived & there was a dance. I stuck out to the bitter end & got back at 2 a.m. . . . I enjoyed it immensely; my 1st ball in London!
> . . . July 8th. . . . to the Duke of Portland's house. . . . my dancing is improving. I got in at 4.
> . . . July 9th. . . . I was up again at 6.00 & walked to Barracks. . . . on to Lady Salisbury's ball. . . . I have now become fond of dancing & love going out!! . . .
> . . . July 10th. . . . I've had no more than 8 hrs. sleep in the last 72 hrs. !!

I was then twenty, and, while my contemporaries and I were enjoying the last weeks of the "old order," my father was wrestling with some of the most troublesome political problems of his reign. He and my mother were harassed by suffragettes at the races, in the theatres, or wherever they appeared in public; and the rejection of the Irish Home Rule Bill in the House of Lords had made Civil War between the Catholic South and the Protestants of Ulster more than a possibility. Ever since June 28, the day the Archduke Franz Ferdinand and his wife were assassinated at Sarajevo, my father had been in constant touch with the Secretary of State for Foreign Affairs, Sir Edward Grey. But it was not until the last days of July that the full international implications of this villainous act became apparent.

My realization that the war clouds were gathering and soon to burst upon my pleasant world is reflected in my diary: ". . . I dined . . . on King's Guard at St. James's Palace. . . . I don't like the look of things abroad." The following Sunday Uncle Henry of Prussia, who had been paying one of his frequent visits over here, called at Buckingham Palace to say good-bye to my father. We were coming out of church when he arrived; Uncle

Henry and I shook hands warmly. I had happy memories of my stay at Hemmelmark the year before, and I felt that his Anglophile sentiments made him dread the awful possibility of war between our two countries as much as we did. I never saw him again.

There were but few indications the last week of July in the barracks of the 1st Life Guards of the seriousness of the situation. The recruits and I still paraded for riding school at 9 o'clock every morning. The Officers' Mess was very deserted because most of the officers had gone to Goodwood for the races. Despite this apparent indifference what I wrote in my diary on July 31 expressed, I am sure, the inward apprehensions of all my friends. ". . . I was reading newspapers all night, & Papa received news of Belgium's mobilization. All this is too ghastly & that we should be on the brink of war is almost incredible; I am very depressed."

CHAPTER VII

THE GRIM SCHOOL OF WAR

O N August 3, 1914, the day before the German Army struck into Belgium, I spent part of the afternoon alone in a squash-rackets court at the Bath Club in Dover Street, batting a small rubber ball against a blank wall. I felt lonely and frustrated. As I watched the 1st Life Guards mobilizing for active service, I realized that unless I got busy I should miss the war we all judged would end so quickly. But I immediately found myself confronted with a unique personal problem: was I to see active service in the field or was I to be kept at home, not to be risked in battle?

Had I been any other youth of twenty that question would never have arisen. In the normal course of events I would have enlisted and been sent overseas, where, in all probability, I should have been killed or certainly wounded within a year. But, as Prince of Wales and Heir Apparent to the Throne, I was to discover that my trophy value exceeded my military usefulness. In any event, my father, in the midst of the crisis, told me that I must wait in London until "suitable employment" could be found for me.

What this order, on the eve of war, meant to me can be judged from the entry I made in my diary the night of August 3 before I went to bed in Buckingham Palace:

> . . . I returned terribly depressed as of course the only topic was the war, & I haven't the remotest chance of getting out with the expeditionary force. The knowledge that I must remain in London (for some time anyhow) totally devoid of a job of any description, is becoming almost intolerable. . . . was out walking with Cadogan [my equerry] from 6.00 to 7.30 . . . to kill time!! I had to come in through the garden on account of a dense crowd

which was airing its patriotism in front of the Palace. The parents went out on the balcony just before dinner at 8.30 & twice again before 10.30 as fresh masses arrived. They sang and cheered the whole evening. . . . Such a relieving sign to feel that the people are backing everything up. . . . Thank God the Gov't have decided that France shall not be deserted. Oh!! God; the whole thing is too big to comprehend!! Oh!! that I had a job.

And this, the next night, August 4:

> . . . At 10.30 came the news that Germany had declared war. . . . A privy Council was at once summoned for Papa to sign our declaration of war, & as soon as this was known in the crowd outside, excitement became intense. Then amid an unparalleled demonstration of patriotism the parents showed themselves at 11.00 before going to bed. But the people remained singing, cheering and whistling for another 3 hrs. & I was lulled to sleep by their fearful shindy at 1.30. The die is cast; may God protect the fleet!!

Crowds stood for days and nights outside Buckingham Palace, collecting, dispersing, and re-forming, filling the great rooms with their tumultuous sounds. I watched them often from my bedroom window; and, reflecting to-day upon that scene across the void of two world wars, I believe that in the behaviour of those friendly, patient, hopeful, and patriotic crowds lies a key to many of the changes that have come over our times. How different was the mood of the great masses of people in 1939. Then so many young men went forth to fight in a hard and cynical frame of mind; they had been raised on sombre tales of the mass slaughters on the Western Front; they had heard all about war from their fathers, its waste and folly and elusive victories. In 1914 the holocaust lay ahead and unknown. The people outside Buckingham Palace were of good conscience. None of the stratagems of the crowd-psychologist leaders of the present-day totalitarian States had been required to herd them there. They had been summoned by the simple loyalties and uncorroded faiths of this country's uncommonly fine common man.

On August 6 my personal crisis was temporarily resolved:

> . . . Then asked [my father] for a commission in the Grenadiers stating that I could no longer tolerate being unable to serve my

country. And dear Papa never hesitated a moment, & immediately instructed Ld. Stamfordham to notify this to the War
Office.... It was a happy moment for me, & now I am an officer
in the army & am going to do active service!! I get away from
this awful palace where I have had the worst weeks of my life!! ...

However, the question of what to do about me was only one
of the private problems the war suddenly thrust into the well-
regulated life of the King and Queen. In the first place, my sister
Mary had a German maid, Else, whom all of us loved for her
devotion and warm-hearted personality. While it was unthink-
able to any of us that Else would ever harm Great Britain, it was
obviously impossible for the Royal Family to harbour a German
maid, while war was being waged against her country. My
mother therefore called Else and told her sadly that she would
have to choose between being interned or returning to the
Fatherland. As a loyal German, Else decided to return to her
home and tearfully packed her belongings. While the crowds
were still cheering outside, my mother, Mary, and all of us
brothers wept as we said good-bye to this fine woman whom war,
with its relentless disregard for human ties, was taking from our
midst.

Another situation involved my father's first cousin by marriage,
the First Sea Lord, Admiral Prince Louis of Battenberg, who
had been born in Austria of a German father. A public clamour
arose. It was said that it would be a dangerous thing to leave the
Royal Navy under the command of a German; but my father,
incensed over what he considered a slander upon one of Britain's
finest and most able naval officers, not to mention his own
cousin, fought hard to save him. The smear campaign was taken
up by the popular Press and finally reached the floor of the
House. In the end "Uncle Louis" had no alternative but to resign.
I called upon him at the Admiralty while all the fuss was going
on; and the hurt showed in his tired, lined face. "This is indeed
an ignominious end to a lifetime of loyal service to the British
Navy," he said, "but I shall not allow this to embitter me against
my country of adoption." The King stood by him to the end.

My Army commission was signed by my father. On being
gazetted to the Grenadier Guards, I was posted to the 1st Battalion,
stationed at Warley Barracks, Brentwood, in Essex. I was further

detailed to the King's Company. This was a special honour, since my modest 5 feet 7 inches failed by a conspicuous margin to meet the minimum height of 6 feet required for officers and men of this Company. I was a pygmy among giants.

Battalion training was hard work. The companies were taken for long route marches, and sent out on field exercises to toughen the reservists who had rejoined the colours on mobilization. There was firing on the rifle ranges. And with the latest-joined ensigns and recruits I paraded under the sergeant-major for squad drill "on the square." Ten days after I had joined, the 1st Battalion moved to London and was quartered at Wellington Barracks, where the comfort of my two rooms was very welcome after the rugged accommodation at Warley. The sudden granting of forty-eight-hour leave in mid-September was a sure sign that the battalion was going overseas. But my immediate transfer to the 3rd Battalion, stationed at the same barracks, confirmed my earlier suspicions that I would be left behind. It was a terrible blow to my pride, the worst in my life. I went at once to see my father at the Palace and, trying to conceal my bitterness, asked why this had to be. My father answered that it was not his wish but Lord Kitchener's. "Lord Kitchener," he said, "does not want you to go to France just now."

It took all the resolve I could muster, but I managed to secure an interview with Lord Kitchener, who by this time had become Secretary of State for War. Face to face with this immense, fierce-looking man, one would have said that all the slow, stubborn purpose of Britain was concentrated behind his somewhat florid countenance. He listened to my case. "What does it matter if I am killed?" I insisted. "I have four brothers."

Lord Kitchener's steely blue eyes met mine. He answered: "If I were sure you would be killed, I do not know if I should be right to restrain you. But I cannot take the chance, which always exists until we have a settled line, of the enemy taking you prisoner." As a subaltern commanding a platoon, or at most forty men, I would have put a lower valuation upon myself. But there was no budging Lord Kitchener. He vaguely mentioned something about a staff job in France later on, but that was little consolation.

Resigned to West End duties, I reported to the 3rd Battalion.

By this time the Adjutant had judged my drill proficient enough for me to go on "King's Guard," and accordingly he passed me "off the square." Then twice a week for the next two months I went on guard. The first time I went on King's Guard I recorded in my diary: ". . . I was ensign . . . & had to carry the colour which is a good weight!!"

Guard mounting was the ceremony that had thrilled me some ten years before, when as a small boy I had watched it with Bertie, Forsyth, and Cameron from the garden wall of Marlborough House. But now with the Army hanging by a thread at Ypres, the fulfilment of a childhood dream seemed to have lost some of its point. The Expeditionary Force had been fighting for its life in France and Belgium. The German rush on Paris had been halted at the Battle of the Marne, and our retreating divisions had turned about and advanced northward across the Aisne and the Somme to Ypres. The slogging match to hold the salient was on and taking terrible toll of our already decimated brigades. Our guns were soon rationed to one round a day, and our attenuated line held through the heroism of the infantry and the deadliness of their musketry.

Soon the dreaded casualty lists began to appear; and I found the names of my friends, including brother officers in the Brigade of Guards with whom I had trained only a few short weeks before. My equerry, Major Cadogan, was killed with the 10th Hussars; one of my cousins, Prince Maurice of Battenberg, and two of my father's equerries lost their lives about the same time, causing me to exclaim in my diary, "I shan't have a friend left soon." Against the background of these incredible sacrifices my subsequent efforts to find an honourable place in the fighting were of small importance, except to myself.

Eventually, on November 16, 1914, I was sent overseas and attached to the staff of Field-Marshal Sir John French, Commander-in-Chief of the British Expeditionary Force. After an unpleasant Channel crossing and a bleak motor ride I reported at Sir John's General Headquarters at St. Omer, a small provincial town in the Department of Pas-de-Calais. With my soldier servant, Finch, now in khaki, I shared a small house with half a dozen staff officers.

Two days before my arrival at G.H.Q. Lord Roberts had died

at St. Omer. This octogenarian Field-Marshal had fought in all manner of Queen Victoria's wars, mostly in India, where he won the Victoria Cross in the Indian Mutiny. As a small boy I had seen him when he returned to London as the victorious general of the Boer War. Lord Roberts had gone to the front on a sentimental mission to see the Indian divisions that had come to France to fight for Britain's cause. But the winter cold proved too much for the old man; he caught pneumonia and died. With heavy fighting still going on for the Ypres salient, only a Territorial Battalion of Gordon Highlanders could be spared for the old Field-Marshal's funeral. But the General Headquarters staff turned out *en masse*, and with them I marched in the grey morning light behind the gun-carriage bearing the coffin. As the small procession made its way over the cobblestones, led by the pipers playing "The Flowers of the Forest," we were all profoundly stirred.

This lonely martial ceremony ended in a gesture illustrating the old-time veneration of the Indians for their British Sahibs. Among the Indians in France who had come to honour Lord Roberts was Sir Pertāb Singh, of Jodhpur, who had also fought for Queen Victoria and had ridden by her carriage at her Diamond Jubilee. When after the funeral service the coffin was placed in a motor ambulance that would carry it to the Channel, this Rajputana warrior without a word climbed up on the front seat. Although it was freezing and the ambulance had no wind-shield and Sir Pertāb no greatcoat, no one could restrain him; and he made the icy, two-hour drive to Boulogne. That impulsive and generous gesture by this old Indian towards his chief made a deep impression upon me, for it revealed in a flash the powerful loyalties and allegiances that had made the British Empire.

At St. Omer I had my first look at war—the General Headquarters view. We were about thirty miles from the front line, out of earshot of all but the heaviest artillery bombardments. Sir John French had surrounded himself with older officers and friends who instinctively thought of fighting in terms of the tactics of the Boer War. They liked their food and their comforts, and in the opinion of the men in the trenches were quite out of touch with what was actually happening in the line. I well recall my father's incredulous expression when, during his first visit to the troops in France in late November, 1914, Sir John assured him that the war would be over by Christmas.

It was no doubt a lucky thing for the Army that not many soldiers were sent off to war in quite the same way as I was. The last order my father gave me was that I should in no circumstances go into the fighting, nor travel the roads behind the front alone. For a long time the nearest I ever got was Divisional Headquarters. My days were taken up with paper work and the carrying of dispatches—made work, I soon realized, designed to conceal my non-combatant rôle under a show of activity.

The concept of duty was part of my inheritance. Is it surprising, then, that I should have rebelled against being held back in safety while my contemporaries bore the shock of battle? My letters to my father had but one theme: that he would allow me to take a more active part. Let it be said he sympathized with me in my frustration; he even intimated to Sir John French that he would not object to my going more frequently to the forward area. But I felt that such occasional escapes from "my glass case" —as I referred to my confinement at G.H.Q.—were far from what I wanted. I was therefore anxious to enlist support for my cause. Searching for an influential ally, I began to appeal in lengthy letters to wise old Lord Stamfordham. He had already been helpful in getting Lord Kitchener to agree to my appointment in France; and his son, John Bigge, a friend of mine, also had a staff job. We used to commiserate on our predicament, for he was as eager as I to return to his regiment. Lord Stamfordham, anyway, would not reject out of hand all the plausible reasons I was thinking up to convince my father that I should be released from St. Omer and the restrictions imposed on my movements by the Commander-in-Chief.

The first tangible result of my pleadings was my being attached to the 2nd Divisional Headquarters at Béthune, only five miles from the front line. From there I wrote to my father with obvious excitement:

March 1, 1915

Dearest Papa,
. . . Here the Germans are rather close so I didn't go into the front trench proper tho. I managed to see the enemy's trenches as well as a lot of their dead. . . . I spent a grand 10 minutes spot-

ting thro. my stalking glass for an officer who had his rifle aimed on a certain spot in a German trench where men could be seen frequently passing & standing. Whenever I saw a man I told him & he fired!! I never saw one drop but the bullets must have gone fairly close for the men used to disappear v. hurriedly!! . . . So I spent a most wonderful 2 hrs. this morning; 2 hrs. that I shall never forget. . . .

Hardly had I removed my eyes, figuratively speaking, from the fascinating panorama framed within the lens of my stalking glass before I was whisked back, by Sir John French's order, to the safety of St. Omer. An attack was to be mounted a little to the north of Béthune with the high ground around Neuve Chapelle as the objective. The Béthune sector, therefore, was in the G.H.Q. view no place for the Prince of Wales during the battle. After this further disappointment I wrote to Lord Stamfordham:

March 20th, 1915   *Very Private*
                                                   Headquarters,
                                                       British Army,
                                                           St. Omer.

Dear Lord Stamfordham
    . . . The "little push" at Neuve Chapelle last week was a success as far as it went, but the casualty list of killed and wounded officers was a staggering one, wasn't it? . . . Our poor 1st Bn. had 7 officers killed and 7 wounded, as you know!! Ghastly. Of course my position at such times as those 4 days becomes all the more painful and depressing when I know I am only to be a spectator. Of course there is no job I am qualified for but that of a regimental officer. . . . tho. it is sad to have to say it, I have no *real* job except that of being P. of Wales. . . . I am awfully sorry for inflicting you with all my small troubles, but you have always been and are so good and kind to me that I can't help it. . . .

It was not until May, 1915, that I finally managed to break loose for good from Sir John French's staff. From then on, although always denied my ambition to return to regimental duties, I was never again kept so far away from and out of touch with life in the forward area. My first appointment away from G.H.Q. was as a General Staff officer attached to the I Army Corps. I lived with the Corps Commander, Lieutenant-General

Sir Charles Munro, in a château near Béthune, where I "messed" with him. I had as personal A.D.C. Lord Claud Hamilton, a brother officer from the 1st Battalion Grenadier Guards, whom I had known at Warley the year before. Claud Hamilton was one of the four surviving officers who brought the remnants of the Battalion—only one hundred and fifty—out of the first battle of Ypres. He was with me as my A.D.C. until the end of the war.

An army-corps headquarters was closer to the front than G.H.Q., but, as I complained to my father, I was still far from satisfied with the mere paper work assigned to me:

> May 19, 1915
> ... As regards myself it's always office work of various kinds & I never see anything or go near the front. ... I feel that in later years I shall ever regret the fact that I was out so long in N. France & yet saw practically nothing of the fighting or got any proper idea of what our troops had to go thro. I shall have to remember the war by the various towns & places far back which were headquarters of generals I was attached to, of meals, etc!! But I have said enough!! ...

During the four months I was with the I Army Corps, I had been in the practice of slipping up to the front to visit my friends in the various Guards and other regiments and to snatch quick glimpses of the devastation of war. But these surreptitious forays proved unnecessary after September 1915, when I was appointed to the staff of Major-General (later Field-Marshal) Lord Cavan, who had been given command of the newly-formed Guards Division, and under whom I was destined to serve almost the whole of the rest of the war. Frederick Rudolph Lambart, tenth Earl of Cavan—"Fatty" to his brother officers and friends—was of my father's generation, a Grenadier and a keen sportsman who was deeply proud of having fulfilled the two ambitions of his life: to command the 1st Battalion of his regiment and to be Master of the Hertfordshire Hounds.

I joined the Guards Division in the midst of the preparations for the abortive offensive by General Haig's First Army to occupy the ridge beyond Loos. One night while the Division was moving up into reserve for the battle I had the job of directing traffic at a crossroads at Nœux-les-Mines. Ankle-deep in mud I watched two green "New Army" divisions move up to the front, sloshing and clanking in the rain. They had been on the march for twenty-four hours without food or rest. At noon the next day they attacked against murderous German shelling and machine-gun fire. They were stopped short of the enemy line by barbed wire, and eventually the survivors were forced to fall back. Then the Guards were ordered to relieve them, and they put on one of the finest exhibitions of discipline ever seen on any battlefield. Topping the flaming ridge, company by company in extended order, they moved into the attack down the shrapnel-raked hill before Loos as seemingly unconcerned as if training at Pirbright.

But even this partial progress into the combat zone was almost stultified by an unfortunate and tragic incident. Three days after the Guards Division went into the line I accompanied Lord Cavan on one of his frequent tours of his Divisional front-line sector before Loos. We had motored to a ruined village called Vermelles, where we left the cars near the church. What happened next is best described by my diary entry for that day:

Wednesday, September 29th, 1915, H. Q. Guards Div.
Nœux-les-Mines.
... Then commenced probably the 4 most interesting hrs. of my life!! We walked along the rd. to le Rutoire, a solitary ruined farm on the open ground which stretches towards Loos, but there was a battery in position ½ way which was being shelled & we were driven to an old communication trench by a big shell which burst 40 yds. from us!! No more above ground strolls for us after that & we had a muddy progress to H.Q. 1st Gds. Bde. in the ruined farm . . . & after a short pow wow . . . forward to an observation sta. at point G.23 b 5.5 in our present 2 line. To get there we had our original system of trenches round "Triangular Fence" to traverse & then climed out over our front parapet into what was "No man's land" & crossed over to the original German front line past "Lone Tree", which we got down into, due S. of the "Bois Carree." In so doing we were able to see exactly what the assaulting parties of the Div. had to undertake on the morning of the 25th: they had to charge a good 300 yds. across the open towards & past "Lone Tree" after the gas had been turned on!! Of course the dead lie out unburied & in the postures & on the spots as they fell, & one got some idea of the horror & ghastliness of it all!! ... Those dead bodies offered a most pathetic & grue-

some sight; too cruel to be killed within a few yds. of yr. objective after a 300 yds. sprint of death!! This was my 1st real sight
of war, & it moved and impressed me most enormously!! . . .
We emerged near Vermelles church, a muddy pair, for it was one
continuous wallow in a foot of mud the whole way in the trenches.
We found our car all right but had a bad shock when we were
told that Green [my driver] had been killed by a burst of shrap-
nel!!!! We went into No. 4 F. A. dressing sta. close by and saw
the poor man's body; he was hit in the heart & death must have
been instantaneous. . . . I can't yet realise that it has happened!!
. . . This push is a failure. . . . I have seen & learnt a lot about war
today. . . .

Two days later the orders for my transfer from the Guards
Division to the XI Corps Staff came as a personal bombshell.
Exaggerated reports of the incident at Vermelles had reached Sir
John French, which said that my driver had been killed beside me.
By good fortune I happened to meet the Commander-in-Chief
riding along a road in our Divisional area and was able to explain
exactly what had happened. When he saw how upset I was, he
told me to "stand fast"; and after he had heard Lord Cavan
confirm my account, he rescinded the order.

However, I was soon to hear the repercussions from Buckingham Palace. Lord Stamfordham wrote me with his usual understanding; but since his only son John had recently been killed in
action there was an undertone of caution as well:

Buckingham Palace
Octr. 1. 1915

Sir,
    You may like a line to say that while the King grieves to hear
that your chauffeur has been killed and realizes that your car,
and I expect, Cavan and yourself were exposed to heavy fire, His
Majesty received the news quite calmly and without blaming
any one; and by His Majesty's orders I have written to Cavan
saying that he is content to leave it to C's decision where and
when you go into the front with the object of seeing the ground
over which the Division is fighting. But, Sir, you who are so
thoughtful of others, will not, *I feel certain*, forget Lord Cavan
& the heavy weight of responsibility resting upon him in his
Command & remember that your safety, your Life, so precious

to your Country, is *another* care which circumstances has devolved upon him. Make it as light for him as you can Sir! To anyone of your nature it is hard, very hard, to be left behind when the others are at the danger points: but plenty of the Staff have to do the same—and after all, things have worked out better than we at one time expected. You will forgive my writing and take it in the spirit which prompts it. God bless and keep you Sir is the prayer of your humble and devoted servant.

STAMFORDHAM

It took me a long time to become reconciled to the policy of keeping me away from the front line. Manifestly I was being kept, so to speak, on ice, against the day that death should claim my father. But in the midst of all the slaughter of the Western Front, I found it hard to accept this unique dispensation. My generation had a rendezvous with history, and my whole being insisted that I share the common destiny, whatever it might be.

This commotion over the Vermelles incident seemed to me all the more galling as a result of a sharp exchange of letters between my father and me only ten days before:

September 19th/15

Buckingham Palace

Dearest David,

. . . Ld. Cavan has written to Bigge about your wearing the ribbon of the Legion of Honour. It is very silly of you not doing what I told you at Easter time, which was to wear the ribbons of the French and Russian Orders that were given you. I know the French order was given you in peace time, but I explained that if you had not had it, you would have been given it for war service, the same as Uncle Nicky sent you his order especially. The French naturally are hurt if you don't wear it. So get both the ribbons sewn on your khaki at once. . . .

Ever my dear boy,
Yr devoted Papa,
G.R.I.

September 22nd, 1915

My dearest Papa,

. . . First I must apologize . . . I think you know how distasteful it is to me to wear these two war decorations having never done any fighting & having always been kept well out of danger!! I feel so ashamed to wear medals which I only have because of my position, when there are so many thousands of gallant officers, who lead a terrible existence in the trenches and who have been in battles of the fiercest kind (many severely wounded or sick as a result) who have not been decorated. No doubt I look at this thing from a wrong & foolish point of view but this is the view I take. . . .

Ever yr. most devoted son,
DAVID

I was only twenty-one, and I believe it will not be misunderstood if I confess how often I deplored my status at this time: "Oh! not to be a prince."

The battle of Loos was one of the great military fiascos of the war. It was the first large-scale attack made by the Expeditionary Force, and was planned without the support of the "creeping barrage" that proved so effective a protection for assaulting infantry in the offensives subsequent on the Somme. The casualties had in consequence been very heavy, out of all proportion to the results achieved. At the end of October, by the time the troops of the First Army had licked their wounds, my father came out to see them. I had a personal interest in his visits to France: he liked to have me with him, and after months of Army rations and crude billets I appreciated to the full the good food and comfort he provided. We stopped in a château near Sir Douglas Haig's First Army Headquarters, and a very important item on my father's busy schedule was a parade for him of the Guards Division on the afternoon of October 28. But, as matters turned out, a serious mishap prevented his attendance.

My father usually visited the troops by car. When he reached a unit scheduled for inspection, he would get out and walk down the ranks. But Sir Douglas Haig had suggested that the men could see the King better if he were mounted and in the morning had produced his own horse, guaranteed to be completely quiet and crowd-trained. My father acquiesced and rode among the troops, reaching an airfield where the 1st Wing of the Royal Flying Corps was drawn up. He was about to pass on from this group when the officer in charge called for "Three cheers for His Majesty the King." The men's response to the order was so lusty that Sir Douglas Haig's charger took fright, reared up, lost its balance, and fell back on top of my father. I was standing a short distance away with the other staff officers when I heard someone shout, "Oh, my God!" I shall never forget the sight of the horse getting up, leaving my father lying still on the ground. For a few terrifying seconds I thought he was dead. We all rushed towards the limp figure; to our immense relief it moved, and our worst fears were further allayed by our hearing groans of pain mixed with indignant rage. We had no idea of the extent of the injuries; but, lifting him carefully from the ground, we carried him to his car. Propping him up in a sitting posture, I rode with him back to the château. Our progress was slowed by columns of troops marching along the road in the opposite direction. Although obviously in agony, he roused himself and asked me in a strained voice who they were. "They are battalions of the Guards Division you were going to inspect this afternoon," I answered. I had to lean over to catch his words; though they were barely audible, there was no mistaking his disappointment.

It developed that my father's pelvis had been fractured, and four days later he travelled back to London on a stretcher. The first stage of the journey in France was made in a hospital train. During this trip he did something that revealed his constant thoughtfulness for others.

During the battle of Loos, Sergeant Oliver Brooks, a reservist in the 3rd Battalion, Coldstream Guards, had been awarded the Victoria Cross for an outstanding feat of courage in the face of the enemy. For twenty-four hours, almost single-handed, he had held a redoubt against recapture by the Germans with no other weapons than a none-too-plentiful supply of hand grenades. My father remembered that but for his accident he would have decorated the Sergeant at the parade of the Guards Division. He had him come to the train; and in a moving impromptu ceremony with his equerry, Sir Charles Cust, reading the citation the King pinned the Victoria Cross on Brooks's tunic while the Sergeant knelt beside the hospital cot.

In December Sir Douglas Haig succeeded Sir John French as Commander-in-Chief of the British forces in France. Whether this dour, high-minded Scot became too absorbed in military strategy to worry over the safety of the Prince of Wales or whether it was because of my continuous "needling" I shall never know, but thereafter, except for a hard-and-fast direction that I was under no circumstances to rejoin the Grenadiers as a combat officer, the policing of my movements in the forward areas was relaxed. And while I continued to rebel against the restrictions always imposed upon me, I saw a good deal more of the grim and sordid side of modern warfare than was generally known.

During the winter of 1915–16 the Guards Division was holding a quiet if wet and muddy sector of the line. In a letter to my father I tried to describe the squalid and monotonous routine of the troops in the forward area, commenting upon its psychological effect upon officers and men:

> H. Q. Guards Div. La Gorgue
> December 11th, 1915.
>
> My dearest Papa,
>
> . . . Except for the wet all goes on the same as ever, both in the trenches & in rear; its a dull and monotonous life for us all, but far worse for the regimental officers!! Poor people they do have a most miserable time. You know well enough the type of man who officers the Brigade of Guards; well his life may be summed up as follows for 18 days:
>
> | | |
> |---|---|
> | 2 days in a ditch | 2 days in a dirty French cottage |
> | 2 days ,, ,, ,, | 2 days ,, ,, ,, ,, ,, |
> | 2 days ,, ,, ,, | 2 days ,, ,, ,, ,, ,, |
>
> 6 days in a dirty French dwelling in a filthy little town!!
>
> What a life indeed & what must be the effect on their brains? Its a terrible thing, this alone, & I almost wonder why some of them don't go mad!! Yet they always seem wonderfully cheery and seldom grouse. . . .

No doubt such a life is more bearable when shared with people of one's own environment and upbringing. That was why I liked serving in the Guards Division, "where are all my friends & what is more the friends of my friends at home. You know what I mean!! . . ." I wrote my father. I knew most of the officers: from childhood dancing classes, from Oxford, from country-house shooting parties, from hunting, and from the West End. The Guards Division was a great club; and, if tinged with snobbishness, it was the snobbishness of tradition, discipline, perfection, and sacrifice. They were the shock troops of the British Army; their prestige was purchased in blood.

In the spring of 1916 I was sent to Egypt to inspect the defences of the Suez Canal. I was glad of an opportunity to see a new theatre of operations, and I also welcomed the chance to get to know the magnificent Australian and New Zealand troops—the Anzacs—who had recently been evacuated from Gallipoli and were resting up for the next offensive.

Fighting was desultory at this time, as we were attempting only to hold the Suez Canal, and the Turks were not pressing the attack. This situation enabled me to make a trip to the Sudan, where at Khartoum I rode over the battlefield of Omdurman with officers who still talked of General "Chinese" Gordon and some of whom had fought the Dervishes on this very field. These stories were especially thrilling to me as I had often seen at Windsor the Bible the soldier-visionary had with him at the time he was run through by the spears of the maddened Fuzzy-Wuzzies on the steps of his Residency.

After six weeks in the Middle East, I was posted to the XIV Army Corps Staff, commanded by Lord Cavan, who had meanwhile been promoted to Lieutenant-General. It was nice to look forward to serving under someone I knew; furthermore, the Guards Division was in the Corps, and I was happy that I should be near my friends, even if I could not actually be with them in the line.

I reported for duty in the Ypres section in May. Two months later the XIV Corps was ordered south to the Somme, where a big offensive had already been under way for several weeks, but the Corps was not actually committed until September. Watching the Guards move up to the attack, I burned with desire to be with them:

> Oh! to be fighting with those grand fellows & not sitting back here doing so little as compared to them who are sacrificing their lives!! There could be no finer death, & if one was spared how proud one would feel to have been thro it. . . .

By then the war had become an indescribable mass carnage, and the slaughter was terrible. As things turned out, I was to spend nine months in these unattractive surroundings, living in a camp of canvas huts through the coldest and bleakest winter of the war. Most of our energies were absorbed in the struggle to provide as much comfort for the troops as the primitive and rugged conditions would allow.

The XIV Corps was spared participation in either of the costly battles of Arras and Messines in the spring of 1917, but we moved back to the Ypres sector in May to prepare for the large-scale operations that have become known under the general name of the Battle of Passchendaele. On July 31 the big push began; and the fighting, which equalled that of the Somme in intensity, did not abate until the first week of November. It was during this phase that I got the most vivid close-ups of the horrible existence that had become the lot of the British soldier.

In an observation post atop the ruins of Langemarck church I had my closest call, being suddenly bracketed early one morning by two near misses and diving to safety as the third shell fell—a direct hit on the heap of rubble. In a field near the Houthulst Forest I crouched for an hour in a dugout with the Welsh Guards while a French battery shelled us enthusiastically in the belief that we were the enemy—a misunderstanding that was happily removed over a fine dinner at the French Divisional commander's mess that night.

After seeing the great offensive begin with optimism and valour, then fizzle out into nothingness from sheer loss of life and human exhaustion, I in time shared the weariness and cynicism of the front line. The general disillusionment, the unending scenes of horror—not to mention several more narrow escapes of my own—had done their work, as shown in a letter I wrote my father:

H.Q. 14th Corps. B. E. F.
31st July 1917

My dearest Papa,
. . . What the ground must be like tonight I shudder to think and we have completely obliterated all roads W. of Pilckem by shell fire. . . . I'm writing this in the office as I'm on watch or night-duty as they call it & it's very cold & damp & still pouring in sheets the rain making a depressing pattering noise on the tin roof of the hut!! The telephone is ringing fairly often so I don't suppose I shall get much sleep tonight. . . . But *how* thankful I am to think I am not living forward tonight & am sitting back here in comfort; one does appreciate this comfort when one has been forward & seen what it's like in the line now!! The nearest thing possible to hell whatever that is!!!!

Therefore, sudden orders to Lord Cavan to take his Corps to North Italy to bolster the Italian Army then in full rout from Caporetto were not unwelcome. On reaching the front, we visited King Victor Emmanuel and found General Cadorna at Treviso cursing socialism as the disintegrating force in Italy. But by November 7 the Austrians were halted on the Piave River, and for almost a whole year we froze in winter and sweltered in summer at our headquarters in the Venetian Plains, without any significant advances or retreats.

Early in 1918 I was recalled home for six weeks to make a tour of the defence plants and happened to be in London in March, 1918, when the Germans made their last and almost successful drive for the Channel. All leave was immediately cancelled, and soldiers in Britain were ordered back to their units forthwith. I asked the War Office to be transferred to France; the Secretary of State for War told me to wait a few days until the desperate situation of our troops had been clarified.

One evening at Buckingham Palace my father suddenly looked up from his war maps and said: "Good God! Are you still here? Why aren't you back with your Corps?" When I explained the reason, he told me I must be off by morning, adding that he could not have me seen around London with the British line broken and the Army with its back to the wall. I left immediately.

By the time I rejoined Lord Cavan in Italy, I found our three divisions holding the mountain sector in front of Asiago. Except for a half-hearted Austrian attack in June and various diplomatic moves on our part to prevent the French Army Corps on our left from turning their guns over our heads on to their Italian allies to our right, the summer passed uneventfully.

As the conflict neared its end, my mind turned increasingly to upheavals that seemed to be rapidly sweeping away the world of my youth, as is shown in this letter to my father:

Headquarters, Canadian Corps
5th November 1918

Dearest Papa,
 . . . There seems to be a regular epidemic of revolutions & abdications throughout the enemy countries which certainly makes it a hard & critical time for the remaining monarchies; but of those that remain I have no hesitation in saying that ours is

by far the [most] solid tho. of course it must be kept so & I more than realize that this can only be done by keeping in the closest possible touch with the people & I can promise you this point is always at the back of mind & that I am & always shall make every effort to carry it out as I know how vitally it will influence the future of the Empire!! . . . I'm sure you wont mind when I tell you that I'm out the whole of every day seeing & visiting *the troops* i.e. *'the people'*!!!!

I remain dearest Papa ever your most devoted son
DAVID

Armistice Day found me a major on the staff of the Canadian Corps, in front of Mons where the Expeditionary Force had had its initial encounter with the Germans in August, 1914. However, I did not leave the Army at once. I was attached to the Australian Corps in Belgium and visited the Occupation troops in Germany, where I had my first contact with the American Expeditionary Force. From a field near Coblenz, Brigadier-General William L. "Billy" Mitchell piloted me in his aeroplane over the Rhine. Later I was the guest of General Pershing at his headquarters at Chaumont and had my first lesson in "crap-shooting" or dicing on the floor of his mess, though not from the General himself.

Obviously it has not been my aim here to write a history of the war but only to set down enough of my activities and experiences to show the profound effect these years had on me. Even an insignificant staff officer has his memories.

I often think I learned about war chiefly on a bicycle. My duties constantly took me back and forth between the various units; and, although entitled to a staff car, I seldom used one within our area. The cars of the brass hats honked infantrymen off the road into ditches, splashed them with mud, and, even under the best of circumstances, were an irritating reminder of the relative comforts of life on the staff.

My green Army bicycle was a heavy, cumbersome machine. But on it I must have pedalled hundreds, even thousands, of miles, collecting material for reports, inspecting camps and ammunition dumps. My brother officers laughed at me for preferring this hard way of getting around, but they missed the point. Just as had my first bicycle at Sandringham, my Army bicycle opened up for me a new world of unexpected associations.

Even now, after three decades, I still meet men who will suddenly turn to me and say, "The last time I saw you, you were on your bicycle on the road to Poperinghe"—or Montauban, or any one of a hundred French villages.

Then there was the rare miracle of leave—rare because officers and men were normally allowed only ten days' home leave a year, and because whenever an offensive was on, all leave was cancelled. But, when my turn did come, the prospect of seeing home again, of savouring once more the comfort and quiet of Sandringham or Windsor, was like a reprieve from the interminable sentence of war. How well do I remember boarding the leave boat at Boulogne. Rusty and battered and jammed with weary troops she might be, but to us she was almost an enchanted bark carrying us back to a world that we had almost forgotten and that we had despaired of seeing again. Perhaps my emotions at that time were best expressed in a letter I wrote to a friend:

> Dear ——
> ... We had a delightful week at Windsor really; riding every morning & golf in the afternoon. I saw a good deal of R who is charming. ... I expect you find as I do, that when one comes home it is rather nice to be with nice looking women again. ... We motored up here this morning: it was a pity to leave Windsor now we have this lovely weather (for it has been glorious there) but still I have a gt. deal to do here as I have only had 3 days in London since Nov.!! Friends to see, gear to sort & put away etc. etc. The King was very pleased with some war loot I brought back & has collared it all for a collection he is making at Windsor. ...
>
> Yours v. sincerely
EDWARD

I am amazed when I hear the young veterans of the second war talk so casually about global war, with its whirlwind sweeps and rushes across oceans and continents. The war my generation fought and in which more than one million Britons perished was a different proposition—a relentless slugging match, contested with savagery and in animal-like congestion. Some 57,000 British fell the first day on the Somme; the slaughter went on at Arras and Passchendaele. I have only to close my eyes to see once more those awful, charred battlefields; miles and miles of duck-board winding across a sea of mud; columns of heavily laden men trudging up to the front; columns of men trudging back, their vitality gone, their eyes dead. I remember the bloodstained shreds of khaki and tartan; the ground grey with corpses; mired horses struggling as they drowned in shell-holes.

While my military duties were circumscribed and my rôle certainly an unusual one, yet my education was widened in war, not through book or theory, but through the experience of living under all kinds of conditions with all manner of men.

CHAPTER VIII

MY ENTRY INTO PUBLIC LIFE

In February, 1919, I returned to the family roof after four years on the battlefields. But only my sister Mary, who had worked through the war in hospitals as a V.A.D., remained at home. Bertie had transferred from the Navy to the Air Force after the Battle of Jutland and long and, for him, disheartening spells on the sick-list. Harry, who had been to Eton, was a "Gentleman Cadet" at Sandhurst, the first step in his Army career. George was in his first year at Dartmouth, standing much higher in the order of his term than either Bertie or I ever had. Our old tutor, Mr. Hansell, his long and painstaking task completed, had retired, although I continued to see him occasionally thereafter.

That spring I suppose was no better than the average, but those of us so recently back from active service thanked God that we had been spared to see one again. Life had never appeared more desirable, and everything I did seemed invested with a sort of magical charm. The pomp and show of Imperial habits remained. Confidence and affluence were returning to the financial and commercial houses of the City of London; and, perhaps because of this outward solidity, we were slow in discovering how much the war had really cost us. It had been a heavy drain upon our capital, the money kind. More seriously still, it had wiped out much of the bravest and most spirited of our youth. That is another form of capital, the most important. Well, history can make but so many calls on the bank, and in both the great World Wars this nation has met the claims of Western civilization in full. I do not know that historians or economists would agree with me, but I feel in my bones that the running-down process that has led to subsequent crises began in 1914.

Lloyd George was soon to cry warningly that "the strength and power of every land has been drained" and that they have all "bled at every vein, and this restlessness which you get everywhere is the fever of anaemia." As I began to move about the country, it dawned on me that people were discontented and disillusioned. The service men not yet discharged were angry over the clumsy demobilization programme; those who had been demobilized were disgruntled over the lack of jobs and homes; the disabled were bitter over inadequate disability pensions. There were strikes and demonstrations disturbing in their frequency and prevalence. And the trouble had infected the armed forces, leading to small, local, socialist-inspired mutinies at certain supply ports.

My father first came face to face with the new discontent one day in London. The War Office, hoping to calm the growing dissatisfaction of the discharged disabled soldiers, asked my father to attend a parade of some 15,000 of these men in Hyde Park. Mounted and in uniform he rode out from the Palace with Bertie and me to review them.

The men, all in plain clothes, were drawn up in divisional formation. At first glance everything appeared in order, the men at attention, the bands playing, and so forth. Most of the men wore on their lapels the "Silver Badge," signifying their honourable discharge for wounds or other disabilities. But there was something in the air, a sullen unresponsiveness all three of us felt instinctively. My father, steady as a rock, rode down the front line. Suddenly there was a commotion at the rear; and, as if by a prearranged signal, hitherto concealed banners with slogans were defiantly unfurled. With cries of "Where is this land fit for heroes?"—a hurling back of Lloyd George's famous election slogan—the men broke ranks and made straight for the King, who was quickly surrounded and cut off from me and my brother by a solid mass. For a moment I feared he would be borne to the ground. Then I saw, with relief, that those who were closest were only trying to shake his hand. These men meant no harm: they had merely taken advantage of an opportunity the War Office had all unconsciously given them of laying their grievances before the King in person. The only danger was that his horse might become scared; and indeed had it started to thrash around in that dense crowd, someone almost certainly would have been hurt. In such a charged atmosphere anything might then have happened.

Fortunately the police were able to extricate us, but the mob was still milling around in the Park as we rode back to the Palace. After my father dismounted, he looked at me, remarking, "Those men were in a funny temper." And shaking his head, as if to rid himself of an unpleasant memory, he strode indoors.

For a while the exact meaning of all this turmoil puzzled those at the Palace; isolated as they were to some extent from the harsh impact of events by the protecting cushion of Cabinet Ministers, much that was then going on seemed remote and unreal. This and other episodes could be conveniently explained away as the unfortunate, but probably inevitable, result of the post-war letdown that the natural good sense of the British people would presently bring under control. But I had seen enough to convince myself that the trouble went far deeper, that the social unrest was related to the slaughter and misery that the first "people's war" had inflicted upon the whole population.

The Russian Revolution of 1917, with the murder of the Czar Nicholas II and his family, had shaken my father's confidence in the innate decency of mankind. There was a very real bond between him and his first cousin Nicky; they corresponded with each other regularly; both wore beards of a distinctive character, and as young men they had looked much alike. When, as Czarevitch, Cousin Nicky came to London in 1893 for my father's wedding, my father was mistaken for him by a well-intentioned diplomat who asked if he had come over especially for the Duke of York's wedding. My father loved to relate the confusion of the embarrassed envoy when he replied, "I am the Duke of York, and I suppose I should attend my own wedding."

It has long been my impression that, just before the Bolsheviks seized the Czar, my father had personally planned to rescue him with a British cruiser, but in some way the plan was blocked. In any case, it hurt my father that Britain had not raised a hand to save his Cousin Nicky. "Those politicians," he used to say. "If it had been one of their kind, they would have acted fast enough. But just because the poor man was an emperor——" Even after the British Government had recognized the U.S.S.R., it was quite a while before he could bring himself to receive the Soviet Ambassador.

My father and I had many talks about the changes that were obviously at work within the political and economic structure not only of Britain but of the whole world; and the more we discussed them the wider grew the divergence of our viewpoints. The ideas and notions that divided us then would, if I were to repeat them, seem of little consequence now; for I was certainly no cosmic thinker, with a blueprint for remaking Britain. More than being a mere product of my Royal upbringing, I was also a product of the war, with ideas of my own, a little on the cynical side maybe, but sure that I knew the answers. My father, on the other hand, was wholly steeped in the Victorian and Edwardian traditions that had been the order under which he had lived the best and most vigorous years of his life.

His visits to the front, combined with his tireless and heartening rounds of the military camps, hospitals, and munitions plants at home, had endeared him to the British people and impressed them with the sincerity of his character. At the same time he had come to know them better. Yet, the strange new concepts that were beginning to permeate our island and the seemingly reckless desire for change in everything both puzzled and vexed him, the more so because his eldest son seemed to share many of these peculiar notions.

But to a bachelor Prince of twenty-five the "fever" of Mr. Lloyd George's metaphor had a glittering and even exciting flush. In June the King's Birthday Parade was revived. As Colonel of the Welsh Guards I rode with my father, who exclaimed that he had never seen it better done. Ascot was brilliant, with everybody out in grey toppers as before the war. The streets of London resounded to victory parades. And, supplying a possibly happy augury of the life awaiting me, I picked that spring at Epsom my first and, as matters turned out, my only Derby winner.

Britain was full of young men just discharged, like myself, from the services, each wondering what to make of his future. Left to my own devices, I would have remained on in the Grenadier Guards, for a while anyway. The Army and war were the only occupations I knew; moreover, I liked Army life. But the choice of career was not left to me. As Heir Apparent my job was to help my father with the serious business of kingship. He was fifty-three when the war ended, and people were already calling him a great King. But the mounting burden of State business had taken its toll of his strength, weakened by the slow mending of his body after the serious riding accident in France. Peace found him aged beyond his years. Some months before I was demobilized he had begun to plan my introduction into public life.

My father had a perfectly clear idea of what he expected of me. It was that I should step without delay into the customary duties devolving upon the Prince of Wales—the laying of cornerstones, the ceremonial tree-plantings, the opening of new highways, appearing before civic groups, and assuming the honorary chairmanships of worthy charities and other institutions. In short, I was required to show myself to the people in order to make my character known, and at the same time to fill the Prince of Wales's traditional rôle of the leader of society. The Prince of Wales has more liberty than the King; he can move around more, travel, mix freely with all kinds of people, and in general act as agent for the Monarch.

At the same time the Prime Minister, David Lloyd George, who still had almost dictatorial powers, also had ideas for my employment in the Empire beyond the seas. The last contingents of the Dominion and Colonial troops, which had fought in Europe and the Middle East, were on their way home; and he was anxious that, before the ardour of the wartime comradeship had wholly cooled, I should set forth at once upon a series of tours to thank the various countries of the British Commonwealth, on my father's behalf, for their contributions to the war. Everywhere the vaunted bonds of Empire showed signs of weakening. India was seething. In Canada, the resistance of the French Canadians to wartime conscription had left an ugly lesion among the people. Australia resounded to radical talk and labour troubles. South Africa had its racial differences. Lloyd George, acutely sensitive to the stirrings of the popular mind, realized that the common people everywhere were fatigued by war and puzzled and disturbed by the new economic forces that were tearing away the foundations of their lives. As he once explained to me, the appearance of the popular Prince of Wales in far corners of the Empire might do more to calm the discord than half a dozen solemn Imperial Conferences.

My father quickly approved the project. These overseas excursions, he reasoned, would in any case provide me with a comprehensive view of the different peoples and conditions of his vast realm while affording his subjects the opportunity of seeing their next King. The Canadian Government having already approached him with the proposal that I should visit Canada that coming summer, it was decided that I should do so in August. The other Dominions at the same time were given to understand that I would visit them in turn as soon as practicable.

How does a Monarch prepare his eldest son for his duties? I had a general idea of what was expected of me. But beyond all that there was no carefully conceived plan for equipping me for eventual assumption of kingship. In that respect, I dare say, my father was no different from most other fathers; he left my mature development pretty much to chance. Perhaps one of the only positive pieces of advice that I was ever given was that supplied by an old courtier who observed: "Only two rules really count. Never miss an opportunity to relieve yourself; never miss a chance to sit down and rest your feet."

About this time my father had a serious talk with me. "You have had a much freer life than I ever knew," he said. "The war has made it possible for you to mix with all manner of people in a way I was never able to do. But don't think that this means you can now act like other people. You must always remember your position and who you are."

Remember your position and who you are—in the years that were to come that injunction was to be dinned into my ears many, many times. But who exactly was I? The idea that my birth and title should somehow or other set me apart from and above other people struck me as wrong. If the levelling process of Osborne, Dartmouth, and Oxford, and the democracy of the battlefields, had taught me anything, it was, firstly, that my desires and interests were much the same as those of other people and, secondly, that, however hard I tried, my capacity was somehow not appreciably above the standards demanded by the fiercely competitive world outside palace walls. In the wisdom

that comes with age I might to-day concede that there are
advantages attached to a position that shelters one from the consequences of one's shortcomings; as a young man, however, I
wanted no part of it. I suppose that, without quite understanding
why, I was in unconscious rebellion against my position. That
is what comes, perhaps, of sending an impressionable Prince to
school and war.

However, I now began to collect a staff to assist me in the
carrying out of my new public duties. Some months before,
indeed, soon after the Armistice, my father's understanding
Secretary, the elderly Lord Stamfordham, had taken upon
himself to advise me in this respect.

Buckingham Palace
22 Decr: 1918

Sir:

. . . And now Sir, I am getting anxious about your securing a
good Private Secretary. . . . The reason for my anxiety is that I
foresee a good deal of work ahead. For instance the King approved of an announcement being made at the annual half yearly
meeting of King E's Hospital Fund that you would take over the
Presidency on your return: and the three Governors who have
been acting for the President, Lord Cambridge, Lord Iveagh &
the Speaker are desirous of "handing over" their duties. There is
a good deal to be done with the Secretaries of the Fund. Then
there is the Royal Coll: of Music. The *University of Wales* is the
most pressing as the King really constitutionally ought *not* to be
the Chancellor. Then your Royal Highness is to be elected a
Trustee of the British Museum, as both the King & King Edward
were. The City of London is waiting to present you with the
Freedom of the City—and finally, *Canada* in the, I assume, near
distance. I know from experience this means plenty for a P.S.
to do. . . .

I remain always your humble and devoted servant,

STAMFORDHAM

Several weeks later he followed up the first piece of counsel
with another:

. . . What Your Royal Highness should have is someone ready
to take up work when you come home for good, especially if you
go to Canada. I am hopeful that you will not think my views

exaggerated when I say that your visits to the Dominions will be made or marred according as you do & *say* the right thing. The Throne is the pivot upon which the Empire will more than ever hinge. Its strength & stability will depend entirely upon its occupant. Your Royal Highness is very popular with the Dominion Troops—and that popularity must be not only maintained but increased by your visits to the respective Dominions. Every year they will expect more and you ought to go well equipped as to their history and politics. A really good man as P.S. is indispensable. Someone with brains, with some Colonial knowledge: a facile pen—a nice fellow. . . .

For this post I turned to Mr. Godfrey Thomas, whom I had first met when he was a junior secretary of Embassy in Berlin, and who had helped with various chores during the War when I was on leave. Five years older than I, he had many qualifications—a sound knowledge of French and German, that faint dash of cynicism that is a diplomat's indispensable ingredient, a diffident manner that disguised perfect confidence in his ability to perform any task he undertook. It meant a good deal to me when he agreed to leave the Foreign Office and join his fortunes to mine. Our close association lasted seventeen years and terminated only with my Abdication.

I also appointed two equerries. This quaint Court term has often puzzled my American friends. During one of my visits to the United States, Will Rogers asked me what it meant; and, after I had explained, he drawled, "Well, Sir, I guess we have the same animal out in Oklahoma, only we call 'em hired hands." Actually an equerry means an A.D.C. to a King or a Prince. One whom I chose was Captain Lord Claud Hamilton, who had been my aide during the war. The other was also a brother officer in the Grenadiers, Captain the Honourable Piers Legh, the second son of Lord Newton. They were in effect my buffers; their job was to accompany me on my official rounds at home or abroad and take care of the mechanics of my daily activities.

Fortunately for the sons of Kings, the ceremonies with which their life abounds afford a series of nursery slopes down which a diffident and inarticulate Royal apprentice may be conducted, by gentle stages, into public life at little risk to his own reputation, and without imposing too much embarrassment upon the public.

That first spring and summer I was presented with the Freedom of the City and other towns, made an honorary Bencher of the Middle Temple and an Elder Brother of Trinity House, initiated into the great fraternity of Freemasons in the Household Brigade Lodge, and admitted a Freeman of the Livery Company of Fishmongers. And with a view to preserving the Royal association with the Fighting Forces of the Crown, I was promoted to post captain in the Royal Navy and appointed colonel of the Welsh Guards and colonel-in-chief of several famous line regiments. One way or another, I really got around a lot those first months after my return. Recalling the kindly crowds that everywhere welcomed me, the generous applause that greeted my hopeful banalities, I marvel at the tolerance with which the world's most democratic people continues to view its Princes.

The more appearances I had to make the more I came to respect a really first-class speech as one of the highest of human accomplishments. No one that I knew seemed to possess that rare or envied gift, the art of speaking well, in so high a degree as Mr. Winston Churchill, who was a sympathetic witness of some of my earliest attempts. "If you have an important point to make," he advised at the outset of my career, "don't try to be subtle or clever. Use a pile driver. Hit the point once. Then come back and hit it again. Then hit it a third time—a tremendous whack." These instructions were subsequently amplified in a letter:

> War Office,
> Whitehall, S.W.1.
> 19th July, 1919.
>
> Sir,
> . . . I would advise your not worrying too much about this speech . . . if you wish to read it out, I should do so quite openly, reading it very slowly and deliberately and not making the least attempt to conceal your notes. Of course it is better if you can find time to memorize it. Rather a good way of dealing with notes at a dinner is to take a tumbler and put a finger bowl on top of it, then put a plate on top of the finger bowl and put the notes on top of the plate; but one has to be very careful not to knock it all over, as once happened to me. . . .

It may have been presumption on my part, but I had begun to flatter myself that these first public appearances had gone off rather well and that the informality that came naturally to me had seemed to please. But a little informality went a long way with my father, as was demonstrated in the affair of the top hat. A stickler for etiquette, he deemed it undignified for the Prince of Wales to appear in public in anything so casual as a bowler; in fact, after seeing newspaper photographs of me in one at a civic function in the provinces, he had reproved me for want of respect to the city Fathers. I defended my position, arguing that my reluctance to wear a silk hat did in fact exhibit a certain sagacity in what are nowadays called public relations. My point was that, since the political cartoonists had, rightly or wrongly, adopted the top hat as a universal symbol of the predatory capitalist, the male members of the Royal Family would be well advised to limit wearing one to formal Court occasions and the weddings of their friends. But my father remained unconvinced.

The attitude of the Court in such matters was further impressed upon me in a conversation I had about this time with my father's Keeper of the Privy Purse, Sir Frederick Ponsonby, an experienced courtier. Valuing his advice, I went to see him one day to discuss a problem that had arisen in connexion with my duties. At the end I asked casually how he thought I was getting on.

"If I may say so, Sir, I think there is risk in your making yourself too accessible," he answered unhesitatingly.

"What do you mean?" I asked.

"The Monarchy must always retain an element of mystery. A Prince should not show himself too much. The Monarchy must remain on a pedestal."

I maintained otherwise, arguing that because of the social changes brought about by the war, one of the most important tasks of the Prince of Wales was to help bring the institution nearer the people.

"If you bring it down to the people," Fritz Ponsonby said coldly, "it will lose its mystery and influence."

"I do not agree," I said. "Times are changing."

He replied severely, "I am older than you are, Sir; I have been with your father, your grandfather, and your great-grandmother. They all understood. You are quite mistaken."

With so many enterprises of my own afoot, the time had plainly come for me to set up a separate establishment. My eye fell on York House, St. James's Palace, which in my early child-hood had been our London home. Lord Kitchener had lived there during the war until he had sailed for Russia on the fateful voyage on which he was drowned. My mother's grandmother, the first Duchess of Cambridge, had died there; and the Duchess's elder brother-in-law, Ernest Augustus, Duke of Cumberland, had had the horrible experience of being attacked in bed there, fortunately without fatal consequence, by his crazed valet armed with a knife. It was a rambling antiquated structure, a veritable rabbit warren, with passages interrupted by unexpected flights of steps leading to unsymmetrical rooms full of ugly Victorian furniture, brass beds, and discarded portraits of former Mon-archs. But I felt I could make it habitable; and it would provide much-needed office space for my staff. I approached my parents, who at first demurred, perhaps because they wished to put off the day when one by one the children would step out from under the parental wing. But, when Lord Stamfordham spoke up quietly for the obvious advantages of the move, my father and mother agreed. I settled at York House shortly before leaving for Canada. Finch followed me there as major-domo, a step which he was afterwards to describe as the beginning of his education.

By August I was ready to set forth. With a view to stressing the official nature of my tour the new battle-cruiser *Renown*, Captain Ernest Augustus Taylor in command, was assigned to transport my party and myself across the Atlantic. My father followed my preparations with an experienced eye. At the last moment, having some intimation of the difficulties into which I would be drawn, the temptations to which I would be exposed, the traps that would be laid for exploiting a member of the Royal Family, he insisted upon my adding an older man to my staff.

I was worried about how to comply with my father's wishes, when Lord Stamfordham, with his usual happy inspiration, came forward with a candidate. His choice was a distinguished naval officer, Rear-Admiral Sir Lionel Halsey. From our first meeting I liked Halsey, who, although he had commanded a Navy gun crew in the siege of Ladysmith and had been Lord Jellicoe's Captain of the Fleet at the Battle of Jutland, was only forty-seven years old, close enough to my generation to be tolerant and understanding. He had served in all parts of the world and was to prove himself a handy reference-book in the manners and customs of many countries into which my travels took me. He brought along with him an old friend and shipmate, Captain, later Admiral, Dudley North; they both accompanied me on the three other official tours.

At the last moment, at Mr. Lloyd George's suggestion, my entourage was broadened to include a political adviser, Lieutenant-Colonel Edward Grigg—a scholar, journalist, and Grenadier with a fine war record, who was an expert on Imperial affairs.

With a retinue of twenty-odd, including clerks, valets, and orderlies, as well as two detectives from Scotland Yard, I sailed from Portsmouth in the *Renown*, which was to be my floating home for many months during the next few years.

My first glimpse of the New World revealed the low, green, misty headlands of Conception Bay, Newfoundland. I went ashore at St. John's, which had prepared a fine reception in my honour. Passing under a unique triumphal arch, I was astonished to observe that it was largely composed of drums of cod-liver oil, and hung with the carcasses of dried codfish.

From Newfoundland and the Maritime Provinces, the *Renown* steamed up the St. Lawrence to Quebec. My party had meanwhile been joined by two Canadian officials who had drawn up my itinerary. One of these was a genial artillery officer, Major-General Sir Henry Burstall, whom I had met during the war. The other was an elderly civil servant, Sir Joseph Pope, who, because he had helped to arrange my father's Canadian tour eighteen years before, had been entrusted with the preparation of mine. The Governor-General of Canada, the Duke of Devonshire, an old friend of my father's, had recommended Sir Joseph to me with the assurance that everything could be left in his "safe and experienced hands." When on our first meeting I went over the schedule prepared for me, it was plain that Sir Joseph had faithfully followed the 1901 model. State drives in horse-drawn landaus with mounted escort, mounted military parades, civic lunches, official dinners, sightseeing detours to notable landmarks—it all had a decidedly Victorian flavour.

"We have tried our best to be civil to and please everyone," my father had written to his mother at the turn of the century in describing what he thought was the proper conduct expected of the Heir Apparent on an Empire tour. But Canada was quick to teach me that mere civility—the polite but distant bow, the right word to the right person, a mild interest in a carefully selected assortment of local projects and good works—was no longer an adequate Royal export. As Lloyd George had shrewdly surmised, the Dominions wanted, if not a vaudeville show, then a first-class carnival in which the Prince of Wales should play a gay, many-sided, and natural rôle.

There were tens of thousands in the streets the sunny afternoon I arrived at Quebec. In company with the Duke of Devonshire I rode up to the Citadel in an open motor-car. By now crowds were no novelty to me. However, the crowds that I encountered in Quebec, and subsequently throughout Canada, proved so volatile and vigorous as to constitute at times an almost terrifying phenomenon. Uncontrolled, almost ferocious in their determination to satisfy their curiosity about me, they again and again broke through and swamped the police lines. They snatched at my handkerchief; they tried to tear the buttons off my coat. Yet, while all this provided welcome proof that the Royal Family still possessed a sure claim upon the affections of overseas British communities, I came to fear not only for my own safety but for that of the Canadians themselves.

Old Sir Joseph Pope, from whose "safe and experienced hands" the crowds were literally snatching me, apologized for their behaviour, saying, "I simply cannot understand what has come over the Canadian people, Sir. This utter lack of control—it is not at all what I would have expected." That part I had not minded at all; in fact, I rather enjoyed it. But I was convinced that these mounted State progresses Sir Joseph had organized on Buckingham Palace lines were an open invitation to disaster. They were all very well in London, where the Royal Mews maintained an ample supply of trained horses, and the escorts of the Household Cavalry through long usage had brought to unrivalled precision the technique of mounted ceremonial. The saddle and carriage horses provided in Canada were unaccustomed to this kind of work, and there was constant danger of their becoming frightened by the crowds, and trampling people underfoot. Yet, despite several close calls, I could not persuade Sir Joseph or General Burstall of the wisdom of dispensing with this obsolescent and cumbersome form of transportation. It required a spectacular incident at Toronto to break down their resistance.

The Great War Veterans Association of Canada had arranged for me to inaugurate "Warrior's Day" at the Canadian National Exhibition. A tremendous parade, at which some 27,000 veterans would be massed at the Exhibition Grounds, was to be the climax of the occasion. My part required that I should mount a horse, pass down the ranks, and then ride solemnly to a platform at the side of the field, where I would dismount, then walk up the steps and make a speech.

When General Burstall had finished outlining the programme, I said, "But, General, do you think it's a good idea for us to ride on this occasion? You know the veterans. They are not going to keep their ranks once I appear. God knows what this horse will do. Frankly, I am all for using a motor."

But the General persuaded me to put aside my apprehensions with the argument that the local military organizers would be disappointed if I did not ride. "The horse, Sir," he said, reassuringly, "has been specially trained." So, at the appointed hour, followed by the General and other officers, I rode out upon the field, still uneasy in my own mind.

What I had feared would happen did happen. The moment I appeared the veterans broke ranks and, cheering and yelling, surged around me. At first my mount showed commendable control. Then, as the human mass engulfed us both, I felt its body quiver. Fortunately, even if its instinct had been to rear up and bolt, the crowd held it as in a vice. The next thing I knew I was being lifted off the horse's back by strong hands and passed like a football over the heads of the veterans. Dishevelled, shaken, and breathless, I eventually found myself on the platform, clutching the crumpled notes of my speech. The roar of cheering had changed to laughter. I wish Papa could have seen this, I thought to myself. I cast a glance back for the horse. It had vanished.

That evening, when Sir Henry came to apologize for the *contretemps* of the afternoon, I looked at him reproachfully and said, "I trust, General, that we have seen the last of horses at these public shows."

"I was afraid you were going to say that, Sir," he answered sadly. "I shall send out the necessary orders."

If it was the last of the horses, it was also, for reasons that by now must be self-evident, the last of Sir Joseph Pope. All his meticulous preparations had collapsed. As the crowds took charge, he had subsided into the background, protesting again and again that "this will never do." Inquiry revealed that he had quietly got off the train with his baggage at an intermediate stop, without even a farewell message.

Sir Joseph's place was taken by a British-born politician, Mr. Martin Burrell, one of the members of Parliament for British Columbia. Mr. Burrell, who was also librarian to the Canadian Parliament, was an altogether different sort—a simple, affable, grass-roots character. Under his agreeable auspices I progressed westwards in a magnificent special train provided by the Canadian Pacific Railway. My quarters were in the rear car, which had an observation platform. This last adjunct, while providing me with a continuous view of the varied Canadian landscape, had, however, the drawback of making me vulnerable to demands for *ad lib.* speeches from the crowds gathered at every stop.

Hoping to please, I would always oblige. As I hurried to the back observation platform, Martin Burrell would usually prime me with such pertinent facts as were likely to appeal to local pride. These I would hopefully weave into the standard three-minute speech I had by then evolved. But on more than one occasion disconcerting bursts of laughter instead of the customary applause informed me that I had made the lamentable blunder of confusing my audience with a rival community some distance down the track. Yet these experiences were all to the good, and taught me to think on my feet. As I became more sure of myself, I began to enjoy these informal meetings. Getting off the train to stretch my legs, I would start up conversations with farmers, section hands, miners, small-town editors, or newly-arrived immigrants from Europe. It was the first time that a Prince had ever stumped a Dominion in quite that way, and the impressions of Canada I formed in this manner proved far more instructive than anything I learned on the formal "red carpet."

My first days in Canada were in some ways the most exhilarating that I have ever known. The veterans, especially, claimed me as their charge. On one pretext or another they were constantly spiriting me away from civic functionaries to offer me a little "nip" or to swap reminiscences of the war. My private evaluation of my own worth had previously not been particularly high, but in their kindly enthusiasm the Canadians almost convinced me that they liked me for myself, an act of open-heartedness that did my ego no end of good. And in a perhaps excessive outburst of gratitude, I undertook to meet, within the limits of human endurance, whatever demands my enthusiastic hosts made upon me.

Everybody seemed so anxious to shake my hand that I decided it would be ungracious to refuse. This rash decision must have been based upon a fallacious idea that Canada was sparsely populated; either that or I failed to appreciate what a feeble and inadequate mechanism the right hand really is. It all started with a man in the crowd thrusting an outstretched hand towards me. "Put it right here, Ed," he said. "I shook hands with your granddad." Within a week my right hand was blackened and swollen and extremely painful; and the sight of an advancing stranger, so welcome only a few days before, now made me flinch. On the advice of my doctor, Surgeon Commander Newport, who warned me that my right hand might be permanently disabled if I went on using it, I retired it temporarily from Imperial service and offered the left instead.

From Balmoral and Buckingham Palace my parents followed the accounts of my journey with approval mixed with dismay, as the following exchange of letters suggests:

> Government House,
> Ottawa.
> August 31st, 1919.

Dearest Papa,
   ... I have not had a moment to myself since landing at Quebec.
... The "Renown" must have looked fine steaming up the St. Lawrence, and it thrilled me to think that she was moored in the same billet opposite the Citadel as occupied by the "Indomitable" during your visit. ...

I got through my long and difficult speech at Friday's Government luncheon alright, (copy of which I enclose), though I was very nervous on account of it being the most important of the trip, and when it was so essential to say absolutely the right thing to the politicians. ...

I'm rubbing it in that altho. not actually Canadian born I'm a Canadian in mind & spirit & come here as such & not as a stranger or a visitor & that goes down well!! These Dominions do appreciate being put on the same level as the U.K. . . . they've done so much to pull the Empire out of the war victoriously that one must recognise their established status as self-governing states of the Empire. . . . I remain ever your most devoted son

DAVID

Balmoral Castle
Septr 7th 1919

Most darling David
. . . One's head almost reels at the amount you are doing & I feel angry at the amount of handshaking and autograph writing you seem compelled to face! In one place I see you had to give yr. left hand as the right was swollen! This does not sound dignified, tho' no doubt the people mean it well & the receptions you are having must be overwhelming. . . . Your speeches quite surprise us, & you must be fairly good now to be able to manage without notes, it is splendid of you to have taken all this trouble about yr. speeches and as you say it will make all the difference in your life, your Papa made himself so miserable over speeches that it often spoilt the pleasure and interest of visiting new places. . . .

ever yr. devoted Mother
MARY

Government House,
Victoria, Vancouver Island, B.C.
Sept. 23rd.

Dearest Papa,
. . . I quite understand what you say about shaking hands & allowing myself to be mobbed & I can assure you that it isn't my fault as you may imagine; you just can't think how enthusiastic the crowds have been & they just go mad & one is powerless!! The staff are marvellous at dealing with crowd situations & never has there ever been an undignified incident!! But it is all so different out here & as I said before so much more is expected & one thing above all others that won't go down & which one has to be careful not [to] put on is "side" & pompousness!! You can trust me not to let down your position or mine either. . . .

I remain your most devoted son
DAVID

143

Buckingham Palace
Oct 12th/19

Dearest David

... You might take things easier during the last month of your visit & give yourself more spare time & more rest from the everlasting functions & speeches which get on one's nerves. I warned you what it would be like, these people think one is made of stone & that one can go on for ever; you ought to have put yr. foot down at the beginning & refused to do so much. . . . All I wish to say now is that I offer you my warmest congratulations on the splendid success of your tour, which is due in a great measure to your own personality & the wonderful way in which you have played up. It makes me very proud of you & makes me feel very happy that my son should be received with such marvellous enthusiasm of loyalty and affection. I have had many letters from all sorts of people in Canada, as well as members of yr. Staff all singing yr. praises. . . .

Ever my dear boy
Yr. most devoted Papa
G.R.I.

The original idea had been to confine this first official tour to Canada alone. But, my association with the American troops during the war having left me with a strong curiosity about their great country, it seemed absurd to be so near the United States without extending my trip across the border and visiting at least Washington and New York. Returning eastwards from British Columbia, I raised the possibility of securing the approval of my father and the Government. After a good deal of cabling back and forth my project was adopted. So, accompanied by my staff, I continued on to Washington, D.C., arriving there on Armistice Day, November 11, 1919.

President Woodrow Wilson, who had been stricken with paralysis a month before, delegated as my principal guide Vice-President Thomas R. Marshall, a shrewd old Hoosier (man from Indiana) who affected the disarming guise of a hayseed. He had an endless fund of stories. He showed me round General Washington's beautiful home at Mount Vernon and the Walter Reed General Hospital, where I humbly paid my respects to some of the American wounded. I met Admiral Dewey's widow, and at a huge evening reception in the Library of Congress I was presented to the members of the two Houses.

I called on the President at the White House. He was lying in Lincoln's bed. We conversed only for a few moments. Leaving him, I thought that his was the most disappointed face that I had ever looked upon. If this was the condition in which the cares of high office left a man, then as a Prince I was happy to be spared the ravages of party politics.

In Washington also I had my first introduction to life under Prohibition. The Eighteenth Amendment to the Constitution, which theoretically turned the United States into a "dry" nation, had come into effect a few months before my arrival; my impression was that this curious law was not taken too seriously. At any rate it would be ungracious of me were I to deny that my American hosts occasionally made tactful provision for the moderate requirements of myself and my staff. But there were times, especially at official banquets, when something more stimulating than water would have imparted more warmth to my response to the usual toast drunk to my health. It was at one such solemn affair, while I was gloomily surveying my empty water glass, that I was approached by a Negro waiter who asked, almost confidentially, "Water or White Rock?"

White Rock? I thought hopefully, recalling my experiences with respected American whiskies of, to me, strange titles, such as "Green River," "Cedar Brook," "Pebble Ford."

"Yes," I whispered to the waiter, "a little 'White Rock' would go very well."

Vice-President Marshall sitting next to me must have seen my face fall as the innocent liquid splashed into the glass.

"Anything wrong?" he inquired solicitously.

"Oh! No," I assured him. "Nothing at all," as I watched the waiter add a large cube of ice.

A few days later I was to be the witness of another aspect of life in the land of the "noble experiment." The occasion was a visit to the Naval Academy at Annapolis, made with a large party that included Secretary of the Navy Josephus Daniels and his vigorous and handsome Assistant Secretary, Franklin D. Roosevelt. This also gave me a chance to observe at close hand another American phenomenon, the motor-cycle escort. A shrieking phalanx of a dozen blue-coated outriders conducted our cavalcade through Washington to a small station in the suburbs at sixty miles an hour, their sirens emitting bloodcurdling waves of sound. While such privileges might be permissible in republics, they would never do in constitutional monarchies, where Kings and Princes were expected to get around with less noise and less disturbance to the general public.

After a bumpy trip on the electric train we arrived at the Academy. I reviewed the regiment of midshipmen on the drill ground and then proceeded to the armoury. As I stepped out on the balcony I heard a midshipman a few feet away shout: "Let's give a 4N for the Prince." Thereupon my ears were assailed with the roar of over two thousand voices all yelling in perfect cadence and unison, a demonstration of mass enthusiasm that would have put to shame the more sedate Hip Hip Hooray's of Osborne, Dartmouth, and Oxford.

It seemed to go something like this: NAV-EE, NAV-EE, NAV-EE, NAV-EE, N N N N, A A A A, V V V V, Y Y Y Y, NAV-EE, PRINCE, PRINCE, PRINCE. This, I was told, was a spontaneous gesture on the part of the midshipmen and not planned by the officers. Touched as I was by such a mark of esteem, I must confess I was a bit stunned and deafened.

We then went to Memorial Hall, which is filled with mementoes and statues of former naval heroes, including Perry's flag, on which are inscribed the immortal words, "Don't Give Up the Ship." There I addressed a few words—appropriate, I hope—to these boys so nearly my own age. And, I might add, nothing is better calculated to make one self-conscious than pontificating to one's own contemporaries.

We then returned to the train and retraced our route to Washington. At the station there we picked up our motor-cycle escort. These men, so alert in the morning, seemed to be having considerable difficulty in starting and mounting their machines; and, as they led us on to the highway, it was plain that their earlier discipline had been replaced by a flippancy that sent them weaving erratically back and forth across the road in front of our long cavalcade.

J. M. Nye, then chief of the State Department's special agents, was riding in the front seat of my car. Tapping his shoulder, I said, "Bill, I hope I'm not speaking out of turn, but these men seem in pretty bad shape; I don't believe they will ever make it back to Dupont Circle." Even as I spoke the nearest pair grazed the front of the car, veering off into the gutter. There they collapsed in a stupor, their legs entangled in the wheels of their machines. Bill shouted something to the driver, and the column pulled up. He walked slowly forward to talk to the men, whose true condition was no longer in doubt: they were undeniably drunk.

When he rejoined me, it was in a state of obvious embarrassment. "This," he said, "could have happened only in my country." He then related a remarkable story. During the long wait our escort had fallen in with a party of Revenue Agents who had just made a successful raid upon a large cache of bootleg liquor. The windfall had been shared, and it was the policemen's misfortune to have committed this lamentable lapse from discipline in the presence of as distinguished a group of high officials as could have been assembled in Washington that day. An irresistibly comic touch was supplied by the fact that an uncomfortable witness of the episode was our host of the day, Mr. Josephus Daniels, a leading Prohibitionist, who had made the U.S. Navy "dry" long before national Prohibition.

Having some intimation that the men would in all probability be dismissed out of hand, I was prompted to intercede with their chief, saying that the pleasure of my stay in America would be forever marred if, through this single slip arising out of an assignment with me, these fine men should lose their jobs. It was one of the few occasions in my life that I ever used my position to defeat the normal processes of the Law. The chief relented, and the men were spared. Later that day before I left Washington they all came to thank me personally.

My first view of New York was from a Jersey City pier. The natural way, then as now, to enter the city by train from Washington was by Pennsylvania Station. But because I was to be honoured with one of the city's fabulous harbour welcomes, my train had been shunted off to Jersey City, where I was met by a formidable and variegated company of municipal authorities, civic leaders, local celebrities, newspaper reporters, and photographers. Borne forward by the weight of these new hosts, I was swept rather than conducted towards an admiral's barge, which was to carry me across the harbour to lower Manhattan.

The din was deafening as scores of vessels in the stream blasted a welcome with their whistles. All the way to the Battery the barge was serenaded from an accompanying tug by a brass band identified as the musical unit of the New York Street Cleaning Department. Even at this late date, cleaning up the streets after horses was one of the principal functions of this municipal department. From their distinctive white dress these artisans were known as "white wings." The idea of having their band welcome me struck me as a stroke of authentic American humour.

We disembarked at the Battery. I had meanwhile unobtrusively scrutinized my hosts. Among them was an impressive stranger whose black moustache, silk topper, and overcoat with velvet collar would have marked him in Paris as a *boulevardier*. In the confusion I had not been able to catch this man's name or determine his exact rôle in the phalanx of welcoming officials, but he was clearly a person of authority.

Students of the America of that period will of course have already identified this stranger as the remarkable Mr. Grover Whalen, who was in charge of the proceedings and was indeed their architect. With this personage at my elbow, I found myself being propelled vigorously towards an open motor. Among the other top-hatted occupants I recognized with relief an old friend of my family, Mr. Rodman Wanamaker, of Philadelphia. He was in fact the generous donor of a beautiful silver altar, to my grandfather's memory, which graces the little church at Sandringham. As I settled gingerly into the back seat, Mr. Whalen asked, "All set, Prince?" On my gesture of acquiescence, he shouted, "O.K., let's go." An instant later I was headed up Broadway, to experience a municipal welcome without counterpart elsewhere in the world.

Peering into the shadowy, steep-sided canyon of Broadway, I discovered that the air between the tall buildings on either side of the street was obscured by what appeared to be a driving snow-storm. "What's that?" I inquired of Mr. Wanamaker, shouting to make myself heard above the roar.

"Ticker tape," he yelled back.

"Ticker tape? What's ticker tape?"

The answer was only partly intelligible; but, knowing that the skyscrapers in this part of New York were chiefly occupied by stock-brokers' offices, I gathered correctly that the snowstorm effect was produced by the release from upper-story windows of torn-up pieces of paper and long narrow strips of tape upon which stock-exchange quotations are printed. Occasionally through the uncoiling paper streamers would hurtle somewhat larger bodies that would land with an alarming thud in the street. These, Mr. Wanamaker explained soothingly, were no cause for concern. "Only parts of telephone books," he shouted. "Some of these people are too damn impatient."

This masterpiece of acclamation in my honour was thrilling beyond description. Half-asphyxiated by the smell of petrol, I found myself sitting up on the back of the motor, bowing and waving like an actor who had been summoned by a tremendous curtain call.

Then suddenly the noise diminished, and the motor emerged from Broadway into a small park, in the centre of which stood a low, two-story building of beautiful proportions. This, Mr. Wanamaker announced, was City Hall. There, still dazed by what I had just been through, I was formally welcomed by the Mayor of New York, Mr. John F. Hylan: ". . . Your Royal Highness, as Mayor I present to you the Freedom of the greatest city of the wonder republic of the ages—a city which in an existence of less than three hundred years has risen to eminence among the municipalities of the world as the dynamic centre of democracy—the all-American city of New York."

With all this I was quite prepared to agree.

I spent four days in New York on this first visit, and my programme tells a good deal about the New York of that day. I was taken to the top of the Woolworth Building (sixty stories high and then the tallest building in the world), to Grant's Tomb, the Stock Exchange, the Metropolitan Opera, and the *Ziegfeld Follies*. Mrs. Whitelaw Reid gave a magnificent ball in my honour at her Madison Avenue house. I visited West Point (whose Superintendent was then a young Brigadier-General, Douglas MacArthur); and at Oyster Bay I laid a wreath on the grave of former President Theodore Roosevelt, who had died early that year. And in Central

Park, by invitation of the municipal authorities, I planted a commemorative tree, as my grandfather had done on his only visit to America shortly before the outbreak of the Civil War.

Politically, at any rate, only one small failure could be charged to me. I never succeeded in wholly penetrating Mayor Hylan's defences. Fearful of offending his Irish constituents, he shied away from all association with me beyond the bare municipal courtesies. Even my innocent invitation, extended as we parted on the steps of City Hall, that he should be my guest at lunch in the *Renown* seemed to alarm him. With a wild glance at his Tammany colleagues, he answered, backing away from me, "Sorry, Prince, can't do it. Everybody here knows that I never eat lunch."

What I saw in North America stirred me deeply—most of all the beauty and grandeur of the Canadian Rockies. In Alberta I met an American-born cattleman, George Lane. My imagination was fired by his tales of life in the foothills of the Rockies, and on impulse I bought a four-thousand-acre ranch, adjoining his, in the valley of the Highwood River, some forty miles south of Calgary. On my return to London my father questioned me closely about this ranch. Mistaking my motive in purchasing it, he warned me that I was setting for myself a dangerous precedent. The Australians would now expect me to buy a sheep station when I visited their country; and if I failed to acquire at least an ostrich farm when I went to South Africa, its people, he pointed out, might construe my neglect as a deliberate slight. The fact is, my impulse in making this investment—the only piece of property that I have ever owned—was far removed from Imperial politics. In the midst of that majestic countryside I had suddenly been overwhelmed by an irresistible longing to immerse myself, if only momentarily, in the simple life of the western prairies. There, I was sure, I would find occasional escape from the sometimes too-confining, too-well-ordered, island life of Britain.

When I arrived home my father, who had never been to the United States, asked me innumerable questions about various American phenomena—the height of New York's skyscrapers, the number of motor-vehicles in the streets, the state of President Wilson's health, and the size of his staff employed at the White House. But most of all he was curious about life in America under

Prohibition. An abstemious man himself, he considered it an outrage for the Government of any country to attempt to regulate
the conduct of its citizens in such a manner. And of all the information that I brought back I think what delighted him most was the
following doggerel picked up in a Canadian border town:

> Four and twenty Yankees, feeling very dry,
> Went across the border to get a drink of rye.
> When the rye was opened, the Yanks began to sing,
> "God bless America, but God save the King!"

My mind was often to travel back to this first visit to America.
My conversations with such men as Mr. Wilson, Mr. Taft, Mr.
Elihu Root, and Mr. Chauncey Depew gave me an insight, however fleeting, into the ideals and aspirations of that great new
country that so baffled us at that time. But curiously what
lingered on in my mind was not so much the grand things that
happened to me—and grand is the only word for the welcome that
was given me—rather it was a haunting little song that I heard at
the *Ziegfeld Follies*: "A Pretty Girl Is Like a Melody." At odd
moments I found myself whistling or humming it—in Australia,
in India, out with the hounds in Leicestershire, or at Sandringham.
Once my father heard me. "What's that damn tune you are
whistling all the time?" he demanded.

"Oh, I'm sorry if it bothers you. It's just something I picked
up in America."

At twenty-five this world, which to-day seems so vexatious,
looked pleasant enough to a young Prince without too many
cares, and with a battle-cruiser to take him around the world.

CHAPTER IX

THEY CALLED ME "DIGGER"

THREE and a half months later I was ready to start off again in the *Renown*, this time bound for Australia and New Zealand, with official calls at numerous places on the way out and back. Just before I sailed, my parents gave a dinner at Buckingham Palace for me and my staff, which remained unchanged except for the addition of Sub-Lieutenant Lord Louis Mountbatten, R.N., known to his family and friends as "Dickie." He came as Flag-Lieutenant to Admiral Halsey, but more than that he was at nineteen a vigorous and high-spirited young man who became the instigator of many an unexpected diversion outside the official programme.

My North American tour had taught me what was expected of a Prince in the post-war world. Mine was after all a simple mission. I was not charged with negotiating treaties with foreign Governments or with propounding high Imperial policy to the Dominions. Primarily my job was to make myself pleasant, mingle with the war veterans, show myself to schoolchildren, attend native "tamashas," cater to official social demands, and in various ways remind my father's subjects of the kindly benefits attaching to the ties of Empire. The message that I carried went something like this: "I come to you as the King's eldest son, as heir to a Throne that stands for a heritage of common aims and ideals—that provides the connecting link of a Commonwealth whose members are free to develop, each on its own lines, but all to work together as one. . . ."

In March, 1920, the *Renown* left Portsmouth and headed southwestwards for New Zealand via the Panama Canal. On April 24 she entered Auckland harbour. There I was greeted just as warmly as in Canada. The lovely bay was filled with a flotilla of small

craft gaily bedecked with flags. Aboard one of them I identified
with delight a Salvation Army band playing hymns, which were
barely audible in the general din. The Governor-General, Lord
Liverpool, a typical product of the old school of country gentleman, came up from Wellington to meet me. The civic festivities lasted for three days and followed the pattern with which I
had become familiar in Canada: a reception at the Town Hall; a
ball in the evening for the local *élite*; a visit to the hospital still full
of New Zealanders wounded in the war; a massed demonstration
by schoolchildren grouped in a formation that spelled the word
"Welcome"; and the inspection of organizations representing
war veterans, nurses, and other patriotic associations. It was all
very heartening; and, as in Canada, I experienced a true sense of
gratitude and even pride that in this "last, loneliest, and loveliest"
of our Dominions the memory of my parents, who had visited
Auckland nineteen years before, should still be so truly cherished.

From Auckland I travelled south over a narrow-gauge railroad
in a special train provided by the New Zealand Government. At
every town or hamlet on the way the train would stop, sometimes for only five minutes, for whatever kind of civic show the
resources of the community were able to provide.

But what was most novel to me in New Zealand was the
Maoris, the race that we had subdued, not without bloodshed, a
little less than half a century before. They gathered to meet me
in various places in their native garb, chanting folk songs, and
performing warlike dances called *hakas*.

Yet, apart from these encounters with the Maoris, I might have
thought myself back in my own country. The New Zealanders,
predominantly descended from English and Scottish stock, are
extraordinarily homogeneous. They are calm, law-abiding, and
industrious. In their far-off land they have preserved almost intact the spirit of their British forbears; even their speech has
remained unaltered by a local accent. In their behaviour towards
me they were enthusiastic but restrained. My schedule was never
upset; even a railroad strike failed to disrupt it. It was a kind of
Royal progress after Sir Joseph Pope's heart.

But Australia, across the Tasman Sea, was to teach me, as Mr.
Lloyd George had warned, that Imperial preferences were not all
the same. On the morning of May 26 the *Renown* approached

Melbourne. From my association with the Australian troops during the war I knew their countrymen to be a tough, independent yet sensitive people, proud of what they had accomplished on their island continent and quick to take offence. Furthermore, Australia was politically the most restless of the Dominions. It had a powerful labour movement, the extreme left wing of which had violently opposed conscription. On this issue the then Prime Minister, Mr. W. M. ("Billy") Hughes, had broken with his colleagues in 1916 and had formed a National Government the next year. Resentment against him still remained; he had been branded a traitor by his former associates. The natural suspicion of British interference that pervaded Australian politics was further accentuated by the presence of big Irish communities in the large cities. Many of these groups were anti-British and anti-monarchical. There had been a good deal of agitation against the Crown. Knowing all this, I was somewhat apprehensive as I approached the dock where were assembled a host of officials.

The first to step forward to greet me was the Governor-General, a wise and charming Scotsman, Sir Ronald Munro-Ferguson, later Lord Novar. I knew of him by reputation as a former distinguished Liberal Member of Parliament. Before the crowd closed in on me, I had time to ask his advice as to the best approach I should adopt. "The Australians," he said, "must be handled with care. They hate formality." Then he smiled, adding, "You are in for a great experience, Sir; and you have nothing to fear for yourself."

As the Governor-General conducted me to the conveyance awaiting me at the end of the pier, I was dismayed to find that it was a State landau drawn by a pair of horses. Turning to Admiral Halsey, I said, "Look! Horses again." Gingerly I stepped into the carriage, and we started out on an eight-mile drive through the city. I was told that there were three-quarters of a million people lining the route. It was a gay and friendly, yet somewhat ribald, crowd. Through the cheers the cry, "Oh! Percy, where did you get that hat?" shouted in good humour, would reach me at intervals. The Prime Minister, Mr. Hughes, rode in the carriage close behind. Farther back in the procession was the Leader of the Opposition. As the cortège made its tumultuous way through the streets to Government House, the predominant political sympathies of the different sections through which we passed were vociferously expressed by alternating boos and cheers addressed to the rival politicians. Happily there were no boos for the Prince of Wales, and the misgivings that had assailed me in the morning were dispelled by a demonstration of loyalty that still remains in my memory.

"The people of Australia," Mr. Hughes, the Prime Minister, had declared in his speech of welcome to me, "see in you the things which they believe." Now it was all very well to be hailed thus as the embodiment of Imperial service. But there were moments in the general excitement when it seemed to me that the people themselves were prone to regard me rather as an Imperial souvenir, to be passed about rapidly from hand to hand, like a lucky talisman. The Australian brand of hospitality was, if possible, even more vigorous than the Canadian. In that Dominion even a car was no sure protection against the hearty greetings of my father's subjects "down under." They called me "Digger"; and, whenever I sallied forth from the sanctuary of Government House, I was in constant dire danger of being waylaid by shouting bands of self-proclaimed "diggers," snatched out of the back seat, and tossed cheerfully about the streets. The unofficial diary kept by my staff—the one not intended for perusal by my father— contains the following entry, recorded in Melbourne: "Confetti is appearing in great and unpleasant quantities, and the touching mania has started, only owing to the hearty disposition of the Australians the touches are more like blows and H.R.H. and the Admiral arrived half blinded and black and blue."

The "touching mania," one of the most remarkable phen- omena connected with my travels, took the form of a mass impulse to prod some part of the Prince of Wales. Whenever I entered a crowd, it closed around me like an octopus. I can still hear the shrill, excited cry, "I touched him!" If I were out of reach, then a blow on my head with a folded newspaper appeared to satisfy the impulse. My staff and I bore stoically our share of knocks and bruises, which we came to regard as part of our daily rounds. The poor Admiral's feet were continually being trodden on, if not by the crowd, then by me or another member of the staff as we ducked and dodged to extricate ourselves from the *mêlée*. His half- choked sailor's oaths could be heard above the happy roar of the crowd. The end of many a hard day found him limping around his room or soaking his crushed extremities in a hot bath.

More than once during these strenuous but friendly encounters with the crowd there was serious doubt whether I would survive at all, were it not for the protection of an obscure but indispensable member of my staff—Sergeant Burt of the Metropolitan Police. Alfred Burt had been assigned to me as personal detective and bodyguard when I embarked upon my public career in 1919. Thereafter he was constantly with me until ill-health compelled his retirement in 1931. His ostensible duty was to protect me from possible assassins and cranks. But his real job was to act as buffer between me and an occasionally too-enthusiastic world.

Whenever I rode in a motor-car, Burt always sat in the front seat, keeping a wary eye for possible trouble. If I were required to leave the car and plunge into a crowd, he would lead the way, his massive frame taking the first shocks. I would be right behind, like a cork bouncing in the wake of an ocean liner. He never seemed to push or shove; yet his firm but polite warning, "By your leave," accompanied by a ramlike thrust, was able to open a path without ever arousing hard feelings.

After a three-day tour of the country towns and communities in the State of Victoria, I re-embarked in the *Renown* and sailed from Melbourne to Sydney. Sydney was Melbourne all over again, with tumultuous progresses through the streets and the by now familiar round of official and civic engagements. If all went well for me, some of the politicians in the official party did not fare so well. During the first procession through the city I was disconcerted to hear boos from a section of the crowd I had just passed. I was informed that the jeers were directed at the Lord Mayor, who had been so indiscreet as to attend a public dinner at which the toast to the King had been omitted.

I had by this time come to understand the difficulties besetting Australian politicians, and the cautious behaviour of the Prime Minister himself on that same occasion was an object-lesson in the skilful use of protective coloration in lulling the suspicions of his volatile countrymen. Decked out in a top hat, Mr. Hughes rode with Ned Grigg and Godfrey Thomas in one of the carriages. They were somewhat surprised and puzzled by the Prime Minister's insistence on taking with him a large hat-box that he deposited on the floor, leaving no room for their feet. The purpose of this encumbrance was soon disclosed as the procession started. With almost a conjuror's deftness, Mr. Hughes whipped off the shiny silk topper, opened the box, and produced a battered soft hat that he donned in its place, saying with a wink, "You can't be too careful. That top hat might cost me thousands of votes." However, as Government House hove into sight, the old felt hat was returned to the box; and the Prime Minister smilingly restored to his head the topper, thus graciously complying with the rules of official decorum.

Of my visit to Sydney the correspondent of *The Times* wrote:

> It is unquestionable that the Prince has made a great impression on Labour opinion, though it would be an exaggeration to say that he has given a permanent twist to the trend of that opinion, so critical of the Monarchy as an institution. . . .
> But Labour is fair minded and perfectly prepared to judge the heir of the Throne as a man. . . . [A] journalist observed that the Prince had silenced criticism of the Monarchy for current lifetimes, and personally I verily believe that that is the simple truth. . . .

Yet I cannot claim to have escaped unscathed. While in Sydney I was one day the guest of the State Legislature of New South Wales at a picnic on the Hawkesbury River. It was a beautiful day; champagne and oysters were the fare. At one stage of this bucolic excursion one of the State Ministers singled me out for a leather-lunged diatribe on the iniquities of princes. His Prime Minister rushed up to intervene and ended the onslaught before I could answer back. I have always regretted that; it promised to be my first real political argument.

I had a fine time in Australia. I liked its bigness, its adventurousness, and its courage. The boundless faith of Australians in their own destiny was perhaps most vividly exemplified for me by their enterprise in creating in the remote back country a brand-new federal capital. When I was there in 1920, nothing was yet to be seen save a few tin shanties, power stations, and numerous cornerstones marking the sites of the proposed Government buildings, to which I contributed one exactly in the city's centre. But I must admit, without wishing to appear ungrateful, that as a personal experience the enjoyment of my journeyings in Australia was somewhat marred by the demands made upon me by the rigorous official schedule.

My official calendar was solidly booked, day after day, for weeks ahead. But what sometimes made my programme a nightmare was the inability of local politicians to resist the temptation to exploit my public appearances. Each State of the Commonwealth submitted for my approval a copy of the schedule the Government wished me to follow; but I discovered all too soon that it availed me little to try to reduce my commitments to a point where it was humanly possible for me to carry them out. Again and again on arriving in another city my staff and I would find ourselves being whisked off to clubs and even private residences we had earlier struck from the programme. In consequence of these sly inclusions my schedule fell further and further behind; punctuality, which has been described as "the politeness of kings," would go by the board. And all too often, before my day was finished, thousands of people, who had been waiting long and patiently to watch me drive by, would have another story to add to the growing legend of the *Unpunctual Prince*.

The trouble was that, as the schedule fell behind, the time allotted to me to catch my breath before dinner or perhaps prepare another speech invariably disappeared. From my last engagement I would have to race back to wherever I was lodged, with scarcely time to dress before being whirled off to a banquet, a ball, or some other form of official entertainment. Midnight often found me with wearied brain and dragging feet, and the orchestra blaring out the by-now hackneyed tunes. If, mindful of next morning's programme, I were to suggest leaving a party early in order to make up some sleep, or if in an unguarded moment my expression betrayed the utter fatigue that possessed me, my hosts, who no doubt had spent weeks preparing an elaborate and expensive party in my honour, would disappointedly attribute my attitude to boredom or, what was worse, bad manners. And so I drove myself many a night to the edge of exhaustion, lest unfounded rumour create the suspicion that I was an *Ungracious Prince*.

Inside a Government House I was fairly safe; there were few opportunities for blunders; but out among the people it was different. God help the Prince of Wales if in the noisy press of a public reception I missed the mild little woman in black who had lost her only two sons in the war. Next day might bring a letter reproving me for being a *Thoughtless Prince.* Once while travelling in the back country of Western Australia my train failed inadvertently to halt at a small community that had been led to expect my appearance. After the train had flashed by the crowd gathered at the station, it vented its displeasure according to Australian custom by loudly "counting me out" of its favour. In this disconcerting rite, the crowd, like a referee bent over a recumbent boxer, counts forward in unison, "One . . . two . . . three . . ." and so on, up to ten, at which point, with an angry cry of "out," it banishes into symbolic oblivion the object of its displeasure. News of this lamentable episode reached me in due time; and on the return journey I managed to undo the damage by stopping at the same place, where the inhabitants graciously forgave the original oversight by counting me back into favour. I lived in terror of little misunderstandings like that. It was so easy to magnify them.

Once, I am glad to say, fate turned the tables upon one of my tormentors. It happened during the part of the schedule that took me into the lumber camps of Western Australia. My guide was a Member of the State Legislature. And, with a view to pleasing his constituents, he had privately arranged with the driver to halt the train at every little station, not only during the day but also throughout the night, in order that his friends might have a chance to shake hands with me. I was out of bed many times that night; and my temper was not improved when I discovered that the Solon was himself slipping off the train at each stop to lead the crowds in their calls for the Prince of Wales.

However, unknown to the officials aboard the train, heavy rains had weakened the track. On a sharp curve my carriage left the rails. I was sitting with Admiral Halsey in my compartment. As the wheels bumped menacingly over the sleepers, we braced ourselves for the shock. Our carriage and the one just ahead toppled over on their sides and slid down the embankment with a terrifying clatter. When the racket stopped, I found myself flat on my back with most of the contents of the compartment, including the Admiral, on top of me. Fortunately, neither of us was hurt, and we were soon extricated through a window. We were congratulating ourselves upon our narrow escape when, from the overturned car ahead, issued a cry for help. It was quickly traced to the toilet; and, on being repeated, its author was identified as our scourge, the M.P. Stooping to listen to the piteous cries issuing from the up-ended toilet, Admiral Halsey permitted himself a rare smile. "If I had planned to square accounts with that old blighter," he growled, "I could not have done it better myself."

And so in numerous ways not to be surmised from a superficial reading of contemporary accounts, this Imperial progress presented me with its own peculiar ordeals and trials. By the time I left Australia, half-killed by kindness, I was physically and mentally at the end of my tether.

During the homeward voyage I had much time for reflexion. The nature of my life came for the first time into clear focus. No one who has ever travelled the globe could have had more kindness showered upon him than I had had. Canada and the United States had almost convinced me that the world was my oyster. But in New Zealand and Australia I had come to comprehend as never before the varied burdens of duty that lie upon a Prince of Wales, imposing far greater mental and physical strains than were generally appreciated at the time. Lonely drives through tumultuous crowds, the almost daily inspections of serried ranks of veterans, the inexhaustible supply of cornerstones to be laid, the commemorative trees to be planted, deputations to be met, and everywhere the sad visits to hospital wards, every step bringing me face to face with some inconsolable tragedy calling for a heartening word from me, and always more hands to shake than a dozen Princes could have coped with—such was the substance of my official days.

The programme was my master; I did my best to obey. Two days here, three days there, any number of one-night stands— much of the time I was like a man caught in a revolving door. I was a wayfarer rather than a sojourner, and never really got to know any place well. Just as I was beginning to absorb a few elementary facts about some place and to know a few people, the itinerary would reassert itself: I would be obliged to move on. One of my staff might remark at the end of a tedious day, "I sat beside a most interesting man at dinner to-night—an old-timer who fought in the last Maori war. You ought to have a talk with him." But more often than not, there was no time. I followed a beaten track; and the opportunities to satisfy my own curiosity about what lay on either side were few and far between.

On October 11, a misty morning, the *Renown* steamed into Portsmouth harbour flying the Prince of Wales's Standard from the fore. We had been gone 210 days, had visited over 200 different towns and places, and travelled by sea and land a total of nearly 46,000 miles.

CHAPTER X

"THE BRIGHTEST JEWEL"

Now followed a year in my own country, my first uninterrupted stay of more than a few weeks since 1914. However, this respite from my travels was no holiday. My public activities continued unabated, and between trips to various parts of the United Kingdom I took up fox-hunting enthusiastically that winter. I began with the Pytchley hounds; and, as my horsemanship improved, I entered two of my best horses in point-to-point races and steeplechases. I won a race at the Household Brigade meeting at Hawthorn Hill with my parents watching from the stand. Lord Stamfordham, a keen rider himself, who was with them, congratulated me, remarking that, as I was the first Heir Apparent to ride in a race, let alone ride a winner, my jacket and cap should be preserved under glass among the memorabilia of Windsor Castle. "And," he added, "I hope, Sir, that you will not risk your neck in a steeplechase again."

I remember the 1921 London season as one of the gayest in my memory. For one thing, full-dress uniform had been restored to the Household Troops. The daily guard-mounting and the King's Birthday Parade were carried out in red tunics and bearskin caps, providing a relief from the drab, wartime khaki. All society seemed to be *en fête*; and the Court, if with the more sedately measured step of protocol, was in a gala mood as well.

Despite the slump and the coal strike, this mood of gaiety seemed to suggest an imminent return to something like pre-war stability. Most of the great houses in London, which had been turned into hospitals during the war, had meanwhile been refurbished and once more opened their doors for a flourish of hospitality such as will never be seen again. That spring I went to parties at many of these fine houses, where formal dinners were still served on gold or silver plates by footmen in the family livery with knee breeches, white stockings, buckled shoes, and powdered hair. One of the most striking of these parties was given by Lady Wimborne at Wimborne House, in Arlington Street, where several hundred guests, including King Alfonso XIII of Spain, danced under the dim romantic light shed by thousands of candles in massive, bronze, *doré* chandeliers.

The season was enlivened by a State visit from Crown Prince Hirohito of Japan, followed a little later by that of the King and Queen of the Belgians. One feature of the latter visit was a brilliant Court ball my parents gave at Buckingham Palace at which they danced the "quadrille" with their Royal guests. As Prince of Wales I took my part in these official festivities. But my attempts to show Hirohito the honours were largely defeated by his ignorance of the English language and mine of Japanese.

That summer I was run down, and my parents gave me a lecture on the necessity of sparing myself. "You know, my dear boy," my father said, "you try to do too much." Since plans for a tour of India by the Prince of Wales that coming "cold weather" were already well advanced, I could not help taking a bleak view of this well-meant advice. However, seeking rest and quiet, I joined them presently at Balmoral, for the first time since 1913, where the bracing air and the healthful days "on the hill" soon restored my strength.

During these days my father talked to me at some length about India and how I should deport myself there. My own knowledge of that great subcontinent—that "brightest jewel" in my father's crown, and briefly in mine, and destined to be lost from my brother's—had been largely coloured by childhood memories of the Kitmatgars who had pushed Queen Victoria's wheel-chair, and the bearded Sikhs who had marched in my grandfather's Coronation procession, and more recently by the Indian troops I had seen in the war. Now my father told me again about his experiences there, first when he toured the country when I was only eleven, and next when he returned in 1911 to be crowned King-Emperor at the great Coronation Durbar at Delhi. Himself the least pompous of Monarchs, my father had gained in India a new conception of the Imperial rôle and of the importance of elaborate display and pageantry in impressing the Oriental mind.

"You seem to have evolved a new technique of your own in the carrying out of your Commonwealth missions," he said, "and, while I do not altogether approve your informal approach, I must concede that you have done very well. But," he continued in a sterner tone, "you must not forget that India is entirely different from Canada, New Zealand, or Australia. What went down well with the white people in those three Dominions will not go down at all in India. You are to do exactly as *they* tell you," he concluded severely. "*They* know best." By "they," I inferred that my father meant the British civil and military authorities in India, into whose presumably safe and experienced hands I was soon to be delivered.

It so happened that among the guests at Balmoral that September was a distinguished, retired Indian Civil Servant, Sir Walter Lawrence, who had been my father's Chief of Staff in India during the 1905 tour. Sir Walter had served in Afghanistan, Rajputana, the Sikh States of Punjab, and Kashmir, as well as being Private Secretary to Lord Curzon when he was Viceroy. His personal knowledge of India, its races, and its problems, was immense. "Go and talk to Walter Lawrence," my father said to me one day, "he will bear out what I have told you." Sir Walter described the complicated caste system and the position occupied in Indian life by the ruling Princes, while expounding at the same time his romantic theory that, under the aegis of Britain, all India should eventually come under princely rule. But the soundest advice he gave me was that I should attempt to learn enough Urdu to converse with as many Indians as possible and to enable me to make simple speeches. "I wish I had had the foresight to suggest the same thing to His Majesty your father years ago," he said regretfully.

At Portsmouth on October 26 I boarded H.M.S. *Renown* once more. My old tutor, Mr. Hansell, now grown quite old, was on the dock to wave good-bye. In the late afternoon, with the crew fallen in and the band playing "Auld Lang Syne" against the booming of a salute of twenty-one guns, the battle-cruiser sailed. This time I was to be gone eight months; for the tour would carry me beyond India to Japan, where I would return the official visit of Crown Prince Hirohito to England that spring. Although I knew full well that I was in for an arduous and exacting time, I set out in a mood of eager anticipation. The East had always fascinated me. Ever since my tour of duty in Egypt during the war, I had longed to explore the lands that lay beyond the Red Sea.

My staff had meanwhile undergone some changes. Ned Grigg had returned to politics; Claud Hamilton had left me to join my father's Household, and his place had been taken by Lieutenant the Honourable Bruce Ogilvy, the son of Lady Airlie, one of my mother's oldest friends and a lady-in-waiting. There was also a new Chief of Staff, the Earl of Cromer—son of the brilliant pro-consul in Egypt during Queen Victoria's reign. As a member of the diplomatic service, Rowland Cromer had served in Cairo, Teheran, St. Petersburg, and later in the Foreign Office. During the war he had been aide to the Viceroy of India, Lord Hardinge, and subsequently one of my father's Assistant Private Secretaries. His knowledge of India had been further extended through his having accompanied the Duke of Connaught to Delhi the winter before. Finally, the *Renown* had a new captain, the Honourable Herbert (Jimmy) Meade, a gallant and competent sailor, son of Admiral of the Fleet the Earl of Clanwilliam, who had commanded the Flying Squadron when my father had sailed round the world as a midshipman in the *Bacchante*.

While the elaborate preparations for my tour were being worked out between Whitehall and Delhi, there remained the unanswered question, how would Mahatma Gandhi and his radical Congress Party react to my visit? Would he try to spoil my show? In Government circles this sworn enemy of British rule, with his loin cloth, his spinning-wheel, his fasting, his public burning of British cloth, his campaign of "non-co-operation" with the Government of India, was regarded as a sinister if somewhat ludicrous figure. Under the Montagu-Chelmsford reforms, inaugurated shortly before, Indians had been admitted into limited participation in the government, as a big step towards eventual but presumably distant self-government. But, far from satisfying the nationalistic aspirations of the Indian politicians, these concessions had been summarily brushed aside by Gandhi and his followers. He had in fact already called upon his followers in Bombay to stage a "hartal"—or strike—on the day of my arrival. He had ordered them to remain indoors as a sign of protest and to bedeck their houses with black bunting, as evidence of their desire to be free of British rule. So when, therefore, one warm November morning, the *Renown* steamed into Bombay harbour, there was general anxiety among the British and Indian officials, shared by my staff, lest I be greeted with empty streets, insulting placards, and perhaps even incidents of violence.

Next morning, while the sun climbed a cloudless sky and amidst the roar of a salute fired by the East Indies Squadron anchored in the bay, I landed at the Apollo Bunder, the famous Gateway of India. There stood the Viceroy, Lord Reading, in a white sun helmet and grey morning coat, with the Star of India pinned on his breast, presenting a grave study in Imperial protocol. With him was Sir George Lloyd, Governor of the Bombay Presidency. Behind them, all in shimmering silks and bejewelled *pagaris*, were arrayed the ruling Princes or their sons who were to be in attendance on me during my tour: the Maharajas of Patiala, Jodhpur, Dholpur, Dahr, and Rutlaim; and the Nawabs of Bahawalpur and Palanpur. And beyond them the masses of Indians gathered to greet the "Shahzada Sahib" stretching as far as the eye could reach. A long red carpet led down to a pavilion topped by gilt minarets with the central dome emblazoned with the Royal coat of arms. To this pavilion I was conducted by Lord Reading, to find myself in a small amphitheatre where several thousand people, European and Indian, were assembled on tiers of seats. Here I delivered a message from the King-Emperor, adding on my own behalf, "I want to know you and I want you to know me. . . ."

Now came a State drive through the streets of Bombay. I rode in a horse-drawn carriage with a Kitmatgar holding a gold-embroidered umbrella over my head. The procession was colourful, with officers in full-dress uniform riding alongside the carriage, and the sunlight flashing on the steel lances of the Governor's Indian mounted bodyguard. Happily Gandhi's hartal was only partially successful. Despite his orders to his followers, there were thousands of Indians in the streets to watch me ride to Government House at Malabar Point. And there came from them a sound such as I have never elsewhere heard issue from human lips —not so much a cheer as an immense murmur of delight, punctuated by the rippling sounds of the hand-clapping that is the Oriental customary sign of approval.

To recount my doings during my three days' stay in Bombay and at near-by Poona would be tedious. But the situation was not lacking in tension. As a result of his call to the natives to boycott my visit, the Mahatma had stirred up the hooligan element of Bombay, which began to terrorize the crowds gathered in the streets to see me. From Government House, one could hear the sounds of distant rioting and occasional shots. Be it said to Gandhi's credit that he tried to stop the disturbances by personal appeals to his followers. But he was too late. I was never certain in my own mind how the trouble began. Most of the fighting was, as usual, communal strife between Hindus and Moslems; but apparently both sects attacked the Parsees and Indian Christians, in what became a general *mêlée*. Street fighting broke out between the contending factions, and the police had to fire on the mobs to restore order. Yet, for all the uproar, the only engagement of my schedule that was cancelled was a visit to a school, which was abandoned rather than expose the children to danger.

Notwithstanding these ominous disturbances, I now prepared to depart into the interior. At Bombay my York House staff had been augmented by officers selected by the Viceroy, each of whom had had many years' experience of Indian affairs. The first of these was my Chief Secretary, Mr. Geoffrey F. de Montmorency, a senior officer in the Indian Civil Service. Of an old Huguenot family, he went to India in 1903. He was steeped in the lore of Hindustan, and he spoke several dialects perfectly; under his coaching Urdu became less of a mystery. Later he was appointed Governor of the Punjab, and is now a distinguished Fellow of Pembroke College, Cambridge. Another was Colonel Rivers B. Worgan, of the 20th Deccan Horse, who became my Military Secretary. In contrast to the scholarly and reserved Chief Secretary, Rivers Worgan was a dashing cavalry officer, who might have galloped straight out of the pages of Kipling. He was always immaculately turned out and, if a trifle pompous, was an eight-goal polo player and a very brave soldier. He is now dead, a sad loss to a world that to-day seems all too full of colourless men. I believe that one of his last experiments was to join a nudist colony, no doubt as an amused spectator, perhaps in search of the complete antithesis of the cherished trappings of his old regiment. His assistant was Lieutenant-Colonel C. O.

Harvey, of the Central India Horse. Tall and slim and almost nonchalant in his approach to life, he was of a piece with Colonel Worgan, a polished product of the same cavalry tradition. In addition there was a doctor from the Indian Medical Service, a police officer, and two A.D.C.'s. Among the latter was a gay, handsome Irishman, Captain Edward Dudley Metcalfe, of the 3rd Skinner's Horse. Another bold and accomplished horseman, he had a sympathetic and understanding nature; during the tour a bond of friendship grew up between us, and on my invitation "Fruity" Metcalfe left India with me to join my permanent staff as equerry. Three years later he married Lady Alexandra Curzon, the youngest daughter of the former Viceroy.

Including servants, my entire retinue numbered at least one hundred Europeans and Indians. To transport this small army around India the Government provided three trains—an elaborate special train for myself, my personal staff, servants, and baggage; a pilot train for the Press and travelling post office; and the third train for the landaus and carriage horses, which were used for the State entries into the cities on my itinerary. There were also twenty-five polo ponies, lent by the Indian Princes. An idea of the style in which I travelled may be judged from the fact that no matter where I was—whether in a Government House, a shooting camp, the special train, or the marble palace of a ruling Prince—my postal address was simply "Prince of Wales's Camp, India."

Setting out from Bombay on November 20 with this magnificent railway caravan, I began an overland tour of India that lasted for four months, and carried me approximately 11,000 miles. Eventually, in mid-February, I reached Delhi, where for a week I was the guest of the Viceroy, Lord Reading, at the old Viceregal Lodge. There I witnessed a display of Imperial pomp and splendour that is to be seen no more. All the high naval, military, and civil officials of India, as well as all the princely rulers of the native States, assembled there. A Viceregal atmosphere of grandeur and magnificence touched all the proceedings—especially the State banquet and ball, attended by 1,500 persons, with the Viceroy flanked by his scarlet-uniformed bodyguard receiving his guests. The grandiose Imperial City of New Delhi was then, like Canberra, an unrecognizable wilderness of unfinished buildings and empty avenues. But I added there yet another cornerstone to my ever-lengthening list, that of Kitchener College, intended to be the "Sandhurst" of India.

The ease with which I moved about was an object-lesson in the technique of British organization in India, a masterpiece of official planning. Nothing important ever seemed to go wrong; nothing was ever left out. From one day to the next, I followed a precise and unalterable schedule, prepared months before. If, for example, the plan for my visit to Bangalore required that I should arrive at the station at 8.30 a.m., inspect a guard of honour, drive in State to the Residency and receive an address of welcome *en route*, inspect a parade of troops and pensioners, lunch at the Residency, take part in a polo game, attend a dinner at the Residency and a dance afterwards, departing from the station at 11.30 p.m.—I would arrive at Bangalore at the exact instant, do exactly what the official programme called for—nothing more, nothing less. Even the All-India Congress Party hartals, proclaimed in most of the cities of British India on my itinerary, failed to interrupt the practised rhythm.

Yet, for all that, Gandhi's ominous shadow fell often across my path; and especially in the native sections of the swarming cities the struggle for the loyalties of the masses seemed to me to be a bidding match between the Government of India on the one hand and Gandhi on the other. The Indians love a "tamasha." Whatever their feelings on the injustices of British rule, they found it hard to resist the great public shows being organized in my honour. In an effort to overcome simple curiosity and scatter the crowds that otherwise would be hailed as proof of the loyalty of the Indian masses to the British Raj, Mahatma Gandhi and his followers went to rather unusual lengths of intimidation and bribery. Storekeepers along the routes of my procession were ordered to close their shops, students to boycott their classrooms, and the rest to remain out of sight in their homes. The Party men spread the rumour that the police had been ordered to shoot any native who approached the route of my procession. It was even said that the Government would poison the food at the "feeding of the poor." The dispensing of this bounty was customary on the occasion of a visit by the Viceroy or by some other exalted person. Whenever it was proclaimed in my honour, Gandhi's lieutenants would circulate a warning among the natives that the free food had been poisoned, adding a diabolical story in explanation. This stated in essence that, having been appalled and shocked by the evidences of widespread poverty, I had commanded the Government of India to remedy the conditions without delay and that the authorities, embarrassed by my Royal command, had decided to eliminate hunger at a stroke with a mass poisoning of the poor.

The Government, I was pleased to observe, countered with certain material inducements of its own. At Lucknow, for example, I noticed trucks circulating through the streets with signs printed in Urdu saying: "Come and See the Prince and Have a Free Ride," a form of enticement that never had to be employed when my father travelled about India.

Only in two cities of the United Provinces, at Allahabad, an industrial centre, and at the sacred city of Benares, a centre of Hindu learning, on the Ganges, was the hartal visibly effective. Allahabad was then the political stronghold of Gandhi's chief lieutenant, Pandit Jawaharlal Nehru, later to be Premier of India; and the British authorities, hoping to disorganize the boycott, had on the eve of my visit clapped Pandit Nehru and his principal associates in jail. But as matters turned out, an opposite effect was produced.

When on the appointed day I emerged from the train, in full-dress uniform, and started off from the railway station in a State carriage, it was to be met in the native city by shuttered windows and ominous silence along the troop-lined, deserted streets. It was a spooky experience. I attempted to maintain a rigid and majestic pose in the carriage in order to show that I had risen above the insult. But curiosity got the better of me; and, peering up the empty side streets, I was gratified to see peeking furtively round the corners of the blocks the heads of many Indians.

However, this incident had an interesting aftermath—a sequel suggesting that, while Pandit Nehru had no doubt scored a victory over the Government, he was not yet master of the Hindu mind. Stationed at Allahabad was a battalion of the Black Watch; and, as often happened, a polo game had been arranged in the afternoon between my staff and the regimental team. I was somewhat surprised to be informed by the Governor of the United Provinces that, if it were still my intention to play polo, he would have to call out some more police.

"Why?" I asked. "Do you expect trouble?"

"On the contrary, Sir," he answered with a smile, "I have reason to believe that there will be a tremendous crowd to see you at the polo field."

"Even after the success of the hartal this morning?"

"If anything, because of it," the Governor went on; "Nehru succeeded in making the population obey him this morning, but he can't control it indefinitely, Sir. The natives will do as they please from now on."

It was as the Governor had predicted. Thousands of laughing Indians were massed along the side lines as I rode out to play. And to judge by the excited applause that greeted my every shot, one might have thought it was Pandit Nehru and not the Prince of Wales who was on the pony. But, while I was still not so naïve as to suppose that the India won by Clive had been saved through my exertions on the polo field of Allahabad, I was thereafter inclined to take with a grain of salt the newspaper accounts of hostile demonstrations against the British Raj. But in spite of the pleasure of the polo I was puzzled and worried, as the following exchange of letters with my father indicates:

Nepal, The Prince of Wales's Camp
16th Dec. 1921.

Dearest Papa,

... Well I must at once tell you that I'm very depressed about my work in British India as I don't feel that I'm doing a scrap of good; in fact I can say that I know I am not. The main reason for this is naturally the boycotting of my visits to the various cities in British India by the non-co-operators but another reason is the police ... no one realises better than I do that precautions have to be taken on a tour of this sort. .... But I do assure you that they (the police) are overdoing these precautions & that they have the wind up unnecessarily; I'm the first to recognise what a splendid force the I.P. are & have talked to & congratulated many of the British Officers & native constables. But the fact remains that by taking too great care of me they aren't helping me. I'm hardly ever allowed even to drive through the bazaars & native quarters of the cities & the crowds if there are any lining the routes through the European quarters are herded together into pens like sheep & guarded by constables who face "outboard" (with their backs to me) so as to watch them. Such severe police tactics can

scarcely be condusive to encouraging even loyal natives to come
& see & welcome the P. of W. can they? . . .

Ever your most devoted son
DAVID

York Cottage, Sandringham, Norfolk
Jan. 25th, 1922

Dearest David,

. . . I greatly regret that it [the situation in India] should have
changed so rapidly for the worse since we were there only 10 years
ago. The War & the situation in Turkey & Montagu's reforms
have no doubt produced the unrest which now exists. . . .

. . . I quite understand that you are depressed & discouraged by
what you have seen, in the way that the natives have boycotted you,
in different places where they have been intimidated by Gandhi.
But I assure you, in spite of it all, you have done & are doing good
work for the Empire & your visit is really giving great pleasure
to the natives although they are not allowed to show it. Anyhow
the Anglo-Indians have given you a splendid reception everywhere & so have the Native States. The Princes are all loyal & if
there was real trouble they would at once come to the assistance
of the Govt. with all their troops, which is quite a different
situation to what it was before the Mutiny in 1857. . . .

Ever my dear boy,
Yr. most devoted Papa
G.R.I.

Yet, whenever I entered the territories of the native States,
Mahatma Gandhi's menacing influence disappeared. There were
then over five hundred of these native States, which in the aggregate contained one-fifth of the population of India, and embraced
two-fifths of its area. The majority of these States were mere
petty chieftainships; but some of them, such as Baroda, Gwalior,
Hyderabad, Jammu and Kashmir, and Mysore, were as large as
countries. And the relative importance of the leading eighty-
eight States was indicated by the number of gun salutes to which
the rulers were entitled on official occasions.

Among these Indian autocrats, I found a way of life, almost
feudal and sometimes barbaric, that had persisted for centuries,
impervious to the growing uproar in British India. And there I
enjoyed Oriental hospitality and sport such as I imagined existed only in books.

At Baroda I found the old Maharaja to be a modern-minded man who knew a good deal about European municipal practices and who had installed the latest American plumbing in his white stucco palace. One evening at Udaipur, in Rajputana, I came upon the water palaces of Jagmandir, lighted up by thousands of oil-lamps. At Jodhpur I learned pig-sticking under the practised eye of the Regent, the gallant old Sir Pertāb Singh, whom I had last seen during the war. The famous Camel Corps marched past me at Bikanir, where I sampled sand-grouse shooting.

On arriving in Nepal to shoot tigers, I learned that for six weeks before my arrival ten thousand Nepalese had laboured to clear the site for the camp and to build miles of roads. In Mysore the Maharaja showed me how wild elephants were trapped and trained; and, besides, he could give me six up at squash rackets. The Maharaja Scindia of Gwalior proudly exhibited his two children, dressed in khaki uniform, whom he had named "George" and "Mary" after my parents; and in Patiala a tall Sikh Maharaja showed me a fleet of no fewer than ten Rolls-Royce cars. In Kashmir, where a Hindu dynasty dominated the lives of three and a half million Moslems, devil dancers wound up an evening of lavish entertainment, and I rode to bed on an elephant.

Outstanding among these rulers was the Nizam of Hyderabad, the largest native State in India. His position, the reverse of that of the Maharaja of Kashmir, was that of being a Moslem ruler over Hindus, and he was supported by British rifles from the near-by garrison at Secunderabad. Birdlike in appearance, he was reputed to be the richest man in the world. The Resident assured me that his palace was honeycombed with secret hiding-places for tons of gold, bushels of precious stones and paper rupees, many millions of which were allegedly destroyed by termites.

Yet, I was to find, as more than one traveller has before me, that the truths about India are elusive. She remained a mystery, fleetingly perceived through an interposed layer of British official-dom and princely autocracy—crowds of natives cordoned off by troops and police, and toiling figures in endless fields seen from the window of my train. Curiously, the thing about India that I remember most to-day was the smell, compounded of the myriad odours of heavily perfumed flowering trees and shrubs, of the sun-baked earth, of Oriental spices, and of burning dung, of the pungent aroma of ghee in millions of cooking-pots, of domestic animals and humanity in the mass. This smell was more fragrant than offensive and pervaded everything.

My contacts with the Indians were by and large limited to a succession of Royal progresses through the streets, a brief appearance at a "mela," or native gathering, a formal conversation with a Hindu or Moslem politician, and distant waves of the hand to murmurous crowds. In the interludes between the public spectacles to impress the native masses I would withdraw into one or another of the British Station communities for a round of official social life centred about a Government House or Residency. Here I would mingle with the Chief Justice, the General Officer commanding the troops, the President of the Legislature, the Indian Civil Service secretaries, regimental officers, inspectors of police, officials of the Indian Medical Service and the public works departments, etc., and, of course, their wives. The precedence on the Station of these civil and military functionaries was regulated by a protocol so rigid that it astonished even me. At dinner I always sat next to my hostess, the Governor's or the Resident's wife—and on the other side I would invariably find the wife of either the Chief Justice or the General. Gazing down the table, I would see the same faces disposed in the same places as the night before. I have but to shut my eyes to find myself again at one of those interminable Government House garden parties, so much alike that they might have been stamped like car bumpers from the substance of Station life. I can see once more the long lines of advancing guests: the women in new print dresses, floppy hats, and long white gloves; the men in grey tropical suits and pith helmets. And once more I see myself standing next to a provincial Governor, shaking hands with one person while trying to catch at the same time, in preparation for the next, the whispered identification of the A.D.C. at my elbow. And as the scene materializes, there come floating into memory the strains of a regimental band, grouped under a banyan tree—the same band that would play lugubrious waltzes for almost exactly the same people at the ball to be held in my honour that evening.

Seen from this vantage-point, British power in India seemed then so solid, secure, and timeless. All that has now been swept away, and I am glad to have seen the machinery of this magnificent example of British rule still at work. In later years I was to hear the British administration of India damned even by my own country-men. And beyond question there was much in our official attitude in India that had become outmoded; the "pukka sahib," with his snobbery based on the authority of the old school tie and his veneration of manners, sport, and etiquette, had become the butt of ribald jokes. Yet, underlying the superficial signs of privilege and luxury were the strict code of duty and the sense of self-dedication that have characterized British stewardship of sub-ject populations. The officers of the Indian Army and the Indian Civil Service were dedicated to an unwearying trusteeship; many of them still represented the third and even fourth generation of their family to have served in India. They bore all the responsi-bilities—for guarding the frontier, putting down riots, alleviating famines, and eradicating plagues—and all too often, through no fault of their own, the resources at their disposal were inadequate. They, too, deplored the contrast between the excessive wealth of the ruling Princes and the abysmal poverty of the masses that so appalled the casual traveller. What is remarkable is not that they failed to eradicate India's countless problems, but rather that they were able to do so much. The more I learned about the British system in India, far from finding it reprehensible or discreditable, the more I came to recognize it as a vast achievement. The im-plantation of the rule of law and justice in a previously oppressed community and the slow teaching of the technique of administra-tion throughout a teeming land that might otherwise have slipped into the anarchy of China—all these were part of the now little-remembered British contribution to India.

Since my father had impressed not only the native Princes but also his own countrymen in India with his skill at tiger-shooting, I was anxious to make my mark in the field of horsemanship. A lucky opportunity unexpectedly presented itself during the last days of my tour, at the Kadir pig-sticking contest, which in those days attracted the boldest and hardest riders in India. Being a keen rider to hounds and having already had my first exciting taste of pig-sticking, I had been eager to try my luck in this famous com-petition. Unfortunately, my schedule prevented my arriving at the meet until the last day, too late to compete for the Kadir Cup itself. However, there remained to be run in the afternoon a point-to-point race for lightweight hog hunters; and a sympathetic artillery officer offered me a ride on his horse, Bombay Duck.

On learning of this, the senior members of my staff tried to talk me out of riding in the race, protesting that I stood a good chance of injuring myself, with consequent dislocation of the remaining part of the tour. The itinerary, however, was almost completed; and I argued that, unless I were so unlucky as to break my neck, there was sufficient time between then and the next important engagement for adequate convalescence. In the end I had my way.

The course was nearly four and a half miles long, over rough country, traversed by deep nullahs, or ditches, and covered with tall grass called *jhow*. Elephants served as the markers. Although the course was completely strange to me, it was fortunately familiar to Bombay Duck, who had won this same race once before. A post entry, I started out against a field of ten. The most I hoped for was to be able to complete the course without falling. But, after Bombay Duck had taken several formidable nullahs in his stride, I grew bolder and began to pass the other horses. The last obstacle was a river. By the time I came to it only two riders remained in front of me. One of them was accounted for when his horse stumbled in the stream and he was thrown into the water. That left only one; and, getting out my whip, I passed him half-way up the bank on the other side. News of this victory spread quickly through the Army cantonments and the princely States, where horsemanship was highly esteemed. I had the feeling thereafter that I was looked upon as something more than a mere Royal figurehead.

One unexpected effect of my visit was to bring Mahatma Gandhi into the open. As my tour progressed, his attacks upon British rule increased in violence; muffled though they were by the boom of saluting guns, the hum of conversation at the garden parties, or the thunder of horses' hooves on the polo fields, I could hear the gathering uproar. This outward clash between the Indian nationalists and the British Government was accompanied by an equally intense but concealed struggle within the Government of India itself over the most effective method to pursue in dealing with Indian demands for independence, to which British policy was committed.

This conflict raged around the new Viceroy, Lord Reading. A

brilliant lawyer and formerly a Liberal politician, he had been sent to India a few months before my arrival to further the Montagu-Chelmsford reforms. He had earlier been Lord Chief Justice of England and during the World War a special ambassador to the United States. But despite these high attainments, his appointment had chilled many of the older British Indian officials to the marrow. In the past, the Viceroys had usually been men of aristocratic descent drawn from what used to be described as the ruling class—men like Lord Elgin, whose earldom went back to the reign of Charles I, and Lord Minto, a gallant Scots Guardsman, who was the envied possessor of a neck that had been broken in the Grand National. Whatever their politics, the Viceroys had adapted themselves to the doctrines of autocratic justice with which the Indian Civil Service, backed by the Army, had run India for two centuries. Lord Reading was the son of a London merchant and ship broker, a circumstance that was deplored by many of the old school, both civil and military, as an unhappy departure from the tradition that had previously limited the choice of Viceroys to the scions of noble families of ancient lineage. On top of this the new Viceroy had unwittingly offended the sensibilities of ultra-conservative elements of the British community by proudly telling one of his first audiences in India—no doubt to reassure the Indian politicians that their aspirations would be judged by an understanding mind—that, when he first came there some forty years before, it was as a seaman. While the producing of such credentials would undoubtedly have made a favourable impression in the United States or Australia, for example, the effect upon the Stations, not to mention the ruling Princes, was quite the opposite. "It is not his having come to India as a common seaman that matters," a certain lady explained to me, "but why did he have to remind us of it?"

This happened nearly thirty years ago, and the lady was then quite old. One can only hope that her sensibilities were spared the shock of the Transport House attitude towards the cherished Indian Civil Service traditions. When the Socialists came into power in Britain in 1945, a former Trade Union official was appointed Governor of one of the three Presidencies. On arriving at his post, this new Governor sought to ingratiate himself in his novel surroundings by taking a whole book from Lord Reading's

tentative leaf. "I understand that my predecessors were all 'toffs',"
he said, "who knew all about shootin', huntin', and fishin'. Well,
having been a railway worker, I had no time for sports; but I can
tell you a lot about hootin', shuntin', and switchin'."

British dominance in India was the product of two hundred
years of war, work, and wisdom. Had anybody tried to persuade
me as I left Karachi, with a regimental band on the quay crashing
out "God Save the King," that all this would be lost in my
lifetime, I would have put the man down as a lunatic.

Yet, the circumstances attending the recent winding up of
British rule in India under the Viceroyalty of Lord Mountbatten
caused my mind to flash back to my tour in 1921–22, on which
Dickie was one of my naval A.D.C.'s. Although he had scarcely
ridden before, he was determined to learn to play polo, and his
initial appearance on a pony startled the Indian cavalry officers
and my staff. But Dickie was nothing if not analytical; and undaunted by his inexperience, he persevered. It was my impression
at the time that his interest in the manifold problems of India was
confined to that part of the country bounded by the white boards
of polo fields. However, not so many years were to elapse
before he was to be established in the Viceroy's House at New
Delhi, engaged in the process of liquidating the immeasurable
Imperial trust he and I, each in our own way, had endeavoured
to defend in our youth.

From Karachi, I proceeded in the *Renown*, with stops at Ceylon,
the Malay Peninsula, and Hong Kong, to Japan, arriving at
Yokohama on April 12.

The Prince Regent, Hirohito, with a host of other Princes,
officials of the Imperial Household, the Cabinet, and admirals and
generals, met me at the railway station in Tokyo; the streets were
solidly lined for miles by schoolchildren holding stiff paper flags,
bowing rhythmically, and shouting "Banzai" in unison.
Mystery surrounded the life of the Mikado, the Prince Regent's
father. He never appeared; it was said that he was mad and was
kept locked up in a room at the Palace.

Altogether I remained in Japan nearly four weeks. The ceremonial obligations of my visit were for the most part discharged
in the capital, and thereafter I was able to travel more freely about
the country. The suspicion with which the Japanese were then

inclined to regard foreigners was apparently lifted in my case; my official hosts seemed eager to show me whatever I wished to see, although their graciousness did not extend to an invitation to visit their warships, about which Dickie Mountbatten, as a young naval officer, had advanced a few hopeful inquiries.

While my countrymen had played a leading rôle in the original industrialization of Japan, evidences of rising American influence were also visible—most conspicuously in the knuckles of the Minister of Foreign Affairs, Count Uchida. One night at a banquet I noticed that these parts of his fingers were knobby and malformed. I asked him out of curiosity what had happened to them. "Oh," he answered proudly, "I hurt them playing baseball while in college in America."

My visit to Japan was further memorable for the golf game that I played with Prince Regent Hirohito—surely one of the most remarkable encounters between representatives of the East and West since Marco Polo's visit to the Celestial Kingdom. Prince Hirohito's observations while in London the year before had apparently persuaded him that golf was our national game. When, therefore, he suggested one afternoon in Tokyo that I should seek respite from the rounds of official engagements by relaxing on the golf course, I eagerly accepted. It was to be a foursome: Prince Hirohito, Admiral Halsey, a low-handicap Japanese player, and myself. Prince Hirohito showed up at the Komazawa Club wearing a cap and plus-fours. It all appeared to be perfectly normal until the Prince took his turn at the tee. Then with no visible signs of impatience or humiliation he fanned several times. And when at last he succeeded in driving the ball down the fairway, he beamed with pleasure.

The Admiral and I exchanged glances. It was plain to both of us that our host had never played the game before. Here was the vaunted courtesy of the Orient at its best. Etiquette demanded from us an equally considerate response. By design I developed a disastrous hook. The Admiral was almost never on the fairway, either. He also kept the score. It suggests a remarkably close match.

However, Prince Hirohito quietly regained "face" in another test of skill in which he was more practised. He took me into the Imperial gardens behind the palace one day to show me how to catch ducks with long-handled nets. He was as deft and quick as I was clumsy. I did not shine that afternoon.

My staff and I rejoined the *Renown* at Kagoshima on May 9. The homeward voyage was not without incident or interest. We stopped three days in Manila, capital of the Philippines, then a dependency of the United States. I was the guest of the Governor, the famous General Leonard Wood, an able, highly respected, and likeable man who was to some extent in political exile. I still carry a scar from Manila. In a polo game between my team from the *Renown* and a U.S. cavalry regiment, my right eyebrow was laid bare by a hard-struck ball—an injury that necessitated three surgical stitches and a shot of tetanus antitoxin. The cure, from my point of view, was worse than the wound: it produced a burning rash, a sleepless night, and marred to some extent an otherwise enjoyable stay.

By then I had seen about as much of the East as one mind could possibly absorb. But more calls had to be made: British North Borneo, the island of Penang off Malaya, and the naval base of Trincomalee.

A sweltering passage across the Indian Ocean in the monsoon brought the *Renown* into the Red Sea; and, as she made her way slowly through the Suez Canal, I went on by train to Cairo to pay my respects to King Fuad, father of the present Monarch. The British protectorate over Egypt had just been terminated, and he himself had just been proclaimed King. But the Egyptian nationalists were agitating for the evacuation of the British occupation forces, and relations between the two countries were strained. My visit was therefore intended to soothe Egyptian sensibility.

The audience with the King took place at the Abdin Palace. I was accompanied there by the High Commissioner, the late Field-Marshal Lord Allenby. The approach to the Monarch's presence was made through endless, ornate, mirrored halls, over miles of parquet floors on which our uniform spurs clanked and jingled. My conversation with the King was one of the most disconcerting I had ever experienced. Owing to an unfortunate impediment in his speech caused by a throat wound suffered in his thirties, his voice under the stress of nervousness or excitement emitted unintelligible sounds that resembled nothing so much as the bark of a dog. My various conversational gambits were un-rewarded; whatever King Fuad wished to convey to me was lost in the staccato bursts from his throat. Lord Allenby, to whom this was no new experience, sat rigid and serious in his chair listening attentively, as if he were pondering and absorbing the weighty things being discussed.

On June 20 Eddystone lighthouse thrust its white tower out of a calm sea and showed the way into Plymouth Sound. I had been gone nearly eight months and had travelled by sea and land nearly 41,000 miles.

By custom the Prince of Wales was expected on his return from official overseas missions to make a public report on his travels at a great banquet at Guildhall as the guest of the Lord Mayor. This I had already done after my first two tours, in the presence of their architect, the Prime Minister, Mr. Lloyd George. This third one was memorable for the felicitous speech with which he welcomed me home—his last official act before he retired for ever from office:

> I have the honour to propose the toast: "His Royal Highness, the Prince of Wales." I regret that so important a toast should have fallen to the lot of a transient although a disembarrassed phantom, but it is a great pleasure to me to have to propose it. I think my colleagues and myself can greet His Royal Highness in the words of the dying gladiators, *Morituri te salutamus.* . . .
>
> Whatever our feeling for him was before he went to India, it is deeper to-day. It was a high act of statesmanship, carried through with inimitable gifts of grace, of tact, and of a drawing attachment which is so very much his dominant characteristic. More than that, it was a high act of courage, carried through with faultless nerve. There were many who doubted the wisdom of the visit. There was no one who was not anxious about the visit. There were difficulties, there were menaces, there was an at-mosphere which gave great concern to everyone. He went there without fear. He went indomitably at the call of duty, and what-ever the Empire owed to him before, it owes to him a debt which it can never repay to-day. . . .
>
> . . . I am proud . . . that the last official function of my Premier-ship is to propose, as I do now, the health and prosperity of His Royal Highness, the Prince of Wales.

CHAPTER XI

MY FATHER AND THE "BRAVE NEW WORLD"

ALTHOUGH the intervals between these tours allowed me to resume my life in my own country, travelling constituted my principal occupation between the ages of twenty-five and thirty-one; and I learned, as others have learned, that a rolling stone has difficulty in coming to rest. The younger countries overseas had taught me newer and freer ways. I had become accustomed to being pretty much on my own, to running my own show. To submerge myself afresh, therefore, in the grave, unhurried, unchanging ways not only of the Court but of ordinary life meant for me no small readjustment.

Meanwhile, certain events had altered the family's structure, so homogeneous in my childhood. While I was in India, my sister Mary had married an older man, Lord Lascelles, and with easy grace had become the chatelaine of his country home in Yorkshire. In 1923, my brother Bertie had married the daughter of a Scottish earl, Lady Elizabeth Bowes-Lyon, who had brought into the family a lively and refreshing spirit. Harry was serving in the Army as a subaltern in the 10th Hussars and was embarked upon a professional military career; George, a lieutenant in the Royal Navy, was away on foreign stations a good deal.

It was especially in my relations with the family that I realized how much my outlook had changed. My life had become one of contrast and commotion; whereas order and perfection ruled my father's. His seasonal migrations were as regular as the revolving planets: at Sandringham in January for the end of the pheasant-shooting season; then to London in February for six months of official and social engagements, with peregrinations to Windsor for Easter and again in June for Ascot Week, and to Newmarket for the Jockey Club race meetings; then to Cowes at the end of July for the Royal Yacht Squadron Regatta; then north to Balmoral during August and September for the grouse-shooting and deer-stalking; then back to London in October for three months, interrupted by journeys to Sandringham for the partridge and pheasant shoots; and finally the family gathering there for Christmas.

As the years wore on, my parents departed less and less from this fixed orbit, which through unchanging repetition took on the authority of tradition. When they did, it was to honour the houses of a few noble families where the proprieties of their generation were defended to the last and where youth walked warily.

Because my father was himself a simple man, the legend grew that his life was simple, too. But it was simple only in that, by contrast with my grandfather's more gregarious, cosmopolitan ways, my father preferred his good times at home. His private interests centred upon his family, his shooting, his sailing, and his stamp collection, one of the best in the world; his small circle of friends was as fixed and constant as his habits. However, that is not to suggest that my father lived under a Spartan régime. He would never have chosen to sleep, for example, as the old Emperor Francis Joseph of Austria did, on an iron bed. On the contrary, I knew no one who liked his comforts more, save perhaps myself. Everything about him was always of the best—his clothes, his fine hammer guns by Purdey, his food, his stationery, his cigarette cases by Fabergé (the famous jeweller of the Imperial Russian Court), the presents he gave to his friends.

My father's life was a masterpiece in the art of well-ordered, unostentatious, elegant living. No matter the place, no matter the occasion, perfection pervaded every detail. The shooting lunches served in a tent in the field at Sandringham were prepared with the same expert care by the chef as the fine banquets set before crowned heads at Windsor Castle or Buckingham Palace. And the approach of the head gamekeeper with the game card to my father's seat at table, after the morning's bag was counted, was as solemn and grave as that of an ambassador presenting his letters of credence. Nothing ever seemed to be forgotten; nothing ever seemed to go wrong. The secret of all this smooth perfection, an old courtier once explained to me, was the system of having the equivalent of a man and a half for every job.

It was to be seen at its best at Windsor in June during the four-day Ascot race meetings. It was my parents' custom to entertain a large house-party of some thirty people; and the old Castle would turn almost gay as the guests arrived. Every day at noon the King and Queen with their guests drove in open landaus through Windsor Great Park to the course. Each carriage was drawn by four horses with bewigged postilions in the special Ascot livery—red jackets, black velvet hunting caps, white buckskin breeches, and top boots. This colourful scene has been brilliantly depicted by Sir Alfred Munnings in a striking picture hanging in the Castle.

The spontaneous ovation accorded my parents as the brilliant cavalcade trotted past the stands was always a gratifying experience for the members of their family.

The order of one of these processions as set forth in *The Times* may be of interest in giving some idea of the composition of one of these Windsor Castle parties for Ascot Week:

First Carriage: The King, the Queen, the Prince of Wales, and the Duke of York.

Second Carriage: The Duchess of York, the Marchioness of Worcester, Viscount Lascelles, and the Duke of Roxburghe.

Third Carriage: The Duchess of Roxburghe, the Duchess of Portland, the Duke of Portland, and the Marquess of Crewe.

Fourth Carriage: The Marchioness of Hartington, the Countess of Mar and Kellie, the Marquess of Worcester, and the Marquess of Hartington.

Fifth Carriage: The Countess of Granard, the Dowager Countess of Airlie, the Earl of Mar and Kellie, and the Earl of Granard.

Sixth Carriage: Viscountess Ednam, Mrs. Fetherstonhaugh, the Earl of Durham, and Lord Revelstoke.

Seventh Carriage: Lady Joan Verney, the Hon. Ursula Lawley, Lord Colebrooke, and Viscount Ednam.

But I shall always remember the dinners at the Castle during that week. A few seconds before 8.30 my father and mother with the other members of the family present would start down the corridor towards the Green Drawing Room. At the door we would be met by the Master of the Household, who, as he backed across the threshold, would bow the King and Queen in. The ladies in evening gowns and sparkling jewels formed a quarter-circle on one side of the room. The men were similarly drawn up on the other. The King, his sons, a few close friends, and members of the Household would be in the Windsor uniform. The rest of the men would be in black tail-coats. All would wear knee-breeches. While my mother shook hands with the men, my father would repeat the same formality with the curtsying women. Then the man who had been commanded to sit on my mother's right would bow and, offering her his arm, escort her to the table while the strains of "God Save the King" issued from a grille in the dining-room behind which was concealed a Guards string band that played during dinner.

One evening the gilt service would be used, on the next an equally magnificent silver one. The courses would be served by pages in blue livery and footmen in scarlet. Occasionally above the soft music my father's voice would rumble out in appreciation of some amusing story or in disapproval of some item of gossip that had just been confided to him. At the end of dinner, which never lasted more than one hour, my mother would catch my father's eye as a signal that she was about to leave with the ladies. The latter as they withdrew would each curtsy to my father.

Then he would motion to two of the men to take the empty chairs beside him. Over the port, coffee, and liqueurs the day's racing and current politics would be discussed. My father never sat more than twenty minutes—there was barely time to smoke even the shortest cigar. Abruptly, as if controlled by a hidden time-clock, he would rise and lead his guests back to the Green Drawing Room to join my mother. At 11 o'clock as if by magic the company would resume the same half-circle in which we had found them, the ladies on one side, the men on the other. Bidding their guests good night, my parents would withdraw with the members of the Royal Family. The door would close silently behind us. The evening was over.

Only once did I observe even a slight disruption in the solemn sequence of one of these evenings. The string band that, as I have already said, played softly throughout dinner, occupied a small

chamber—almost a cubby-hole—off the dining-room. One unusually warm June evening on her way out my mother was moved
to express to the bandmaster her pleasure over the rendering of
one of her favourite pieces. Opening the door into the chamber,
she peered inside. A second later came a gasp, and my mother
was heard murmuring consoling sentences. When she reappeared,
she seemed upset and beckoned to the Master of the Household as
she continued into the drawing-room. It was some time before
the reason for this slight commotion was divulged to the rest of
the party. Behind the grille my mother had discovered a veritable
Black Hole of Calcutta—a windowless, airless chamber in which
the bandsmen in their tightly buttoned tunics sat drenched in
sweat and half-fainting in their chairs.

"Is it always as warm as this?" my mother had asked.

"Not always, Your Majesty," was the honest response.

Sumptuous as was the scale of entertainment, life at Windsor
for young people was a trifle overpowering, to say the least.
Nothing was lacking but gaiety; and the abrupt ending of the
evening at 11 would leave us subdued and at a loss. One evening
my brothers and I were emboldened to try to enliven the atmosphere for the younger members of the party. We had arranged
with the band to wait for us in the Green Drawing Room. When
my parents had gone to bed, we returned; the rugs were rolled
back; and the musicians, more familiar with classical music and
martial airs, made an earnest attempt to cope with outmoded fox-
trots, which were as close as they could come to jazz. But our
efforts to be gay were a failure. The ancient walls seemed to
exude disapproval. We never tried it again.

No other man that I ever knew was more content with his own
mode of life than was my father. He was already thirty-five years
old when Queen Victoria, whom he revered, died. His habits,
tastes, and views reflected the era when his grandmother ruled
over the British Empire and the British aristocracy stood admired
and envied throughout the world. The first rending of the social
fabric by the Liberal politicians in his father's reign had filled him
with foreboding. But the acceleration in change, brought on by
the war, shaking the foundations of convention, almost outraged
him. It would not be correct to say that he rejected the twentieth
century. It was only that he was determined to resist as much of

it as he could. How often did I hear him say, "Well, we never did that in the olden days."

In January, 1924, the Conservative Government fell; and my father, charged by the constitution with forming a new one, summoned to Buckingham Palace the Labour leader, Ramsay Mac-Donald, who had begun life in a thatched cottage in a Scottish fishing village. Hoping for the best but troubled, he confided to the diary that records every day of his life: "I had an hour's talk with him. He impressed me very much, he wishes to do the right thing. To-day 23 years ago dear Grandmamma died, I wonder what she would have thought of a Labour Government?"

While my father could have had little doubt as to what she would have thought, he was in considerable doubt as to how the Socialist leaders would conduct themselves towards him in their new rôle of Ministers of the Crown. Many of them, in their youth, had publicly scoffed at the Monarchy. And my father was not only apprehensive that some of his new Ministers might refuse to participate in the State ceremonies, but he also had some grounds for believing that they might even refuse to wear at Court the official uniforms that were *de rigueur*. Fortunately Mr. Mac-Donald proved to be a reasonable man; the new Prime Minister and his Cabinet in due course made their debut at Court colour-fully clad in the uniform of Ministers of the Crown—a blue, gold-braided tail coat and white knee-breeches with sword—a courtesy that went far to reassure my father.

The things that my father found wrong with the "Brave New World" would have made a long list, at the head of which he would almost certainly have put what was coming to be known as the "new woman." His distaste for the extreme styles affected by the emancipated flapper led to an amusing incident one afternoon at Windsor. A group of women were sightseeing on the terrace below the Royal Apartments. My father, peering down from the windows, suddenly cried out: "Good God, look at those short skirts; look at that bobbed hair." These scornful comments delivered in his resonant voice carried out across the terrace. My mother hurried to the window; a moment later the King fell silent and was seen to withdraw.

He disapproved of Soviet Russia, painted fingernails, women who smoked in public, cocktails, frivolous hats, American jazz, and the growing habit of going away for week-ends. While I shared my father's mistrust of Communism, I couldn't see anything glaringly reprehensible about the others. Our differing views on these and related trends of my generation not unnaturally made for occasional misunderstandings between us.

I think I can say in all humility that I have come to understand my father better since those days. Now, to my surprise, I discover myself standing in relation to the new war-fostered generation in much the same position as he stood to mine in the early 1920's. He was then fifty-six years old and disappointed that the way of life which he had known before the First World War had not returned. I am the same age to-day; and, having lived the most active part of my life between the two wars, I now find myself regretting the pushing aside of many things I knew and understood. And just as I once found myself thirty years ago as a young man at variance with my more conservative father, so I now find myself unable to agree with some of the political ideas held by my young friends. It is not that I fear change, for I have never been reactionary. What I fear, and what I now realize my father always feared, was violent change, change that would sweep away fundamental and hard-bought things.

But mine was a generation of evolution, and my exalted position did not make me immune to the stirrings. On the contrary, I was full of curiosity, and there were few experiences open to a young man of my day that I did not savour. I used to say that I liked to try everything once, and there was plenty for me to try. I rode in steeplechases; I went to night-clubs. If I worked hard, I also played hard.

My own Household had meanwhile been reinforced by the addition of a gallant and charming Grenadier Guardsman, Brigadier-General G. F. Trotter, known to his friends—and I never knew a man who had more—simply as "G." His post was that of my Assistant Comptroller, which implied that he assisted Admiral Halsey. But "G's" and my association went beyond his ostensible duties. Although more than twenty years older than I—he had lost his right arm in the Boer War while I was still in the nursery—he became my constant companion in the things pertaining to the lighter side of the Princely rôle. If I had learned constitutional history from Sir William Anson at Oxford and Imperial politics from Ned Grigg, I suppose I learned from "G" Trotter that life should be lived to the full.

But, if life could be lived to the full, it had in my case to be lived within certain strict rules. And no other person of Royal birth that I ever encountered seemed to blend in his own character such a tolerant understanding of human nature combined with a rigid sense of duty as my great-uncle, the Duke of Connaught. Born in 1850 and therefore fifteen years older than my father, he was Queen Victoria's third son. The "Iron" Duke of Wellington was one of his godfathers and was present at his christening. With such a beginning, it was destined that he should follow an Army career. Educated at Woolwich, he later served in the infantry and the cavalry and saw service in Canada and Egypt and as a General Officer in India. Although he was eventually made a Field-Marshal, it was a matter of personal disappointment to him that he never attained in the prime of his life the command of the British Army. During the early part of the First World War he was, as Governor-General, an important influence in Canada's great contribution to the Empire's forces.

Uncle Arthur had of course been a revered figure of my childhood. However, I did not really begin to appreciate his sterling qualities until I entered public life. He was then in his seventies —still a fine, soldierly figure, if somewhat bent. If he was not the most brilliant of military tacticians, he was without a peer in matters of uniform. There were more than a hundred regiments in the British Army, each with its own sacred idiosyncrasy of dress—lacings, badges, buttons, belts, and head-dresses. Uncle Arthur seemed to carry in his head an exact catalogue of every uniform, its history, and how it should be worn. News that he was going to inspect a unit would strike terror into all ranks. He would scrutinize each officer and soldier from head to toe.

"My dear fellow, you are a Grenadier, aren't you?" he was once heard to ask sarcastically of an unsuspecting field officer in the guttural accent that was a characteristic of all Queen Victoria's children.

"Sir," was the officer's affirmative answer.

"Then why the devil," asked Uncle Arthur, "are you wearing Coldstream spurs?"

It was once my unhappy experience to have "my name taken"

—to use the Brigade of Guards' term for being put in the report book—by Uncle Arthur before a King's Birthday Parade, the first at which I was ever on duty in full dress. Having accoutred myself with considerable care at York House, I mounted my horse and rode over to Clarence House to fetch my great-uncle and accompany him to Buckingham Palace to join the King's procession to the Horse Guards. He was waiting for me on the steps. As I saluted, his eagle eye darted over my uniform to rest finally for interminable seconds at my waist. "My dear boy," he said coldly, "don't you realize that you are improperly dressed? You are in 'guard order' when you should be in 'review order'." The first prescribed a crimson silk sash and white leather sword slings and knot; the other, a gold and crimson net sash, and gold-lace sword slings and knot. I turned my horse around and trotted shamefacedly back to York House, where, without my dismounting, the correct accoutrements were girt around me. The idea of having thus saved me from so embarrassing a military error evidently gave him satisfaction. At every Birthday Parade thereafter he never failed to remind me of the incident. "Do you remember that day when you started for parade in the wrong order? Wasn't it lucky I spotted it in time?"

The stories about Uncle Arthur were legion; but it is not as the stickler for punctilios that I remember him. As if by a hidden balance-wheel his life was regulated by a code of personal rectitude and an unflawed sense of duty. His manners were faultless; his courtesy invested his simplest action with dignity and naturalness. I would not have called him a completely happy man. His family life had not been without sadness. As a younger brother and later the uncle and great-uncle of successive Sovereigns he had always had to play second fiddle in the affairs of the Royal Family. Yet, he never shirked the onerous demands made upon his services. As a sponsor of a multitude of national institutions and undertakings he was a distinguished figure in public life. In his personal philosophy, he was urbane, tolerant, and wise. Even when I sometimes found myself in rebellion against some of the things of the world of which he was a part, I nevertheless felt that, while he might not necessarily approve the course I had in mind, he would view it in a sympathetic and understanding light. He died during the Second World War, aged ninety-one; in him the nation lost a devoted servant, and I a revered and sympathetic friend.

In the early 1920's the forces of change had not yet thrust so deeply into the texture of society as to have obliterated much of the old elegance. It was my good fortune to enjoy the hospitality of many of the stately homes of England before taxation and death duties closed most of them for ever. In these ancestral country seats was still to be found a way of life that was the product of the centuries-old system of primogeniture and the prerogative of the aristocracy and landed gentry. And the houses themselves were of infinite variety, each one reflecting the tastes and idiosyncrasies of its successive masters. One might be famous for its architecture, another for its collection of pictures or tapestry; still others for their silver, their china, or furniture. And nearly all were surrounded by lovely gardens and grounds. One by one these hereditary "palaces," "castles," "halls," "manors," "parks," or "houses" have passed to the National Trust or been sold for only a fraction of their value under the auctioneer's hammer.

During the whole of the London season, the West End was an almost continuous ball from midnight until dawn. One might receive invitations for as many as four parties the same evening— at Londonderry House, Wimborne House, Forbes House, Derby House, Chesterfield House, Crewe House, or the foreign embassies. If the first failed to please, one could always move on to another. And however one fared at the more formal affairs, the evening could always be saved by recourse to one or another of the gay night-clubs, which had by then become fashionable and almost respectable. There were the Café de Paris, Ciro's, the Kit-Kat Club, and the one I went to most, the Embassy Club in Old Bond Street, run by the famous Luigi Naintre, an Italian restaurateur with an enormous cranium and an unequalled sense of discretion.

Like most young men, I loved to dance, and almost every year brought forth some new step or rhythm; for a brief period I counted the music of the "Charleston" and the "Black Bottom" among the foremost American exports to Britain.

My father, never having been inside a night-club, assumed from the term that these establishments must be dimly lit, smoky, disreputable dives, closely allied to the American "speak-easies" and infested with gangsters. The fact that the Embassy Club was, on the contrary, a brightly lit, expensive, and altogether respectable, even staid, restaurant with an elegant international clientele failed to alter his prejudice. Since he himself always started for bed at 11.10, it was difficult for him to believe that anything but mischief could result from staying up later.

My father could not understand why I was not more like him. For one reason or another there would be occasional lectures on the theme that I must always remember who I was. Yet, despite these passing storms of disapproval, I was happy in my parents' company and always spent at least a month out of every year with them at one or another of their country residences. If anything can be said to have come between us, it was the relentless formality of their lives, never wholly relaxed and regulating their every action. It was this that inhibited the natural and spontaneous expression of emotions and ideas. Much that might have been mutually enriching between us often remained unexpressed and unattempted. The difficulty, I believe, was in large measure implicit in our circumstances: Kings and Queens are only secondarily fathers and mothers. Because my official life was already ridden with formality, I instinctively sought relaxation in company where, though there was no lack of respect for my position, there was no tedious standing on ceremony. Had I been of a studious nature, I might have sought refreshment in highbrow circles; I might have cultivated an amateur's interest in literature or listened to Sir Ernest Rutherford discourse on the splitting of the atom. But it so happened that I preferred physical to intellectual exercise. No sport provides this in greater degree than riding to hounds.

Although I was taught to ride as a small boy and had done a little fox-hunting at Oxford, I did not take it up seriously until 1920-21, when I began to hunt with the Pytchley in Northamptonshire. In this formidable country, I went through an exacting apprenticeship. As I gained confidence, I began to ride in steeplechases and point-to-point races.

Two seasons later I hunted with the Duke of Beaufort's hounds in Gloucestershire. The old Duke, then seventy-five years old, was too heavy and infirm to get on a horse any more, but the instincts of the chase were still strong in him. From his ancestral seat, Badminton House, he would set out in a Ford to follow his hounds, scooting through the coverts, bumping in and out of ditches, all but sending his clattering vehicle over the fences.

After a season with the Beaufort, I moved to Leicestershire. A rambling, red-brick house at Melton Mowbray, called Craven Lodge, had been turned into a hunting club. The rooms were simple but comfortable, the stabling first class. I engaged a flat there, and began to collect a string of hunters. In this I was assisted by "Fruity" Metcalfe.

Melton Mowbray is the focal-point of three famous hunts: the Quorn, the Cottesmore, and the Belvoir. This little town was surrounded by miles of undulating grassland stretching as far as the eye could see. In the Vale of Belvoir one could gallop for twenty minutes at a stretch without drawing rein. The going was marvellous. The fences were well cut and laid; one seldom met barbed wire. I have been one of six riders taking the same fence abreast—a wonderful feeling.

But, in addition to providing ideal country for the chase, the hunts centring on Melton Mowbray formed a sturdy and cosmopolitan society. Intermixed with the local landed gentry, who form the sure base of any hunting community, was a lively sampling of dashing figures: noblemen and their ladies; wealthy people who had discovered that the stable door was a quick if expensive short-cut into society; a strong injection of Americans from the famous eastern hunts; ladies whose pursuit of the fox was only a phase of an even more intense pursuit of romance; retired admirals and generals; cavalrymen and Guardsmen; good riders on bad horses; bad riders on good horses. And last but by no means least were the yeomen farmers, keen sportsmen in spite of the fact that their land was often a dismal scene after the "field" had galloped over it, smashing the fences and leaving the gates open for cattle to stray.

Of all the outstanding hunting personalities of the Leicestershire of those days, I shall pause to mention only one, the late Major Algernon Burnaby, the Squire of Baggrave Hall and a famous master of the Quorn Hunt. With a weather-beaten complexion, a hawklike nose, piercing eyes, and the intellect of a statesman, Algy Burnaby kept his hard-riding field under perfect control by means of an unrivalled combination of polished wit and sarcasm. If, for example, some of the ladies rode too close to hounds in their eagerness to keep ahead of each other, his cry of "Hold hard, all the pretty women; the others can go on" would stop them in their tracks. Or, if a thrusting young man jumped a fence where the hounds had checked to pick up the lost scent, and I was within earshot, Algy would upbraid him with some such caustic remark as, "Come back, young feller. Who the hell do you think you are, the Prince of Wales?"

In this vigorous, untrammelled company I revelled. There is no thrill to equal that of riding a good, keen horse on a line of one's own as he takes in his stride the stake-and-bound fences standing out black in the wintry light.

Hunting and steeplechasing were more than exhilarating exercise to me. In the hunting field I could forget my round of duties. I was too busy riding my horse and scanning the next fence for a place to jump to worry over my next engagement or my next speech. Besides, they satisfied the latent desire in me to excel; to pit myself against others on equal terms; to show that, at least in matters where physical boldness and endurance counted, I could hold my own. Just as my father was one of the best shots in the country, so it was my ambition to be a good rider to hounds.

People who ride to hounds or in steeplechases must expect their share of spills. There used to be a saying among hunting folk that, if one went too long without a fall, the next one would hurt. I had plenty, some painful but none, to me at least, too serious. Had I been anybody else, these mishaps would have been shrugged off as part of the natural hazards of a robust sport. But, because I was the Prince of Wales and because newspaper readers then had less serious problems in the world to distract them, the mere report from some obscure village that I had been seen with "mud on my back" or with my top-hat stove in would momentarily assume world importance.

This was particularly true of the American Press, which about this time began to follow my falls with the relentless curiosity that marks its approach to Royalty. Jokes about the Prince of Wales falling off his horse became almost as commonplace in American vaudeville acts as topical wisecracks on Prohibition. All this fun at my expense finally got under my skin; after all, I didn't ride that badly. Just as I was beginning to despair of ever living down these gibes, the famous American humorist, Will Rogers, came to my defence with a series of dry commentaries on riding that no one appreciated more than I did. "England is all worked up over the Prince's numerous falls," Will Rogers said, "but up to now no one has manifested much interest in any of mine—only for laughing purposes. In my falls I am not fortunate enough to spill any royal blood, but it's my blood, and it's all I got. No matter how common our blood is, we hate to lose it." Will Rogers then asked: "Are the Prince and I supposed to fall with the horse, or are we supposed to stay up in the air until the horse gets up and comes back under us?"

The public fuss about my falls would have remained in the realm of humour had it not been my misfortune in the winter of 1924 to suffer quite a serious one. In a race for Lord Cavan's cup in the Army point-to-point at Arborfield Cross I fell at the first fence. The ground was hard; and, since my head was the first part of my body to hit, I suffered a concussion and was knocked out for half an hour. The injury was sufficiently serious to keep me in a dark room for a week and in bed for nearly a month. In consequence of this accident the question of the right of the Prince of Wales to hazard his neck in steeplechasing quickly flared up into a public issue. A Member of Parliament, himself a skilled and fearless sportsman, was moved to ask from the Conservative benches of the House of Commons whether the Government should not restrain me from engaging in so dangerous a sport. And the Prime Minister, Mr. Ramsay MacDonald, was sufficiently disturbed to address to me a letter, probably without counterpart in the long annals of British official correspondence.

> 10, Downing Street,
> Whitehall, S.W.1.
> 19 March 1924
>
> Sir,
> Pray do not put me down as an interfering person who having no zest in life himself wishes to knock it out of others. But you know how much we are all concerned about you, not only for public but, if you would permit me to say so, for personal reasons. . . .
> Would you please not consider it an excess either of my duty or of my interest, if I begged you to refrain from taking chances

that no doubt offer you an exhilarating temptation but [consider it] as nothing but a timorous apprehension? No one in these days can do more good than you, Sir, to your people, through them, to the world, & were a serious mishap to come upon you, who could take your place? Even if someone could, it would not diminish the heartiness of the appeal I make to you, for you must know the personal affection in which you are regarded by your people quite apart from the high office & dignity which are yours.

If I have gone too far in writing this, I crave your forgiveness. I am sure that both in its substance & in its spirit it expresses what is in the hearts of everybody in this country.

Pray accept my felicitations on your speedy recovery and believe me to be in faithful service, Sir,

Your obedient servant,
RAMSAY MACDONALD

This was followed eleven days later by one from my father:

Buckingham Palace,
March 30th 1924

Dearest David,

I am very glad you came to luncheon today & delighted to see that you had practically recovered from your fall. You have no doubt seen the various articles which appeared in the newspapers at the time of your accident, these only express what is the general feeling of the country, which you know is also the very strong opinion of Mama and myself, that you should not expose yourself to unnecessary risks in riding point to points & steeple chases. You have shown great courage & horsemanship which everyone appreciates, but the time has come when *I must ask you to give up* riding in the future in steeple chases & point to point races. I know how fond you are of riding, but I am sure you will get plenty of enjoyment & exercise in hunting & playing polo which you can do as much as you like. . . .

Ever my dear boy
Yr most devoted Papa
G.R.I.

Let it not be assumed that I took these admonitions lightly. The end of my convalescence saw me calling first upon my father and then upon the Prime Minister. I assured them that I rode no more recklessly than anybody else, that this last fall was just an unlucky break, that my horses were all good jumpers, and that I always kept myself in good shape—all the plausible arguments that could be mustered by a young man determined not to be put off from doing what he enjoyed most. But spring was already at hand; the point-to-point season was over, and the question receded into the background.

That summer the international polo matches between Great Britain and America were to be played at the Meadow Brook Club on Long Island, and I crossed the Atlantic to watch the games and to see something more of the country. I might not have set forth so blithely, however, had I realized what a furore my subsequent adventures in the United States would cause in conservative British minds.

After paying my respects to President Calvin Coolidge in Washington, I repaired to Syosset, Long Island, where Mr. and Mrs. James A. Burden had lent me their lovely house, Woodside. All around were fine homes with well-kept lawns and swimming-pools. Compared to the creature comforts Americans took for granted, the luxury to which I was accustomed in Europe seemed almost primitive. Seen from Syosset, my American prospects were most agreeable; and the proximity of New York offered assurance that the hours not occupied with polo could be spent satisfying my curiosity about the varied activities of that great city.

Everything seemed to go well amid a gay round of sport and entertainment. And I was congratulating myself upon having made a small contribution towards the partial eradication of anti-British prejudices in America when certain editorials began to appear in the Chicago *Tribune*. Colonel McCormick was then engaged in one of his private wars with Britain, and my appearance on Long Island had evidently aroused his suspicions. Convinced that my ostensibly innocent connexion with polo in truth concealed a sinister scheme to undo the immortal work of 1776, he felt impelled to warn his fellow citizens.

If the polo matches were, as the Colonel suspected, a plot to advance British prestige, they were a dismal failure. Despite the last-minute inclusion of a ten-goal Anglo-Argentine player, Lewis Lacey, to play at back for the British side, the invincible American team, composed of Devereux Milburn, Jr., Watson Webb, Thomas Hitchcock, Jr., Malcolm Stevenson, and Robert

E. Strawbridge, Jr., won by lopsided scores, two matches to none.

A striking discovery I soon made was the strange attitude of the American public towards polo. I had played it with considerable pleasure, if without marked proficiency, both in India and in England, where, as in other countries, it was regarded as an altogether admirable sport, despite the fact that only the comparatively wealthy could afford the expenses involved. However, in reading the American newspaper reporting of the international matches, I noted with surprise an unmistakably derisive and even mocking tone towards the game. In analysing this point of view, it dawned on me that in popular journalism the term "polo player" was practically synonymous with the derogatory term "playboy." This was clearly a class distinction, for no apparent stigma was attached to golf, hunting, tennis, or fishing. Though puzzled, I was nevertheless forced to conclude that anybody in public life who was photographed in white riding-breeches and a helmet and armed with a mallet was only storing up future trouble for himself. Although this reasoning in no way influenced me in my decision to sell my ponies after the matches were over, I am now inclined to regard my action as a wise one. A quick if not too comprehensive glance at the world stage to-day reveals the fact that only four prominent figures have succeeded in overcoming this bad publicity—my brother the King, Mr. Winston Churchill, Mr. Averell Harriman, and Lord Mountbatten; and of the four only Mr. Churchill has ever run for public office.

But this attitude impressed me as being only one of the minor vagaries of good sense to which every country is entitled and of which none is innocent. Basically, America meant to me a country in which nothing was impossible. And the scale of hospitality purveyed on Long Island did nothing to disabuse me of this conception. Some of the parties given in my honour were fabulous. My American hosts spared no expense in demonstrating the splendour of a modern industrial republic. Not one but two orchestras and the stars of popular Broadway revues were brought out from New York in relays to provide entertainment at parties that lasted until dawn.

Perhaps the most elaborate of all these was the one given by the late Mr. Clarence H. Mackay at his country home, Harbour Hill.

A copy of a French château, it stood on top of a wooded rise over-looking Long Island Sound. I spent the day going through the place, marvelling at all it contained. The art treasures alone would have sufficed the needs of an ordinary museum, and I particularly remember a vast hall lined with figures in armour that had been obtained from various old European collections. Now, paintings, tapestries, old china, and armour would have been commonplace enough in an English country house; what was surprising was to find on the same property a squash-rackets court, a gymnasium, an indoor swimming-pool, and a Turkish bath.

As darkness fell and the guests, who included General Pershing, Secretary of War Weeks, and Dr. Nicholas Murray Butler, began to arrive for the ball, the trees lining the winding avenue leading to the house were illuminated with orange-coloured lights. Towering above the roof was the Stars and Stripes in electric lights, which must have been visible for miles around.

The dance music was provided by two bands directed by the great Paul Whiteman, who at a later stage was inspired to lead his musicians in a march around the hall, weaving in and out of the shadowy figures in armour.

It was only as I prepared to leave that I noticed in the entrance hall an object strangely different from all the rest: a small statue of what appeared to be a workman with a pick in his hand.

"What is that?" I asked Mr. Mackay.

"A replica of a statue of my father I have erected on the campus of the University of Nevada at Reno," he answered proudly. I admired Mr. Mackay for that.

As soon as the polo matches were over, I paid a quick visit to my ranch in Alberta, stopping on the way back at Chicago and Detroit. These stops gave me my first glimpses of the American Middle West and the prodigies of American industry. In Detroit the late Mr. Henry Ford took me along his assembly line at River Rouge, where I saw a car assembled in sixteen minutes; and while in Chicago another leading captain of industry, Mr. Louis F. Swift, showed me how a steer could be dismembered in about the same time.

By the time I had to return home, I had picked up quite a full line of American slang, acquired a taste for bathtub gin, and had decided that every Englishman in a position to do so should make a practice of visiting that great country at least once every two or three years. Unfortunately for my own ambitions in this direction, the American Press had been following my research into American life all too thoroughly. And anticipating from past experience that the more colourful reports would no doubt be finding their way to my father's desk at Balmoral, I thought it wise to disarm his suspicion in advance. With the idea of diverting his attention from the emphasis on parties, I wrote him an account of my more prosaic activities, ending with the following observations:

> E. P. Ranch
> Pekisko, Alta
> 20-IX-24
>
> . . . I have learnt a great deal about the U.S. Press . . . you can't compare it in any way with the British Press because it is a far bigger *industry* than ours. . . . It indulges in queer & extravagant headlines *daily* which means that they are forgotten the next day. Sometimes they don't look so good . . . but being a daily habit their 'bark' or . . . their '*look*' is worse than their '*bite*'. . . .
>
> Ever your devoted son
> DAVID

But I was not quick enough. There was already an ominous letter on the way.

> Balmoral Castle
> September 18, 1924
>
> Dearest David
>
> I was glad to get yr. letter of the 4th & to hear that you were enjoying yourself at Long Id. But according to the daily telegrams in the papers you must be having a pretty strenuous time, as besides playing polo & various other things in the day at most of which you are mobbed, you dance till 6 o'clock every morning, including Sundays. It is a pity the Press can't be induced to leave you alone, when you are supposed to be on a holiday. . . .
>
> Ever my dear boy
> Yr. most devoted Papa
> G.R.I.

When upon my return to England I saw my father again, it was to find that my surmise had been correct; on his desk was a heap of American newspaper clippings, some two months old.

Picking up one and tapping it sharply with a pencil he asked, "Did you see this when you were in New York?" The headline that stared back at me cried:

PRINCE GETS IN WITH MILKMAN

While I had seen many headlines of the same type, this particular one I had missed, and I so informed my father. "Fancy their saying that about you," said my father. Turning over the clippings, he produced more samples for my inspection:

HERE HE IS GIRLS—THE MOST ELIGIBLE BACHELOR YET UNCAUGHT
OH! WHO'LL ASK H.R.H. WHAT HE WEARS ASLEEP?
PRINCE OF WALES HAS 'EM GUESSING IN THE WEE HOURS!

I tried to calm my father's apprehensions by telling him that Americans themselves did not take headlines too seriously. But the damage was past repairing. My father's ideas of America had been chiefly based upon his agreeable acquaintance with such eminent figures as Mr. J. P. Morgan, Ambassadors Whitelaw Reid, Walter H. Page, and John W. Davis, as well as families like the Vanderbilts and the Astors. But the sensationalism with which the American Press had reported my doings so upset him as to nullify temporarily his otherwise favourable impressions of the United States. The British Press still abstained from commenting on the private doings of the Royal Family; he was therefore outraged at what he called the "effrontery" of American editors in daring to portray his eldest son so flippantly. In his severest tones he said, "If this vulgarity represents the American attitude towards people in our position, little purpose would be served in your exposing yourself again to this kind of treatment."

However, there was one question asked me by an American journalist on this 1924 trip about which I never told my father. As the *Berengaria* steamed into New York Harbour, the ship-news reporters swarmed around me, asking all manner of questions: what ties and socks I wore, did I like America, and what was I going to do. Suddenly there popped out through the front row of burly newspapermen, the pert figure of a young woman. In a piping voice she asked, "Would you marry an American gal if you fell in love with one?" In the delighted laughter of the other reporters and the somewhat disdainful guffaw of my British companions my affirmative answer was lost.

The net effect of all this uninhibited journalism was that my father privately broke off relations between America and the members of his family, though it would not be correct to say that he actually banned my returning to the United States. Yet, whenever my brothers and I tentatively advanced some project that would take us there, a series of vague but irremovable obstacles always appeared to block us.

This was always a bitter disappointment to me. In the years that followed I was the poorer in experience for being denied access to that stimulating country.

Looking back, I have no doubt that one of the things about me that puzzled and disturbed my father was my continued bachelorhood. Neither he nor my mother ever really tried to push me into marriage; nevertheless, signs and hints were not wanting that in their judgment the time had come for me to take a wife and settle down. I knew exactly what was in my parents' minds: it was that in the interest of assuring the line of succession I should take my chance in what I used to call the "grab bag" of the Royal marriage market.

My father had, of course, married under precisely these conditions; and the happy union with my mother that resulted convinced him that wedding bells were the true answer to a young man's restlessness.

With marriage, both as an institution and a possible condition of happiness, I had no quarrel. Indeed, it was very much in my mind to marry some day. But the idea of an arranged marriage was altogether repugnant to me; moreover, such a union as a means of maintaining the purity of the Royal Line no longer offered so wide a range of choice as in the past. Before the war the Imperial and Royal non-Catholic dynasties of the Continent of Europe had for centuries provided the British Royal House with a continuous supply of suitable brides and grooms. For example, all but one of Queen Victoria's daughters, my greataunts, had married German princes; of her four sons one took to himself a Danish princess, another a Russian grand duchess, and the two youngest married German princesses. However, the break-up of the German and Russian Empires, not to mention the war's bitter legacy of British distrust for Germanic associations, had effectively eliminated from further consideration this once-fertile source of Royal matrimonial prospects. Furthermore, the fact that the war had been fought with unmitigated ferocity between nations led in considerable part by Queen Victoria's grandchildren had discredited the dynastic marriage as an efficacious instrument of foreign policy.

Thus, when first my sister Mary, the Princess Royal, and then my brother Bertie married outside Royalty, the British public approved. No doubt the same dispensation would have been extended to me had I sought the hand of some unmarried daughter of a peer of the realm. But, because no one in such a category had stirred my blood or been sentimentally drawn to me and because I was determined under no circumstances to contract a loveless marriage, the question did not arise. I had seen too many unhappy unions of this kind to wish to risk one myself—all the more so because my particular circumstances would have made the dissolution of an inharmonious partnership almost impossible. From the first I was determined that my choice of a wife would be dictated not by considerations of State but by my own heart.

This is not to suggest that my emotions during these youthful years of travel and intermingling had escaped being moved. There had been moments of tenderness, even enchantment, without which a Princely existence would have been almost intolerable. But in so far as marriage was concerned, I was determined not to be hurried. Therefore, my life went along pervaded, as I realize now, by a sense of incompleteness and inner discontent.

CHAPTER XII

A PROPHETIC DATE

THE winter of 1925 found me preparing for my fourth and last official tour, this time to Africa and South America. Although Mr. Lloyd George had fallen from power, his original plans for me had not been abandoned; and this voyage would complete his design for a Princely odyssey to all the British communities scattered about the globe. The great South African Premier, General Jan Smuts, had also urged upon my father and the British Government the wisdom of continuing with the project. However, in 1924 General Smuts had suffered the same fate as Mr. Lloyd George. His South African Party, dedicated to a policy of closer relations with Great Britain within the framework of the British Commonwealth, was defeated in a general election by the Nationalists under General Hertzog, who had been extremely critical of the relationship. Because the Nationalist party was built around a core of irreconcilable Boer farmers, who still cherished the belief that the Union would one day become an independent republic outside the Empire, the view was expressed by some in Whitehall that the chances of my being received with unanimous goodwill were no longer as certain as would have been the case had General Smuts remained at the helm of government. Happily reassurances on this score were received from the new Premier, and I sailed from Portsmouth on March 28, 1925.

For this voyage the battle-cruiser *Repulse* (Captain Herbert W. W. Hope) replaced her sister ship *Renown*, which was in dockyard hands. Despite the lapse of three years since my last official tour, my staff, headed by Admiral Halsey, had changed but little. Dickie Mountbatten was well launched on the career in the Royal Navy that was to bring him fame. Bruce Ogilvy had returned to his regiment, and his place as equerry had been taken by Lieutenant (now Brigadier) W. D. C. Greenacre of the Welsh Guards—a South African by birth.

A tranquil voyage through quiet seas down the west coast of Africa brought us in quick succession to our colonies of Gambia, Sierra Leone, the Gold Coast, and Nigeria. At each of these places a "Palaver" was held with the local chiefs who had travelled from the hinterland to greet the first Prince of Wales ever to set foot on this steaming malarial coast of scattered settlements, which had long been known as "the white man's grave." The most spectacular of these ceremonies was held at Kumasi, in the Gold Coast, where were forgathered scores of Ashanti chieftains, each squatting under his umbrella of State and surrounded by black retainers adorned with ornaments and insignia overlaid with gold. Here I met a famous character, Prempeh, the King of the Ashanti, who had defied the might of Britain three decades before, only to have his capital seized by our troops and to be exiled along with his family to a lonely island in the Indian Ocean. Prempeh had been a tyrant and a scourge of the Gold Coast; his tribesmen had raided the white settlements. Worse than that, under him they had practised human sacrifices—a common and gruesome adjunct of his reign. It was said that he had painted the walls of his palace with human blood, and testimony to these lurid stories was supplied by huge piles of human skulls and bones found in the near-by forests. Some months before my visit the British Government had ended Prempeh's exile and had allowed him to rejoin his people, establishing him in a fine house with a pension of a thousand pounds a year. He was brought to the Royal stand at the Palaver and presented to me. Having heard all the stories about him, I was gratified to discover that the old tyrant had indeed been tamed by his thirty years of lonely reflection and contemplation. Turned out in European morning dress, he explained in voluble but broken English that he had become a Christian, was deeply interested in missionary work, was studying books on sanitation, and hoped before long to be elected mayor of Kumasi. In any case, the word "progress" cropped up in every sentence. Here, I thought to myself, is an encouraging example of the beneficence of British rule, proof of its justice, humanitarianism, and sagacity.

In the vast territory of Nigeria, which I visited next, a great

Durbar had been arranged in my honour at Kano in the Northern Provinces. To reach it I travelled 700 miles by train from the coast through a wild country traversed by the Niger River. And there is no question but that I was privileged to witness a marvellous spectacle—20,000 Moslem horsemen, some of them in chain armour, the rest in white turbans and flowing cloaks, led by their emirs and sheiks, galloping past me in serried ranks across the desert plain in a charge that would have stunned a motion-picture director.

On April 30 the *Repulse* reached Capetown, anchoring below Table Mountain. My introduction to South Africa was made easier by the fortuitous presence of my uncle, the Earl of Athlone, then Governor-General, and his wife, Princess Alice. Uncle Alge was my mother's youngest brother. Formerly a cavalry officer, and possessed of a fine soldierly bearing, he was a popular and admired figure throughout the Union. The rival political leaders Generals Hertzog and Smuts were with him on the dock to greet me. Then came the usual progress through the streets to Government House with most of Capetown's population thronging the route.

I spent five days in the capital, making the customary rounds and meeting all sections of the community. Then my caravan, consisting of two special trains and carrying, among other things, six cars, plus two cows to provide fresh milk, set out on a thirteen-week tour that would carry me almost 10,000 miles. First I visited the towns and hamlets of the Cape Province, and then travelled through the Orange Free State, Natal, and Zululand, with excursions into the protectorates of Basutoland and Swaziland. Then up to the Transvaal and across to Bechuanaland, turning finally north-east, into first Southern and then Northern Rhodesia.

I saw many remarkable things—the diamond workings at Kimberley; Cecil Rhodes's grave in the Matopo Hills in Southern Rhodesia; and the great, boisterous, gold-mining city, Johannesburg, where I descended 6,700 feet to the lower workings of the City Deep Mine, where I surveyed the still visible scars left by the bloody insurrection of 1922, when a Communist-led mob gained brief control of the city. At Eshowe in Zululand near Durban I witnessed a war dance of thousands of Zulu warriors armed with assegais, knobkerries, and oval shields. These were the grandsons of the same fierce warriors who had defied Queen Victoria's soldiers in 1879 and at Rorke's Drift had surrounded and cut up a company of the 24th Regiment. Indeed, present among the chieftains was a grizzled old warrior of ninety, clad in a faded, ill-fitting frock coat, who had fought in the Zulu War and who gave me blood-curdling imitations of the groans and cries of the dying British soldiers.

Africa is a continent of ceaseless wars—Europeans against Europeans for the control of its resources, and Europeans against the native races for survival. And in South Africa even the most unobservant tourist could not for long miss the ominous fact that the Boer War at the turn of the century had left a lasting bitterness between the Dutch and the British communities that time had failed to heal. It made itself known to me in many ways—in the refusal of a Boer Cabinet Minister to be seen riding with me in Johannesburg, and in the cold declaration of another, also an Afrikander and educated at Oxford, that he could never forgive the British for what he called their wanton attack upon the two Boer republics.

"But surely," I remarked to this second Minister, "this bitterness will eradicate itself as the generations move further away from that war?"

"No, Sir," was his emphatic answer, "never."

And as I visited the old battlefields—Talana Hill, Elandslaagte, Colenso, Spion Kop, Belmont, Enslin, Modder River, and Magersfontein—I began to understand why. At Ladysmith my guide was Admiral Halsey, who, as has already been mentioned, survived the siege as a young lieutenant. From him I naturally saw the campaign through British eyes. But more often my companions were Boers themselves. From them I heard possibly exaggerated tales of the burning of farms and the concentration camps. For ten days the Minister in Attendance was Mr. N. C. Havenga, presently Minister of Finance in the Nationalist Government. At one battlefield his description was so vivid that I asked him whether he had fought there himself. Pulling up one trouser leg he exhibited the scar of what must have been a serious wound. "Sir," he said, "your British put nine bullets into me that day."

Nevertheless, such memories did not restrain the Dutch from showing me hospitality in full measure. As I travelled about the back veld, my train was often met at the outskirts of some dorp by a column of burly Dutch farmers riding shaggy horses—the same men who as Boer commandos armed with Mauser, Bible, and the inevitable coffee-pot had harassed the British columns. If they had brought along a spare mount for me to ride, I would leave the train and gallop into the town at their head, a gesture that seemed to please them and that also gave me much-needed exercise.

On my return to Capetown, General Smuts asked my impressions of his country. My answer was that the tour had thrust me into so great a variety of communities that I hardly knew where to begin. But it had at least given me a comprehension of the unique and complex racial problems besetting the Union. And it had further given me a measure of the greatness of Smuts himself, who almost alone of the old Boer leaders worked ceaselessly and hopefully to hold South Africa within the Empire.

So far as I was concerned, this journey had been a marvellous experience. It had been replete with pleasant episodes, not the least of which was the acquaintance I had formed with a remarkable character, Mr. Thomas Boydell, the Minister of Posts, who accompanied me for a considerable part of the time. Born in England, Tommy Boydell had gone to Natal as a young man to seek his fortune. Instead he found his true talents were for politics. Forceful, plausible, and a good storyteller, he soon became one of the best-known personalities in South African politics. He was abstemious, he never wore a hat, and was always game for a prank. When I bet him five pounds that he would not dare to be photographed alone with a lion, he managed to make a deal with a travelling circus and was able to produce a picture the same evening showing him stroking a large lion with no one else in sight. When I bade Tommy Boydell farewell, I said I hoped to be able to return to South Africa and that if I did it would be unofficially so that I would be able to move about more freely. "In that case," he said, "you had better come under an entirely different name."

"What name do you suggest?" I asked.

"Fourie, Sir." Fourie is a common South African name, as common as Smith or Brown in England.

"But why of all your names, Fourie?" I asked.

"Because," answered Tommy Boydell without more than the suspicion of a smile, "wherever you go you hear the people singing, 'Fourie's a jolly good fellow'."

Now it had been arranged before I left England that this fourth tour should be extended across the South Atlantic to South America. One reason for this extension was to enable me on my father's behalf to return the State visit made three years before to London by the President of the Argentine Republic, Señor Marcelo de Alvear. But there was also present another motive previously unknown in these Royal excursions—trade. Britain had an investment of £400,000,000 in the Argentine; but, while she was by far the Argentine's best customer, the British position in the Argentine market, which before the war had been paramount, had been greatly weakened. The hope of the Government was that whatever popular enthusiasm might be generated by my visit would redound to our commercial advantage. The Republics of Uruguay and Chile having also extended invitations for me to visit them, it was decided to include these other countries as well.

When in due course I arrived in the River Plate I was in condition to resume the strenuous routine—and strenuous it proved to be. Latin Americans, like the Spaniards, never seem to have a good reason for going to bed before 4 a.m. With the day crowded with official rounds and the night given over to Latin hospitality that seemed inexhaustible, there were moments of sheer desperation. But in the warmth and gaiety my spirit found unexpected sources of refreshment that sustained me.

From Montevideo I went on to Buenos Aires. There were a hundred ships in the harbour jammed with people welcoming me with shouts of *"Viva el Principe!"* and from the tops of the highest buildings were released, as I entered the city, clouds of doves, their wing-tips dyed red, white, and blue. After ten exciting days in the Argentine capital and some visits to the largest near-by *estancias*, I travelled by train across the pampas and over the Andes to Santiago de Chile and on to Valparaiso on the Pacific coast.

On October 16, 1925, I arrived back in England. That marked the end of my last official overseas tour. These four voyages, which were my principal occupation between the ages of twenty-five and thirty-one, took me into 45 different countries and colonies, and carried me a total distance of 150,000 miles, equal to six circumnavigations of the globe. In this age of air travel such mileage spread over a period of six years may not seem impressive. Moreover, those long and leisurely progresses by both cruiser and train, although there were occasions when they seemed hardly leisurely to me, had the advantage of allowing me to savour something of the atmosphere of hundreds of different communities. When I had finished poking into the corners of the world, I could have qualified as a self-contained encyclopædia on railway gauges, national anthems, statistics, local customs and dishes, and the political affiliations of a hundred mayors. I knew the gold output of the Rand, the storage capacity of the grain elevators at Winnipeg, and the wool export of Australia; and I could even have held my own on the subject of the chilled-beef trade of the Argentine. The number of memorial trees I planted, if they have survived the vicissitudes of climate and the depredations of man, must to-day constitute a substantial forest. And the number of public buildings and institutions whose foundation-stones I laid would comprise, could they be brought together, a sizable city.

It has been said that my education was completed on the trade routes of the world. That strikes me as a happy judgment. As I travelled the vast Imperial hinterlands with their wheat-laden prairies, the forests, the rubber plantations, the rich mines, the raw, bustling, half-finished cities, and the harbours everywhere filled with British shipping, I was astonished to discover how much of the world's hard work, the dirty work, was being done by a relative handful of my countrymen. It used to depress me on my return home to find that this magnificent effort and sacrifice were by all too many taken for granted. The complacent attitude that characterizes a certain type of ignorant Englishman like Mr. Podsnap was all too evident and most discouragingly so even in the great industrial cities whose prosperity depended in so great a degree upon world trade: "Although his business was sustained upon commerce with other countries, he considered other countries, with that important reservation, a mistake."

Although the significance may have been lost upon me at the time, I realize now that my tours could hardly have been undertaken at a more important period. The British Empire was slowly moving towards another fateful turning-point in its long history. The British Commonwealth as it stands to-day is radically different from what it was when I tramped its outer marches only a quarter of a century ago. I was to be the last King to traverse it with all its diverse parts still in place.

Before attempting to resume my duties at home I took a month's rest, which was largely spent cub-hunting in Leicestershire. This pleasant, healthful interlude was interrupted by the sad news that my grandmother, Queen Alexandra, had suffered a serious heart attack at Sandringham. Next afternoon, with Bertie and Lord Stamfordham, I went there from London by train. When in the early evening we reached Wolferton station it was to be told that my grandmother had already passed away. We arrived at the Big House just in time to join my parents and other near relations for prayers around the bedside.

With my grandmother's death, the last light of the Edwardian era flickered out at Sandringham. She had lived there since the 1860's; and by now many of her contemporaries of that gay company that had made the Big House the symbol of an age had preceded her into the shadows. Sir Dighton Probyn had died the year before; of her intimates, only Miss Charlotte Knollys, bent but seemingly ageless, remained to mourn "the Beloved Lady." My father established her in a comfortable flat in London, where he often visited her. He also naturally made arrangements for his sister Princess Victoria, settling her in a snug little property at Iver near Windsor. Some months later my parents moved from York Cottage to the Big House; except for the addition of their personal possessions, it was left very much as it always had been.

By now I had had sufficient experience both in the outer world and within the tight little island of Britain itself to understand better the rather curious nature of my position, which at times seemed to leave me dangling futilely in space between the ceremonial make-believe symbolizing the power of high and mighty princes and the discouraging realities of a world that insisted upon relegating even a conscientious Prince to a figure-head rôle. The Prince of Wales is the King's deputy, the "King-in-Waiting," so to speak. But he has no specific, routine job in the sense, for example, that a vice-president has a job. Though I was next in the line to the Throne, with all that position implied, I actually possessed no prescribed State duties or responsibilities. I was never present when my father gave audiences. Nor was I ever allowed to examine the contents of the red despatch boxes containing the submissions of the Prime Minister and the heads of the different Government departments. The only concession ever made to my interest in high matters of State was my being allowed occasionally to peruse Foreign Office telegrams pertinent to my various foreign missions. Until I myself became King, the evolution of Government policies remained outside my ken. Indeed, my father, who was inclined to attribute—much as the rest of us do to-day—most of the world's ills to the politicians, frowned upon any conspicuous association on my part with men of this calling. Yet, at the same time, in a manner never defined, I was expected to remain conversant with all that was going on in the world and to give the impression of being knowledgeable and well informed.

But my life was not wanting in its demands. There were certain set ceremonies and Court fixtures that recurred annually on my calendar. These included the Opening of Parliament, the winter and spring levees held by the King, the Courts at which the year's débutantes were presented, and at least one of the huge garden parties the King and Queen gave at the Palace to wind up the London season. I was also expected to go to the Derby, as well as to sit opposite my father at the banquet at Buckingham Palace afterwards, when he entertained the members of the Jockey Club. Then, too, I always joined my parents at Windsor for Ascot Week and, of course, never missed the family gathering at Sandringham for Christmas.

In addition there descended to me numerous honorary quasi-hereditary positions in various public and charitable institutions that my father and grandfather had held before me. In becoming Chancellor of the University of Wales, a trustee of the National Gallery, and president of various charitable foundations, including Christ's Hospital, King Edward's Hospital Fund for London, the Royal National Life-Boat Institution, I fulfilled my oft-repeated declaration that "I consider it a great honour to follow in the footsteps of my grandfather and my father in assuming this high position, thus carrying on the Royal association with your illustrious body." Happily perhaps for the administration of these institutions, my other duties prevented my exercising the executive functions such posts ordinarily carry with them. Nevertheless, whenever there was the necessity for a public drive for funds, my services were always called upon and most willingly given. And there were always new bridges to be opened, highways to be dedicated, foundation-stones to be laid, and municipal projects inaugurated—all the standard, ever-repeating public functions for which the Royal Family by ancient custom supplies the principal actors.

When, in the preparation of these memoirs, I had occasion to thumb through my old calendars, I was surprised at the wide variety of things that I did. I attended Pilgrim dinners to welcome American Ambassadors. I inspected the Welsh Guards. I awarded prizes at the Metropolitan Police Boxing Tournament. I opened the new premises of the Chartered Auctioneers' and Estate Agents' Institute in Lincoln's Inn Fields. I handed out diplomas to the Society of Apothecaries. I unveiled Lord Kitchener's statue in the Horse Guards. I spoke at the Swan Dinner of the Worshipful Company of Vintners. I presided over the proceedings of the Master Mariners' Company.

Although few would consider attendance at public banquets as work, I hasten to add that I rarely went with any idea of having a good time. Many an evening would find me at some great corporate banquet, seated at the chairman's table, just another performer in what I used jokingly to call "the decorated circus"— that indefatigable guild of after-dinner speakers, masters of the apt quotation and the unwearying anecdote, the celebrities of the day, all clad in white ties and tails, resplendent with orders and neat, glittering rows of decorations won in the service of the King. Other men might be chained to their desks; I was metaphorically chained to the banquet table. And, if sometimes I got up in the morning somewhat later than the hour recommended by business traditions, it was often because, between my service at some public dinner followed by my appearance at a charity ball, and a brief call for relaxation on my way home, possibly at the Embassy Club, the night was well along before I realized it.

The extent to which I employed my talents beyond these stereotyped rôles was left pretty much to me. I was free to do as much in the public interest or as little as I liked. The job of Prince of Wales, as I tried to interpret it, was, first, to carry on associations with worthy causes outside politics and clothe them with the prestige of the Prince's high position; and, second, to bring the Monarchy, in response to new conditions, ever nearer to the people. I was encouraged to feel that I was succeeding to some degree at least by a remark Lady Astor once made to me at York House. Known as she was for her forthrightness and critical mind, I was surprised and gratified to hear her say, "You know, Sir, that you and I do not always agree. But by reinterpreting the Monarchy in modern terms you have rendered a great service to your father and will have made the way easier for your successors."

The aftermath of the war saw the emergence of a wide variety of ex-service men's organizations throughout the British Empire; because I had been in the war, many of these ex-service groups asked me to become their patron. In another direction the rising social consciousness of the upper classes had already begun to express itself, belatedly perhaps, in the founding of college and public-school missions in the slums of London and other big cities. Many an evening I slipped down to the East End to look in on one or more of these clubs, where I mingled with the boys, watched them boxing, or joined them in a game of darts. And it was from the dedicated men who had given up lives of leisure to run these places that I learned most about the poor.

One way and another I was always on the go. The monotony of my London engagements was broken by quick trips to other parts of the country: perhaps to visit an agricultural fair, a public school, launch a new life-boat at some lonely station on the coast, inspect a regiment, or make a three-day tour of one or another of the great industrial areas of South Wales, the Midlands, the North, or Clydeside. It was also my habit to go once a year at least to one of the large rural estates of the Duchy of Cornwall, which was my particular stewardship, providing, as it did, the revenues from which I paid my expenses.

But the industrial tours were usually the most interesting. Having sailed the trade routes and seen the world markets, I usually had something to say on my own account. Yet, there was an inescapable sameness about even these expeditions. In saying this I am reminded of a conversation I once had with the Lord-Lieutenant of a county in the Midlands, a friend of mine, who was any host on one of those tours. We had just returned to his house after several gruelling days.

"Thank God that's over," said my friend.

"It may be for you," I answered, "but it is never over for me."

These provincial forays were miniatures of my Imperial tours. They carried me back again and again to the well-springs of national life. In York House I kept a large map of the British Isles with pins stuck into it to show the places that I had visited. From time to time I would consult it. If, for example, I had not been to Shropshire or Westmorland, I had my Private Secretary write to inquire either of the Lord-Lieutenant or the mayor of the largest town whether some useful purpose would not be served by my paying a visit to the county. The answer was invariably yes. In this way I came to know my country, from Land's End to Caithness, from Rothesay to Dover. And while it may not be correct to say that I ever felt exactly "at home" on Clydeside or in the dingy mining villages of the Rhondda Valley, I nevertheless came to know these sad and poverty-ridden places as none of my ancestors ever had.

Wherever I went, I was usually expected to make a speech. I strove for a light and friendly touch, and for new ways of saying the ever-recurrent clichés to which my public utterances were in so great a measure restricted. But my efforts in this direction, however much they might be appreciated by my audiences, were not always approved by my father. He maintained that humour had no place in the public activities of members of the Royal Family. His views were once set forth by Lord Stamfordham in a letter to Godfrey Thomas.

Buckingham Palace

Dear Godfrey,

. . . The King argues that he never made jokes in any of his public speeches: but I ventured to point out that His Majesty takes rather an extreme view of what he calls the flippant style and that I myself was answerable for what was considered undue flippancy in a speech made by Prince Henry at the Royal Academy Dinner, most of which I had written. I also humbly urged that a little humour lightened what otherwise might be a ponderous after-dinner speech: and I *did* call His Majesty's attention to the very high praise given by Austen Chamberlain and Steel-Maitland both of whom have had exceptional experience in listening to after-dinner speeches.

Yours ever,
STAMFORDHAM

By and large, however, my father let me have my head in the matter of making speeches.

The only time he ever evinced alarm over the possibility of my getting beyond my depth was in 1926 when I undertook to address the British Association at its annual meeting, held that year at Oxford. Since science had never been one of my specialities, my first instinct was to side-step the invitation. But the scientists seemed so anxious to have me, perhaps in the belief that my presence would attract desirable publicity to their important work, that I was persuaded to accept, all the more so after Captain Alan Lascelles, my Assistant Private Secretary from 1920 to 1929, had promised to take care of the speech himself.

A few days before I went to Oxford I was dining with my parents when my father suddenly turned to me and said, "Oh, by the way, I see that you are going to address the British Association."

The remark startled me. "Yes, I am," I said, though I must confess a little nervously.

"What are you going to talk about?"

"Oh, the usual thing," I said. "I shall congratulate them for their magnificent contributions to science, praise the unselfishness of scientific research, and so on."

"Good God!" exclaimed my father. "You evidently don't seem to realize, my dear boy, what you have taken on. Don't you know who these people are?"

I answered humbly, "I know only too well who they are. I have been worried all along, but they have been very insistent."

Almost reproachfully my father said, "Your audience will represent the most formidable collection of brains in the country. The last member of the family, indeed the only one, who ever felt equal to the task was your great-grandfather the Prince Consort, *and he was an intellectual*." After pausing a moment to allow this judgment to sink in, my father added, "These people once asked me to address them. I refused."

I was crestfallen, but there was no escape. In trepidation I went to Oxford. Happily my fears proved groundless; I read "Tommy"

Lascelles's speech, and it was a success. A handsomely bound copy of this masterpiece survives to-day in the King's Private Secretary's office at Buckingham Palace, where Tommy Lascelles now holds sway. He recently described it to a friend as the finest speech that the Prince of Wales ever made. He ought to know.

And so the 1920's spun for me their bright magic. Austerity is now the rule of the day in Britain. Yet, I should be ungrateful were I not to render a fond salute to the elegant pleasures that were available in my youth under capitalism. Nowadays I note with regret a tendency to write off the 'twenties as a lost and decadent decade. On the contrary, I remember them as a bright era in which the Royal Navy still ruled the seas and the pound sterling was still the world's foremost unit of exchange. It was, I imagine, the last time in this tortured century that a man could enjoy himself in good conscience; the last time that Princes could circulate easily and without embarrassment through all levels of society.

Then almost without warning there came a skip in the gay rhythm, the General Strike, which paralysed the country for nine incredible days.

I have decided to record my impressions of that portentous episode, not because of the part I played in it, but more for the part I could not play because of my position—a Prince debarred from politics. With the exception of the war and each succeeding general election no other happening made me so acutely aware of the perpetual conflict within me between my natural desire to share in the tremendous experiences of my times and the constitutional restraints requiring me to remain aloof from controversial turmoil.

Ever since the end of the war the British working classes had been agitated by chronic unemployment and a general dissatisfaction with their lot—the "fever" of Lloyd George's metaphor. But coal lay, as it has lain so often, at the root of the trouble. On April 30 the miners struck. Two days later the powerful Trades Union Congress, which included the strategic Transport Workers Union, called a general strike in support of the miners. Overnight the trains stopped. No buses ran. Power plants and factories lay idle. No newspapers were published. And as a result of that single stroke the pulse-beat of British power, which had throbbed across the centuries into the farthest corners of the earth, all but died away.

What was unique about the strike of 1926 was the reaction of the upper and middle classes. They regarded it as a blow aimed at the constitutional foundations of English life. In response to the Government's appeal thousands left their business desks and their suburban homes or emerged from their landed estates, their clubs, and their leisure, determined to restore the essential services of the nation. The people I knew felt that they were putting down something that was terribly wrong, something contrary to British traditions. And they put on a first-class show.

I happened to be at Biarritz recuperating from a minor ear operation when the trouble started. Hurrying back, I arrived on the first night of the strike. Along with many of his thoughtful subjects my father was plainly confused in his own mind as to whether the strike ought to be classed as party politics in the accepted meaning of the term or whether it smacked of revolution. However, because of the deep split that had been produced within classes he counselled me and my brothers to abstain from all public or private comment on the issues and to remain more or less out of sight until the trouble blew over. But that was like asking a man in a burning building to retire to his room while the firemen coped with the blaze.

Within the limits of my father's counsel I nevertheless managed to follow the daily developments of the strike pretty closely. The first thing every morning I would hurry off to one or another of the Government departments to get the latest news. In the afternoon with Bertie I would repair to the House of Commons, where from behind the clock in the Peers' Gallery he and I would listen, with rapt interest, to the acrimonious debates. The evenings might find me making the rounds of London, usually in the company of friends in the Metropolitan Police. As in the war, it irked me to be only a spectator; and my frustrations found release in watching the goings-on at the divisional police-stations, the docks, at power plants, and at Paddington Station, where amateurs were successfully manning the Great Western Railway. At this late date I am sure that I will not be accused of having departed from the non-party rôle of the Royal Family when I confess that I lent my chauffeur, George Ladbrook, and my car to trans-

Four generations of the monarchy, 1894: the author, the future King Edward VIII, on the lap of his great-grandmother, Queen Victoria, flanked by the Prince of Wales, later King Edward VII, his grandfather and by the Duke of York, later King George V, his father.

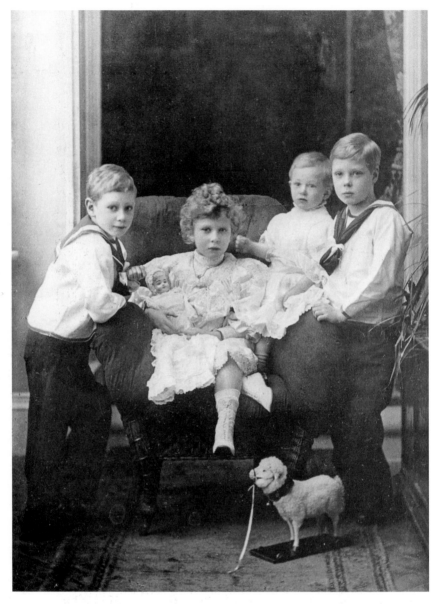

The royal children: the author on the right with, from the left, Bertie, later King George VI, Princess Mary and Prince Henry.

The British and Russian royal families on the Isle of Wight, 1909. *Left to right*
Standing: the author, Queen Alexandra, Princess Mary, Princess Victoria, Grand Duchess Olga, Grand Duchess Tatiana.
Seated: the Princess of Wales, Tsar Nicholas II, King Edward VII, Empress Alexandra, the Prince of Wales, Grand Duchess Marie.
On the ground: Tsarevitch Alexis, Grand Duchess Anastasia.

King Edward VII, seated, flanked by his son, soon to be King George V, and his grandson, soon to be Prince of Wales.

The author's investiture as Prince of Wales, Caernarvon Castle, 1911.

Contributing to the *Entente Cordiale*. The author being greeted by the British Consul, Calais 1912.

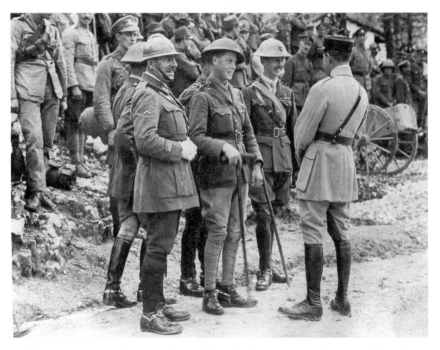

The young prince talking to Italian and French officers on the Italian front during the First World War, 1918.

The Duchess of Windsor's favourite portrait: the author on his first Dominions tour, Canada 1919.

Canoeing at Waikiki, Hawaii, en route to Australia, 1920.

Taking a dip with Louis Mountbatten on board *The Renown*, 1920.

As Colonel-in-Chief of Jacob's Horse, the Indian Army cavalry regiment, Delhi 1921.

The author inspecting the Jodhpur Lancers during his Indian tour, 1921.

The author and the Begum of Bhopal walking to the Durbar Hall, 1922.

Fort Belvedere, Sunningdale, where the author lived from 1930 until his abdication.

The author with a favourite cairn terrier at the Fort, 1930.

The author aged 36.

The author in the uniform of the Welsh Guards, 1932.

The author, on the right, with Stanley Baldwin, Prime Minister, 1927.

The author, now King Edward VIII, walking through cheering crowds during his tour of South Wales, 1936 – evidence of his great popularity in spite of the Depression.

The King and Wallis Simpson: one of the first pictures of them together on the Adriatic cruise of 1936.

Although there was an agreement among the British press not to mention the affair, the *Nahlin* cruise was widely reported in America. The Adriatic, 1936.

Crowds outside Buckingham Palace during the abdication crisis, December 1936.

The author making his abdication speech, 11 December, 1936.

The Duke and Duchess of Windsor in France, January 1939.

port to Wales the Government newspaper, the *British Gazette*, edited by Mr. Winston Churchill.

In the end the strike failed. The workers went back to their jobs—all but the coal-miners, who stayed out until the autumn. My friends returned to their normal pursuits. The general feeling was that all had stood up rather well under the test. A dangerous social crisis had been overcome in the traditional English way, without bloodshed or reprisals and leaving no lasting scars.

In 1927 I made two trips abroad with my brother George— first to stay with King Alfonso of Spain at his Court in Madrid and Seville, and then to visit Canada, where at the invitation of the Canadian Government I took part in the Diamond Jubilee of Confederation.

The trip to Canada was made noteworthy to me for bringing me for the first time into intimate contact with the political leader who was destined to oppose me in 1936, Mr. Stanley Baldwin. At the time he was invited to join the celebration he had been Prime Minister for three years. His wife, Lucy, was also in the party, and the four of us crossed the Atlantic together.

Delighted as I was to return to Canada, I was momentarily disconcerted upon landing at Quebec to find that I was expected to ride in an open landau again. It was almost as if the ghost of old Sir Joseph Pope had made a reappearance. "Those damn horses again," I muttered to George. "I thought I had talked these Canadians out of this eight years ago." My own misgivings certainly had not abated with the passage of time; and when, upon clambering in with the Governor, the carriage started off with so violent a jerk as almost to snap our necks, I became alarmed.

"A fine pair of horses," exclaimed the Governor-General, mistaking my anxious glance for one of approval. He was in high spirits as we raced through the streets; so were the horses. By the time we had reached the suburbs the landau began swaying and lurching from side to side, and it was evident that the horses had bolted. Only after the Governor-General had cautioned and instructed the straining, sweating coachman in French did he manage to steady the frantic animals and get them under control.

Delivered shaken but intact at the Governor-General's residence, I was recovering from this harrowing experience when his daughter arrived with my brother. They had watched from the carriage behind as we had rocketed out of sight. This charming lady, apologizing for what had happened, then divulged that her father's hobby was driving horses; that the speed with which he drove was the terror of the Province; and that with the idea of paying me a compliment he had brought out his liveliest pair. "I begged my father," she said, "not to do it. I knew this would happen. But he would not listen." Mr. Baldwin had of course decided upon a safer if less spectacular form of transportation—Mr. Mackenzie King's car. Watching them drive up, I thought to myself wistfully that there are occasions when not so much is expected of Prime Ministers.

The celebrations in Ottawa and Toronto were followed by the inauguration of the International Peace Bridge across the Niagara River. With George and Mr. Baldwin I took part in an unusual ceremony. Advancing from the Canadian side across the bright new span, I was met exactly in the middle by an American delegation headed by the Vice-President, Mr. Charles Dawes, and the famous Al Smith, then Governor of New York State. Mr. Dawes and I shook hands across a wide silken cord, which I proceeded to cut.

We continued westward to Alberta; I to stop at my ranch, Mr. and Mrs. Baldwin to do some sightseeing in the Rockies. I saw a good deal of them on the train. The Prime Minister was a fluent conversationalist. Listening to him expounding on such varied topics as the apple husbandry of Worcestershire, cricket, and the revision of the Prayer Book—then a subject of violent controversy in Parliament—I was impressed by his erudition even more than by his reputation for political sagacity. However, as I studied Mr. Baldwin, I thought I detected traces of the arrogance that some Englishmen display when travelling abroad. The deeper we penetrated the North American continent, the more he became the embodiment of old John Bull himself. In my hour of Sovereignty I was to rediscover that side of him.

Life seemed pretty good to me in 1927 and throughout 1928. I was then thirty-four, with ten years of intense and continuous public activity behind me. My travels and the varied experiences that had come my way had given me more confidence in myself; even public speaking, which had never come easily, ceased to be so much of a nightmare. Moreover, my personal ambition to excel in the sport that I liked best had been to some extent re-warded. I had gained a reputation in the hunting-field; and in spite of my father's and Mr. Ramsay MacDonald's objections I had continued steeplechasing and had even won a few races. Yet, once again England seemed a trifle cramped.

Therefore, when my brother Bertie recommended to me the fascination of big-game hunting, I decided to satisfy my recurrent wanderlust with an extended shooting expedition to East Africa. I was drawn there as well by reasons of Empire. For some time my old Imperial travelling companion, Ned Grigg, who had meanwhile become Governor of Kenya, had been inviting me to visit him in his equatorial domain.

With my second brother Harry, the Duke of Gloucester, who was organizing his own safari, and three members of my staff, including "G" Trotter, I left Great Britain in early September. After several official days in Nairobi, Harry and I separated. He went south to shoot in Tanganyika and Northern Rhodesia, while I continued my journey westwards across Lake Victoria to Uganda with the intention of rejoining him at Capetown for Christmas.

My excursion into Uganda was not without incident. In the steamer on Lake Albert poor "G" Trotter nearly died of a heart attack and had to be sent back to Kampala. I likewise had two misadventures. While hunting on the shore of the lake, I was put to flight by a charging elephant, a terrifying experience that caused me thereafter to regard these huge creatures with new respect. A few days later, while walking back from the lake to Fort Portal with twenty native porters, my guide, one of the game wardens, lost his way and was the cause of my having to spend a wet, uncomfortable night, floundering through almost impene-trable elephant grass ten feet high, the hunting-ground of lions and snakes.

In mid-November, my engagements in Kenya and Uganda being completed, I started on safari to Tanganyika. Because I and my party would have to travel light, we shipped most of our clothes to South Africa. Stripped down to "bush shirts" and shorts, we made our way south in a small convoy of station wagons and light lorries.

I enjoyed this open-air life of hard exercise, so much so that I found it difficult to believe that anyone would ever voluntarily choose to return to civilization. But this idyllic existence was not to last. After we had been out only ten days, my party was overtaken by a message from the Reuters news agency reporting that my father was ill but giving no details. The news did not immediately alarm me, for my father had long been subject to chronic colds. Nevertheless, I cabled Buckingham Palace for more information. Several days later at Dodoma, one of the provincial headquarters, I found a serious communication from my father's doctor, Lord Dawson, awaiting me. The King had had a relapse. There were also cables from the Prime Minister, Admiral Halsey, and Godfrey Thomas, urging me to return to London with all possible speed.

Even while I was debating the quickest way to get back, word came that the light cruiser *Enterprise* of the East Indies Squadron had been ordered to proceed from Aden to Dar-es-Salaam, the capital and main port of Tanganyika, where she could be expected in three days. Dodoma was on the railway, and by a fortunate coincidence the Governor's rickety little train was even then waiting to take my party westward to Tabora on Lake Tanganyika. So next morning before dawn we started down to the coast, arriving at Dar-es-Salaam the same evening. There I fretted for three days awaiting the *Enterprise*. She finally appeared shortly after breakfast on the morning of December 2; and, as soon as I had boarded her, she was under way again, her propellers thrusting her across the glazed, burning sea.

The race against time that followed, first by sea northward up the Indian Ocean, through the Red Sea and the Suez Canal, and westward half the length of the Mediterranean to Brindisi in Italy and then by train across Europe, was a gruelling experience. The *Enterprise*, driven as I had never seen a ship driven before, completed the 4,700-mile voyage to Brindisi in eight days. Stepping ashore, still in the safari clothes in which I had left East Africa, I was met by Godfrey Thomas, who had thoughtfully brought me a change of clothing more suitable for European December weather. Mussolini had sent his own train to transport me across Europe. It started immediately, and the breakneck race to the Channel was facilitated by personal orders from Il Duce to clear the tracks all the way to the Swiss frontier.

Godfrey Thomas also brought me some letters from London, and I settled down to read them in the train. There was a long, technical report from Lord Dawson, concluding with the hopeful observation that "the most dangerous part of the illness is in the way of being conquered." And then there were two letters from Bertie:

145 Piccadilly W.1.
December 6th 1928

My dear old David,

I am glad you will be home so soon now. We have had a very anxious & worrying time over Papa this last fortnight. It was touch & go on Sunday night & the whole of Monday. The whole cause of the anxiety has been the heart. Some time during these last few months Papa has damaged the valves of his heart, probably overdoing the shooting, & when he went down with this lung trouble of course he started minus in the way of physical resistance.

But thank God since Monday he has rallied a good deal & he is much quieter & is stronger. He is not out of the wood yet, but as things are at the moment, he is going on as well as can be expected. It will be a long time before he is well again, I'm afraid. . . .

She [Mama] is delighted at your decision to come home. . . .

I am here of course now & am longing to see you. I shall meet you at the station no matter at what time you arrive.

Best love to you from us both from
BERTIE

145 Piccadilly W.1.
December 6th 1928

My dear old David,

Since writing to you this evening I have seen Dawson. Papa's temperature has again gone up to-night which is a worry but has not altered Papa's condition very materially as he is stronger physically. . . .

There is a lovely story going about which emanated from the East End that the reason of your rushing home is that in the event of anything happening to Papa I am going to bag the Throne in your absence ! ! ! ! Just like the Middle Ages. . . .

Ever yours
BERTIE

The next evening found me at Boulogne, whence a packet-boat sped me across the Channel to Folkestone, where Mr. Baldwin was waiting to accompany me by train back to London. In the dining-car he confided gravely that despite the improvement in my father's condition the convalescence was bound to be protracted. The likelihood that my father would have to curtail his public activities in the future meant, Mr. Baldwin suggested, that more of his duties would of necessity devolve upon me. The implications of the Prime Minister's warning were plain: the sombre responsibilities of the Throne had begun to claim me.

My meeting with Bertie at Victoria Station further deepened my anxiety over my father. During the three-minute car drive to Buckingham Palace he prepared me for the shock that my father's appearance would bring. "You will find him greatly changed," he said, "and now Dawson says that an operation will be necessary in a day or two." Then he spoke admiringly of my mother. "Through all the anxiety she has never once revealed her feelings to any of us." This seemed to trouble him, for he quickly added, "She is really far too reserved; she keeps too much locked up inside of her. I fear a breakdown if anything awful happens. She has been wonderful."

At the Palace she was awaiting me. "I am so relieved you are back," she said. "Papa keeps asking where you are." She took me at once to his bedroom, the same room Bertie now uses as his study. Although he was desperately weak, he recognized me instantly and mumbled something about hoping I had had good sport in East Africa. He had plainly endured a terrible ordeal. He was sixty-three. If he were to recover at all, the process would be painful and prolonged.

It was December 11, 1928, a curiously prophetic date. Exactly eight years later almost to the hour, I would be leaving my country, having relinquished the inheritance that had brought me racing back this night across two continents.

CHAPTER XIII

I FIND THE FORT

O N December 12, 1928, at Buckingham Palace, my father underwent a serious operation for a streptococcus infection. Thereafter, because the surgical wound in his back seemed stubbornly slow to heal, his convalescence was long. The King's impromptu sick-bed strictures on the ineptitude and incompetence of the British medical profession, from which his chief physician, Lord Dawson, was not excluded, were marvellous to overhear. But my father was, in truth, a very sick man, far sicker than the public ever knew.

While I was racing back to England aboard the *Enterprise*, my father had set up a Council of State, consisting of my mother, my brother Bertie, the Archbishop of Canterbury, the Prime Minister, the Lord Chancellor, and me, with authority to conduct State business in the Sovereign's name. In this capacity we approved Orders in Council, submissions, Government appointments, and signed commissions for the armed forces. For me this shared responsibility was all the more interesting because I was enabled for the first time to read various secret official communications, including Foreign Office telegrams, but not the minutes of Cabinet meetings, which only the King's Private Secretary, the venerable Lord Stamfordham, was allowed to see.

A letter that I wrote my father at the time suggests the different ways in which during his incapacity I acted for him.

St. James's Palace, S.W.1.
February 20, 1929

Dearest Papa
 Mama tells me that I may write to you now which is good news. . . . Mama will have told you of our visit to the Industries

Fair at the White City. It was very kind of her to go as it encourages the manufacturers who need that now. Her energy is amazing & she had everyone tired out that morning. . . .

I received the new Japanese Ambassador this morning & accepted his credentials on your behalf & this afternoon I gave your cup away at the shire horse show in Islington.

So we are trying to keep things going while you are still laid up & there is no reason for you to worry your head over a thing. . . .

Your devoted son
DAVID

The winter of 1928–29 was one of the coldest in European history. The lake in Buckingham Palace garden froze over, a rare occurrence, and my brothers and I invited our friends for skating parties. The ring of the skates on the ice and our shouts reached my father's room and seemed to bring him pleasure.

In February the King was moved to Bognor, on the Sussex coast, where I often visited him. Although he gained strength at the seaside, my mother remained worried. One afternoon as I was starting back to London she asked me to her room for a private talk. She expressed her satisfaction with the way I was carrying on for my father. Then with that quiet indirection that marks her approach to delicate situations, she took me by surprise by asking whether I did not think it might be better on the whole if I were to give up steeplechasing.

"Is it because you think I might get hurt?" I asked.

"Partly that," my mother answered. "But with Papa so ill and unable to get around and your having to do so much more, it would seem better if you did not take these chances."

"But I don't fall very often," I protested.

"No, I realize that. Nevertheless, I know it would please Papa if you would give up race-riding and be content with fox-hunting."

"If it will save you further anxiety," I assured her, "I shall, of course, do what you and Papa wish."

And so I reluctantly abandoned the one pursuit that gave outlet to my competitive spirit. The question of my continuing to hunt was academic because my string of horses was largely built around steeplechasing. That winter I sold them all and gave up the comfortable rooms at Craven Lodge, Melton Mowbray.

Thereafter the fields of Leicestershire saw little of me; and for relaxation I turned increasingly to golf.

About this time I had an unexpected meeting with Mr. Baldwin, the Prime Minister. While the episode in itself was of no particular importance, it was in a sense my first object-lesson in the workings of an astute political mind.

The coal industry was already in a bad way and indeed had been so since the end of the war. Many collieries were being forced to shut down uneconomic pits, leaving whole communities without work and on the dole. The tragic story was gradually unfolded in the correspondence addressed to me as Prince of Wales. Because of my long-standing association with ex-servicemen's organizations many former sailors and soldiers looked to me as their Royal patron; and, perhaps not knowing where else to turn, miners who had served in the war wrote me of their pitiable circumstances and begged me to use my influence with the Government to do something for them.

It therefore seemed only right that I should concern myself with this sad development, and I was debating how best to proceed when a North Country business man, Sir Alexander Leith, approached me with a proposal that I should make an extensive tour of the Durham and Northumberland coal-fields, which were among the hardest hit. I was assured by Sir Alexander that my appearance might put some heart back into the miners and show them that they were not entirely forgotten. "The Government doesn't seem to understand," said Sir Alexander, earnestly, "how serious the situation is up there." My Princely journeys having taken me into this region in better days, it seemed all the more important that I should see it in its adversity. And since Sir Alexander was a pillar of the Conservative Party, and a former chairman of the Northern Counties Area, I accepted his sponsorship without question, leaving it to him to arrange for me a three-day tour of the coal-fields.

It was January, 1929, and bitterly cold. The afternoon before I was to leave London I received from Mr. Baldwin a message asking me to come to see him without delay. Puzzled as to the reason for so urgent a request, I went at once to the House of Commons and was ushered into the Prime Minister's office. Offering me a chair, he said, "Sir, I have just heard about your proposed trip to Durham. I should like to know under whose auspices you are going."

"But why, Mr. Baldwin?" I asked, truly astonished. "It has never been my understanding that I am expected to notify the Government of my movements."

"No, Sir," he answered. "The difficulty here is that your visit to the coal-fields of the North Country is bound to have political repercussions."

"I don't understand," I replied. "You know that I stand outside politics. My only reason for going is to see for myself what the shutting down of so many mines has done to the people who depend upon them for a living."

Mr. Baldwin seemed not to hear, and said almost coldly: "The Government is well aware of the conditions in some coal-mining districts. It is doing everything possible to ameliorate them. But as you know, a general election is only four months away, and unemployment may well be used as a stick with which to beat my Party."

Only then did I grasp the hidden basis of the Prime Minister's concern. Could he suspect that I had allowed myself to be "used" by the Opposition? The idea was so preposterous that I hesitated to dignify it with a disclaimer; yet, the Prime Minister was so obviously exercised that I thought it best to reassure him.

"As a matter of fact, Mr. Baldwin," I said, "the idea of this trip originated with a member of your own Party, Alexander Leith."

At the mention of the name, the Prime Minister leaped to his feet. "Oh, so it was Alexander Leith who suggested that you should go to Durham," he said, incredulously.

"Yes, and for that matter he is in charge of all arrangements."

The Prime Minister exuded relief. "A first-class man," he said jovially, "you could not be in better hands. Of course, this information puts quite a different face on the matter. Forgive me, Sir; I'm afraid I must go back to the House." Showing me to the door, he said, "I hope you have a successful trip, and don't find the cold too trying."

As I left the House of Commons, I was somewhat puzzled as to the precise difference between Conservative and Socialist humanitarianism.

In the spring of that year the King was well enough to leave

Bognor and return to Windsor, but his convalescence continued
to be harassed by frequent relapses. In May the general election
brought down Mr. Baldwin's Conservative Government and
returned to power the Socialist chief, Mr. Ramsay MacDonald,
an event my father, despite his high personal regard for the
Scottish leader, could hardly have taken as an encouraging sign.
On top of everything else, the new Archbishop of Canterbury,
the Most Reverend Cosmo Gordon Lang, had been pressing my
father's secretariat to allow him to set aside a Sunday in the near
future as a day of national thanksgiving for the King's recovery.
The difficulty was that the plan envisaged the King's appearance
at a great service in Westminster Abbey, conducted by the Archbishop himself.

Since the true state of the King's health was still far removed
from the condition hopefully anticipated by Dr. Lang, those of
us who were close to the sickroom were inclined to regard the
Archbishop's project as a trifle premature. However, Dr. Lang
was an old and close friend; my father was reluctant to disappoint
him; and in the end his doctors decided—against their better judgment, I always believed—that Sunday, July 7, would be a safe
date.

When early that month my father returned to Buckingham
Palace, which he had not seen since the previous February, his
temperature unaccountably rose. Yet, the day before the elaborate
religious display intended to celebrate his recovery, he received
one of his Socialist Ministers, Mr. J. H. Thomas, who always had
a marvellous fund of vernacular stories. My father was laughing
in full-chested enjoyment at one of these when he suddenly
checked himself as if in pain. As the too-successful storyteller
looked on aghast, my father ran his hand down his back, saying,
"I must excuse myself. Something seems to have happened to
this damn wound." When his shirt was opened, it was discovered
that under the stress of his laughter an abscess below his ribs had
burst. Although Mr. Thomas was at first overcome by remorse,
he was later relieved to learn that his story had had the fortunate
effect of exposing the real cause of my father's continued weak-
ness—the presence of tiny bone splinters left behind in the wound
after the first operation. I suppose this is probably the only case in
medical history in which a side-splitting joke literally and figura-

tively has achieved happier results than the surgeons succeeded in effecting.

Fortunately the temperature subsided; though weak, my father insisted on going through with the service next day. Whether the Archbishop ever truly appreciated how much my father suffered that Sunday in the interests of national rejoicing I never knew, but certainly the thousands who cheered the King as he drove through the streets with my mother to the Abbey and the distinguished congregation within had no inkling. Despite my father's distress, it was all very moving. However, he himself was not unaware of the underlying irony; and on returning to the Palace he remarked to his physician, Lord Dawson, "Fancy a thanksgiving service with an open wound in your back."

A second operation successfully dealt with the sources of infection, and by the end of August my father was strong enough to journey to his beloved Sandringham. There he presently resumed his shooting, though never again on the same vigorous scale. When I returned to the Big House for the annual family Christmas party, I noted the addition of a lift to save him the strain of walking upstairs.

One of the things I did while deputizing for my father during his illness was to hold levees on his behalf. There were four of these ceremonies each year, and they took place at 11.30 a.m. in the Throne Room of St. James's Palace. In essence they provided opportunities for the Diplomatic Corps, the Cabinet, governors, officers of the forces, and selected private citizens to pay their respects to the Sovereign. Another duty was to act as escort to my mother when she had to hold a Court without my father. Like the levees, there were four of these a year. They took place in the ballroom at Buckingham Palace at 9.30 in the evening.

Dress regulations at Court were meticulous. Although they had been relaxed somewhat because of the changed conditions after the First World War, they were well understood. At the Court of St. James's it was the custom for diplomats—for all men, in fact—to wear knee-breeches whenever the Queen was present at formal functions in the evening; indeed, this custom extended to unofficial dinner parties in private houses given for the King and Queen.

This costume consists of a black velvet tail coat, black velvet breeches that buckle below the knee over black silk hose, and a pair of pumps. Knights of the Garter wear the Garter below the left knee. Indeed, for men with a well-turned calf, knee-breeches can be flattering; for others less favoured the reverse is equally true.

Of all the causes for an Anglo-American "incident" this custom would seem the most unlikely. Ever since the days of John Jay, a succession of American envoys had found almost everything else to hold against us, but never this. However, when in 1929 Mr. Herbert Hoover sent Brigadier-General Charles G. Dawes to London as Ambassador, the problem of knee-breeches suddenly assumed large-scale proportions in the eyes of the American Press.

Mr. Dawes, a former Vice-President of the United States, was a Chicago banker with a flair for picturesque speech. It was confidently expected that he would bring to the staid confines of the Court the spirited, independent outlook that made the American amateur an admired and often terrifying figure in diplomacy. Mr. Dawes lived up to the part. Before leaving his own country, one of the questions he was asked at a Press conference was whether he proposed to wear knee-breeches at Court. Had Mr. Dawes been a foreign-service careerist, this particular point would never have been raised. However, for him the question was fraught with dangers peculiar to American domestic politics.

The idea was then widespread among his countrymen that we were clever and adroit and versed in all Machiavellian tricks for deluding and beguiling simple Americans. In the 1920's this distrust was at its height, and nothing would have been more damaging to an American political figure in England than the suggestion that he was putting on airs. In this respect Mr. Dawes was in double jeopardy, for he hailed from Chicago, where the mayor, "Bill" Thompson, had recently campaigned for re-election on a platform "obligating" him, among other things, to punch my father on the nose were the latter ever so imprudent as to set foot inside the city limits. Under the circumstances Mr. Dawes's negative was no doubt the only possible answer to the reporter's question.

I rather suspect that Mr. Dawes, on second thoughts, hoped that would be the end of the matter. And in the normal course of events the Court, which, in common with other British institutions, is endowed with unusual powers of adaptation, would have found a mutually satisfactory way out of the impasse. An institution that could receive a Gandhi in a *dhoti* could surely have come quietly to terms with an American Ambassador. But all possibility of a discreet private compromise vanished after the American Press seized with loud cries upon the Ambassador's veto as a new and commendable variation in the popular American sport of twisting the British lion's tail. When in June Mr. Dawes duly appeared in London, the question of whether he would or would not wear the usual knee-breeches had become a burning issue, if not in Mayfair certainly in Peoria. The Lord Chamberlain, Lord Cromer, thus found himself in an extremely awkward position. More than the etiquette of the Court was at stake; the Queen's dignity was by implication involved. This was unsuspected, I am sure, by Mr. Dawes, who, in spite of a blunt manner, never lacked in courtesy and was contemplating no personal insult to my mother whatsoever.

However, while the British public at large was unconcerned about the whole matter, I foresaw that the repercussions in Court circles of Mr. Dawes's remark would be no less profound than those that would have been caused by the appearance of the State gilt coach hitched to a team of camels. And I was not far wrong, for the first officials to recover from the initial shock of the news story left their breakfasts uneaten and began to discuss the appalling implications of Mr. Dawes's declaration with their colleagues over the telephone. The King, convalescing at Windsor, was of course informed of the *contretemps*. He was indignant that this apparent lapse of good taste should be visited on my mother, especially when she was obliged, because of his incapacity, to hold the Court alone.

Fortunately a brief trip to the industrial North removed me from the turmoil before there was time for me to become involved. Much as I was amused by the furore, I still did not relish returning to London, for the Court knew that Mr. Dawes and I had become friends, outside the official world. No sooner had I set foot within York House than the Lord Chamberlain was on the telephone to report that all the cajolings and entreaties of his Embassy staff, of the Foreign Office, of the Marshal of the

Diplomatic Corps, and finally of the Lord Chamberlain himself had failed to budge Mr. Dawes an inch. He asked to see me at once. I told him to come immediately.

Lord Cromer was a man of the world, urbane and suave; years of diplomatic experience had reinforced a naturally gracious manner with a remarkable outward calm. Nevertheless, it was instantly clear that his first encounter with this Midwestern American had exhausted all the resources with which a lifetime of experience at Court had equipped him. He explained that my father had suggested that I should call upon General Dawes myself and explain why it was really most important for him to wear the proper dress. "The King," Lord Cromer concluded, bleakly, "is extremely upset."

My sympathy for Lord Cromer's predicament was genuine enough. But I had a glimmering of Mr. Dawes's predicament as well. Were he to worm back, so to speak, into the breeches, he would expose himself to the ridicule of the American public. Reasoning, then, that the situation was past redeeming by ordinary methods, and having in addition more sympathy for Mr. Dawes's position than it seemed advisable to divulge to the Lord Chamberlain, I proposed what I considered an ingenious solution. It was that on the evening of the Court, Mr. Dawes should issue from the American Embassy wearing the usual knee-breeches, but concealed under the black evening trousers he had sworn he would wear. This camouflage would throw off the reporters who were certain to be watching outside the Embassy door and at the Palace gate. Upon arriving thus normally attired, the Ambassador would be met by an equerry and conducted to a room where a footman would be waiting to help him remove the trousers. There would no doubt be a decanter of Scotch whisky on a tray to refresh him and make easier his reappearance decked out according to protocol. Then on leaving the ballroom, he could retire into the same room, don once more the long trousers, and return safely to his own Embassy with no one the wiser.

"It's a little devious," I conceded, "and I imagine Mr. Dawes may take persuading. But of this much I am sure: he'll never leave his own Embassy in knee-breeches."

"Will you lay this proposal yourself before the Ambassador, Sir?"

"I'm sorry, but I'm afraid I can't," I answered firmly. "I'm not going to forfeit a friendship I value over an incident that is actually no concern of mine. Besides, good Anglo-American relations mean far more to me than a breach of Court etiquette, and I don't want to spoil any good will I may have built up for myself in America by offending so important a citizen. While I deplore the Ambassador's attitude, I am not going to run the risk of his turning me down, which I am confident he will do."

"In that case," said Lord Cromer, gloomily, "I suppose I am still left with the hot potato."

The following evening, it devolved upon me to conduct my mother by the hand into the vast ballroom and escort her to the solitary gilt chair on the dais. From my position at her right I had a commanding view of the familiar scene, into which the speculation attending Mr. Dawes's début had injected an unwonted tension. It was an impressive spectacle, this stately procession of ambassadors, ministers, counsellors, secretaries, and attachés of embassies in Court dress or uniform, with their wives in trains and feathers, the men making their bows before the Queen, the women their curtsies. But all eyes were straining for the first glimpse of the American Ambassador. Fortunately we did not have long to wait before he appeared in the line. At a glance it was obvious that he had won the day; his trousers flowed unbrokenly to his shoes. My mother must have looked glacial, while I hid a mildly disapproving glance behind the bearskin cap I was cradling in my right arm. Did I detect a certain self-consciousness in Mr. Dawes's demeanour as he advanced to make his bow? If I did, it was only a flash, for he walked with the same deliberation and self-assurance with which he might have taken the chair in the United States Senate.

When it was all over, my mother murmured, "Papa will not be pleased; what a pity such a distinguished man should be so difficult."

My parents bore no rancour, and the incident was soon forgotten. Mr. Dawes proved himself to be an able and popular Ambassador, and his continued appearances in the wrong garb ceased to be regarded as an affront. When twenty years later I visited him while he was wintering in Florida, then past his eightieth year, the word "knickers" was never once mentioned

during the hour we reminisced over old times. If he ever remem-
bers the incident at all, I am sure he would pass it off as one of the
least important episodes in the course of a long and notable
career.

The new year of 1930 found my father's health so restored that
I was able to plan another trip to East Africa. This time I was
lured back not to shoot big game with a rifle but rather with a
motion-picture camera, my new hobby. Having observed how
vanity had betrayed my friends into defacing the rooms of their
otherwise handsome homes with unsightly stuffed trophies of the
chase, I had decided that for me a living record on film of my
expeditions would be a more satisfying, and certainly less cumbersome, souvenir. Beginning with a two-week walking safari in
the elephant country around Voi, in Kenya, I progressed through
Uganda, into the Pygmy forests of the Belgian Congo, whence
by steamer and aeroplane I made my way down the White Nile
through the Sudan past Khartoum to Cairo. A wonderful trip,
productive of fine pictures, it was marred only by my contracting
malaria, a prevalent disease in those parts. Yet even this unlucky
break had its lighter side: when I arose weak and thin from my
fever-racked bed, a white planter remarked half-jokingly, "Now,
Sir, you are one of us."

My return in the month of April, 1930, introduced me to a
new and absorbing interest. The summer before, one of the
"Grace and Favour" houses near Windsor—i.e. houses at the
Sovereign's disposal—fell vacant. It was a castellated conglomera-
tion called Fort Belvedere, situated on Crown land bordering the
Great Park near Sunningdale. When I went to my father to ask
whether I might live there, he was surprised. "What could you
possibly want that queer old place for? Those damn week-ends,
I suppose." But then he smiled, "Well, if you want it, you can
have it."

I thanked him. My real reason for desiring the property lay
deeper than a mere wish for a place to spend week-ends at. I was
thirty-five years old; the rolling stone was beginning to seek a
resting-place. Until then my only residence had been York
House, which, because it was so much the centre of my official
life, was more an office than a home. Moreover, I was, like my
father, a man who loved the country. However much I might

enjoy London's metropolitan amenities, I preferred them in small doses. If my work kept me in the city longer than a few days at a time, I would begin to feel caged. It had therefore been my practice since the conclusion of my Imperial voyages in 1925 to spend my week-ends and holidays in small, rented, country houses, selected because of their proximity to good golf courses. But I was already weary of living in other people's homes; and, when chance led me to Fort Belvedere, I knew instantly that here was the place I was looking for. The initial work of reconditioning went forward while I was away in Africa, and on my return I moved in.

Because The Fort—as I chose to call it—became my home, some description of its charm and atmosphere is, I believe, desirable.

It was begun in the eighteenth century by William, Duke of Cumberland, the third son of George II. Some eighty years later, the famous architect, Wyatville, whom George IV had commissioned to restore Windsor Castle, was directed by the same Monarch to enlarge the structure—so the legend goes—for one of the King's favourites. One of Wyatville's happiest additions was a tall tower, higher than the surrounding trees, which enhanced the effect of an ancient castle in a forest. In 1912, at the outset of my father's reign, the structure underwent a further extensive modification to make it habitable. By the time I came upon it, it had become a pseudo-Gothic hodge-podge. An intrusion of yew-trees kept one side of the house in perpetual shadow, staining the walls with green, acidulous mould. The garden was untended; the surrounding undergrowth was wild and untidy. But the half-buried beauty of the place leaped to my eye.

Northwards the land descends in a gentle slope towards Virginia Water, where as a child I had paddled in rowboats with Mary and my brothers. Here the grassy approaches were guarded by a broad arc of stone battlements, with more than a score of handsome, eighteenth-century bronze cannon mounted in embrasures. Windsor Castle was six miles away, on the opposite side of the Great Park; and from the top of the tower on a clear afternoon one could see London and with a spyglass make out the dome of St. Paul's nearly twenty-five miles away.

I had a wonderful time fixing up The Fort, both inside and outside. It was a joy that I was loath to share with others; though I naturally sought professional advice, the final result in the main represented my ideas; and, being mine, they were modern. Inside I introduced, to the extent that space and the old walls allowed, many of the creature conveniences that I had sampled and enjoyed in the New World—a bathroom to nearly every room, showers, a steam bath, built-in cupboards, central heating —the so-called modern comforts that were seldom found in profusion in English houses. Outside, the changes also went on apace. Down came the gloomy, encroaching yew-trees, to let in light and air. A muddy lily pond below the battlements was transformed into a swimming-pool. I cleared away acres of dank laurel and replaced them with rare rhododendrons. I cut winding paths through the fir- and birch-trees, revealing the true enchantment of the woodland setting. As the sheer pleasures of creation took possession of me, the landscape gardener displaced the fox-hunter and, to some extent, the golfer. I found a new contentment in working about The Fort with my own hands—planting the herbaceous borders, moving shrubs, mowing the hay in the summer, building a rock garden with cascades supplied by water pumped up from a dam I had installed below Virginia Water.

I was in such a hurry to make the place perfect that I begrudged as lost a daylight hour that did not see the work progressing. Saturday afternoons and Sundays, when my gardeners were off, I pressed my week-end guests into arduous physical labour to which some of them were unaccustomed. Groaning and grunting, they joined me in hacking out the undergrowth, pruning trees, and transplanting shrubs; but presently they began to share my enthusiasm. Even my brother Bertie, who lived near by in the Great Park at Royal Lodge, would come over to lend a hand.

The Fort laid hold of me in many ways. Soon I came to love it as I loved no other material thing—perhaps because it was so much my own creation. More and more it became for me a peaceful, almost enchanted anchorage, where I found refuge from the cares and turmoil of my life.

One of the unexpected pleasures associated with The Fort was my discovery of the true charm of Windsor Castle. In my youth I had been inclined to regard its vastness and formality as almost overpowering; despite the magnificence of its chambers and galleries, it had seemed to me more of a museum than a residence for the Sovereign. However, now that I was a neighbour sharing the beauties of the Great Park, there grew up in me a reverence for the immense grey pile Pepys had described as "the most romantique castle that is in the world." I formed the habit of browsing around the library, a veritable treasure-trove of rare books and drawings and archives of the Royal Family; or of showing my friends the Rubenses and the Vandykes in the State apartments, acting the guide and relating historical anecdotes I had picked up over the years. On Sunday afternoons I would sometimes go to St. George's Chapel for evensong, where, sitting in my stall as a Knight of the Garter, I listened to the singing of its fine choir, deriving an inner comfort of the spirit that I had seldom known elsewhere. In the life that I was leading, Windsor became an island of tranquillity; and, as I came to know it better, it evoked in me an ever-deepening appreciation of the glories of the British past.

A great deal of what I knew about the Castle came from my mother, who, in her own right, is one of the foremost authorities on the lore of English Royal residences and the history and associations of the innumerable treasures they contain. She has a profound sense of order, a photographic mind, and a housekeeper's infallible memory.

Ever since becoming Queen, she had set herself the task of rearranging and redecorating the Palaces, restoring each to its original and authentic period, getting rid of the anachronisms, and, as she used to say, "bringing the right things together." Queen Victoria had allowed her large family to borrow freely from the Royal appointments. As a result, sets of pictures, furniture, even silver, lacked the completing pieces. From the old inventories my mother gradually tracked them down. Her search led her to obscure family sources in Great Britain and the German principalities. Tactfully she would initiate a correspondence with the current holders of the missing items, seeking their return. This quest, pursued with pertinacity and diligence, has continued throughout her lifetime, providing her with unending interest and satisfaction. "You remember those missing candlesticks from the Cumberland silver," she would ask. Then without waiting for an answer she would continue delightedly. "Where do you think I found them? Amongst poor Cousin Lilly's things, of all places!" Through her unflagging efforts, the Royal collection has been brought together, and is to-day as nearly complete as such things can ever be.

Let it not be supposed that this restoration proceeded without some objections from my father, whose aversion to change extended even to the Palaces where he lived. As my mother proceeded serenely with her self-appointed task, he would sooner or later notice that something had been moved from its familiar place. Protesting against the constant tinkering with the order of things he had accepted, he would be heard to mutter, "What is the good of moving that picture from the place where it has always hung?" Yet in the end, when my mother had given an excellent reason, he usually acquiesced.

Fixing up houses—if one can indulge the luxury—eventually becomes a kind of disease. Once the taste has been indulged, it is never satisfied. In the flush of my success with The Fort, I now laid confident hands on York House. Its drab, gloomy rooms, furnished according to the sombre Victorian style prescribed by the Office of Works, cried for redecoration.

One result of my taking over some of my father's work was that I became increasingly involved in more sophisticated official and social duties. More important people came to see me—statesmen, business men, foreign diplomats, men distinguished in all professions, and people whom I had met on my travels. I was obliged to give more formal dinners than before; and, sensing the need of a more dignified setting in which to entertain, I rearranged and refurnished the reception rooms of my London residence.

In the course of these changes I provided at one end of the house two rooms for my brother George, who, leaving the Royal Navy after ten years' service, came at this time to live with me. Nearly nine years younger than I, George was sharply different in outlook and temperament from the rest of us. Possessed of unusual charm of manner and a quick sense of humour and talented in many directions, he had an undoubted flair for the arts. He played the piano, knew a good deal about music, and had a knowledgeable eye for antiques. Being somewhat Bohemian by inclination, he had understandably found life in the Navy a bit confining. And I dare say that he received with relief a suggestion that he should take his share of the increasing burden of public duties falling upon the King's sons. Bertie and I, who until then had carried most of the load, were pleased to be able to count upon his reinforcement.

In moving his things to York House, George came, so to speak, under the wing of his older brother. We were together a great deal during the next few years, and it was a happy association. He left my roof in 1934 to marry Princess Marina of Greece. His tragic death in an aeroplane accident in 1942 while on active service cut short, at thirty-nine, a promising career.

By 1930 flying had already made considerable progress. Colonel Charles Lindbergh's pioneer flights had aroused in this country, no less than in his own, a tremendous interest in aviation. With all the travelling I had to do, air transportation seemed to offer unique advantages for me. I had, as a matter of fact, flown a little at the front towards the end of the First World War, and might well have gone on to qualify as a pilot had I not been so injudicious as to attract publicity by making a flight near London with a Canadian ace, a V.C., who, at the time, had a wounded arm in a sling and was obliged to fly the machine with only one hand. Taking a poor view of this incident, my father sternly ordered me to stay on the ground. A decade passed before I flew again. However, by 1929 aviation had made such spectacular progress that I approached my father again. My airmen friends had encouraged me to believe that if I travelled about Britain in my own aeroplane the example would give much-needed impetus to the struggling aircraft industry. My father offered no objections to my buying a small De Havilland Gypsy Moth—a surprising concession in view of his ban on steeplechasing only a few months before.

Hardly was I again in the air before the old desire to learn to fly myself revived; and, unknown to my father, I began to take lessons from a pilot at Northolt aerodrome. Meanwhile Harry and George had also taken up flying; and, as there had always been keen rivalry among us brothers, it became a race between them and me as to which of us would fly solo first.

Then one memorable day my great test came. I had already to my credit many hours of dual instruction, and that summer evening I had made a number of successful practice landings. Suddenly, without explanation, my instructor jumped from the front cockpit, and I noticed with surprise that he had his control stick in his hand. With a dramatic gesture he waved me into the air alone. Taking off, I completed two extremely lonely circuits of the field and landed twice without cracking up the machine. Once out of the aeroplane, my first act was to telephone my two younger brothers. "I've beaten you to it," I announced triumphantly to each in turn. But, although I travelled a lot thereafter by air, I was content to leave the piloting from then on to experts.

In January, 1931, I set out for South America with my brother George upon what proved to be the last of my overseas voyages in the interests of my country. My ostensible purpose was to open the British Empire Trade Exposition at Buenos Aires. My real mission, however, was to try to recapture for British commerce the great South American markets into which the competition of the United States and other countries had made deep inroads. Assisting me was a lifelong friend who had been at Oxford with me, the present Lord Dudley, whose successful management of his family coal and steel properties had established him as one of our leading industrialists. Also in the party were my Assistant Private Secretary, Mr. Hugh Lloyd Thomas, of the Foreign Office, and my equerry, Major John Aird, another Grenadier. On my first trip to Latin America in 1925 I realized I had lost a good deal through not being able to speak Spanish. Determined this time to make a more effective impression, and also to widen my own understanding of these countries, I made a serious effort to master the language. With a Spanish professor from the University of London I studied every day; he even came to The Fort for week-ends.

Because this trip was only semi-official, there was no provision of a battle cruiser. I made the voyage in the *Oropesa* through the Panama Canal to Callao, the principal port of Peru. Despite the unofficial nature of my visit, I was received in Lima with full honours; and, indeed, the parties contending for power postponed an imminent palace revolution until my departure from the capital. The Provisional President, Sanchez Cerro, was a small, swarthy, and voluble "mestizo" who had risen to power from a humble position in the Army. At a dinner at the British Legation the President sat at my right. The place at my left, reserved for the Vice-President, was empty. "I wouldn't wait for my colleague," Señor Sanchez Cerro advised with a sardonic smile; "I happen to know that he is plotting to have me shot. But I am planning a little surprise for him; I am going to have *him* shot." However, the missing Vice-President eventually appeared and took his seat next to me, apologizing profusely for his tardiness.

This explosive atmosphere seemed hardly conducive to discussions of the dull details of trade, and after four days in Lima I moved on. The revolution so considerately delayed on my account had already broken out by the time my plane reached Arequipa. Such was the speed with which Latin American Governments rose and fell in those days that when next I heard of Señor Sanchez Cerro, he was already aboard the *Oropesa*, occupying the same cabin that I had, bound for France and exile.

From Cuzco I crossed Lake Titicaca into Bolivia and thence down through Chile and across the Andes again to the Argentine and on to Brazil by sea. My time was largely taken up with matters of trade. With Eric Dudley at my elbow, I had long conversations with the leading financiers and industrialists of the Republics I visited, addressed the British Chambers of Commerce, and inspected many factories. But beyond all that, with a view to obtaining a true picture of what was going on in South American markets, I made a practice of poking around department stores and wholesale mercantile establishments, comparing the products they were receiving from Britain with the competing exports of other countries. It was plain that, while British industry was still dominant in the field of railways and public utilities it was losing ground in other lines: textiles, flying, cars, agricultural and road-construction machinery, and scientific instruments. I discovered, for example, that even in the cheaper merchandise, such as costume jewellery, which had long been profitable to Birmingham, clever Czechoslovak designers were capturing the market. Hoping to impress on my countrymen the inroads foreign competition was making, I began to collect samples of the kinds of foreign goods that were in demand.

Throughout the trip I persevered with Spanish. In my speech inaugurating the great exhibition at Buenos Aires, delivered in the presence of President Uriburu and the members of his Government, I had sufficient command of the language to deliver half of it in their tongue. It was broadcast to the world. From the

Opposition benches in the House of Commons came by cable an encouraging tribute: WELL DONE SIR STOP MY WARMEST AND MOST RESPECTFUL CONGRATULATIONS ON YOUR SPEECH STOP SPANISH PUNDITS DELIGHTED WITH YOUR PRONUNCIATION. It was signed, STANLEY BALDWIN.

On my return I tried to put to practical use the lessons in the realities of post-war trade that I had learned. It was no easy task with all Britain bogged down in the gloom of the world slump. I went to Manchester, where in the Free Trade Hall I warned a large audience of hard-headed business men that our industrial prestige was no longer what it had been; that important markets were being lost through the failure of English manufacturers to alter their designs in line with the new trends; and that they would be wise to take a leaf from American techniques, especially in the field of advertising.

In Birmingham I dumped some of my foreign samples on the desks of the jewellery manufacturers. But instead of being seized upon avidly, they were regarded with brooding suspicion and almost disdain. I particularly remember the attitude of an elderly jeweller when I pulled out of my pocket pieces of cheap Czech jewellery—sham emeralds, bogus rubies, and imitation diamonds set in the latest Cartier styles, that the *caballeros* were buying for their *señoritas*.

He said severely, "We don't make such flashy, tawdry stuff."

"Then what do you make for the South American market?" I asked. At his order an assistant appeared with a small tray of trinkets and ornaments—a drab display alongside the Czech finery.

"Do these things sell?" I asked.

The business man shook his head. "They did," he answered, "but no longer."

While I was away on this commercial mission, my father suffered two grievous blows in the deaths of the two members of his Household closest to him. The first to go, in January, was Sir Charles Cust, with whom he had been associated for fifty-four years. They had joined the Royal Navy together in 1877; their relationship was far more that of friends than of Sovereign and courtier: Charles Cust never hesitated to challenge the King's opinions. Only two months later his Private Secretary, Arthur

Bigge, Lord Stamfordham, died at eighty-one. Of him my father's biographer wrote, "If ever a man upheld King, Church and State, it was he." Although nearly half a century separated us, he was never wanting in his understanding of my problems and difficulties; he was truly a friend at Court to my brothers and me. The sorrow that overwhelmed us all was touchingly expressed in a letter from my mother:

Windsor Castle
April 3, 1931

Darling David,

   . . . I cannot say what a real grief this is to us both for we had such confidence in him & in all our many worries & difficulties always turned to him for advice. As to poor Papa he is quite knocked over by the blow, he has had a tiresome cough for some time owing to the fearful east winds we have been having all March, & the depression & grief caused by Bigge's death has made him worse & to-day he is very sorry for himself & is keeping in his rooms. . . .

Ever David darling
Yr devoted Mama
MARY

That summer the depression struck the country with full force. More than two and a half million men were out of work. There were hunger marches from the provinces and angry street demonstrations when the marchers reached London. By mid-summer the finances of Mr. Ramsay MacDonald's Labour Government were on the verge of collapse, and a Coalition Government was the only hope of saving the situation. Hastening to London from Balmoral, my father intervened in a constitutional impasse for the third time in his long reign, to bring about the formation of a National Government under the Socialist leader.

Blow now followed blow. Only a month later the Government's attempts to economize led to a mutiny of the Atlantic Fleet at Invergordon over inequalities in a general reduction of pay. Nothing that had ever happened before during my lifetime was more wounding to British pride. I had served in the Navy; I could not bring myself to believe that it had happened. Then, while the public was still half stunned by the Invergordon affair, the Government announced that the country had gone off the gold standard, an event as shattering to our position as the world's banker as the mutiny of the Fleet had been to our prestige. For a dreadful moment one had the feeling that the foundations of British power were being swept away. Fortunately the country rallied from these tribulations.

As I look back over the events of 1931, one occasion stands out. The scene was the Picture Gallery at Buckingham Palace, where my parents in November received the delegates to the India Round Table Conference. The screen of black morning coats suddenly parted; and I descried an extraordinary figure: a bald, wizened Indian clad in a *dhoti* and sandals, advancing towards my father. It was Mahatma Gandhi. Only nine years before, when I was in India, the Viceroy had thrown this man into jail for sedition. Now the King-Emperor was shaking his hand. Standing with me and looking on were a group of bejewelled Indian Princes whom I had known and with whom I had played polo. Nodding his head, one of them murmured, "This will cost you India."

By the summer of 1932 the stigma of the Invergordon mutiny had faded. The disgruntled naval ratings had been placated by a judicious redress of their grievances; an able and vigorous admiral had been put in command and had restored the confidence and discipline of the men. That July my father spent three days with the Home Fleet, and I was with him aboard the *Victoria and Albert*. During a conversation the First Lord of the Admiralty, who was in attendance upon my father, said to me: "It has come to my knowledge that the men of the Mediterranean Fleet are taking a poor view of this visit of His Majesty to the Home Fleet. They argue that, since they did not mutiny last year over the reductions in pay, why are the mutineers being thus honoured while they are ignored? I know the King cannot go out, but could you?" I talked it over with my father, who approved the idea. Flying to Corfu, where the Mediterranean Fleet was assembled, I passed some interesting days with Admiral Sir Ernle Chatfield aboard his flagship *Queen Elizabeth*, in which I steamed back with the Fleet to Malta. The men seemed to appreciate my going out to see them, and I was happy to have been able to contribute to the removal of any lingering hard feelings.

The implications of these stirrings in the body politic were not lost on me, and I was beginning to look on life with a seriousness that might have surprised those who had known the debonair Prince of a few years back. I was by now well aware of what the depression foreboded, and a trip to Scandinavia that autumn served to make me increasingly aware of the dangerous international situation building up on the Continent. After opening an Anglo-Danish exposition in Copenhagen, I went on to Sweden. In Stockholm I had a long talk with King Gustav. Then seventy-three years of age, he was the doyen of European rulers and had analysed the workings of political forces for over half a century from his neutral vantage-point. He was also strongly pro-British in spite of the close ties his Court and subjects traditionally maintained with Germany.

With logic he dissected the Treaty of Versailles: "that hodge-podge of conflicting ideologies that neither reconciles the vanquished to accepting the *status quo* nor destroys their power to rise against it." He went on to discuss the Polish Corridor: "that jagged gash in German national pride that will some day be the destruction of Poland." He concluded with this statement: "Your treaty has sowed the whirlwind, and unless you can effect peaceful adjustments very quickly you will reap it. Your only other hope is to become strong, very strong." On my return I duly passed on the old King's cogent comments to Whitehall, where they were received with the complacency that passed for statesmanship in those days.

In making the rounds of my father's depression-ridden realm I witnessed many grim sights—throngs of idle men everywhere, with nowhere to go. In town after town, village after village throughout the industrial areas, one would come upon dejected groups aimlessly milling in the streets or standing about outside the labour exchanges, and in front of the pubs they lacked the means to patronize. The saddest fact of all was that tens of thousands of these unemployed had come to judge themselves useless and unwanted. And in common with many thoughtful men at the time, I felt that unless the despair was arrested a large part of our manhood would sink into a slough of despond from which they would never rise.

A conversation I had in Newcastle-upon-Tyne about this period made a deep impression on me. The war had transformed Tyneside into a great shipbuilding centre. Thousands of workmen from all parts of the country had settled there with their families. Then with the decline of trade, Tyneside began to die slowly. Few ships were built, but the people remained—there was no work or home for them elsewhere. Walking about the dismal cottages on the riverbank, I came upon a man. He was about forty, poorly but cleanly dressed, erect and with an honest face. I singled him out for a talk.

"What is your trade?" I asked.

"Foreman riveter, Sir," he answered.

"How long is it since you have worked?"

"Five years, Sir."

A riveter was a key worker in the shipbuilding industry. The man mentioned the wages he had formerly earned, high even for those times. His eyes searched mine. Manifestly he expected me, the King's son, presumably privy to the secrets of Government, to be able to offer him some hope. But what response could I make to that tragic disclosure? That the Monarchy was not responsible for his plight? That the Government was doing all it could? That he had only to be patient? What possible solace would that have given to a man who had been on the dole for five years?

From 1931 onward various schemes were put forward by individuals and groups for mitigating the lot of the jobless by voluntary action. One heard a curious term in connexion with unemployment—"enforced leisure." And to provide these unfortunate people with some means of recreation, some escape from their cheerless homes and the dull defeatism of the streets, there evolved an ambitious plan for establishing throughout the so-called "depressed areas" social centres for unemployed working men. Financed by voluntary contributions, it became one of the activities of the National Council of Social Service.

One of the prime movers of this scheme was a remarkable character, Commander J. B. Adams, R.N. (later knighted), whom I had first met in Durham in 1929. "Bill" Adams was that curiosity—a man of action turned social worker. A retired Naval Commander, he had served with Shackleton in the Antarctic. A landowner in Yorkshire, and a member of White's Club, which was as poles removed from the accustomed haunts of "do-gooders," he unconcernedly went about twentieth-century Britain garbed in the tweed Inverness cape and curly-brimmed bowler of a Victorian squire. He had opened in 1910 in Yorkshire the first labour-exchange office in Great Britain. "I like to work with human beings in a Christian way," he once told me. And, as the depression deepened, he took the lead in organizing all kinds of social-service projects in the North Country.

"Bill" Adams saw nothing wrong about a Prince with a social conscience. With him as my guide I made several extensive tours of coal-mining villages and industrial centres in his area, visiting working-men's clubs that he had organized. I used to admire and envy his rare gift for getting along with people; in "Bill" Adams's world everybody from the highest to the lowest was "mate." His bluff, seafaring ways generated trust and confidence, and the atmosphere of good will that surrounded him made easier my passage through these dispirited communities. Yet, on occasion these calls could be for me a severe ordeal. Despite sincere attempts to make these clubs cheerful, they were for the most part dreary places—unused public halls, makeshift wooden structures often ill-lit and shabbily furnished with hard, almost forbidding, benches and tables. The walls were bare, except for coloured lithographs of my parents and other national figures. The prevailing despair and resentment were often too heavy even for "Bill" Adams's salty buoyancy to lift. More than once I found myself walking the length of one of these big rooms past row after row of crowded but silent benches, hearing nothing save the creak of the floor-boards under my weight.

This reproachful, almost sullen, silence was a new experience for me; I was accustomed to cheers. I was expected to talk to the men, but it was hard to decide what to say. About all that could be said was that I sympathized with them in their hardships. I would remind them that the Government was engaged in measures designed to overcome the existing economic problems. I would express the hope that their club would make their days less dreary. Whether these reassurances ever saved any of them from despair, I cannot say. But I had the feeling that empty as was my mission, my appearance among them was in large measure appreciated and taken as a sign that the Monarchy had not forgotten them in their misfortunes.

Nevertheless, as I circulated among these people, I came to realize that something more was needed than merely to make their idleness less dreary. Unemployment, the basic cause of their distress, obviously involved economic forces that were world-wide and outside a Prince's scope. However, in going down as I did again and again to the slums I presently discerned a field where-in my intervention might do some good—and that was housing. Some of the conditions that I saw sent me back to The Fort almost ill. How could one hope to build a healthy nation on such wretchedness?

It was a visit to Liverpool with my father's old friend, Lord Derby, that supplied me with an idea. Lord Derby was a great figure in Lancashire—Lord-Lieutenant of the county and the owner of extensive property. Whenever I visited those parts, I always stopped with him at his country seat, Knowsley Hall. On this occasion he was showing me around a new housing project built on the site previously occupied by one of the worst slums of Liverpool. While these new working-class dwellings represented an encouraging start in the right direction, they were, we both agreed, only drops of water in the ocean of human need.

Lord Derby grumbled over the tardiness and lack of initiative displayed by the Government. "Perhaps I may be able to help," I said. And on a sudden inspiration I asked him what he thought of the idea of my inviting the Prime Minister to York House to discuss housing with a few leading men who held the same views as we did.

"That's a capital idea," said Lord Derby. "I should be honoured to come myself."

A dinner party struck me as the most advantageous approach. By the time I finally settled upon the men I wanted Mr. Ramsay MacDonald to meet, the capacity of my dining-room was taxed to the full. He sat on my right and Mr. Neville Chamberlain, Chancellor of the Exchequer, on my left. The Minister of Health, Sir Hilton Young, sat opposite. The talk went on until midnight. No doubt every argument advanced had been brought up earlier at a hundred housing conferences. But I dare say that it was the first debate on housing that ever took place under the auspices of the Prince of Wales. If the Prime Minister had accepted my invitation with pleasure, he took his leave in a different mood.

Under the steady cross-fire of criticism he made what struck the rest of us as rather a lame defence of the Government's housing programme.

The Royal power in British politics is limited to the power of suggestion. Beyond this I could not go. However, in the ways that were open to me I tried to bring the subject of housing more and more to the fore. I also had a practical interest in the question. As Duke of Cornwall I was both beneficiary and administrator of the estates of the Duchy. More valuable even than the 120,000 acres of agricultural properties in the west of England were some 80 acres of real estate in London at Kennington. In the management of the Duchy properties the normal desire for profit was subordinated to the Duke of Cornwall's responsibility to be by example the most enlightened landlord in the country. Because the estates were extensive and had always been well run, the revenues were substantial. Nevertheless, a larger proportion than was the usual practice was ploughed back for the improvements that were part of the Duchy's long-range policy of management. However, by 1934 certain blocks of low-rent houses built in Victorian times had deteriorated, despite steady repairs, to a condition only a degree or two removed from that of a slum. To have replaced them with modern buildings incorporating the latest ideas would have required a much bigger outlay than the Duchy could afford. Since it was in a way a trust for the support of the Heir Apparent, it had long been a hard-and-fast rule of the Duchy Council that it should not speculate or borrow. These blocks of old houses were therefore sold to the London County Council, which had at that time embarked upon a large slum-clearance project. The houses were torn down, but for various reasons part of the site remained vacant.

About this time I made the acquaintance of a brilliant young architect, a Scot, who had just come home primed with new ideas for the mass production of a low-rent housing that he had picked up in America. My conversations with this enthusiastic man started me thinking about the possibility of developing this unused site. It occurred to me that if I could stimulate the interest of far-sighted, public-spirited men in the City, the Duchy's former land might well be transformed into a model housing development. My old friend, Sir Edward Peacock, the senior partner in

Baring Brothers, who was also Receiver-General of the Duchy, was all for the scheme. It was not long before he had collected a keen and influential group who were prepared to risk the necessary large investment with only a token return.

The next step was to persuade the L.C.C. to release the land for the experiment. Towards that end I invited its Socialist leader, Mr. Herbert Morrison, to meet the men from the City at York House. He turned up one afternoon with certain Council officials, including the architect and surveyor. As the meeting progressed, it became clear that even had Sir Edward's group envisaged the building of a Garden of Eden on the former Duchy site, the L.C.C. planners were not going to yield the ground they had captured for their own experiments. They listened respectfully, but in the end Mr. Morrison rejected the idea; his architect supported him, insisting that the project was impracticable. So the scheme came to naught. But my instruction in the expediencies of party politics, begun some years earlier under the Conservative Mr. Baldwin, thus progressed under the example provided by the Socialist Mr. Morrison.

The incident, however, had an amusing sequel. Having escorted Mr. Morrison to the door, I was hardly back with my friends before he returned with a roguish glint in his eye. "Forgive me, Sir," he explained, "but I appear to have forgotten my brief-case. Have I by any chance left it in the dining-room?" My butler went to look and soon returned with the mislaid portfolio.

"Ha!" exclaimed Mr. Morrison, tucking it under his arm. "It would never have done to leave the secrets of the Socialist Party at York House, would it, Sir?"

"Mr. Morrison," I chided, "it would be hard to imagine a safer place."

But my growing interest in such matters went beyond mere domestic issues. As I have already said, I was becoming increasingly disturbed over the conflict of opinion as to whether our foreign policy should be based on realism or on the League of Nations. And, careful as I had been to suppress any indication in public of what was in my mind, two occurrences eventually moved me to speak out. But in so doing I came into collision with the inescapable political restraints binding the Prince of Wales.

The first of these took place in connexion with the British

Legion, of which I was the patron, at its annual Whitsuntide meeting in London. A proposal had been advanced within that organization that, as a gesture of friendship and good will, a small group of members should visit Germany in the near future and shake hands with some of those whom they had fought so bitterly in the past. This struck me as an eminently reasonable idea, and at the suggestion of the Chairman of the Legion I agreed to commend the proposal in the speech I was to make at the closing session in the Queen's Hall on June 11, 1935. My brief reference to this project was duly reported next day in the newspapers. That same afternoon my father sent for me. He was disturbed. "How often have I told you, my dear boy," he began, "never to mix in politics, especially where foreign affairs are concerned. The views you expressed yesterday, however sensible, are, I happen to know, contrary to those of the Foreign Office."

"But, Papa, it was not entirely my idea. I was only endorsing a resolution adopted by the British Legion," I said.

"That is beside the point," my father replied. "You must never speak on such controversial matters without consulting the Government."

The rebuke disturbed me. It seemed to settle nothing; our foreign policy, the more I thought about it, seemed paralysed.

The second incident happened two days later, when I visited Berkhamsted School, one of the oldest public schools in the country. While flying there in my aeroplane, I happened to read in the newspapers that the London County Council had banned the use of even wooden guns by the boys in the Cadet Corps of the schools within their jurisdiction. This action filled me with fury. On the one hand the Government discouraged intercourse with a former enemy whose revived power was feared, and on the other an influential Socialist wing, mostly pacifist, was determined to obstruct any revival of the martial spirit that might hold Germany in check. Berkhamsted, I happened to know, had a first-class O.T.C. Remembering my pride of membership in the O.T.C. at Oxford many years before, I determined to throw caution to the winds and to speak out for the right of patriotic men to prepare themselves for the defence of their institutions. When, therefore, I addressed the school, I spoke not from notes but from the heart. There was only a reference to the "misguided" and to the "cranks" who sought to abolish the Cadet Corps, one of the cornerstones of defence. My extemporaneous address brought a sharp if somewhat humorous rebuke from an ageing but prominent Socialist leader who, reminding me that "a crank is a very important part of an engine," suggested that I might to better advantage lead a deputation of the British Legion to Russia.

These examples of visionary thinking born of political expediency struck me as portents of exceedingly ill omen.

No word came from Buckingham Palace. But my father could hardly have been pleased, not because he disagreed with me, but because I had embroiled myself once again—and so soon—in politics.

CHAPTER XIV

"THE HEART HAS ITS REASONS"

HOWEVER, despite these occasional restraints my life was in many ways a free and ample one. I was, up to a point, my own master, a Prince in a democratic society. Nevertheless, there was always something lacking, something not supplied. Given my character, my roving curiosity and independence, my life appeared to form a disconnected pattern—duty without decision, service without responsibility, pomp without power.

Meanwhile something had happened that, although I did not realize it at the time, was destined to change the whole course of my life. I met Wallis Warfield Simpson.

It was during the winter after my return from South America in 1931. I had gone to Melton Mowbray with my brother George for a week-end's hunting. Mr. and Mrs. Simpson were guests in the same house. It was one of those week-ends for which our winters are justly infamous—cold, damp, foggy. Mrs. Simpson did not ride and obviously had no interest in horses, hounds, or hunting in general. She was also plainly in misery from a bad cold in the head. Since a Prince is by custom expected to take the lead in conversing with strangers, and having been informed that she was an American, I was prompted to observe that she must miss central heating, of which there was a lamentable lack in my country and an abundance in hers. The affirmative answer that, in the circumstances, any Briton had reason to expect would then have cleared the way for a casual discussion of the variety of physical comforts available in America, and the conversation would have been safely anchored on firm ground. But instead, a verbal chasm opened under my feet. Mrs. Simpson did not miss the great boon that her country has conferred upon the world. On the contrary, she liked our cold houses. A mocking look came into her eyes. "I am sorry, Sir," she said, "but you have disappointed me."

"In what way?"

"Every American woman who comes to your country is always asked that same question. I had hoped for something more original from the Prince of Wales."

I moved away to talk to the other guests, but the echoes of the passage lingered. Central heating had its merits, beyond doubt, but I had clearly taken too much for granted.

So began our acquaintance. During the next few years we met occasionally in the company of friends at dinner parties in London and more rarely at week-ends in the country. Of the slow unfolding of our friendship Wallis tells an amusing story. Not long after our first meeting at Melton Mowbray, we were at a party in London. I am supposed to have asked my hostess, "Haven't I met that lady before?" Then I saw her again at a Court at Buckingham Palace, being presented to my parents. I was as usual standing behind their gilt thrones as Wallis approached in the slowly-moving line of women brilliant in Court feathers and trains. When her turn came to curtsy, first to my father then to my mother, I was struck by the grace of her carriage and the natural dignity of her movements.

The Simpsons had a small but charming flat in Bryanston Court, Bryanston Square. Everything in it was in exquisite taste and the food, in my judgment, unrivalled in London. Having been raised in Baltimore, where a fine dinner is considered one of the highest human accomplishments, Wallis had an expert knowledge of cooking. But beyond all that, she had a magnetic attraction for gay, lively, and informed company.

I travelled a good deal during this period. But, whenever I was in London, I liked to drop in at Bryanston Court for tea or cocktails, where one met young British and American men of affairs, foreign diplomats, and intelligent women. The talk was witty and crackling with the new ideas that were bubbling up furiously in the world of Hitler, Mussolini, Stalin, the New Deal, and Chiang Kai-shek.

Subtle and discriminating, Wallis had an intuitive understanding of the forces and ideas working in society. She was extraordinarily well informed about politics and current affairs. I was impressed by her habit of reading the four leading London newspapers every day, from cover to cover. She kept up with the latest books and knew a good deal about the theatre. Her conversation was deft and amusing. But most of all I admired her forthrightness. If she disagreed with some point under discussion, she never failed to advance her own views with vigour and spirit. That side of her enchanted me. A man in my position seldom encountered that trait in other people. Never having believed that my offhand judgments were infallible, I always welcomed a chance to argue them—perhaps because I had so few opportunities of doing so.

And even if nothing else had ever come of our friendship, I should have been eternally grateful to Wallis for one thing: she was genuinely interested in how the Prince of Wales went about his job. It all began with something as simple as that.

One evening I invited a few friends, Wallis among them, to dinner at the Dorchester Hotel. The conversation turned to my interest in the new social-service schemes for the unemployed. It so happened that only that afternoon I had returned from Yorkshire, where I had been visiting working-men's clubs in towns and villages. In the company to which I was accustomed the disclosure of such a chore would usually have brought some such sympathetic response as, "Oh! Sir, how boring for you. Aren't you terribly tired?"

Wallis had read in the newspapers about the Council of Social Service. She wanted to know more about it. I told her what it was and what it was trying to do. And, being an American, she was curious to learn just what a Prince's working day consisted of. Although the orchestra was making a good deal of noise, I did my best to explain that, too. I have always remembered that evening.

In character, Wallis was, and still remains, complex and elusive; and from the first I looked upon her as the most independent woman I had ever met. This refreshing trait I was inclined to put down as one of the happier outcomes of the events of 1776.

And then one day she began to mean more to me in a way that she did not perhaps comprehend. My impression is that for a long time she remained unaffected by my interest. In ancient times the love of a Prince would have been lauded by the poets. The modern folk-tale, however, has taken a more rigid form; a Prince's heart, like his politics, must remain within the constitutional pale. But my heart refused to be so confined; and presently and imperceptibly the hope formed that one day I might be able to share my life with her, just how I did not know.

That the fulfilment of this hope would entail grave difficulties was clear to me from the outset. In the first place an immediate difficulty confronted me in the shape of the Royal Marriages Act of 1772. Under the provisions of this Act the marriages of Princes of the Blood Royal are under the Sovereign's control and ultimately Parliament's. Thus a veto power over my choice of a wife rested with my father. And for several reasons, among which the element of divorce was not the least, I was convinced that it was unlikely that he would give his consent.

To write about divorce is to provoke contention. Yet, because the difficulties that eventually beset me arose in predominant measure from the prejudices pertaining to divorce, I am constrained to set forth here, in humble spirit, certain observations of my own relating to a human situation, proper under the Law and increasingly accepted, which brought me to an agony of decision and cost me my Throne.

Divorce is not recognized by the Church of England, of which the King as Defender of the Faith is the titular head. And, because the Monarch is expected to give force in his private as well as his public life to the tenets of the Established Church, the Court by its very nature is bound to maintain a strong position on this question. Even as late as my grandfather's era the rule was that no divorced person, even if the innocent party, would be received at Court. In response to the widespread breaking up of hasty wartime marriages, this rule was relaxed during my father's reign to the extent of allowing the innocent party to continue to enjoy the social distinction an invitation to Court bestows. The guilty parties, however, were with a few rare exceptions still thrust out into limbo. Invitations no longer arrived from the Lord Chamberlain to levees, garden parties, or the Royal Enclosure at Ascot. One's name never appeared again in the Court Circular.

Because of this interdict, which rightly or wrongly I regarded as outmoded and hypocritical, an ever-increasing number of otherwise worthy and blameless men and women were forced to stand apart in a permanent state of obloquy. And the Sovereign and indeed the whole nation were thus deprived of the full services of many able people. To be sure a few rare exceptions were from time to time made; but these represented, so far as the Court was concerned, a convenient averting of the eyes rather than a frank acknowledgment of the changing attitude of society towards divorce. It had long been in my mind that, were I ever to succeed to the Throne, I should strive tactfully to end this form of social ostracism. However, as matters turned out, there never was time for that.

But the one point that matters is that with regard to my private hopes I foresaw that, even though my intended wife was beyond reproach under the Law, as indeed she was, the prevailing attitude of the Court was still powerful enough to impose almost insurmountable barriers in the way of my marriage. The mere avowal of intent was certain to raise a storm of opposition inside the Church and ultra-conservative Court circles. And it was bound to bring discord into the family.

It was all quite vague but none the less vivid, this dream of being able to bring into my life what for so long had been lacking, without which my service to the State would seem an empty thing. It was, of course, my intention to discuss the matter some day with my father; but that was not going to be an easy thing to do. He was almost seventy and steadily failing as his reign entered its twenty-fifth year in 1935. Moreover, I could not discount the possibility of my having to withdraw altogether from the line of succession if my hope were ever to be fulfilled. However, I took comfort from the fact that my brother Bertie, to whom the succession would pass, was in outlook and temperament very much like my father. The patterns of their lives were much the same, with the steady swing of habit taking them both year after year to the same places at the same time and with the same associates. Strongly rooted each in his own existence, they tended to be withdrawn from the hurly-burly of life that I relished. Both were devoted family men, a quality that goes a long way for a King in a constitutional monarchy.

These were my thoughts that momentous spring of 1935, as the country prepared to celebrate my father's Silver Jubilee. Although the unstinted outpourings of affection from all parts of

the Empire gratified him, the continuous ceremonies and functions wore him out. It was hardly a propitious time to disturb
him. The summer saw him off as usual for Balmoral and me on a
shooting trip in Austria and Hungary.

Then, when we were together again in London, a remarkable
concatenation of events left me no opportunity to talk things over.
First my brother Harry, following George's example of the year
before, was married in the private chapel at Buckingham Palace,
on November 6. His bride was Lady Alice Scott, the third
daughter of my father's old friend, the Duke of Buccleuch, who
died just before the wedding. In his diary my father wrote, "Now
all the children are married but David."

A week later a general election returned to power the Conservative Party led by Mr. Baldwin, establishing a Government
that was to hold office for five momentous years. These events
engrossed my father's attention. Then, in the early morning of
the day he was to open Parliament, my aunt, Princess Victoria,
died. Aunt Toria was not only my father's favourite sister but
also his cherished friend. For many years his days had begun at
9.30 with a telephone call to her. His grief was such that he could
not bring himself to face the crowds of London, and the State
ceremony was cancelled. My father never again appeared in
public.

Meanwhile, events were on the march that all too soon would
convulse Europe. The Italian legions were driving into Abyssinia,
and the tension between Italy and Britain over sanctions added to
my father's anxiety. Absorbed by the gathering world crisis, I
slipped into the House of Commons one afternoon, and from the
Peers' Gallery listened to my friend, Sir Samuel Hoare, make his
moving speech of resignation as Secretary of State for Foreign
Affairs in deference to the fierce public outcry that had arisen over
the pact that he and M. Pierre Laval had concluded in Paris.
Knowing much that had gone on behind the scenes, I was sorry
that Sam Hoare had been made the scapegoat for what was, in
the last analysis, Mr. Baldwin's own policy, and that the popular
clamour had been focused on him to the exclusion of his Party
leader.

A few days later I was at Sandringham for the family Christmas
gathering. My brothers and their wives were already there. My

father had grown thin and bent; we all shared a sense of foreboding that this might well be his last Christmas; so we tried to make it an especially happy one. In the spacious white ballroom of the Big House, where we had all had such fun in my grandfather's time, a fourth generation had begun to assert itself. Bertie's two children, Elizabeth, who was then nine, and her sister, Margaret Rose, romped around the twenty-foot tree. Yet, in this closely-knit fabric of family ties I felt detached and lonely. My brothers were secure in their private lives; whereas I was caught up in an inner conflict and would have no peace of mind until I had resolved it. But again this was hardly the time or the place. My father died before another opportunity presented itself.

CHAPTER XV

MY FATHER DIES

O<small>N</small> Thursday afternoon, January 16, I was out shooting with friends in Windsor Great Park. An urgent note from my mother was brought to me in the field. "I think you ought to know that Papa is not very well," the note began, and in the calm way that I knew so well my mother went on to say that, while she herself did not consider the danger immediate, Lord Dawson was "not too pleased with Papa's state at the present moment." She therefore suggested that I should "propose" myself for the coming week-end at Sandringham, but do so in such a casual manner that my father should not suspect that she had warned me of his condition.

Rather than wait until the Saturday I flew to Sandringham the next morning in my own aeroplane. The air was clear; and as the semicircle of the Wash came slowly into view, leaden grey under the winter sun, a sudden impulse made me signal the pilot to make a wide circle around the estate. Here was my father's home, a place he preferred to palaces and where since boyhood he had known happiness to a degree experienced by few men and almost never by kings. The Big House, set off by formal lawns from the surrounding woods, seemed the embodiment of my father's life and philosophy—secure, unchanging, apart. It was impossible for me to believe that his life might be coming to an end.

My father was in his bedroom. Dressed in an old Tibetan dressing gown, a faded relic of his visits to India, he was sitting in his favourite chair in front of a crackling fire. He seemed to be half asleep. Although the small sounds attending my entrance aroused him and the light of recognition momentarily flickered in his eyes, he did not seem to be wholly aware of my presence. From

261

the bay window he could look out across the sunken garden and over the tops of the trees, now wintry bare, towards the square church tower from which the Royal Standard flew. In one corner was a simple brass bed in which my grandfather had slept before him.

Mary had come from Yorkshire at my mother's summons. While we were whispering together in the room, my father suddenly roused himself. He asked Mary whether she had been skating. There had been a sharp frost during the night, and the pond below the house was covered with thin ice. My father's mind must have been travelling back into the past and to the wonderful skating parties that he and the rest of us had had there. Then he dozed off again, and Mary beckoned me to leave the room.

Next day my father's condition grew worse. It was plain, now, to all of us that nothing could save him; but so far we had refrained from admitting the dreadful fact to one another. That afternoon, however, my mother suggested that Bertie, Mary, and I should join her for a walk in the grounds. "It will do us good," she said, "to get out of doors for a little while." As we were all walking together, she put into words the grave thoughts that were in our minds and began to discuss the changes that my father's passing, now imminent, would bring to us all.

On Sunday I motored back to London to inform the Prime Minister that the King was not expected to live more than two or three days. I went directly to No. 10 Downing Street. It happened to be Mrs. Baldwin's birthday; she invited me to join the Prime Minister and herself for tea. When I had finished relating to him the grave news from Sandringham, he murmured his sympathy, adding almost wistfully, "I wonder if you know, Sir, that another great Englishman, a contemporary of your father's, died yesterday." My expression must have been blank, for Mr. Baldwin continued, "But, of course, Sir, you have a great deal on your mind. I should not have expected you to know. It was Rudyard Kipling, my first cousin." He seemed a little resentful of the injustice of a situation that allowed the death of one of our great writers to go unnoticed while the nation was absorbed in the passing of a Sovereign. However, he swiftly suppressed his personal emotions. Expressing his sympathy for the loss about to overtake my family and me, he commented on the exalted position about to descend upon me, a position that would necessarily bring us into close association. We had known each other since 1923, shortly after he had become Prime Minister for the first time. On the strength of his long acquaintance he was inspired to say that both of us had good reason to contemplate the future with confidence. I replied in like spirit. We parted, giving voice to those reassurances of mutual personal esteem that in constitutional society show the hereditary and representative systems at their harmonious best.

During these last days, while my father lay beyond recovery, the boxes containing State papers requiring his attention and signature had steadily accumulated on his desk. In order to break this block in constitutional business the Lord President of the Council and some Privy Councillors had been summoned from London on the Monday morning so that my father might hold a Council and appoint a Council of State, similar to that set up during his first serious illness in 1928. This time it was to consist only of my mother, my three brothers, and me. When I returned to Sandringham in the afternoon, this Council had already been held, and I had been spared witnessing what must have been a most pathetic scene. The Privy Councillors had assembled in my father's study adjoining his bedroom. Too weak to stand, my father sat propped up in a chair, just visible to the Councillors through the open door between. He could not even muster the strength to sign the enabling document; only by immense effort, with Lord Dawson holding the pen, was he able to manage two shaky marks.

During the few hours the Council of State was in being, we, the five members, set ourselves to the task of dealing with the boxes. Signing documents provided a distraction from the strain of waiting. It is a harrowing experience to watch anyone die, let alone one's father, and especially when one's father is a King. When a King starts to die, the whole world crowds in for the death-watch, to follow with morbid curiosity every detail in the pathetic process of mortality. Inside the Big House a sad quiet came over our family circle. The members of the Household-in-Waiting subsided into the background. Of the shadowy figures that slipped in and out of my father's room as the end approached

I particularly remember two. One was the doctor, Lord Dawson, as much courtier as physician, who composed the memorable bulletins; the other was the Archbishop of Canterbury, a noiseless spectre in black gaiters.

All was still as we—his wife and children—stood together by my father's bedside waiting for life to be extinguished. Death came to him five minutes before midnight. And while my mind was still trying to comprehend the profound event that had in that instant occurred, my mother did an unexpected thing. She took my hand in hers and kissed it; before I could stop him my brother George, who was standing beside her, stepped forward and followed her example. I knew, of course, that this form of homage was now by custom my due. But like my father the action embarrassed me. I could not bring myself to believe that the members of my own family, or indeed anyone else, should be expected to humble themselves before me in this way. Nevertheless, these two spontaneous gestures served to remind me, however needlessly, that I was now King.

According to ancient usage the first public act of the new Sovereign is to present himself before an Accession Privy Council composed principally of Princes of the Blood Royal, present and former Cabinet Ministers, and other eminent persons who, in combination with the High Commissioners for the Dominions and India, as well as the Lord Mayor and Aldermen of London, are charged with proclaiming the fact of the accession of the new King to the Throne.

For this purpose I repaired next morning to London in my aeroplane, thereby creating, without realizing it, a kingly precedent, for my father had never flown in his life. That afternoon more than one hundred Privy Councillors assembled in the Banqueting Hall at St. James's Palace. There they swore allegiance to me after the Clerk of the Council, Sir Maurice Hankey, had read to them the following sonorous proclamation:

". . . We, therefore, the Lords Spiritual and Temporal of this Realm . . . do now hereby with one Voice and Consent of Tongue and Heart, publish and proclaim, That the High and Mighty Prince Edward Albert Christian George Andrew Patrick David, is now, by the Death of our late Sovereign of Happy Memory, become our only lawful and rightful Liege Lord, Edward the

Eighth, by the Grace of God, of Great Britain, Ireland, and the British Dominions beyond the Seas, King, Defender of the Faith, Emperor of India. . . ."

A moment later I presented myself to this distinguished company, composed in large measure of men whose lives had been associated with my father's reign. My appearance before them was brief; yet I dare say the emotions of some were as tense as mine as I addressed them in the following terms:

"When my Father stood here twenty-six years ago he declared that one of the objects of his life would be to uphold constitutional government. In this I am determined to follow in my Father's footsteps and to work as he did throughout his life for the happiness and welfare of all classes of my Subjects.

"I place my reliance upon the loyalty and affection of my peoples throughout the Empire, and upon the wisdom of their Parliaments, to support me in this heavy task, and I pray God will guide me to perform it."

Then I had to arrange for the burial of my father, and towards that end I called a meeting of a committee of the civil and military officials responsible for the ceremonial. The funeral of a Sovereign inevitably requires a vast public show—a display of State pomp and circumstance that inescapably runs counter to the bereaved family's desire for privacy and simplicity. My mother shrank from a repetition of the prolonged manifestations of grief that marked the obsequies of my grandfather. Her one request to me before I left Sandringham was that my father should not remain unburied more than a week. When I conveyed her wish to the committee, they readily offered to comply.

That night I slept at York House. My accession was to be publicly proclaimed at four different points in London—first by the Garter King of Arms at St. James's Palace, then by Heralds at Charing Cross, Temple Bar, and the Royal Exchange. I arranged for a few personal friends, including Wallis, to watch the first ceremony from a room in St. James's that provided a good view of the proceedings in Friary Court. Then at the last moment I asked myself what was wrong in my watching myself being proclaimed King? So I hurried across Ambassadors' Court and joined them. The impulse was well rewarded, for the scene was picturesque and colourful, with mace bearers and trumpeters in attendance in State dress. As the tremendous words rolled out, the symmetrical polished words of sovereignty and dominion, I was swept by conflicting emotions. There was a flash of pride in becoming King-Emperor of the vast and liberal Commonwealth I knew so well. At the same time these words seemed to tell me that my relations with Wallis had suddenly entered a more significant stage.

"It was all very moving," she said, as we walked away. "But it has also made me realize how different your life is going to be."

And so for some sad days we parted.

While I was still in London, I had ordered a bearer party from the King's Company, 1st Battalion Grenadier Guards, to be sent to Sandringham. This Grenadier Company, which since the reign of Charles II by right guards the Sovereign's person in life, also has the right to carry his body in death. When I returned to Sandringham on the Wednesday afternoon, it was to find that my father had been placed in a coffin made from an oak-tree felled on the estate, and, escorted by the Guardsmen from the Big House, taken to the little church near by. I went there directly. The coffin rested before the altar, watched over by gamekeepers, gardeners, and other faithful retainers, who in this way were able to pay a last tribute not only to their King but to a beloved squire. As I stood there, it came to my mind that my father would have preferred that his earthly remains be spared the huge State funeral and buried in the peaceful churchyard at Sandringham. But Windsor claims the bodies of British Monarchs: next morning the coffin was placed on a gun-carriage drawn by a Royal Horse Artillery team, which set out for Wolferton Station three miles away, where a special train waited to carry my father's body to London. I followed to the station on foot with my brothers and my brother-in-law, Lord Harewood. My mother and my sister rode in a carriage. Then came a groom leading my father's white shooting pony, Jock. Bringing up the rear of the simple procession were some hundreds of plainly dressed men and women, tenants and workers on the estate, neighbours, friends, and gamekeepers in green liveries and black bowler hats. With them marched the old piper, Forsyth, playing "The Flowers of the Forest."

The morning was bright and frosty; a biting cold wind blew off the North Sea. Just as we topped the last hill above the station,

the stillness of the morning was broken by a wild familiar sound
—the crow of a cock pheasant. My brothers and I glanced up in
time to see a solitary bird flying across the road directly overhead.
In the symbolism of that felicitous incident our sadness momentarily disappeared. The thought occurred to all of us that had my
father been vouchsafed the choice of one last sight at Sandringham
he would have chosen something like that: a pheasant travelling
high and fast on the wind, the kind of shot he loved.

The Royal train reached King's Cross that winter's afternoon.
The family followed the draped gun-carriage through the streets,
across Trafalgar Square to Westminster. That simple family
procession through London was, perhaps, more impressive than
the State *cortège* on the day of the funeral, and I especially remember a curious incident that happened on the way and was seen by
very few. The Imperial Crown, heavily encrusted with precious
stones, had been removed from its glass case in the Tower
and secured to the lid of the coffin over the folds of the
Royal Standard. In spite of the rubber-tired wheels, the jolting of
the heavy vehicle must have caused the Maltese cross on the top
of the Crown—set with a square sapphire, eight medium-sized
diamonds, and one hundred and ninety-two smaller diamonds—
to fall. For suddenly, out of the corner of my eye, I caught a flash
of light dancing along the pavement.

My natural instinct was to bend down and retrieve the jewels,
lest the equivalent of a king's ransom be lost for ever. Then a
sense of dignity restrained me, and I resolutely marched on.
Fortunately, the Company Sergeant-Major bringing up the rear
of the two files of Grenadiers flanking the gun-carriage had also
seen the accident. Quick as a flash, with scarcely a missed step, he
bent down, scooped up the cross with his hand, and dropped it
into his pocket. It was one of the most quick-witted acts that I
have ever witnessed. It seemed a strange thing to happen; and,
although not superstitious, I wondered whether it was a bad
omen.

In Westminster Hall a magnificent catafalque had been prepared. There, under the lofty hammer-beamed roof, my father's
body lay in state. During the four days it rested there nearly one
million people filed past, forming a continuous river of humanity
that flowed on through day and night.

Five rulers came to my father's funeral—King Christian of
Denmark, King Haakon of Norway, King Carol of Rumania,
Czar Boris of Bulgaria, and Leopold III King of the Belgians.
President Lebrun represented the French Republic. There was in
addition a host of foreign princes, ambassadors, statesmen, mar-
shals, and other dignitaries sent by their respective countries. On
the night before the funeral I was obliged by custom to give a
State dinner and reception at Buckingham Palace for these distinguished mourners. It was a brilliant but, as matters turned out, an
ill-fated company. In the French delegation was Marshal Pétain,
then France's most honoured soldier, the hero of Verdun. For
Soviet Russia there were Marshal Tukhachevsky, Vice-Commissar
for Defence, who was destined to be shot a little more than a year
later in the bloody purge; and M. Litvinov, Commissar for
Foreign Affairs, who was temporarily in high favour as the plausible agent of Moscow's short-lived *rapprochement* with the West.
For Germany there were Baron von Neurath, the Minister of
Foreign Affairs, who was to become "Protector" of part of
Czechoslovakia; and General von Rundstedt, who became Commander-in-Chief in the West. King Victor Emmanuel of Italy
sent his son, Umberto, then Prince of Piedmont; representing
Austria was the dashing Prince Starhemberg, who two years
later would be driven from his country by the *Anschluss*. And
for Finland, Field-Marshal Baron Carl von Mannerheim, whose
country would be the first to resist the shock of the Red
Army. However, the occasion was hardly one to induce crystal-
gazing. Such feasting and commingling, with my father still unburied, seemed to me unfitting and heartless. Yet there was no
escaping the duty. When finally the last guest had departed, my
three brothers and I slipped quietly away to carry out a plan upon
which we had decided in the afternoon.

All the time my father lay in Westminster Hall, officers of the
Household Troops, together with the Gentlemen-at-Arms and
Yeomen of the Guard, maintained a continuous vigil around the
coffin. I had been to the Hall and was greatly moved by the scene.
It occurred to me that here was a way in which my brothers and
I might pay our respects to our dead father in a simple and wholly
appropriate way. Having earlier taken the General Officer Com-
manding the London District into our confidence, Bertie, Harry,

George, and I changed into full-dress uniform and motored to Westminster, arriving there shortly after midnight. Without the public being aware of our presence we descended the staircase into the hall and stationed ourselves around the catafalque between the officers already on vigil. Even at so late an hour the river of people still flowed past the coffin. But I doubt whether many recognized the King's four sons among the motionless uniformed figures bent over swords reversed. We stood there for twenty minutes in the dim candlelight and the great silence. I felt close to my father and all that he had stood for. Then from the gloomy heights above us the great clock chimed the half-hour—its lingering reverberations obliterating momentarily the sound of countless shuffling feet.

From Westminster my father's body was taken to Windsor for burial; and the funeral procession was a brilliant and impressive spectacle. As my father had been a sailor, I decided that he should have a sailor's funeral. With five-score bluejackets manning the drag-ropes of the gun-carriage, his body was taken to Paddington Station. The march at slow time took two and a half hours. Days afterwards the wail of the massed pipe bands echoed in my ears. And I shall never forget the crowds.

The final rites took place in St. George's Chapel beneath the silken banners of the Knights of the Garter. As the coffin began to sink on slow and noiseless pulleys into the vault below and the Archbishop of Canterbury recited the passage from the burial service—"Earth to earth, ashes to ashes, dust to dust, . . ."—I scattered over it the symbolic earth from a silver bowl handed to me by Sir Derek Keppel, the Master of my father's Household and his lifelong friend.

CHAPTER XVI

SOME REFLECTIONS ON
BECOMING KING

So ended a harrowing and exhausting week. The tumult died; the captains and the kings departed; for a little while I had the uneasy sensation of being left alone on a vast stage, a stage that was the British Empire, to play a part not yet written. It was a part that I had known since childhood would probably be mine, and that I had watched and studied. Yet it was some time before I became accustomed to identifying the term "King" with myself. It had so long been the appellation of my father that at first, whenever I was so addressed, I automatically assumed, before I could catch myself, that it still referred to him.

In certain outward respects my life went on much as before. My mother stayed on at Buckingham Palace while I remained at York House. However, in order to be closer to the Palace secretariat, running smoothly under the experienced direction of my father's Private Secretary, Lord Wigram, I transferred my office to the Palace, occupying on the ground floor a small wait-ing-room, decorated and furnished in Oriental style. It looked out upon the great Courtyard through two windows; on all but the brightest days I kept a light burning on my desk. I would motor there every morning in one of my father's Daimlers. Had I had my way that immense, sombre vehicle, known to my brothers and me as the "Crystal Palace," would have remained in the garage, and I would have walked to my office as many of my subjects were wont to do. But caution restrained me. The appearance of the Daimler, with a painted metal miniature Royal Standard displayed on the front of the roof, had come to mean to the public that the King was passing by on his business. On the single occasion (which will presently be related) that I dispensed with the hallowed conveyance and set out from the Palace on foot, the cry of wounded tradition that went up could not have been louder had I travelled third class by train to Windsor.

To be sure, signs were not wanting that many welcomed the advent of my reign as an event of happy augury. And in the light of the tensions gathering beneath the surface it is interesting to record now that perhaps the most felicitous expressions of confidence emanated from the sources of power that eleven months later were to be so influential in bringing that reign to an end.

First, *The Times* enumerated with gratification a rather extensive catalogue of kingly attributes that it professed to find in the new Monarch. It spoke flatteringly of my physical courage. It discerned in me "an unerring eye for the distinction between dignity and solemnity," by which was meant, I suppose, that I was not taken in by the pompous. "Men, not books," *The Times* observed approvingly, "are his library." It perceived as well an interest in all sorts and conditions of people, "which more 'democrats' profess than feel." Then, remembering that the new King was a bachelor, it reminded its readers, with sudden solicitude, that "in the life of responsibility, day in and day out, which will henceforth be his, he will lack the help and counsel of a consort." That sentimental sentence was to echo mutely in my ears at the end when *The Times*, once again the "Thunderer," turned its wrath against the woman of my choice.

Shortly before my father died the Archbishop of Canterbury, Dr. Cosmo Lang, at a public dinner, had spoken glowingly in my presence of my manifold public services as Prince of Wales "for all that belongs to our common life, for the sick and not least for the unemployed, and for that embassy of Empire, which the Prince fulfils in every part of the world, and, I begin to think, in almost every language." The Archbishop had added, perhaps with more eloquence than accuracy, "It is no exaggeration to say that future historians will look to the Prince's speeches to learn the best that can be said of the industrial, social, and commercial life of his day and generation."

And finally the Prime Minister, in a statement in the House of Commons, found much to praise in welcoming my accession to the Throne. He reminded Parliament of my broad experience in public affairs, of the universal good will that had been the fruit of my travels, and of my own unique knowledge of the varied conditions under which my subjects lived not only in the British Isles but throughout the Empire. Almost joyfully Mr. Baldwin exclaimed, "He has the secret of youth in the prime of age."

The secret of youth in the prime of age—this exciting ingredient, or elixir, whatever it was that the Prime Minister had detected, sounded fine—exactly the right thing for a King inaugurating his reign in an era that had put the highest premium upon youthful vigour and adaptability.

Anyone who has had much experience in public life eventually learns, and not necessarily with cynicism, that official eulogies should not be taken too literally. And my father's body had hardly been laid to rest before I myself had reason to recall these fine sentiments with some disillusionment.

The day after the funeral, the Archbishop called at Buckingham Palace to pay his respects to my mother. Word was sent down to me that he would like to see me afterwards if it were convenient. I said I would receive him.

Before describing this meeting I shall digress for a moment to explain my feelings toward this strange, brilliant man whose influence, if only remote and passive, was to weigh so heavily against me. The Most Reverend Cosmo Gordon Lang as Primate of all England occupied the most exalted ecclesiastical post in the realm, ranking in fact in the Table of Precedence immediately after the Royal Family and before the Prime Minister. But what counted even more than his high position was his long-standing, intimate friendship with my father. A sombre but impressive figure in black clericals, he had been a frequent guest of my parents as long as I could remember; and he was very close to my father's Private Secretaries. He had undoubted charm of manner; and, when we were all younger, he had made a favourable impression upon us, perhaps because, in the habit of confirmed bachelors, he had made a point of ingratiating himself with the children of his contemporaries. However, as I grew older my opinion of him changed. The mannerisms that had appealed to a youthful mind as being kind and unfeigned were later to give the impression of an over-anxiety to please. When I had occasion to watch him conduct a religious service or hear him speak at a public dinner—an art in which he had few equals—I was to decide that for a prelate he was almost too polished, too worldly. He seemed to me to be rather in the tradition of the medieval church-man, accustomed to the company of princes and statesmen, more interested in the pursuit of prestige and power than the abstractions of the human soul. In fact, while he was at Oxford the Law as a stepping-stone to politics had been his first choice of a career. The Church called him only later. My father's simple but sturdy views upon religion could scarcely have held for long the interest of so subtle a mind. Yet there was no doubting the sincerity of the friendship between them. When, therefore, the Primate glided into my office that afternoon I could not bring myself to greet him with perhaps all the warmth to which he had been accustomed in his dealings with the Sovereign. Dr. Lang opened the conversation by saying that he was sorry that over the years we had failed to come to know each other better. Announcing that he intended to be frank and forthright with me, he said that he supposed that I must be aware that my father had at various times discussed me with him. "It would be a pity, Sir," he said, "if you were to misjudge me in this connexion. Believe me, I appreciate that you are different from your father in your outlook and temperament. I want you to know that whenever the King questioned your conduct I tried in your interest to present it in the most favourable light."

My conduct, I wondered. What was Dr. Lang driving at? No man likes to be told that his character has provided a topic of conversation between his father and a third person. At any rate, the Archbishop's disclosure was certainly an unpropitious note with which to inaugurate the formal relations between a new Sovereign and his Primate. It was unfortunate, but there it was. However, hiding my resentment, I turned the conversation in the direction of my new responsibilities as head of the Church. Even on this subject, I could not seem to impress him; for, when I brought up the names of several clerics whom I knew and liked, his cool almost negative response implied that my acquaintance with Church affairs was too naïve to be pursued. No doubt he was as relieved as I was when the audience came to an end.

There was nothing more. Yet, the air in the room was heavy with portent when the Archbishop left. During the months that followed my mind was to travel back to that conversation many times. Wallis's name had of course not been mentioned, but I knew that the Archbishop intended that I should know that she was the hidden burden of his discourse. He was clearly against our continued friendship. He would undoubtedly muster powerful forces in opposition to my project when I came to press it. That encounter was my first intimation that I might be approaching an irreconcilable conflict.

Until then I had taken my inheritance more or less for granted. With due allowance for the restraints imposed upon me as Prince of Wales I had succeeded, at least to my own satisfaction, and certainly without audible criticism from the public, in so composing my life as to establish a generally harmonious balance between official duty and personal interests that made existence tolerable. But now the Royal Standard flying from the clock tower of St. James's Palace was a signal that my freer days as Heir Apparent were over; and that my life and actions, already dedicated beyond recall to a secret hope, had by the circumstances of my new position become the presumptive property of a vast Imperial community that might seek to obstruct that hope.

What was at stake, of course, was the question of my right to make a life on the Throne in terms of my own philosophy. Afterwards it was to be suggested that my actions were governed by a "craving for private happiness." The inference was that I sought for myself a life within a life, a private life separate from a public one. This was an unhappy, even an unjust imputation. I had always known that the existence of a constitutional Monarch is indivisible in all its aspects. Yet, man himself is always changing; and, while the parts played by Kings tend to become somewhat stereotyped, the sons of Kings do not. Unfortunately for the standards of uniformity that would seem desirable in the line of succession, the Heirs Apparent cannot be stamped out of sheet metal. Certainly it had not been so with me.

I am something of a fatalist. I believe that man is seldom master of his own fate. When great issues are invoked, forces are let loose that are beyond the limited powers of personal decision. There was no way of telling then, at so early a stage, how my private problem could be resolved on the Throne, if it could be resolved at all. But my encounter with the Archbishop, if it had served no other purpose, had at least revealed how wide was the gulf between the outlook he represented and mine. Yet I continued to hope with all my heart that time would produce a solution to my problem. And so I resolutely turned to deal with what one of my equerries, gloomily surveying my crowded calendar, once described as "the King business," of which a Monarch has more than is commonly appreciated.

By long-standing custom the members of the Household of the deceased King remain undisturbed in their posts for six months. This period of grace, by guaranteeing the *status quo* at the outset of the new régime, assures the Monarchy an unhurried continuity.

It also enabled me to take stock of the many obligations now devolving upon me, and gradually to gear my habits to the slower but more sustained tempo of the Palace routine.

Although the Court mourning restricted my public appearances, these first months of my reign saw me continuously occupied. Almost every day found me with one or another of my Ministers. The international situation was steadily deteriorating. Mr. Anthony Eden, who had succeeded Sir Samuel Hoare as Foreign Secretary four weeks before my father's death, appeared in the little Chinese Room to tell me of his hopes of saving the peace of Europe by strengthening the policy of collective security fostered by the League of Nations. Mr. Duff Cooper, Secretary of State for War, described the first feeble beginnings of British rearmament. The Minister of Labour, Mr. Ernest Brown, came to report to me on the slow progress made by the Government to combat the demoralization in the "depressed areas," where youth was in danger of entering into manhood without ever experiencing the rewards of prosperity or knowing the security of work.

Provincial mayors, lieutenant-colonels of the Brigade of Guards, industrialists, Royal Academicians, journalists, and scientists, alternated with ambassadors, cabinet ministers, bishops, maharajas, and colonial governors in the ever-lengthening list of those having business with the King. And then one day early in my reign I was informed out of the blue that I would have to begin to squeeze into my already crowded calendar delegations from the so-called "Privileged Bodies."

"The Privileged Bodies!" I exclaimed. "What are they?"

I was told that they represented the leading corporate elements of the community and that under an ancient right they separately possessed the privilege of equal access to the Monarch for the purpose of presenting loyal addresses upon the occasion of his accession.

"How many of them are there to be received?" I asked.

I was told that there were twenty and that they included such bodies as the University of Oxford, the University of Cambridge, the Society of Friends, the University of Edinburgh, the Corporation of the City of London, the Royal Society, the Jewish Board of Deputies, the Governor and Company of the Bank of England, the Archbishop and Clergy of the Province of Canterbury, and the Royal Academy of Arts.

"But must I receive each delegation separately?" I asked.

"Yes, Sir," said my Private Secretary, "and each group will read its own address."

"Will I have to reply to each one?" I asked.

The answer was in the affirmative. It did not take me long to figure that, unless I put aside my more pressing daily business, it would take at least a month to run through the list. That seemed to me an excessive amount of time and work to devote to what had become a mere ritual, whatever its ancient significance. After a quick glance at my diary, I proposed that these separate identical ceremonies be merged into one, with all these Privileged Bodies coming to the Palace *en masse*, each bearing its own scroll of loyal congratulations. My reply would be addressed to them all. Although the officials of most of these bodies acquiesced with good grace to my proposal, several were to express their disappointment over what one of them described as "His Majesty's unfortunate decision"; and the Lord Mayor of London was placated only after I had agreed to receive him and his Aldermen separately in an ante-room before the ceremony. I have digressed to describe this unimportant incident only to illustrate the extent to which mere formality still, even to-day, claims the time of the King.

It was afterwards suggested that because of my obvious concern for the underprivileged I aspired to be the first radical King. As a matter of fact, had an assessment been made at the time of my private views on various issues of the day, in the manner of public-opinion polls, it would have revealed, I am sure, what would have been classified as a distinctly conservative outlook.

I believed, among other things, in private enterprise, a strong Navy, the long week-end, a balanced budget, the gold standard, and close relations with the United States. At the same time, while regarding with misgivings the continued encroachments by governments upon private prerogative, I had become convinced that it was their duty to intervene in the economic system whenever the failure of the free play of the market brought distress to the working classes or impeded the rational development of housing. And at the risk of inviting a shower of brickbats, I must admit that I was not a supporter of the League of Nations. It was not that I was opposed to the dream of a universal society wherein mankind should learn to dwell in amity. On the contrary, as a man who knew the horrors of war, I shared that dream. But as a realist with some knowledge of international politics I could not help but look upon it as a will-o'-the-wisp, in pursuit of which my country might foolishly neglect the strength that had been its sure recourse in the past against aggression. In spite of Hitler's phenomenal sway over the German masses, their Führer struck me as a somewhat ridiculous figure, with his theatrical posturings and his bombastic pretensions. Nevertheless, with my pre-war experiences in Germany I admired the people, sympathized with many of their aspirations, and continued to hope that their solid virtues would overcome their terrifying ambitions and vanities and restore them to the ways of good society. At the same time I was all for Mr. Winston Churchill in his campaign to rearm Britain, although I was against anything, including the controversial imposition of sanctions, that might tend to throw the Italy of Mussolini into the arms of Hitler.

These were scarcely the views of a radical. It might be said that I did not set quite so much store by the dicta of officials merely because of the offices they held as had been the wont of Monarchs in the past. This is not to say that I was in any way indifferent to all that this powerful and interwoven hierarchy stood for. But in the course of a life lived in large measure outside the more restricted confines bounded by the Court Circular, I had discovered that good and stimulating company was also to be found elsewhere. And having decided that ready access to contrasting minds had been indispensable to my existence as Prince of Wales and to whatever mental development I might claim, I did not intend, as King, to withdraw into the tight, possessive world of officialdom from which, first at Oxford, and still more during the First World War, I had begun to escape.

It was even said that I never wanted to be King at all. No doubt as I had grown older, maturing as I had in the world of action, it is entirely possible that, had the choice been left to me, I might not have consciously chosen the Throne as the most desirable goal of all my aspirations. But not to wish to be King was something else. Only my death or some precipitous action on my part could have prevented my becoming King when my father died. Now that he was dead I *was* the King. And what was more, I wanted to be a successful King, though a King in a modern way.

I was, after all, the first King of the twentieth century who had not spent at least half his life under the strict authority of Queen Victoria. My father was already halfway through his life-span when his grandmother died; and by the gravity of his temperament it was to her, rather than to the livelier example of his own father, that he looked for a model of the Sovereign's deportment. His Court retained a Victorian flavour to the end; and I had come to look upon it as at least sexagenarian in composition and outlook.

Whereas my great-grandmother took the Monarchy back into the tradition of the masterful executive, and my grandfather associated it with brilliant successes in the field of foreign diplomacy, my father conducted it with skill and sureness into "the realm of clear and unambiguous constitutional procedure." Because the high office I inherited had been moulded and altered to greater or less degree under the influence of their personalities, and most recently by my father's, I feel bound to set forth certain reflections of my own, in order to explain what I hoped to be able to do, and to set forth the difficulties as I assessed them at the time.

It has always seemed to me that one of my father's great contributions to monarchical practice was the manner in which, without apparent design, he managed to resolve the internal contradiction of Monarchy in the twentieth century that requires it to be remote from, yet at the same time to personify the aspirations of, the people. It must appear aloof and distant in order to sustain the illusion of a Monarch who, shunning faction, stands above politics and the more mundane allegiances. At the same time, it must appear to share intimately the ideals of the multitude, whose affection and loyalty provide the broad base of constitutional Monarchy. My father, with the instinctive genius of the simple man, found the means of squaring the apparent circle within the resources of his own character. By the force of his own authentic example—the King himself in the rôle of the bearded paterfamilias, his devoted and queenly wife, their four grown sons and a daughter, not to mention the rising generation of grandchildren—he transformed the Crown as personified by the Royal Family into a model of the traditional family virtues, a model that was all the more genuine for its suspected but inconspicuous flaws. The King, as the dutiful father, became the living symbol not only of the nation, but also of the Empire, the last link holding together these diversified and scattered communities.

My father was greatly beloved. And the undoubted popularity of my brother Bertie, whose life is so much like that which my father led, suggests that irrespective of whatever other forms the Monarchy might have taken under the impress of a different personality, the British people are rightly pleased with his faithful carrying on of my father's ways. But any chance of my presenting myself to my subjects in this admired and ready-made rôle of King as family man was unfortunately made impracticable, not to say impossible, by the simple fact of my being a bachelor.

Nevertheless, despite this obvious handicap, I began my reign in good heart and with high aspirations. Having already enjoyed some success in adapting the rôle of Prince of Wales to the "embassy of Empire," I had reason to hope that the same energy, and the same quality of mind would find useful employment in discharging the duties of King.

At forty-one I had seen about as much of life as my position had allowed. To be sure, a labouring man or an economist might have argued that much that was important had remained outside my experience. Nevertheless, I believe that I can claim without bombast that no Heir Apparent had travelled so far as I had or been thrown in with so many different kinds of people under such violently contrasting conditions. The First World War had made it possible for me to share an unparalleled human experience with all manner of men. I had visited practically all the important countries of the world, except Soviet Russia, and many of the smaller ones. I had seen the good and the bad in the Empire, its triumphs and its failures. Princely progresses, diplomatic and commercial missions, not to mention the continuous travelling that I did on my own account, had taken me again and again into realms previously unknown to Royalty.

Ever since I first started travelling in the public interest after the war I had become fascinated by commerce. I knew about raw materials—where they came from, how they were produced and later processed industrially for the use of mankind. I enjoyed the company of business men. I had seen the workers at their jobs and in their homes; I had some idea of what was in their minds. No other King can have inspected so many factories, gone down so many mines, tramped so many shipyards, or followed so many assembly lines as I had. Of all the titles ever applied to me, hereditary or complimentary, the ones that gave me the most private satisfaction were the newspaper sobriquets acknowledging these services—"Britain's First Ambassador" and "Britain's Best Salesman."

One way or another the people had contributed a great deal towards my preparation for kingship. It was my hope to be able to repay them by concentrating upon that which I knew best: by reminding them in the limited ways open to me of their Imperial stake in world trade and by throwing the prestige and glamour of the Crown's solicitude around the workaday matters of commerce.

However, contrary to a belief held by some, I brought to the Throne no ambitious blueprints for reform—no Royal counterparts of the Five-Year Plan. I had no desire to go down in history as Edward the Reformer. Edward the Innovator—that might have been more to the point. Yet I had no notion of tinkering with the fundamental rules of Monarchy, nor of upsetting the proud traditions of the Court. In truth, all that I ever had in mind was to throw open the windows a little and to let into the venerable institution some of the fresh air that I had become accustomed to breathe as Prince of Wales. My modest ambition was to broaden the base of the Monarchy a little more: to make it a little more responsive to the changed circumstances of my times.

Actually only two innovations in the Royal Establishment are chargeable to me. To supplement the traditional forms of Royal transportation supplied by the King's horses and the King's motorcars under the Master of the Horse's department I created a "King's Flight," consisting of my own aeroplane under the direction of my personal pilot, Wing-Commander (now Air-Commodore) Edward H. Fielden, to whom was give the romantic appellation, "Captain of the King's Flight." About the same time I dispensed with the requirement that the Yeomen of the Guard should grow beards in a Tudor style. Recruitment in the Beefeaters had fallen off. Inquiry had revealed that long-service retired soldiers who would otherwise have joined had been discouraged by their wives' objections to their growing whiskers. In response to an appeal from the Captain of this bodyguard, I made the wearing of beards by the Yeomen optional; and the recruiting problem disappeared.

However, I was to discover that, although according to the familiar axiom the King can do no wrong, immunity clothes him only so long as he stays prudently within the stock rôle. Even so innocent and logical an action as my turning back the clocks at Sandringham to Greenwich time produced a shaking of old heads and a muttering in the beards over my presumption in tampering with an old family idiosyncrasy. But it was the experience with an umbrella that really awakened me to the risks that were inherent in even the most innocent divergences from kingly practice.

There being no Prince of Wales, I continued as King to administer the Duchy of Cornwall estates. Early in my reign I called a meeting of the Duchy Council. The afternoon was rainy; but, since it was only a two-minute walk from the Palace to the Duchy offices, I decided not to order the Daimler but to walk instead. So, calling for my bowler hat and umbrella, and accompanied by an old member of my staff, Admiral Sir Lionel Halsey, similarly equipped, I sallied forth. And that for me would have been the end of the episode, but for the chance that a newspaper photographer who had stationed himself at the door of 10 Buckingham Gate for a routine picture of the King disembarking from the

Royal motor-car happened to spot the Admiral and me as we came striding across the street.

What he saw was a scene that must have been repeated ten thousand times that day in London—two men in City clothes, one with a brief-case, the other with upturned collar, striding along under umbrellas on their way to a business appointment. But because one of the two men was the King, the picture was widely published and its informality appeared to please many of my subjects. However, as Wallis was to discover, there was at least one whom it failed to please.

At a dinner party in London a few days later she found herself placed beside a prominent Member of Parliament and a confidant of the Prime Minister. Halfway through dinner this man turned to her and said gravely, "I am told that you know the King." Her answer that she did encouraged him to bring up a matter over which he had obviously been brooding. "Did you see that newspaper photograph of His Majesty walking from the Palace in the rain?" Wallis had of course seen it and was about to remark that she had thought it natural and amusing when her neighbour exclaimed with a visible shudder, "That umbrella! Since you know the King, won't you ask him to be more careful in the future as to how he is photographed?" His undoubted disapproval took her aback. After all, what could be the harm in the King's using an umbrella? Was it not as useful and characteristic a convenience to a Briton as a ten-gallon hat is to a Texan? However, the Member seemed so perturbed that she suppressed a temptation to make light of the matter. Instead she countered by suggesting that it would be presumptuous of her, an American, to advise the King of England upon a point of behaviour. The man seemed not to hear. "The Monarchy must remain aloof and above the commonplace. We can't have the King doing this kind of thing. He has the Daimler."

But I had been criticized before. These petty pinpricks were not going to ruffle my equanimity. Besides, no man worth his salt, least of all a King, can expect to be popular with everybody. Still, however solidly I may have stood with the mass of the people, I was soberly aware that my popularity was not quite so complete as a superficial reading of the Press and the utterances of public men might have led me to believe. So far as I could tell there was no actual animosity or hostility. It was something in the air—the first nip that presages an autumn frost—and I tried to explain it to myself this way: It is only natural that those who have participated in and influenced the ways of one reign are apt to regard the advent of another with some suspicion. And human nature is understandably loath to yield privilege and influence easily. Having known some of the members of my father's Household all my life, I was far too conscious of their integrity and rectitude to suppose that merely selfish considerations controlled their thinking towards me. But they had been part of a régime that had held sway for a quarter of a century. They were accustomed to a Monarch of their own generation; and those who had known me since childhood continued to look upon me, even at forty-one, as somewhat independent and perhaps even a trifle unconventional. It had been quite all right for me as Prince of Wales to be gay and dashing and even original in my approach to various undertakings. But were these same characteristics desirable in a King? In short, might I not one day upset the Royal apple-cart?

And this air of discountenance I suspected went beyond the confines of the Court. It extended into Whitehall and through certain sections of society whose influence throughout the country was, at least in my day, dominant. Many of these people were my friends; I was a product of their own environment; they were admirable people; and, because many of them could point to a record of generations in the service of the Crown, they instinctively regarded the Monarchy—"the fountain of honour"— as their own particular trust. And my father's slowly turning wheel of habit, leading him year after year in unchanging rotation from one Royal residence to another and from one Royal pursuit to another, had provided a self-repeating pattern of kingly life by which they and indeed the whole nation could mark the seasons.

They were accustomed to a King who went to church every Sunday; who unless some State emergency or serious illness interfered never missed the Two Thousand Guineas or Cowes Regatta; who would be on the grouse moors every August 12; and who on the rare occasions that he dined out graced with his presence only the tables of noble friends. But this new young Monarch was different. While he worked overtime in so far as his duties were concerned, August would probably find him playing golf at

Biarritz or swimming off Eden Roc, or stooking wheat on his ranch in Canada. He had abandoned hunting for the less virile pursuit of gardening. He preferred golf to yacht racing, and in place of the stereotyped shooting parties still in vogue for those who could afford them, he would be off stalking chamois in the Tyrol, or shooting partridges as a guest of Regent Horthy of Hungary. His free evenings were more likely to be spent *en petit comité* with a few intimates or at the Embassy Club than in the great houses or salons of London. And so, because he had to some extent departed from what had come to be regarded as the King's accustomed mode of life, many of the more conservative had begun to shake their heads.

My first few weeks on the Throne therefore supplied me with a good deal to think about. It became increasingly plain to me, as I reflected upon my new circumstances, that however wholeheartedly I might adapt myself to the familiar outward pattern of kingship—not merely with regard to the discharge of the formal State duties, but equally in the carrying out of the personal pursuits, the race-horse breeding, the yacht racing, the stamp collecting, and the continuation of the sporting amenities of Sandringham and Balmoral—I could never expect wholly to satisfy the expectations of those for whom the rigid modes of my father's era had come to exemplify the only admissible standard for a King.

In the clash that presently followed, some professed to see the workings of fate. But the fault lay not in my stars but in my genes. I was what I was—a man with a profound faith in God and an ingrained sense of duty. But I was also acutely conscious of the changes working in the times, and I was eager to respond to them as I had always done. And it therefore seemed important that the nation should know that even though I had become King my philosophy had not changed.

An opportunity presented itself when on Sunday, March 1, Saint David's Day, I broadcast for the first time as King to the people of the British Empire. Whenever a Sovereign makes an official speech it is the function of the Secretary of State for Home Affairs to make sure that he says nothing that might conflict with the policy of the Government. The Home Office therefore submitted a draft—a noble example of Whitehall rhetoric—that I painstakingly rewrote in my own simple style.

The broadcast was to be for the most part a heartfelt tribute to my father's long reign, a reminder of his services to the Empire, and an expression of my desire to carry on his work. But I decided to close with a statement of my own. This I embodied in a final paragraph that, after some thought, I decided not to include in the text sent back to the Home Office. There was no question of the omitted paragraph possibly embarrassing my Ministers, for the content could not have been further removed from politics. I only wanted that part of my speech to be purely personal. This is what it was: "I am better known to you as Prince of Wales—as a man who, during the war and since, has had the opportunity of getting to know the people of nearly every country of the world, under all conditions and circumstances. And, although I now speak to you as King, I am still that same man who has had that experience and whose constant effort it will be to continue to promote the well-being of his fellow men. . . ."

CHAPTER XVII

THE FIRST SIX MONTHS OF
MY REIGN

THAT simple statement was meant to give notice that I did not intend to allow my activities as Monarch to be impaired by much that had become antiquated, or that my way of life should be bound by a social outlook that to me and others had begun to lose touch with reality. In my sensitive state of mind I was no doubt prone to impute to my words a sense that was not fully comprehended by the nation, which at that time could hardly have been aware of the tensions surrounding me as King. But I felt better for having said what I said, believing that it would at least help to prepare the ground for what might eventually follow. The public response to the broadcast was all that I could have desired. These first encouraging echoes, however, were almost immediately drowned in the uproar that developed a week later in consequence of the dramatic reoccupation of the Rhineland by troops under the orders of the German Führer, Adolf Hitler. The reverberations of that defiant gesture dominated for the moment all thought, driving from the foreground of my mind the question of my personal problem.

For a little while war seemed very close. London bustled with European statesmen, and I talked with most of them. One after the other they entered the little Chinese Room to give me their separate interpretation of the drama that had begun. Some of my visitors advocated a policy of standing up to Germany; others wanted my Government to pursue the opposite course. While I saw the pros and cons of both courses of action, I must confess that I was not convinced that either would lead to a peaceful solution. Intuitively I felt that another great war in Europe was all too probable; and I saw but too clearly that it could only bring

286

needless human suffering and a resurgent Bolshevism pouring into the vacuum of a ravaged and exhausted continent.

Then the crisis over the Rhineland ebbed. It was as if a great wave had swept over human affairs, momentarily inundating the day's wonted concerns, and then had passed on. Yet that convulsive movement of the Germans had disclosed the power of the forces stirring in Central Europe; and I turned back to my routine work gravely troubled in spirit.

Even among people whose ideas of a modern Monarch go beyond the story-book picture there still persists a suspicion that a King is, on the whole, an unusually fortunate mortal, with plenty of courtiers to dance attendance upon him, no money troubles, no serious decisions to make, a large choice of residences in which to enjoy the passing seasons—in short, a man with few cares. Having in recent years moved within closer range of the stresses and strains that rule the fiercely competitive world outside the hereditary system, I am prepared to concede that the picture possesses a certain modicum of truth. But the ceremonial façade that provides the public with a romantic illusion of the higher satisfactions of kingship actually disguises an occupation of considerable drudgery.

This fact was hardly a discovery for me. From long observation of my father's activities, I knew only too well what I was in for. The picture of him "doing his boxes," to use his own phrase, had long represented for me the relentless grind of the King's daily routine.

There were Foreign Office despatches and telegrams to be studied, as well as Colonial Office surveys and reports concerning relations in all parts of the globe. And when the Cabinet met there would come to me next day the secret minutes of the meeting locked in a special box, of which, outside the Cabinet, only my Private Secretary and I had keys. I also had to approve and sign the appointments of Ambassadors and ministers in the Foreign Service, of Governors-General to the Dominions and Governors to the Colonies, of bishops, of clergy to Crown livings, the commissions for officers in the armed forces, and warrants conferring honours in the various orders of Knighthood.

This interminable amount of desk work was all the more taxing for me because, if the truth must be known, I have never had much zest for paper work. Much more to my taste was what I called my "field work"—the business of inspecting and visiting the diverse organizations and undertakings that claimed the interest and encouragement of the King. These sorties took me away from the Palace and out into my realm, for many varied purposes.

For example, since the Sovereign's associations with the armed forces of the Crown are of a somewhat personal nature, I was anxious to continue the close touch with them that was one of the traditions of the Monarchy. On his accession the King automatically becomes Admiral of the Fleet, Field-Marshal, and Marshal of the Royal Air Force, regardless of his previous naval or military service. These honours naturally fell to me. And one of the most affecting incidents of my reign came when my Uncle Arthur brought to the Palace the other ageing Field-Marshals, among them Lord Cavan, to present to me my baton.

As titular head of the Royal Navy I went to Portsmouth to visit the Naval and Marine establishments. By air I toured a number of stations of the Royal Air Force. As the guest of Major-General Lord Gort, then the Commandant, I dined with the students of the Staff College at Camberley, where my brother Harry was completing a two-year course. Being also Colonel-in-Chief of each of the seven regiments of Household Troops, I made it my business during the first months of my reign to inspect the units that were on home service in their barracks in London, Windsor, and Aldershot.

I tramped what seemed to be miles of exhibits at the British Industries Fair; and, attended by the Archbishop of Canterbury, distributed the King's Maundy in Westminster Abbey. Then there was Chelsea Flower Show, and an agreeable forenoon in Windsor Great Park, which I toured in the company of a group of eminent arboriculturists, not so much as King, but rather as the amateur gardener of The Fort, who hoped that his own ideas would not clash too much with theirs. As I was still responsible for the administration of the Duchy of Cornwall, I followed my habit of touring some of the properties in the spring.

The completion of the 81,000-ton liner *Queen Mary* was an important item in the public events of 1936; eighteen months earlier I had seen my mother launch the great ship from John Brown's yard on the Clyde. Early in March, while the vessel was undergoing her final fitting-out before being delivered to the Cunard White Star Line for service on the North Atlantic run, I travelled to Glasgow with the object of calling the world's attention to this stupendous product of British industrial skill. Two and a half months later I visited her again at Southampton. She was to sail on her maiden voyage to New York on May 26, the birthday of Queen Mary, who the day before in my presence had presented the vessel with a silken replica of her own Standard.

Compared to the routine of men of other callings, these excursions might seem to form a disconnected and aimless pattern. Yet they are the means by which the Sovereign reminds his people of their great, continuing institutions. Besides, they were instructive and diverting for me, providing welcome breaks in the monotony of Palace days. But the King's business covers a great deal more territory than the daily items reported in the Court Circular suggest. The King himself, apart from his constitutional functions, is quite a busy executive as well. In a general sense he is ultimately responsible for maintaining all the panoply of Monarchy in its various expressions—for the appointment of his own considerable Household, for the interior economy of the Palaces in and outside London, as well as for the management of the two private Royal estates, Sandringham and Balmoral. In short, he is charged with the direction of the entire Royal Establishment and all its adjuncts.

In common with most cherished British institutions, the Royal Establishment is a mixture of ancient and modern usage—a unique and more or less self-contained community in which an aeroplane and a garage full of the latest motor-cars exist in congenial juxtaposition with Plantagenet ritual, Tudor costumes, and Victorian etiquette. Monarchs come and go, but the apparatus of the Monarchy goes on for ever, adapting itself slowly to the changing times, yet preserving within its own anachronisms the sense of continuity that is so marked a feature of our national life.

The cost of this Establishment is borne by moneys voted by Parliament under the Civil List Act, which provides for the support of "the honour and dignity of the Crown and the Royal Family." In early times the King's income was identical with the national revenues, except as regards defence; i.e., the King paid for the civil portion of the Government as distinct from military expenditure. Hence the term, Civil List. These expenses were defrayed from the revenues of Crown Lands and other hereditary sources.

However, as the Government services increased with the growth of population, the King's resources were subjected to an ever-increasing strain; and the recurring deficits were covered by Parliamentary grants. Therefore, on the accession of George III in 1760, Parliament took a tighter grip than ever on the Royal purse. In return for a fixed Civil List of £800,000 the King surrendered his claim upon the revenues of Crown Lands in England and Wales and later Ireland, while still holding the Crown Lands in Scotland. Finally William IV had to part with most of the Scottish Crown Lands. By Queen Victoria's time the Crown had divested itself of responsibility for all Government services, and Parliament had instituted the practice of supporting the Monarchy by means of a fixed annual payment under the Civil List Act.

In the constitutional sense the Civil List might be regarded as something of a bargain on Parliament's part in return for the relinquishment by the King of the hereditary revenues of Crown Lands. Indeed, one of my first acts after my accession in 1936 was to send a message to Parliament formally surrendering to the State these hereditary revenues, and placing myself, as the phrase goes, "at the disposal of the House of Commons with regard to the Civil List." On the whole, Parliament has done well under the bargain; for, whereas the Civil List of 1936 paid the Sovereign only £410,000, the Crown Lands yielded the Treasury £1,350,000, after paying all costs of administration.

By law a new Civil List must be voted within six months after the demise of the Crown, and the sum that is then fixed by Parliament becomes the new King's annual income for the duration of his reign. A few weeks after my accession, therefore, the Chancellor of the Exchequer, Mr. Neville Chamberlain, sought an audience to inquire as to my probable financial requirements, in the light of the circumstance of my being a bachelor and the changed conditions since the old Civil List had been voted a quarter of a century before. However, it is not to be assumed that the Monarch's drafts upon the Treasury are settled privately with the Chancellor of the Exchequer. A Select Committee of twenty-one—drawn from all parties in the House of Commons, including such diversified personalities as the Prime Minister, Mr. Baldwin; the Conservative statesman, Mr. Winston Churchill; the Liberal leader, Mr. Lloyd George; and the Socialist, Mr. Clement Attlee —was appointed to consider my message and, in consultation with the Keeper of the Privy Purse, to review the expenses of the Royal Establishment. An annual sum of £410,000 was agreed upon by the committee and in due course passed by Parliament without serious challenge.

As few people are familiar with the operation of the Civil List, I propose to devote a little space to explaining it. There are actually four classes of expenditure. The first is the Privy Purse, which covers the personal outlay of the Sovereign. It might be described as the King's drawing account and is disbursed by the Keeper of the Privy Purse. It pays for the upkeep of the estates of Sandringham and Balmoral, the King's stud and racing stable, and all his private expenses, including many subscriptions and donations to charity. There being no longer a Duke of Cornwall, the amount of the Duchy revenue that had previously provided my income as Prince of Wales was now diverted to finance my Privy Purse as King, thus effecting a considerable saving to the Treasury.

The three remaining classes of expenditure under the Civil List are of a less personal nature, being to a large extent devoted to maintaining the State and administrative side of the Establishment. These accounts, which represent the major part of the Monarch's income, are audited by the Treasury and disbursed by the Keeper of the Privy Purse in his capacity as Treasurer to the King. The salaries of the King's Household from the Lord Chamberlain's down to the coal porters' are paid out of one class.

Paid for under another class of the Civil List is the maintenance of the Household—the King's table, the Palace furnishings, the liveries of the indoor and outdoor servants, the procurement and upkeep of the horses, coaches, and motor-cars in the Royal Mews, and the wages of the charwomen, known in the Palace terminology as the "daily women."

The last class includes Royal Bounty and Alms, which are distributed through the Royal Almonry in the form of Maundy Money and other gifts. For instance, every year one hundred poor people chosen by their parishes receive ten shillings from the King as a Christmas gift. It is also the custom for the King to recognize the parents of triplets born within his realm by the payment of £3 in each instance from his Privy Purse.

While the amount of money voted by Parliament for the Civil List may seem ample, it is a fact that in contrast with other agencies of Government, the cost of the Royal Establishment, despite greatly increased wages and the rising cost of material and services, has remained more or less stationary since the turn of the century. Only by economizing in his personal expenses has the King been able to meet his public liabilities without asking Parliament for additional funds. When, therefore, I was confronted with the problem of further retrenchment I initiated a business-like survey of the entire Royal Establishment with a view to eliminating certain redundant or wasteful offices and functions that were consuming too great a proportion of the Civil List. However, before intruding upon the long-established workings of the Court and the Palace machinery I decided to begin with my private commitments under the Privy Purse.

There my inquiring gaze fell upon the Sandringham accounts, and the figures startled me. To my father it had always been "dear Sandringham," and his love for it had defied the encroachments of time. There, in remote Norfolk by the Wash, his private war with the twentieth century had ended in almost complete repulse of the latter. Sandringham had been allowed to suffer but few changes since my grandparents' days; in his affection for the place my father had seen to that. No expense had been spared to maintain Sandringham as a model property; but that praise-worthy reputation had been preserved only by dipping into the Privy Purse with a prodigality that was the wonder of my father's neighbours. And game birds for the King and his guests to shoot were still being raised on a scale that could hardly have been surpassed in the country.

Knowing that I would inherit this voracious "white elephant" and that in the event of my death Bertie might conceivably have to administer it, he and I had often discussed privately between ourselves just how we should be able to run it after my father died. We had concluded that certain retrenchments were desirable and possible, and that they could be effected without profaning the tradition of Royal abundance. Besides, much as I had loved the place in my boyhood, I had by this time ceased to regard it in quite the same way. The Fort had become for me a spiritual "Sandringham." I therefore asked Bertie to spend a week or two in Norfolk and to advise me how the running expenses could be most effectively reduced. He took with him a mutual friend, Lord Radnor, the Lord Warden of the Stannaries of the Duchy of Cornwall and also a large and successful landowner. The two of them devoted a fortnight to surveying the estate and produced an excellent report.

But I was soon to find that any tampering with tradition is fraught with trouble. The King, more than most men, is a prisoner of the past. The resistance to any move he may make towards the most trifling change is illustrated by an encounter between me and the Deputy Master of the Mint in the matter of the design of the new coinage to be used for my reign.

British coins and postage stamps bear the profile likeness of the reigning Sovereign. It is the practice, whenever a new Monarch ascends the throne, for the Royal Mint and the General Post Office to invite artists to submit designs in competition for the new coins and stamps. When, therefore, the Deputy Master of the Mint, Sir Robert Johnson, asked if I would pose at the Palace for the two artists whose designs had been accepted, I agreed to do so. On the appointed day Sir Robert appeared with the artists. Examining their drawings, I was interested to observe that all showed the right side of my face. Long experience in public life had taught me that the first rule of good public relations is to present oneself whenever possible in the most favourable light. After having had to contemplate thousands of pictures of myself in the Press I had come to the conclusion—and not merely out of vanity—that my left profile was better than the right. I therefore asked the artists why they had both chosen to draw the right side, explaining at the same time my own reasons for preferring the left. The answer was that the Mint had so directed them. However, after carefully scrutinizing my face, they agreed that the æsthetic appearance of the new coins would undoubtedly be improved if the other side were shown. At this point the Deputy Master of the Mint, who until then had kept his silence, intervened in the discussion.

Clearing his throat, Sir Robert Johnson explained that the direction in which the King's head was turned on the coins and stamps had nothing to do with æsthetics. It was simply a long-standing custom to reverse the profile of the Sovereign with the advent of each new reign. "Your grandfather, King Edward VII, looked to the right, Sir," said the Deputy Master, "and his late Majesty your father looked to the left."

"Ah," I interposed, "so now it is my turn to look to the right."

Sir Robert was visibly distressed and mortified at finding himself at odds with the King. Hoping to lift the discussion to a lighter plane, I added, "Now I see. It is just as if the Sovereigns of England were following a perpetual tennis-game from the side lines."

But the hoped-for smile of agreement failed to appear; the Deputy Master stood his ground. I then assured him that, while I had no desire to upset tradition, there was logic in my argument; and I therefore asked him to direct the artists to prepare new drawings. "After all," I concluded, "it is *my* face that is to be used. Isn't it only reasonable that I should at least have the privilege of deciding which side is to be put on public display?"

The Deputy Master, clearly torn between a sincere desire to placate the King and still serve numismatic tradition, promised to do whatever he could and retired.

A few days later the artists were back at the Palace with new sketches. My head, I noted, still faced in the same direction as before, but an ingenious attempt had been made to meet my desires by transferring to the right side of my face the features of the left. Surveying that anatomical fabrication, I decided that, if blind allegiance to form could induce the Royal Mint to take such licence with the King's countenance, it would be better to dispense with form entirely. Finally I told Sir Robert politely but firmly that my instructions were to be followed. He yielded. The pundits of the G.P.O., who had no doubt been following the duel between the King and the Deputy Master of the Mint, must have been impressed by my determination. For, when the essays of the new stamps were submitted to me, they showed the Monarch facing, I am glad to say, to the left. In this form they were printed and issued. There never were any coins.

However, I should not like to leave the impression that these occasional brushes with officialdom were in themselves significant or that I took them seriously. Perhaps they only represented an occasional tilting at the creaking windmills of custom. Where custom and ceremonial were truly interwoven with the continuing realities of our national life, I eagerly and humbly lent myself to them, believing that here was something important for a King to uphold.

In my dealings with my Ministers I was more than once drawn into situations that called for tact, human understanding, and even a sense of humour. A painful incident occurred in May, when one of the members of the Cabinet, Mr. J. H. Thomas, the Secretary of State for the Colonies, was so unfortunate as to become involved in a public scandal. It was just one of those distressing episodes from which politics the world over are not entirely free. Jim Thomas was accused of having disclosed to several cronies details of the 1936 Budget before the Chancellor of the Exchequer had presented it to Parliament. In the end he had to resign from the Cabinet and the House of Commons, bringing to an end a long public career that had carried him to the Cabinet from a humble beginning as engine-driver.

Custom required that he should deliver up to the King his seal of office, and the audience in the Palace was all the more embarrassing to both of us because he had long enjoyed my father's confidence. In fact I knew that, in addition to their conventional relations as King and Minister of State, my father took occasional advantage of his friend's intimate knowledge of the racecourse to consult him as to what horses to back. Jim Thomas was in obvious distress as he entered the Chinese Room. He dropped with a bang on my desk the box containing his seal of office. "It's all a bloody conspiracy," he cried, sinking into an empty chair. I tried unsuccessfully to comfort him. As he left the room in tears, he paused to say a wonderful thing: "Thank God your old Dad is not alive to see this." A few days later when I was commiserating with Mr. Ramsay MacDonald on the misfortune that had befallen his old colleague of the Labour Party, the former Prime Minister threw up his hands and exclaimed in his rich Highland brogue, "Poor old Jim. There goes the only member of the Cabinet with whom I could be gloriously indiscreet."

Another audience with one of my Ministers forced me into a personal decision in connexion with foreign affairs. Early in May, the Italians entered Addis Ababa and completed their conquest of Ethiopia. The luckless Emperor Haile Selassie, evading Marshal Badoglio's legions, had meanwhile fled to Djibuti in French Somaliland on the Red Sea, whence a British light cruiser had transported him and his family to safety. The collapse of Ethiopian resistance having proclaimed the failure of the League of Nations' policy of sanctions against Italy, there was some speculation as to what the British Government's attitude towards the fleeing potentate would be. When, therefore, the Negus eventually turned up in London, Il Duce and the rest of the world were in effect given notice that Britain did not propose to abandon Haile Selassie in his exile. In the course of an audience with me a few days after the Emperor's arrival, the Foreign Secretary, Mr. Anthony Eden, advanced the suggestion that it would be a popular gesture on my part were I to receive the Negus at the Palace. "Popular with whom?" I asked; "certainly not with the Italians." Sorry as I was for the Ethiopians, I nevertheless maintained that far from serving the cause of peace, my action in receiving the Negus might well give unnecessary offence to Mussolini and drive him closer to Hitler. Mr. Eden, though disappointed, did not insist. But rather than have him go away completely empty-handed, I agreed that it would be proper for my brother Harry, who had represented my father at Haile Selassie's coronation in Addis Ababa six years before, to call upon him at his hotel.

In the perspective of recent history, some might think that my attitude lacked magnanimity. Yet, I can take some comfort from the fact that I was by no means alone in my quandary. The Prime Minister himself was also dubious whether it would be expedient for him to meet the exiled Abyssinian ruler, as was shown by an extraordinary incident, no doubt more deserving of the pen of Lewis Carroll than of mine. However, I shall endeavour briefly to describe it, as a revealing sidelight upon the Ethiopian drama.

One fine June afternoon, Mr. Baldwin was on the terrace of the House of Commons having tea with one of his colleagues. Looking up, he perceived in the distance a small group of sightseers, in the midst of whom was a diminutive, dusky figure in a long cape and a strange hat. Conducted tours of the Houses of Parliament for visitors from all over the world had accustomed the M.P.'s to the almost daily spectacle of tourists in native costumes of all descriptions. But, as this group advanced slowly towards the table where Mr. Baldwin was sitting, an intuitive sense of risk made him inquire of one of the waiters who the visitors were. "Haile Selassie, the Emperor of Ethiopia, and some Ethiopians, Sir," he was told. The Prime Minister gave a start. The path for a normal dignified exit being cut off by the oncoming party, his only apparent alternative to a meeting with the Negus was to leap on to the parapet of the terrace and dive into the Thames or to duck around the tables hiding his face with his hands. This latter course he chose, and by a circuitous route eventually gained the sanctuary of his office. The story adds that he locked the door.

Behind all this lay an important, if concealed, difference of opinion between my Ministers and me regarding Italy. They had embarked upon a futile policy of coercing Mussolini, which had utterly failed of its purpose and was only forcing him into ever-closer relations with Hitler. While I would be the first to con-demn aggression and to advocate any forceful measures that would put it down, I could see no point in indulging in half-measures that could not succeed. It was more important in my eyes at this stage to gain an ally than to score debating victories in the tottering League of Nations.

By and large, the carrying out of my kingly duties that spring and early summer proceeded smoothly. Only two *contretemps* occurred. The first, a novel experience for me, provided a sensa-tional sequel to a presentation of colours by me to some battalions of Foot Guards. The other episode had to do with a Palace garden party that was interrupted by an inadvertent shower. I shall describe these two incidents, not because either was in any way important, but only because each is an example of the hazards of kingship.

The battalions of the Guards Regiments, like all battalions of infantry save the Rifle Regiments, have two colours: the King's colour, a crimson silken flag; and the Regimental colour, a silk Union Jack—both richly embroidered, one with the Royal cipher and the other with the regiment's battle honours. As colours wear out, the War Office issues new ones at prescribed periods, and those for the Guards are presented ceremonially by the Sovereign.

It so happened that in 1936 the battalions of the three senior regiments, the Grenadier Guards, the Coldstream Guards, and the Scots Guards, were all due for new colours. The 2nd Battalion Grenadiers and the 1st Battalion Scots Guards were stationed in Egypt. The six battalions on home service were paraded in Hyde Park in the forenoon of July 16, and I rode out from the Palace to make the presentations. It was one of those perfect English days, sunny and warm. The rigid ranks of Guardsmen in scarlet tunics and bearskin caps, their bayonets flashing in the sun, made a bright splash of colour against the green trees. I have always been proud of being a Guardsman; and, although I had been through the ceremony many times and this one deviated in no detail from the drill as laid down in standing orders of the Brigade of Guards, I was nevertheless deeply stirred. After the battalions had formed three sides of a square, I dismounted and took my place on a low platform. The colours were consecrated by Army chaplains; on bended knee the ensigns detailed to carry them received each pair in turn from my hands. And I then addressed the troops with a short speech that I had asked Mr. Winston Churchill to read and embellish.

At the close of the ceremony I remounted my horse and led the battalions away through the Park. Major-General Sergison-Brooke, the General Officer Commanding the London District —known to his friends as "Boy"—rode on my right; and Bertie, as Colonel of the Scots Guards, was on my left. Just as we emerged from the Arch at the top of Constitution Hill, I noticed a slight commotion in the crowd on my left. A man pushed himself through the police line, and an instant later something bright and metallic flew through the air. It was well aimed for it struck the pavement close by me, skidding first under my horse, then under the General's.

For one icy moment I braced myself for a blast that never came. There was a convulsive stir in the crowd as several policemen threw themselves upon the man. General Sergison-Brooke, himself a man without fear, threw an anxious look in my direction. Turning to him, I said, " 'Boy,' I don't know what that thing was; but, if it had gone off, it would have made a nasty mess of us." The General gave a smile of relief, and we rode on as if nothing had happened. At the Palace I took the salute of the battalions. Afterwards in the courtyard, when the troops had passed, I was informed by one of my equerries that the missile that had been thrown at me was not a bomb but a loaded revolver.

"A revolver?" I asked. "But if that man wanted to kill me, why didn't he shoot? Why did he only throw the revolver?"

"He apparently meant Your Majesty no harm," said the equerry. "He only wished to create a scene."

By evening Scotland Yard had unravelled the mystery. The gun-thrower was a frustrated Irish journalist, one George Andrew McMahon. By some feat of tortured reasoning this man had convinced himself that the Secretary of State for Home Affairs, Sir John Simon, had conspired to prevent his publishing in London a journal called the *Human Gazette*. Foiled in his efforts to reach the Home Secretary himself, McMahon had resolved to publicize his fancied injustice by causing a public disturbance. The presentation of the colours offered such an opportunity; having armed himself with a gun, he had joined the crowd assembled near the Arch, knowing I would pass through it. Special Constable A. G. Dick, made suspicious by McMahon's agitated behaviour, was actually watching the man when he raised his arm, gun in hand. The policeman had thrown himself at McMahon, and in the struggle over the weapon it had been flung violently into the street.

The incident impressed me as a notable example of the illogicality of human behaviour. By what possible line of reasoning, I asked myself, could anybody possibly mistake the King in a bearskin riding at the head of his Guards for so eminent a legal pundit as Sir John Simon?

McMahon was tried, convicted, and sent to jail for one year. Afterwards I used to refer to the incident jokingly as "The Dastardly Attempt," the phrase used by one of my older courtiers in indignantly describing it.

Next day I was gratified but also surprised by the number of congratulatory messages from my subjects of both high and low degree, including the Archbishop of Canterbury, the Prime Minister, and Mr. Winston Churchill, who were doubtless under the impression that the risk had been greater than it actually was. *The Times* reported the episode next morning under the flattering headline:

THE KING'S CALM
NO INTERRUPTION OF PROCEEDINGS

All this was very fine in its way. But a few days later an untimely interruption of the first garden party I gave as King was
to teach me that, while an elementary exhibition of self-control
by a Monarch could be a signal for national applause, the exercise
of common sense under other circumstances would not necessarily
guarantee the same response.

As the six months' period of full Court mourning for my
father would end on July 20, I had already begun to make
arrangements to resume some of the Court functions that had
been in abeyance. Among these were the four annual Courts at
which women of position and debutantes are presented. When
the Lord Chamberlain, Lord Cromer, had gone over his lists, it
was discovered that some six hundred ladies were awaiting the
opportunity of receiving this particular form of Royal recognition.

It has always seemed to me that women are prone to attach an
excessive importance to these affairs. Nevertheless, he would be a
foolish man who would question their reasoning. Yet, because a
formal Court would have been too quick a turn from the sombre
mood of mourning, it was suggested by Lord Cromer that the
existing social bottle-neck should be cleared by combining the
presentations with two garden parties. It was therefore arranged
that the six hundred should be presented in the garden of Buckingham Palace on the successive afternoons of July 21 and 22.

When that first afternoon I joined my guests in the garden, I
found pitched near the lake the huge silken Durbar canopy with
hammered silver poles that my parents had brought back from
India. Under it was a large gilt chair for me to sit on. Members
of the Royal Family, the Diplomatic Corps, and the Household
were seated directly behind; a Guards' band alternating with the
pipers of a Highland regiment played under the trees a little distance away. The scene was undeniably charming as the attrac-
tively-dressed women advanced down the red carpet to make
their curtsies to the King.

Nevertheless, I was inwardly disquieted from the start. The
morning weather forecast had warned of showers; and the ceremony had scarcely begun when a menacing cloud loomed over
the immense pile of the Palace. Between my bows to the curtsying ladies I followed the development of that cloud with increasing apprehension. It expanded with incredible swiftness. If only

the tempo of the curtsying could have been speeded, the day might have been saved. But these Court presentations, like an assembly line, have a cadence all their own: ten seconds for each débutante to make her curtsy and pass on. Meanwhile the wind came up; and the first big, wet drops began to fall. Then came the downpour. Prudently, the other guests who were not being presented scampered into the protection of the tea tents. But with scarcely a waver the débutantes came on. Their costly hats and dresses, which had taken weeks to make, became progressively more bedraggled; and their expressions increasingly woebegone. From the shelter of the thickly-embroidered Durbar canopy, I was put in mind of Lord Chesterfield's sage observation: "It is not to be imagined in how many different ways vanity defeats its own purpose."

Beckoning to Lord Cromer, I whispered, "We can't let this go on. All the dresses will be ruined. I'm going to stop it."

The Lord Chamberlain agreed that it would be the most dignified and sensible thing to do. Rising from the gilt chair, I made a bow in the direction of the still unpresented young ladies, and with a gesture intended to convey my regret over the inadvertent shower that had necessitated cutting the garden party short, I retired into the Palace.

Since all the cards had been taken up, it seemed to me that there was no doubt as to the social status of those débutantes who had been left, so to speak, at the far end of the red carpet. Apparently, however, there were some parents who felt that without the Sovereign's personal bow of recognition, the presentation was not quite genuine and that the social position of their daughters was in consequence left in doubt. Why, I am still at a loss to understand.

CHAPTER XVIII

BALKAN HOLIDAY

WITH the termination of the Court mourning, the list of appointments to my Household was officially published. During the first six months after my father's death, I had carried on with his old Household, reinforced by my York House staff. Many of my father's officials were by this time well advanced in years and ready to retire. Two of them were seventy-three: Sir Derek Keppel, the Master of the Household, had been on my father's staff since 1893, and Captain Sir Bryan Godfrey-Faussett was in the *Britannia* with my father as a naval cadet in the late 1870's. Lord Wigram, the Private Secretary, a former cavalry officer in the Indian Army, was sixty-three. He had joined the King's Household in 1910. Throughout that spring, therefore, I had given much thought to the delicate question of replacing some of the members of my father's Household with younger men who had served me as Prince of Wales or whom I had come to know over the years.

While the posts to be filled were numerous, many were for the most part ornamental and concerned only with the ceremonial side and State functions. Still, I had to select them with care; for, even if the emoluments are small, these posts are nevertheless sought after, first because of the prestige surrounding them, and secondly because in the cases of some Court officials, they provide welcome additions to their incomes. Other appointments are made by the Government in power with, of course, the King's approval, such as the Treasurer of the Household, the Captain of the Gentlemen-at-Arms, and the Captain of the Yeomen of the Guard.

For filling the ecclesiastical and medical establishments I followed custom and relied largely upon the recommendations of the Church and the medical profession respectively. And with regard to all the others I drew upon the counsel of my father's trusted friend, Lord Cromer, who generously consented to continue to serve me as Lord Chamberlain.

However, when I came to decide upon the two key posts in my Household—the Private Secretary and the Keeper of the Privy Purse, the men with whom I would conduct the day-to-day business—it was a different matter. Ever since the death of Lord Sysonby (formerly Sir Frederick Ponsonby) the year before, these two full-time jobs had been combined temporarily in the person of Lord Wigram. The Keeper of the Privy Purse is the King's disbursing agent. He budgets for the income made available under the Civil List and is responsible for the management of the King's private estates. Obviously the post calls for a man with a financial background. Fortunately a man of high ability was available—Major (now Sir) Ulick Alexander—an Etonian who had joined the Coldstream Guards from Sandhurst and had been Adjutant of the 3rd Battalion of his regiment during the first months of the heavy fighting in 1914. Although his health had been greatly impaired, he served for six years in the Egyptian Army. I first met him in South Africa, where he was Political Secretary to my uncle, Lord Athlone, when the latter was Governor-General. Major Alexander later on was associated with a South African mining interest and a large insurance company, and in addition looked after the affairs of my brother George. It was in this connexion that I became impressed by his fine qualities.

When I came to the post of Private Secretary I found myself involved in a more complex problem. A King's Private Secretary is a personage of higher order than the current usage of the term might imply. He never "takes a letter" or answers the telephone for his master. Apart from personal contacts the Private Secretary is the only channel of communication between the Sovereign and his Ministers. In this function he is expected to keep the King informed of developments in Whitehall that might not be apparent from even a close scrutiny of the contents of the red boxes— the falling-out of a member of the Cabinet with the Prime Minister or an imminent attack by the Opposition on some point of Government policy. But beyond all that that entails, the Private

Secretary is responsible for the good public relations of the King. In that sense he is the Monarch's contact with the world beyond Whitehall, and should keep his ear to the ground so as to advise his master in the moulding of Royal policy.

The importance of the post, which demands a rare combination of personal gifts—a grasp of constitutional procedure, tact, and political sagacity—is self-evident. The Sovereign must have the unswerving loyalty of his Private Secretary. The Private Secretary on his side must have the trust and confidence of his Sovereign. In the absence of either, the transaction of State business would be seriously impaired. And the high prestige the Monarchy had enjoyed for a century before was due in no small measure to the fact that the position had passed in sequence to wise and able men. Queen Victoria relied upon Sir Henry Ponsonby, who features in her biographies where her disagreements with Mr. Gladstone are described. My grandfather had a faithful adviser in Francis, Lord Knollys; and my father, when his turn came, was able to lean on Arthur Bigge, Lord Stamfordham, whose training began in Queen Victoria's secretariat under Sir Henry Ponsonby.

Now, I already had a man whom I felt could meet the exacting traditions of the office, Sir Godfrey Thomas, who had been my Private Secretary for seventeen years. He had been with me on all my official overseas tours; he had shared my princely vicissitudes and had in no small measure contributed to the development of the technique with which I had conducted my duties as Prince of Wales. However, I am sorry to say that he did not rate his own qualities quite so highly as I did. When I offered him this most important post, he modestly refused it, preferring to take his place in my new secretariat as an assistant. On his recommendation I turned to Major Alexander Hardinge—a son of Lord Hardinge of Penshurst, a former Viceroy of India—who, having been Assistant Private Secretary to my father since 1920, was, of course, thoroughly versed in the Palace ways. Although he and I had had few dealings with each other, the combination promised on the surface to work well. Yet, this appointment was a fateful one, as events soon to unfold will show.

A week after these new appointments to the Household had been announced in the Court Circular, I went to France to discharge my last official engagement before the summer holidays. The Canadian Government had acquired from the French nation Vimy Ridge; there they had erected a noble monument in memory of the Canadians who lie buried in France, including those who had carried that bloody rise of land in the famous assault that began in the mud and icy rain on Easter Monday, 1917.

I had been invited to inaugurate the monument in the presence of 6,000 Canadian veterans who had made a pilgrimage across the Atlantic for the ceremony. M. Lebrun, President of the French Republic, came from Paris to be present. The countryside was bright and green. New trees had grown up to replace those scarred and shattered by shell-fire; the old trenches had been filled in; the survivors of that charge up Vimy Ridge had themselves become middle-aged. Looking out upon that scene, I thought to myself how much time had already passed over my generation. My speech, I think, went well; and I flew home.

It had long been my habit as Prince of Wales to spend a part of the summer holidays abroad. Apart from the fact that I like to travel, I used to contend that it was a good thing for a man in my position to remove himself at least once a year from his own country in order to view it, however fleetingly, as foreigners do, and to hear, if he can, their criticisms, which are often more important than their compliments. And now that I was King, I saw no reason for abandoning this agreeable and enriching practice, even if it meant the absence of the King from the grouse moors at the opening of the season. I had hoped to go that August to the Côte d'Azur. But the turmoil in France in the summer of 1936, produced by the combination of sit-down strikes and the civil war in Spain, had convinced my Ambassador in Paris that it would be unwise for me to go there just then. I therefore chartered a large yacht, the *Nahlin*, for a cruise in the Adriatic along the Dalmatian coast, which I had long wanted to see. But the trip was not concerned merely with pleasure. My Government was then making strong overtures to Turkey, which under the Montreux Convention had repossessed the Dardanelles and had begun to fortify them. Discussions were going on between the Turkish President, Kemâl Atatürk, and Whitehall concerning commercial credits and other loans. When plans for my trip were announced, my Ambassador at Ankara urged the Foreign Office to propose to me that, as a gesture of friendship, I should extend my cruise in order to pay a call on the Ghazi at Istanbul. This I was ready to do.

To save time and avoid the long sea passage through the Bay of Biscay and the Straits of Gibraltar into the Mediterranean, I had despatched the *Nahlin* ahead, intending to board her at Venice. But such was the delicacy of the international situation at that hour, with the Italian Press fulminating against Britain, that my Foreign Secretary, Mr. Anthony Eden, felt impelled to persuade me not to enter Italy. Almost on the eve of my departure he came to the Palace to explain why he was tendering this advice. When he had finished, I was not quite sure which he feared most —that I might be jeered at by the Italians, because my Government had imposed sanctions, which would be bad for British prestige, or that I might be cheered by the same people as a friend of Italy, which would have offended the faithful supporters of the League of Nations. In any case I agreed to switch my embarkation point across the Adriatic to Sibenik, a small fishing-village on the Dalmatian coast. In thus bending my plans to suit the expediencies of British foreign policy, I subjected myself to an indescribable night journey by train into Yugoslavia with a clanking and jolting such as I had never before experienced.

Along with an Assistant Private Secretary and an equerry, I took with me some friends, among whom were my Minister for War, Mr. Duff Cooper, and Lady Diana Duff Cooper. Wallis was also a member of the party, although she and I were both by then well aware that my interest in her had attracted attention and speculation. During those first six months of Court mourning, I had had but few social engagements. My week-ends were spent in the quietude of The Fort; and Wallis was sometimes there with our friends. She had also been my guest at two official dinner parties at York House when I had entertained, among others, the Prime Minister and Mrs. Baldwin, Mr. and Mrs. Winston Churchill, and Colonel and Mrs. Charles A. Lindbergh. Her presence at my table was duly recorded in the Court Circular. Secrecy and concealment were not of my nature. We saw each other when we could. Her strength and sympathy supported me in my loneliness.

It would be difficult to imagine anything having less relevance to the affairs of to-day than the details of a yachting trip of fifteen years ago. The special charm of a large yacht lies in the circumstance that it enables presumably responsible people to combine, in a manner not otherwise possible, the milder irresponsibilities of a beachcomber's existence with all the comforts of a luxury hotel. In this respect the cruise of the *Nahlin* did not disappoint me. Nevertheless, as the yacht made her leisurely way through the ruffled waters of the Balkans, I was conscious of the clouds that were rolling up on the horizon—not only clouds of war but clouds of private trouble for me; for the American Press had become fascinated with my friendship for Wallis, and now pursued us everywhere.

Escorted by two destroyers, *Grafton* and *Glowworm*, the *Nahlin* put out from Sibenik on August 10. The destroyers had been sent from Malta in the double capacity of guard-ships and despatch vessels for carrying to me from British diplomatic posts *en route* the red boxes that arrived from Whitehall throughout my holiday. The first ten days we steamed southward, down the Dalmatian coast, calling at picturesque old towns or island fishing-villages, and stopping for a picnic and swim whenever a fine sandy beach was sighted.

Arriving at Corfu off the southern frontier of Albania, we found there King George II of the Hellenes, who had taken a villa to escape the summer heat of Athens. We were second cousins, for like me he was a great-grandson of Queen Victoria. He had been recalled to his throne only the year before, after an eleven-year exile in England, where he had lived quietly and inconspicuously at Brown's Hotel in London. There he had impressed me as a contented man, but on meeting him again in his own land he seemed disillusioned. When I asked him, as one King to another, how he was getting along, he answered almost bitterly that he wasn't getting along at all. He had returned to Greece to find the loyalties of his people divided between innumerable factions and cliques; if he tried to approach one, the others were instantly suspicious. He had therefore given up trying to see anybody. The dictator, Metaxas, had just compelled him to dissolve Parliament and proclaim martial law. "I am a King in name only," George said. "I might just as well be back at Brown's Hotel." As

I took leave of him he gripped my hand and said, "I hope you have better luck."

The voyage continued through the Corinth Canal to Athens and beyond to the beautiful Greek islands in the Ægean Sea. Before entering the Dardanelles on our way to Istanbul we went ashore on the Gallipoli Peninsula to inspect the British war graves and the monuments raised in honour of the victims of the bloody landings at Cape Helles, Anzac, and Suvla Bay. At Istanbul, Kemâl Atatürk, the Dictator of Turkey, greeted me as I stepped ashore, and drove me in an open motor through the city—a rare compliment, my Ambassador assured me, since the Ghazi only travelled in a bullet-proof limousine. As mine was not a State visit the entertainment provided by Atatürk was informal. This was an advantage, as on the several occasions we were together I had the opportunity to study this ruthless soldier-revolutionary, who had accomplished within his own country one of the most violent social upheavals ever to be achieved by one man in modern times. We conversed in German. He told me how he had broken the Moslem dominance, abolished the fez, closed the harems, and emancipated the Turkish women by giving them the vote. Atatürk's features were sharply chiselled, and his eyes were the most piercing I have ever looked into. And as I listened to the Ghazi discourse on his triumphs, the melancholy echo of George of Greece bemoaning his fate provided a counterpoint in my mind of a theme on the realities and illusions of power in the modern world.

By now I had been away almost a month, and the time had come to start for home. After a day's cruise up the Bosporus into the Black Sea we boarded the Ghazi's special train at Istanbul, leaving the *Nahlin* to proceed independently back to her home port. The next day found us traversing the rugged countryside of Bulgaria. Czar Boris III boarded the train before we reached Sofia. Boris was a versatile monarch. He spoke six languages, was a keen botanist and an excellent mechanic whose chief hobby was to drive the locomotives of his State railways. He is quoted as saying that he had no fear of losing his throne through revolution because he could always get a job in the United States as an engineer or a college professor. He became Czar at the end of the First World War after his father, Ferdinand, had been forced to abdicate for his miscalculation in alining Bulgaria on the losing side with Germany. Despite this final blunder the old Czar had steered his country through the maze of Balkan politics with an adroitness that earned for him in the Courts and Chancelleries of Europe the sobriquet of "Foxy Ferdinand." Some of this flair for diplomacy Boris had inherited, and he was fond of saying that, while his queen, Giovanna, the attractive third daughter of King Victor Emmanuel, was pro-Italian, his Ministers were pro-German, and his people were pro-Russian, he himself was neutral.

From Sofia, Boris and his brother Kyril accompanied us north, and the afternoon passed pleasantly in an exchange of views to the clacking of the train wheels. The leave-taking at the Yugoslav frontier was somewhat perfunctory owing to an argument between the Czar and his brother as to who should drive the locomotive of the train waiting to take them back to the capital.

Passing through Yugoslavia I met yet another Balkan ruler in the person of the Regent, Prince Paul, who had been at Oxford with me. When King Alexander had been assassinated at Marseilles two years before, leaving as his heir Peter, then only eleven years old, Paul became Regent for the young King. He was an altogether different type from Boris; his tastes ran all to the arts. During two short hours in Belgrade he took us to his residence, where he showed us with pride his fine personal collection of pictures and furniture. But what I remember most clearly of that evening was the large, empty, white-marble palace in which the late King Alexander had had constructed a vast moving-picture theatre, where, according to Paul, he would often sit in solitary majesty while the latest American films were shown for his exclusive benefit.

Nowadays, when I read about the Balkan countries, all save Yugoslavia, Greece, and Turkey closed off behind the Iron Curtain, and where the monarchical system survives alone among the Hellenes, I sometimes reflect on what has befallen these four heads of state. Only Paul of Yugoslavia is alive to-day, and he, like King Peter, is in exile. Atatürk was dead of cirrhosis of the liver within two years. Boris died mysteriously in 1943. He had followed in his father's footsteps by alining Bulgaria with Hitler's Germany. George of Greece, after having had to flee his country a third time, succumbed to a heart attack in 1949.

A pleasant five days in that most charming of capitals—Vienna
—wound up my holiday. While there I visited President Miklas
and Chancellor von Schuschnigg, who were still oblivious to the
growing menace of their neighbour to the north. Atatürk's train
having meanwhile returned to Turkey, I continued westward
across Europe with my party in the Orient Express. My own aeroplane met me at Zurich; and with an equerry I flew home, to
resume my duties and to deal with a personal problem which
it had become increasingly clear could not be held much longer
in abeyance.

CHAPTER XIX

THE PRIME MINISTER SEEKS AN
AUDIENCE

On my first night back in England, September 14, I dined with my mother at Buckingham Palace. She was in the midst of moving her things to Marlborough House, a melancholy task of no mean magnitude, for in the course of her active life she had assembled an immense collection of *objets d'art* and historical souvenirs of the Royal Family. She had lived in the Palace for twenty-six years, and although she appeared quite pleased at the prospect of moving back to Marlborough House, I realized that inwardly it must have been a severe wrench for her to give up her pleasant rooms overlooking the garden. Greeting her, I wondered how much she knew about the stories appearing in the American Press. But her conversation told me nothing.

My mother asked whether I had enjoyed the cruise. I assured her that I had had a wonderful time. "Didn't you find it terribly warm in the Adriatic?" she asked. Her curiosity about the simple details of the voyage reminded me of how she used to talk to us when we returned from school. She had read in *The Times* of my meeting with King George of Greece at Corfu, and wondered how he was getting on. I told her that he had lost weight, and that he was homesick for his friends in London.

"Poor George," said my mother. "I don't envy the rulers of those Balkan countries."

The news that I intended to spend the last two weeks of September at Balmoral pleased her. To my mother the habits and customs of the family meant almost as much as the official obligations devolving upon us: she hoped now that I had become head of the family, that I would return more to the ways of my father.

Having handed over York House to my brother Harry and his bride Alice, and with my mother still in Buckingham Palace, I found myself temporarily without a London residence. So I stayed at The Fort, and for four busy days motored back and forth to my office in the Palace. From the red boxes that had pursued me throughout my holiday I knew that the international situation had not improved during my absence. One of my callers, Anthony Eden, informed me that the Government, after many vacillations, had decided to follow France's example and remain aloof from the Spanish Civil War. Trouble smouldered in Palestine: the British garrison there had been reinforced. In my turn, I gave the Secretary of State for Foreign Affairs the benefit of my conversations with the monarchs and statesmen of the countries I had visited.

"Of course, Anthony," I chided him, "I am in no position to tell you about the Italian situation."

This joking reference to the Foreign Secretary's ban upon my having any traffic whatever with the Duce's Italy brought a fleeting smile to his grave countenance. He parried by complimenting me upon the success of my visit to Kemâl Atatürk.

After the enervating heat of the Balkans, I looked forward to a fortnight in Scotland. If in the past I had sometimes found the transplanted routine of the Court at Balmoral a trifle too formal for my tastes, still I loved the life in the Highlands.

The deer-stalking would be at its best; there would still be plenty of grouse on the moors; and the exhilarating air and hard exercise would put me in condition for the heavy list of appointments awaiting me that autumn and winter.

When, in mid-September, I arrived at the castle, it was to find Bertie and Elizabeth already at Birkhall about six miles away. Harry and Alice were near by at Abergeldie Mains. And the various other houses on the estate were already occupied by the senior members of my household and their families.

There was, however, one slight departure from custom. Since Queen Victoria's time the guest-book at Balmoral had annually recorded the descent of a succession of Cabinet Ministers, archbishops, admirals, generals, and so forth, to enjoy the Sovereign's hospitality. But because I was still on vacation, and much of my time in London was always occupied with such dignitaries, I decided to confine my first house-party there as King to a number of friends to whom I was indebted for hospitality over the years. None of my guests, except my brother George and his wife Marina, had ever been to Balmoral; now that I had the property, I wanted the others to see it and enjoy with me its famous sport and amenities. Naturally Wallis was included in the house-party, and her arrival with Mr. and Mrs. Herman Rogers a few days later was duly recorded, in accordance with my instructions, in the Court Circular.

Despite the rumblings abroad, life within the castle was extremely pleasant and, by present-day house-party standards, entirely normal. My guests enjoyed themselves as much as I did. The days were spent "on the hill" or the moors: in the evening one relaxed with bridge or the latest films. At the foot of the stairs stands a life-size white marble statue of the Prince Consort, in full Highland dress, complete with dog and gun. If the austere figure of my Saxe-Coburg great-grandfather seemed to register disapproval whenever the tray of cocktails was carried into the drawing-room before dinner, it must have noted with approval my mastering the rudiments of a truly authentic Scottish accomplishment of which there is no mention amongst Prince Albert's activities as I recall from my reading of Queen Victoria's *Leaves from the Journal of our Life in the Highlands*. I was the first member of the Royal Family to play the "pipes." My old teacher, Henry Forsyth, who was still in my service, was proud to have the King play in the Balmoral pipe band, which he led around the dinner table before the coffee was served.

October 1 found me back in London. My mother by then had established herself at Marlborough House. From the train I went straight to Buckingham Palace: the Royal Standard was broken from the mast as I drove through the gates. I took up residence in that vast building without pleasure; the dank, musty smell I had always associated with the building assailed me afresh the instant I set foot inside the King's Door. Out of respect for my father's memory, I was reluctant to occupy his rooms on the second floor. At my mother's suggestion, I moved into the "Belgian suite" on the first floor, named after Queen Victoria's uncle, Leopold I, King of the Belgians, and kept for visiting foreign monarchs. This five-room suite had tall french windows opening on the gardens, and was conveniently adjacent to the private Garden Entrance which is always used, except on State occasions, by the Royal Family. One never tinkers much with palaces; like museums, they seem to resist change. Besides, a curious presentiment induced me to leave the rooms as they were. Somehow I had a feeling that I might not be there very long. About the only changes I made for my comfort were to add a shower to the bathtub and to replace the ornate four-poster bed with a single one of my own. I installed a small extra switchboard to handle my personal calls, and added a private line to The Fort. During the two months I lived at Buckingham Palace, I never got over the feeling of not quite belonging there. I felt lost in its regal immensity.

I threw myself into my work with energy. My calendar was filled right up until Christmas. Audiences at the Palace; a State Opening of Parliament; a quick visit to the Home Fleet at its Portland base; a tour of the South Wales coal-fields; the Fat Stock Show at Smithfield for the Christmas market; a tour of the Potteries—except for week-ends, I should be on the job every day.

Wallis's divorce petition was put down to be heard at the Ipswich Assizes on October 27, and in preparation for that event she rented a small house at Felixstowe. She had retained a London solicitor, Mr. Theodore Goddard, to handle her case. The American Press almost instantly got wind of the divorce proceedings, and predictions were made that she would marry the King as soon as she was free.

In the face of this challenging display of enterprise by American journalism, what was the British Press likely to do? Apart from the unadorned publication of Wallis's name in the Court Circular, so far there had been no overt attempt by any British journal to couple her name with mine. This was not for want of enterprise on the part of the editors, who were well aware of what was being printed by their American rivals. What had stayed their hands was Fleet Street's long-standing reticence where the privacy of the Royal Family was concerned. There is nothing servile in this tradition. The reason for it is honourable: it is founded on the premise that if the exalted position of the Monarchy is to be preserved in the face of the encroaching cynicism of modern life, it must be held above carping and criticism. That is the explanation for the long silence. Nevertheless, with the divorce petition pending, it seemed too much to hope that this general self-restraint could be long maintained in the face of the terrific pressure building up on the other side of the Atlantic. Something was bound to give before long; and, believing in the direct approach, I decided to try to enlist the aid and understanding of two powerful newspaper friends—Lord Beaverbrook and the Hon. Esmond Harmsworth, now Lord Rothermere. Max Beaverbrook controlled the *Daily Express* and the *Evening Standard*, the former having the largest daily circulation of any newspaper in the British Isles. Esmond Harmsworth was the son of the late Lord Rothermere, who owned the *Daily Mail* and *Evening News*.

At my request, Max Beaverbrook came to the Palace on October 16. I told him frankly of my problem. I had no thought of asking him to use his influence on other newspaper publishers for the purpose of hushing up the news of the imminent divorce petition. My one desire was to protect Wallis from sensational publicity, at least in my own country.

Max heard me out. "All these reasons," he said, "appear satisfactory to me—I shall try to do what you ask."

Without delay he began a prodigious task, unique in the annals of Fleet Street, where the mere suggestion of censorship offends. With the co-operation of Esmond Harmsworth and several others, he achieved the miracle I desired—a "gentlemen's agreement" among newspaper editors to report the case without sensation. The British Press kept its word, and for that I shall always be grateful.

Meanwhile, intervention from an unexpected quarter threatened to sweep away the coffer-dams I was anxious to erect around Wallis.

The following Sunday found me at Sandringham. I had gone there to inspect the progress of the changes which Bertie had recommended earlier in the year, and at the same time to enjoy four days' partridge shooting with a few friends. On arriving at the Big House I found a message from my private secretary, Alec Hardinge, who was at Windsor, asking that I should telephone him without delay. I did so, and was informed that the Prime Minister desired to see me on an important and urgent matter. The request appeared to me particularly surprising, because I had seen him only a few days before, in connexion with the Fleet Air Arm. "Where is the Prime Minister now?" I asked. I was told that he was near The Fort, week-ending with Lord FitzAlan at his residence, Cumberland Lodge, in Windsor Great Park, and had, indeed, tried to reach me at The Fort before I left that morning. "Well," I said, "if it is all that important, let him come here, to Sandringham." Alec Hardinge seemed to hesitate. He went on to say that Mr. Baldwin was quite prepared to do so, but because his sudden appearance in the midst of a shooting-party was almost certain to excite comment and speculation, he thought it wiser that we should meet at Sunningdale. "The Prime Minister," said Hardinge, "regrets putting Your Majesty to this inconvenience. But he stresses the importance of secrecy, and hopes you will be able to receive him at The Fort on Tuesday."

This I agreed to do, fixing the hour at 10 a.m. I was in no doubt as to the object of the Prime Minister's urgent request for an audience. Nevertheless, his sudden intrusion perplexed me. If it were, indeed, his intent to proffer Prime Ministerial advice in the matter of my friendship with Wallis, I wondered how far he would go. Plainly a crisis of some kind was imminent in my personal affairs.

On Monday night I drove back to The Fort. The next morning, refreshed by a good night's sleep, I was at the door to receive the Prime Minister when, punctually at ten o'clock, he crunched up the drive in a tiny black car which did not seem half big enough for him.

Friendly, casual, and discursive, he might have been a neighbour who had called to discuss a dispute over a boundary fence. He complimented me upon the beauty of the grounds, the arrangement of the garden, the silvery radiance of the birch-trees, and the delicacy of the autumn tints. We repaired to the octagonal drawing-room and sat down in front of the fire, he in an armchair and I on a sofa. Yet he could not have been as calm and composed inside as he looked, for he became restless and finally asked, almost apologetically, if he might have a whisky-and-soda.

Somewhat startled by the request for a drink so early in the day, I rang the bell and told the butler to bring some whisky. He reappeared with a tray, which he placed on a table behind the sofa. When he had withdrawn Mr. Baldwin rose and, picking up the decanter and a glass, looked inquiringly at me, asking, "Sir, when?"

As gravely as I could, I hoped even severely, I answered, "No, thank you, Mr. Baldwin; I never take a drink before seven o'clock in the evening."

The Prime Minister seemed to give a slight start, then went ahead and poured his own drink. When, however, he produced his pipe and tobacco pouch, I also produced mine. The familiar reciprocal action seemed to put him at his ease.

Mr. Baldwin's side of this first conversation was extensively set forth in his famous statement on the Abdication made to the House of Commons on December 10. In general, the substance of the conversation was much as he described it. Yet my own recollection of the same occasion, constant through the years, is not so much that of a generous Prime Minister trying to help his Sovereign through a personal situation of almost indescribable complexity as that of a political Procrustes determined to fit his regal victim into the iron bed of convention.

Mr. Baldwin's business did, indeed, concern my friendship with Wallis; and in justifying his intervention in this most delicate matter, he hastened to say that he had been moved to do so not alone in his capacity as Prime Minister but also as a friend who was anxious to help. The rumours and criticisms appearing in the American and Canadian Press had given him great anxiety; if continued, they might, he said, endanger the position of the Monarchy.

On this subject Mr. Baldwin and I talked for about an hour, with him doing most of the talking. Although he never came right out and asked me in so many words to do so, it slowly dawned on me that his real object was to persuade me to prevail upon Wallis to withdraw her divorce petition. With the petition not yet heard I could not at this stage allow myself to be drawn into a discussion of my hopes.

Finally the Prime Minister asked almost bluntly, "Must the case really go on?"

"Mr. Baldwin," I said, doing my best to hide my feelings,

"I have no right to interfere with the affairs of an individual. It would be wrong were I to attempt to influence Mrs. Simpson just because she happens to be a friend of the King's."

The Prime Minister seemed to be sounding the depths of my feelings, trying to decide whether this was just a fleeting attachment or the real thing. However, the conversation ended without his ever asking me whether it was my intention to marry Wallis if she became free. Rising to leave, he mentioned something about being glad that the ice had been broken. It was on the tip of my tongue to say that so far as I could see the only ice that had been broken had long since melted in his drink. But Mr. Baldwin's sense of humour being intermittent and unpredictable, I thought better of it. We parted, perhaps not with lively expressions of mutual esteem, but certainly without bitterness. In fact, as he took his leave he complimented me again on the beauty of my garden, and volunteered an excellent suggestion for replanting the herbaceous border in the coming spring.

My talk with my Prime Minister perturbed me. A friendship which so far had remained within the sheltered realm of my private solicitude was manifestly about to become an affair of State. It was about to become, along with the air estimates, the Polish Corridor, the civil war in Spain, and the value of the pound sterling, a matter for the concern of the Government. If the Prime Minister's approach to my particular problem were to prove to be no more statesmanlike than his handling of other complex political problems of the hour, then I had little reason to hope for a happy solution.

At this stage I decided to talk to an old friend, Mr. (now Sir) Walter Monckton, K.C., who had just come back from a professional trip to India. My acquaintance with this brilliant barrister, who was destined to play a leading rôle in the events leading up to my abdication, began at Oxford, where he had been President of the Union. I lost track of him for some years during the war, in which he served with distinction; and the relationship was not resumed until he was appointed, in 1932, Attorney-General to the Prince of Wales and legal adviser to the Duchy of Cornwall. I admired his mind, respected his judgment, and had been attracted by his charitable nature. A few days later I invited him to The Fort for lunch. Afterwards I took him for a walk in the grounds and gave him an account of my conversation with Mr. Baldwin. As we strolled under the beautiful cedar-trees, I stopped short and faced him. "Listen, Walter, one doesn't know how things are going to turn out. I am beginning to wonder whether I really am the kind of king they want. Am I not a bit too independent? As you know, my make-up is very different from that of my father. I believe they would prefer someone more like him. Well, there is my brother Bertie."

In fairness to Walter Monckton, I should say that I do not believe he wholly agreed; nevertheless, he conceded the logic of my argument.

Four days later Wallis's petition for divorce was heard at the Ipswich Assizes. From the Court Circular recording the King's official engagements for the morning of October 27, faithful readers would have judged that business was as usual in the Palace.

> The King held a Council this morning at 11.30 o'clock. There were present:—The Right Hon. J. Ramsay MacDonald, M.P. (Lord President), The Earl of Cromer (Lord Chamberlain), The Earl Stanhope (First Commissioner of Works and Public Buildings) and the Right Hon. W. L. Mackenzie King (Prime Minister of the Dominion of Canada).
>
> The Duke of Sutherland (Lord Steward), The Duke of Beaufort (Master of the Horse) and Major the Hon. Alexander Hardinge (Private Secretary to The King) were sworn in Members of His Majesty's Most Honourable Privy Council.
>
> Colonel Sir Maurice Hankey was in attendance as Clerk of the Council.
>
> The Right Hon. J. Ramsay MacDonald, M.P., had an audience of The King previous to the Council and the Right Hon. W. L. Mackenzie King had an audience of His Majesty after the Council.
>
> The Lord Brownlow (Lord in Waiting), the Master of the Household, and Commander Charles Lambe, R.N. (Equerry in Waiting) were in attendance.

But all the morning, while I strove to carry out these duties with my usual punctiliousness, part of my mind was preoccupied with what was taking place at Ipswich.

The message that I was waiting for came shortly after lunch. It was a telephone call from the lawyers to say that the court had granted a decree nisi.

"Nisi" is a Latin word meaning "unless." A decree nisi under English law is the first of two stages in obtaining a divorce, the second being the decree absolute, which at that time entailed a delay of six months. Wallis, therefore, could not remarry before the end of April 1937. However, with my Coronation fixed for May 12, this seemed to allow ample time for me to work things out. Inwardly relieved—mistakenly, as it proved—I returned to my engagements.

CHAPTER XX

THE KING RECEIVES A
DISTURBING LETTER

THUS, as my personal affairs moved ever closer to decision, the Royal minuet went on, its stately measures undisturbed. The rôle of a successful constitutional monarch consists in no small measure of appearing to be not only above politics but also above life. To be above politics entailed no particular strain on me: discretion had by this time become instinctive. And under normal circumstances one could depend upon the affectionate mystery the world's most democratic people weave about their monarchy to support and sustain the illusion of being safely above the human comedy. But now that I myself was caught up in a struggle of the heart and spirit, the old easy sense of security crumbled away. And as I discharged my kingly duties, the ceremonial parts, especially, took on an air of unreality.

Of the many official personages who called upon me that last week in October, only one now stands out in sharp relief in my memory—the new German Ambassador to the Court of St. James's, Herr Joachim von Ribbentrop. On October 30 Herr von Ribbentrop came to Buckingham Palace to hand me his letters of credence from his Führer. It was a full-dress uniform ceremony. With Mr. Anthony Eden, I awaited Adolf Hitler's envoy. The occasion was not without strain. This intimate of the Führer had been, among other things, a champagne salesman, a circumstance that had offended the sensibilities of those who had been accustomed to a long sequence of distinguished German Ambassadors. Furthermore, relations with Germany had not improved since the spring, and the appointment of this polished but bombastic opportunist was not calculated to ease British apprehensions.

At the stroke of 11.30 the double doors of the audience room opened, and there advanced towards me a tall, rigid figure in fault-less tail coat and white tie. The Nazi salute with which the Ger-man Ambassador was to outrage the officials of the next reign was not employed. He bowed, we shook hands, and he handed me his letters of credence, which I passed to Mr. Anthony Eden. He then presented his full Embassy staff, who had followed him into the room. After they had withdrawn, I invited Herr von Ribben-trop to be seated. Anthony Eden remained with us. The formal-ity of this kind of ceremony restricts conversation to an exchange of stereotyped compliments. Herr von Ribbentrop spoke of his Führer's desire for peace; I wished him a successful mission to my country. The double doors swung open again, and the Lord Chamberlain entered to conduct the Ambassador to the carriage waiting at the Grand Entrance. As the Secretary of State turned to leave, I remarked, "Well, Anthony, that passed off all right." "Yes, Sir," he answered pensively, "if only German diplomacy were as correct as its manners, the rest would be easy."

The sense of unreality deepened as I prepared for my first State Opening of Parliament on November 3. By an ancient custom each parliamentary session is inaugurated by the reading in the House of Lords, by the Monarch himself when he can be present, of the "Most Gracious Speech from the Throne," in which he reviews the state of the realm and outlines the legislative programme which his Government proposes to enact in the forth-coming session. Like many of the cherished Royal rituals, the ceremony celebrates an authority long extinct; yet in pomp and pageantry it is second only to a coronation. When the King sets out from Buckingham Palace, he drives in the gilt State coach drawn by eight grey horses. The mounted Household Cavalry and Yeomen of the Guard on foot provide a glittering and colour-ful escort down the Mall. The streets are lined with troops of the Brigade of Guards. And the scene that awaits the Sovereign inside the House of Lords is impressive in the extreme—every bench occupied, the Lords Temporal in their scarlet and ermine robes; the Lords Spiritual in their episcopal gowns; the Diplomatic Corps in brilliant uniforms; the peeresses in décolleté, adorned with be-jewelled tiaras and parures.

No other event in the Monarch's calendar is more calculated to remind him of the figurehead nature of his rôle. The Gracious Speech is itself a composition to which he may not contribute a single word. The Government of the day sets the policies that he solemnly enunciates; its draftsmen supply the lines he reads. Thus, in the act of opening Parliament, the King occupies a position quite the opposite of that of the President of the United States when he delivers his annual State of the Union message to a joint session of Congress. The President is judged by what he says; the King by how he says it. Be that as it may, my father used to say that he knew of few worse ordeals than being obliged to deliver somebody else's speech, at the same time balancing on his head a 2½-lb. gold crown.

However, these State openings are cut-and-dried affairs, following a ritual that never varies. Having often watched my father on such occasions, I anticipated no particular difficulty so far as ceremonial went, although, owing to circumstances peculiar to myself, certain departures were necessary from the routine to which my noble audience had been accustomed during my father's reign.

First of all, because I was a bachelor only one throne would be placed under the canopy behind the Woolsack, where for a quarter of a century a second one had been provided for my mother. Secondly, the Opening of Parliament is ordinarily the only occasion except the Coronation on which the King wears his crown. But because I had not been crowned yet was required by custom to be covered during the reading of the "Most Gracious Speech," I decided to wear, in place of the massive, bejewelled headgear of kingship, the cocked hat that went with the uniform of Admiral of the Fleet. Even the detail of the cocked hat raised a weighty point. Should I enter the House of Lords with it on my head or should I carry it in my hand? No one still attached to the Offices of State remembered how my father had handled this detail of his head-dress at his first state Opening of Parliament: the contemporary accounts were hazy. Eventually, however, after prolonged research, a learned opinion was handed down by some venerable official that custom and usage would be correctly served if the King made his entrance holding the cocked hat in his hand.

Finally, as this would be my first appearance before Parliament since my accession, I was obliged to make what is called the Declaration ensuring the maintenance of the Protestant faith by the Crown:

> I, Edward VIII, do solemnly and sincerely in the presence of God profess, testify and declare that I am a faithful Protestant, and that I will, according to the true intent of the enactments which secure the Protestant Succession to the Throne of my realm, uphold and maintain the said enactments to the best of my powers according to law.

I was brought up in the Protestant faith; yet the duty of uttering this outmoded sentiment was repugnant to me. In spirit it seemed wholly inappropriate to an institution supposed to shelter all creeds. I actually inquired into the possibility of dispensing altogether with this ritual. But on learning that the Sovereign's subscription to the declaration is, in fact, a mandatory matter, going back to the Bill of Rights in 1689, I decided not to make an issue of it.

As it was, I had ample reason for approaching my début in this majestic ceremony with apprehension. My audience would be exacting—the bluest blood, the finest brains in the realm. Inevitably, my performance would be compared with that of my father, who was always superb on these occasions. But beyond that I realized that many in my audience—the Ministers of the Crown who knew what Mr. Baldwin had already said to me; the Press barons who were well aware of what was being published in the American newspapers—would be measuring me with more curiosity than the occasion ordinarily warranted. I was therefore determined to play my part well—as well as I had ever done anything in my life.

Pageantry needs sunshine. There are few sadder spectacles than that presented by a dripping *cortège* splashing down a half-empty street, its finery bedraggled, its once resplendent participants soaked to the bone. One needs a certain amount of luck in these outdoor spectacles; I was doomed to be disappointed. When I awoke at eight o'clock it was pouring with rain. Reluctantly I gave instructions for the State procession to be cancelled, and when I started out from the Palace it was in the less spectacular

Daimler, summoned, ironically enough, by the Master of the Horse.

Well do I recall the hush inside the House of Lords as I mounted the steps to the Throne. As I looked out over the brilliant scene, my senses were suddenly assailed by an almost suffocating smell of moth-balls given off by the colourful robes removed from storage for this formal airing. It was nauseating, and sitting there on the Throne I could feel the pumping of my own heart.

"My Lords," I said solemnly, according to ancient usage, "pray be seated." An immense rustle filled the chamber as my audience settled back upon the benches. The Lord Privy Seal, Lord Halifax, one of the great Officers of State, advanced with the Declaration. I read it aloud, and then signed my name to it. Now the Lord Chancellor, Lord Hailsham, a resplendent figure, approached, bearing the Gracious Speech. Placing my cocked hat on my head, I took it from him. My nerves were taut. Momentarily I felt exactly as if I were approaching a big fence in a steeplechase, a little apprehensive but braced for the test. Summoning all the resources of will and spirit, I began to read. Slowly the tension went out of me; the sound of my own voice in my ears was strong and vigorous; as I read on, there welled up inside me a feeling almost of defiance. My confidence grew. I had cleared the fence, I was safe on the other side.

It was all very solemn and not a word of it was mine. Nevertheless, _The Times_ reported next morning with satisfaction: "One more page in the history of Parliament has been written. A young King has made his first speech from the Throne. Not alone the fact that his was a Throne by itself, but his whole Royal demeanour bade one feel that 'in himself was all his state'."

Eight days passed. My next ceremonial duty, and it turned out to be my last, was in connexion with the celebrations of Armistice Day at the Cenotaph. As I bent to lay a wreath at the foot of the simple monument to the Empire's warriors of the First World War, I was reminded how often I had seen my father's bearded figure stooped over in this same gesture of reverence.

That night I took the train for Portland, where I spent two blowy days with the Home Fleet, moored in its snug anchorage.

They were good days. Engrossed in inspecting the ships, talking to sailors and reminiscing with old shipmates, I was able to put aside for a few hours the burning issue that was pressing for decision.

On the evening of November 13 I was back at The Fort. My butler informed me as I entered the door that there was a letter from Major Hardinge, who was anxious that I should open it without delay. On top of the usual pile of red despatch boxes lay one marked "Urgent and Confidential." I was very tired. The visit to the Fleet had been exhausting; the chill of the Portland gale was still in my bones, and I had looked forward to a hot bath. But there was that box. It must be something of unusual importance. So, before immersing myself in the steaming water, I opened it and took out the letter from Alec Hardinge. An instant later I was confronted by the most serious crisis of my life.

The letter was short and precise. It began:

Sir,
    With my humble duty.
    As Your Majesty's Private Secretary I feel it my duty to bring to your notice the following facts . . .

Alec Hardinge went on to inform me categorically that the Prime Minister and senior members of the Government were meeting that day in London to discuss the Government's possible action in the light of "the serious situation which is developing" —i.e. the possible clash with the Government over my intentions towards Wallis. The silence of the Press, he warned me, was not going to be maintained: "It is probably only a matter of days before the outburst begins." And the resignation of the Government was, he stated, an eventuality which could by no means be excluded—an eventuality that, he insisted, could hold no solution for me since he had "reason to know" that I should find it impossible to form a new one. The letter ended with the following paragraph:

If Your Majesty will permit me to say so, there is only one step which holds out any prospect of avoiding this dangerous situation, and that is for Mrs. Simpson to go abroad *without further delay*, and I would *beg* Your Majesty to give this proposal your earnest consideration before the position has become inevitable. Owing to the changing attitude of the Press, the matter has become one of great urgency.

I was shocked and angry—shocked by the suddenness of the blow, angry because of the way it was launched, with the startling suggestion that I should send from my land, my realm, the woman I intended to marry.

My first instinct was to seize the telephone. Then I thought better of it. I took the tub instead. The warm water relaxed me. After dinner I read the letter again. The longer I studied it the more puzzled I was by the motives that could have prompted Alec Hardinge to write it. As to his right to address such a communication to his Sovereign there could, of course, be no question. If, indeed, a Cabinet crisis impended over any issue, it was the duty of the King's Private Secretary to warn his master. But what hurt was the cold formality with which so personal a matter affecting my whole happiness had been broached. How was I to construe this—a warning? An ultimatum? There was the phrase, "I have reason to know." Who could have told Alec Hardinge all this but the Prime Minister? But what was Mr. Baldwin's purpose? Was this move an attempt to test the strength of my attachment? If the real intention was to try to induce me to give Wallis up by pointing at my head this big pistol of the Government's threatened resignation, they had clearly misjudged their man. I was obviously in love. They had struck at the very roots of my pride. Only the most faint-hearted would have remained unaroused by such a challenge.

There was little sleep for me that night. This was not the crisis of a Prince; it was the crisis of a King. And because it was not my nature to watch and wait, I resolved to come to grips at once with Mr. Baldwin and the nebulous figures around him. The challenge could not have come at a worse time. I was scheduled to leave London the following Tuesday evening on a tour of the South Wales coal-fields. Rather than put the matter off, I decided to have it out with the Prime Minister before leaving London.

Although the King's Private Secretary is the normal channel of communication between the Palace and No. 10 Downing Street,

Alec Hardinge's attitude might have made it awkward, to say the least, for me to continue to work through him in the difficult negotiations ahead. I decided to establish a new connexion through Walter Monckton. Accordingly I asked him to meet me at Windsor Castle on Sunday afternoon.

Wallis and her aunt, Mrs. D. Buchanan Merryman of Washington, D.C., who had recently arrived from America, were spending the week-end with me at The Fort. Not wishing to worry them until I had discussed this serious situation with Walter Monckton, I carried that disturbing secret locked up inside me for two days, pressing with deadly weight upon my every thought and action. The Kents, who lived at Iver, near Slough, had invited Wallis and me to tea that Sunday afternoon. Excusing myself on the plea of business with the Librarian, I left soon after lunch for my rendezvous with Walter Monckton, telling Wallis that the motor would return for her so that she could pick me up an hour later.

Driving into the Great Park, preoccupied with my thoughts, I suddenly caught sight of the Castle, its massive grandeur dominating the countryside. How solid, secure, and changeless it was—something left over from the Middle Ages, it seemed remote, unconcerned with the urgent decisions of the hour.

As the motor turned into the Frogmore Gate the gate-keeper, a former Royal Marine, clumped down the path on the wooden leg that replaced the one he had lost at Zeebrugge. He bowed and gave me a warm and friendly smile as he let me through. When I looked back he was hobbling up the path towards his cottage, thrusting himself forward with powerful jerks of his body. I said to myself, "There no doubt is a contented man, wooden leg and all. Little does he know of the problem that confronts me this day."

Walter was waiting in my old rooms on the second floor. I showed him Alec Hardinge's letter. He read it slowly. His expression left me in no doubt that it had shocked him as much as it had me. He agreed that it could hardly have been written without some discussion with Mr. Baldwin. And he also agreed that time would not wait.

"The first thing I must do," I said, "is to send for the Prime Minister—to-morrow. I shall tell him that if, as would now appear, he and the Government are against my marrying Mrs. Simpson, I am prepared to go."

"He will not like to hear that," said Walter gravely.

"I shall not find it easy to say."

I then asked Walter whether he would act as my personal adviser and liaison officer with No. 10 Downing Street. I realized that I was asking for a good deal. With a gallantry consistent with his generous spirit, he immediately volunteered to serve me.

In the events that followed he played his part with a skill that impressed Mr. Baldwin as much as it helped me. Despite the passions that all too soon were to envelop us, neither the Prime Minister nor I ever once had reason to complain of any mis-representation or misunderstanding of our individual views. Undisturbed by the deafening hullabaloo in the Press, the intri-cate constitutional negotiations were handled calmly, expertly, and always with dignity. And while Walter might have wished on more than one occasion that I had taken another line, he carried out without question the exacting responsibilities he had undertaken.

Word came that my motor was back with Wallis; I left Walter Monckton and hurried down to join her. We drove on to Iver, where we paid an agreeable but brief visit to George and Marina. Although Wallis had as yet no intimation of the powder-keg locked up in the red box, it was no longer possible for me to conceal my concern behind a mask of gaiety. Back at The Fort I drew her aside, saying, "A most serious thing has happened. I have kept it from you since Friday evening. But since it concerns you no less than it does me, you must know what is involved. Alec Hardinge has written me a letter—here, you had better read it yourself."

Slowly Wallis read the ominous communication. Before she could speak, I said, "To use a good American expression, they are about to give me the works. They want me to give you up." She was stunned. I took her hands in mine. "I intend to see the Prime Minister to-morrow. I shall tell him that if the Govern-ment is opposed to our marriage, as Alec Hardinge says in his letter, then I am prepared to go."

"You must not be impetuous," Wallis said, "there must be some other way."

"I don't believe there can be—after this. I cannot leave this challenge hanging in the air another day."

The first thing Monday morning I asked one of my secretaries to notify No. 10 Downing Street that I wished to see the Prime Minister at 6.30 that evening.

I had, meanwhile, sought out Max Beaverbrook once more. Inquiry at Stornoway House produced the disconcerting information that he was no longer in Great Britain. A chronic sufferer from asthma, he was even then *en route* across the Atlantic in the liner *Bremen*, bound for the healing climate of the Arizona desert. The loss of so powerful an ally just at this stage disturbed me. Alec Hardinge's letter had served blunt notice that the self-imposed silence of the British newspapers that Max had engineered was about to end. By telegram and telephone I appealed to him to return. The answer I sought might jeopardize his health, but it was given from mid-ocean in good heart. He agreed to come back in the same ship when she completed her turn-around in New York. I could count on seeing him in twelve days.

My second meeting with Mr. Baldwin took place at Buckingham Palace on Monday evening, November 16, at 6.30.

I came at once to the point. "I understand that you and several members of the Cabinet have some fear of a constitutional crisis developing over my friendship with Mrs. Simpson."

"Yes, Sir, that is correct."

Mr. Baldwin went on to say that he personally was disturbed, and further that he knew his senior colleagues in the Cabinet were likewise upset over the prospect of the King's marrying someone whose former marriage had been dissolved by divorce. Marriage? Until this moment the word "marriage" had never been mentioned between us. Whether or not Mr. Baldwin had taken my refusal to stop the divorce case at the Ipswich Assizes as evidence of my intention to marry Wallis, the assumption that marriage was my object was implicit in his conversation. For now he stated frankly that the difficulty arose from the fact that whoever I married would have to be Queen.

And commencing with this dogmatic assertion, the Prime Minister launched confidently upon a dissertation concerning the moral outlook of the British people. "I believe I know," he said, "what the people would tolerate and what they would not. Even my enemies would grant me that." He might have been the Gallup Poll incarnate.

Mr. Baldwin had a curious habit of imparting emphasis to his discourses by snapping and cracking his fingers with a quick flip of the hand past his right ear. This distracting mannerism had first forced itself upon my attention not quite a decade before when he, Mrs. Baldwin, my brother George, and I travelled westward across Canada in a private railway car. Then it had provided a fire-cracker accompaniment to a mildly interesting stream of reminiscences of the lighter aspects of British life. Now, like an orchestral instrument carrying the theme, it accompanied a homily upon the duties of kings.

I never underestimated the weight and authority of the group whose views the Prime Minister represented. His senior Ministers, the men closest to him, were deeply conservative, not alone in their politics but equally in their way of life. Behind them, I suspected, was a shadowy, hovering presence, the Archbishop of Canterbury. Curiously enough, I did not once see him throughout this period. He stood aside until the fateful fabric had been woven and the crisis was over. Yet from beginning to end I had a disquieting feeling that he was invisibly and noiselessly about.

On the other hand, I fully appreciated the quandary in which I had placed Dr. Lang. For in order to shore the ebbing influence of the Church among people he was preparing to use my Coronation as a sounding-board for an emotional call for Christian revival—a "recall to religion"—in which a main theme would be an attack on the growing practice of divorce. Thus the Archbishop and I were both fighting for a principle; I, to marry someone who possessed all the womanly qualities that I desired in a consort, and he, to prevent the marriage because the lady had been divorced, albeit the innocent party.

Men do not all live by the same rules. As I strove to relate my own philosophy to that expounded by the Prime Minister, the idea grew that this entire discourse was pervaded by a paradox. What separated us was not a sinful wish on my part but rather the question of my right to marry as other men do. No idea would have been further from Mr. Baldwin's wholly respectable

331

mind. Yet it seemed to me that if his argument were carried to its logical conclusion, then I should have taken a mistress. A discreet house near by, a key to a garden door, decorous associations—the relationship might be privately deplored, but it had had notable precedents.

Then, dispassionately as I could, I told Mr. Baldwin that marriage had become an indispensable condition to my continued existence, whether as King or as man. "I intend to marry Mrs. Simpson as soon as she is free to marry," I said. If I could marry her as King, well and good; I would be happy and in consequence perhaps a better King. But if, on the other hand, the Government opposed the marriage, as the Prime Minister had given me reason to believe it would, *then I was prepared to go.*

Mr. Baldwin heard me out, pulling deeply on his pipe, his massive head wreathed in a cloud of smoke. But at the mention of the possibility of my leaving the throne, he was startled. The Prime Minister, in his parliamentary account of this conversation, quoted himself as replying: "Sir, that is most grievous news, and it is impossible for me to make any comment on it to-day."

Out of courtesy, I escorted Mr. Baldwin to the Garden Entrance. Standing under the glass canopy, I watched him wriggle into the same undersized little black box in which he had made his first descent upon The Fort. As the box with its portly occupant shot away into the dark, it began to take on the guise of a sinister and purposeful little black beetle. Where was it off to now?

When last we separated, the Prime Minister had expressed his satisfaction over the ice being broken. From this tentative beginning I certainly had carried on the process a good deal further than I could ever have expected. The ice had indeed been broken up, and like Eliza in *Uncle Tom's Cabin*, I found myself facing a perilous dash to shore across the disintegrating floe.

Now came something even more difficult than dealing with the Prime Minister. That was to tell my mother. I wished her to hear from my own lips what had passed between the Prime Minister and me, before anybody had padded off to her with a distorted version of this momentous conversation. That morning, when arranging for the audience with Mr. Baldwin, I had "proposed" myself to my mother for dinner. Punctually at 8.30 I appeared at Marlborough House in white tie and tailcoat. With maternal intuition she must have guessed that I had something serious to tell—indeed, I rather suspected that she knew what it was, for when I entered her boudoir I found my sister Mary there as well.

My mother had leaned more and more on Mary since my father's death, and had therefore asked her to be present, realizing that the meeting might be painful. For Mary's presence I was grateful: it would spare my having to repeat the same story to her. But I was somewhat nonplussed to find my sister-in-law, Alice, Harry's newly wedded wife, there as well. She was a newcomer, almost a stranger to the family. However, my mother put both of us at our ease by announcing, with a reassuring smile, that Alice was tired and would go to bed directly after dinner.

The meal, for which I had little appetite, seemed endless. I was preoccupied with what I was going to say afterwards; no matter how gracefully I proceeded, the evening was bound to be difficult for all of us. I tried to ease the tension by keeping the conversation on a light plane. I congratulated my mother upon the record contribution of garments to her favourite charity, the London Needlework Guild. She was glad to hear that I had arranged to have the outside of Buckingham Palace painted before the Coronation next year: "It is high time," she said. I asked Mary whether she and her husband had bought any yearlings at the Newmarket sales. But I felt especially sorry for poor Alice. Shy and retiring by nature, she had all unwittingly sat down at my mother's table only to find herself caught up in the opening scene of one of the most poignant episodes in the annals of the Royal Family. Never loquacious, this evening she uttered not a word. And when at last we got up to leave the table she eagerly seized upon the interruption to protest that she was extremely tired and to ask that she be excused. After making her curtsy she almost fled from the room. My mother, Mary, and I retired to the boudoir. We were alone.

Settling down in a chair, I told them of my love for Wallis and my determination to marry her; and of the opposition of the Prime Minister and the Government to the marriage. The telling was all the harder because until that evening the subject had never been discussed between us. Neither my mother nor Mary reproved me; in fact, they sympathized with me. But as I went on and they comprehended that even the alternative of abdication would not deter me from my course, I became conscious of their growing consternation that I could even contemplate giving up the Throne of my forebears. My mother had been schooled to put duty, in the stoic Victorian sense, before everything else in life. From her invincible virtue and correctness she looked out as from a fortress upon the rest of humanity, with all its tremulous uncertainties and distractions.

To my mother the Monarchy was something sacred and the Sovereign a personage apart. The word "duty" fell between us. But there could be no question of my shirking my duty. What separated us was not a question of duty but a different concept of kingship. I was, of course, eager to serve my people in all the many ways expected of the King as the head of the State. I had already assumed with pride the manifold duties whereby the King identifies himself with all the phases of national and imperial life. But I would stand on my right to marry on my own terms.

All the while I was waiting for the right moment to make a request I did not believe would be refused. "Please won't you let me bring Wallis Simpson to see you?" I asked. "If you were to meet her you would then understand what she means to me, and why I cannot give her up. I have waited a long time to find the person whom I wished to marry. For me the question now is not whether she is acceptable but whether I am worthy of her." But they could not bring themselves to unbend even this much. It was not, I was sure, because they were wanting in understanding: it was rather because the iron grip of Royal convention would not release them.

For all her self-control, my mother was obviously distressed. Yet she made no effort to dissuade me from the action I contemplated. Perhaps it was because, knowing me so well, she realized that the chances of my turning back were remote indeed. Then, too, I was also something more than just her eldest son: I was the King. This may also have restrained her. As we parted, my mother expressed the hope that I would make a wise decision for my future, adding that she feared my imminent visit to South Wales would be trying in more ways than one.

Over the next several days I took my three brothers into my confidence. Because we had always been a somewhat complicated quartet, I preferred to see them separately, knowing that each would react in his own fashion. As I had anticipated, Harry appeared little moved by what I had to say. Apart from our mutual interests in horses and riding, we had little in common, and our lives in recent years had tended to diverge. All the same, I sensed that he was disappointed. The only one of us brothers who had pursued a professional career was Harry. A regular soldier, he had passed into the Staff College, and until that moment he had looked forward with confidence to promotion achieved through merit. I suspected as I talked that Harry foresaw that if I abdicated he would be required to leave the Army and take more part in the Royal show.

Bertie was so taken aback by my news that in his shy way he could not bring himself to express his innermost feelings at the time. This, after all, was not surprising, for next to myself Bertie had most at stake: it was he who would have to wear the crown if I left, and his genuine concern for me was mixed with the dread of having to assume the responsibilities of kingship. He waited a few days before confiding his thoughts to a letter. He wrote that he longed for me to be happy, adding that he of all people should be able to understand my feelings; he was sure that whatever I decided would be in the best interests of the country and the Empire.

George I saw last of all. Because we had lived in close companionship, he was bound to have guessed what was in my mind. Yet when I told him my story, he seemed genuinely upset. Notwithstanding his somewhat unconventional tastes, George set great store by the Monarchy. I think I can say without being immodest that George had a stout brotherly confidence that I would make a useful King. Nevertheless, because he had had better opportunity than the others to observe the nature of my love for Wallis, he was reconciled to my decision.

From this point on I saw but little of my mother, my sister, or my brothers until the very end. The bonds that united us as a family remained as strong as ever; and throughout the ensuing three and a half weeks of personal trial I was strengthened by the knowledge that I had their affection and that their counsel would not have been withheld had I sought it. But because a constitutional issue was at stake, rather than a family one, I purposely kept the others out of the negotiations with the Government. If I had to go—and even at this point I saw no alternative—it would fall upon them to carry on the institution of Monarchy. No purpose would be served, therefore, by involving them in the hurricane that I felt I should face alone.

My affairs had by this time plainly reached a highly explosive state, and a careless spark from outside might touch off the charge. With so much at stake I was loath to leave London, but the King's business had to go on. Thirty-one hours after my meeting with Mr. Baldwin I was on the night train to South Wales, for a two-day tour of the coal-fields.

As the train clanked and rattled through the night, I lay in my berth reflecting on the turmoil that I knew must by this time have gripped Whitehall. Yet I was at peace with myself. My spiritual struggle was over. I had passed the climax. The public struggle remained, and in many ways it would be more pitiless. But I had declared myself.

CHAPTER XXI

A MOMENTOUS CABINET MEETING

In the atmosphere of suspicion that then prevailed, even this sad journey to the coal-mining valleys of South Wales gave rise to rumours that tended to widen the breach between me and my Government.

Some were to argue afterwards that my real purpose in undertaking this trip was to curry favour with the Opposition, and to use whatever good feeling accrued therefrom as a shield between me and Mr. Baldwin.

In truth, the trip had been on my calendar for months, long before the first little cloud had cast its ominous shadow over my affairs. It was meant to mark my resumption as King of the industrial tours that I used to make as Prince of Wales. Far from having opposed the trip, the Prime Minister welcomed it, believing that the King's appearance in Wales would bring favourably to public attention the Government's efforts at rehabilitation of the "depressed areas."

It was to occur to me that Wales was a truly prophetic place in which to wind up the many years of my public life. From Llantwit-Major, where I got off the train, it is not over one hundred and fifty miles to Caernarvon where, one July morning a quarter of a century before, in the pomp and splendour of the mediæval setting of the ancient castle, my investiture as Prince of Wales had taken place. Its famous Member of Parliament, Mr. Lloyd George, who as Constable of the Castle then had led the trembling young prince into its crumbling mossy walls, was by this time the father of the House of Commons and still vigorous at seventy-three. And the then-tempestuous Home Secretary, Mr. Winston Churchill, who on that same occasion had proclaimed my titles from its "sunlit battlements," now was out of power, feared and mistrusted by much the same people who were closing ranks against me. And the young Royal protégé of Mr. Lloyd George's fanciful promotion had himself become a middle-aged Monarch whose life subsequently had taken him among multitudes of people in many lands. In place of brilliant flags and princely paraphernalia, I was now met by humble arches made of leeks from Government-sponsored co-operative farms, and of un-lighted Davy lamps strung together by jobless miners.

For two days I travelled among the little mining villages of the Rhondda and Monmouth valleys—Penygraig, Pontypridd, Merthyr Tydfil, Dowlais, Penrhiwceiber, Mountain Ash, Cwm-bran, Pontypool, Blaenavon, Blaina, and ending at Rhymney on the borders of Glamorgan. Rhondda's black hillsides, its slag-heaps and dingy houses, were familiar to me: I had been visiting the valley with some regularity since the First World War. But the once-rich coal-mines upon which the wealth and power of Britain so largely depended had become a monument to the transitoriness of human institutions. Even a king, who would be among the last to feel the pinch of a depression, could see that something was manifestly wrong.

However, an incident occurred that momentarily brought tension into the atmosphere surrounding the journey. I was quoted as having said, in the midst of some dismal scene of ruined industry, that "something must be done" to repair the ravages of the dread-ful inertia that had gripped the region. The statement was the minimum humanitarian response that I could have made to what I had seen. The Liberal Press naturally took approving note. But certain Government circles were not pleased. It was intimated that by saying that "something must be done" I had suggested in effect that the Government had neglected to do all that it might have done.

Fortunately the flurry soon passed, and the episode is important only in that it reveals the unfathomable complications that the economic issues of the twentieth century have introduced into the technique of kingship, rendering it almost impossible for a Monarch to continue to play the rôle of the Good King, free to move unhindered among his subjects, and speak what is in his mind.

Back in London it was impossible to delay coming to grips

with the major issue. Mr. Baldwin and the senior members of the Cabinet already having taken their stand, clearly there was little hope of my being able successfully to reverse their opinion unless influential members of their own Party could be persuaded to step forward and speak for me. A few of his colleagues were my personal friends—some of them were my contemporaries; I had reason to believe that with a number of them the old objections to divorce had lost some of their relevance in modern society. With this thought in mind I had, in fact, asked the Prime Minister at our previous meeting whether I might, without a breach of constitutional practice, seek the independent advice and counsel of members of his Cabinet. He had agreed. I turned to two— Sir Samuel Hoare (the present Lord Templewood), whom Mr. Baldwin had brought back into the Government as First Lord of the Admiralty, and Mr. (now Sir) Duff Cooper, then Secretary of State for War.

Sam Hoare I saw first. Although he had never been one of my intimates, our acquaintanceship went back to the First World War, and we had often been thrown in contact in the intervening years while Sam slowly but steadily progressed up the Conservative Party ladder to posts of increasing importance. A product of Harrow and Oxford, well off and descended from an old Norfolk family, he exemplified in his career and outlook the solid virtues of the Tory politician. He was a vigorous, far-sighted and hard-working Minister. He did much to develop British air power during the period just before "the locust years" of the 1930's. During my short reign I had seen rather more of him than I had of most of the other Ministers: in fact, he had been in the shooting-party at Sandringham when Mr. Baldwin sought the first audience at The Fort. Besides, he had been my Minister in Attendance only two weeks before, on the wind-buffeted visit to the Fleet at Port-land.

The First Lord of the Admiralty's temperament was not such as to encourage the belief that I might convert him into a champion of my cause. The most that I hoped from our meeting was that after hearing my story he would understand the compulsions working upon me, and might be moved, when the matter came up for formal discussion in the Cabinet—as soon it must—to speak up in defence of my right to marry.

But I failed to win him as an advocate. He was sympathetic; but he also was acutely conscious of the political realities. Mr. Baldwin, he warned me, was in command of the situation: the senior Ministers were solidly with him on this issue. If I were to press my marriage project upon the Cabinet, I should meet a stone wall of opposition.

I saw Mr. Duff Cooper at the Palace later the same day. Because of our closer association, the facts I had to tell came as no surprise to him. He was as encouraging and optimistic as Sam Hoare had been pessimistic and discouraging. He urged upon me a subtle suggestion. It was based upon the proposition that, since Wallis would not be free to marry again until her divorce became absolute, the question of my marriage therefore would remain abstract for another five months, and the Government could not press me into a decision on a constitutional issue that did not exist. His advice was that I should be patient, that I should ignore the furore, go ahead with the Coronation, and in due time, after the people had become accustomed to see me as King, raise in a calmer atmosphere the question of my right to marry whom I pleased.

This was the counsel of a sophisticated man of the world. But as I considered it I realized that there was an aspect of the Coronation service that he had overlooked. It is essentially a religious service. The King is anointed with holy oil; he takes the Sacrament; and as Defender of the Faith he swears an oath to uphold the doctrines of the Church of England, which does not approve of divorce. For me to have gone through the Coronation ceremony while harbouring in my heart a secret intention to marry contrary to the Church's tenets would have meant being crowned with a lie on my lips. The Archbishop of Canterbury might then justifiably have reproached me for being wanting not only in Christian spirit but also in sincerity. My soul contained enough religion for me to comprehend to the full the deep meaning attached to the Coronation service. Whatever the cost to me personally, I was determined, before I would think of being crowned, to settle once and for all the question of my right to marry.

However, a practical suggestion for resolving the constitutional difficulty emanated from Mr. Esmond Harmsworth. A friend of Wallis's no less than of mine, he invited her to lunch with him at Claridge's, ostensibly to discuss certain aspects of the American newspaper publicity, which was continuing with unflagging volume and inventiveness. In the middle of lunch, without warning, he asked Wallis whether she had ever thought of marrying the King morganatically.

"Morganatically?" she asked. "What do you mean?"

Esmond Harmsworth had evidently made a thorough study of the subject, because he proceeded to answer Wallis's question in detail. A morganatic marriage, he explained, is a legal marriage between a male member of a Royal or princely house and a woman not of equal birth. The wife is as much married as any other wife, but she does not take her husband's rank, and their children, although legitimate, are without rights of succession to the dignities of the father, and their claims upon his estate are restricted to his personal property. This type of marriage was not unknown among Royal houses on the Continent of Europe, but it has never been recognized under British constitutional law.

"Would you be willing," Esmond Harmsworth continued, "to marry the King under these conditions; that is, become his morganatic as distinct from his queenly wife, taking the customary marriage vows but without the title and position of Queen?"

Wallis replied that the matter was hardly one upon which she could with propriety comment. She went on to say, however, that she had reason to believe that the King wanted to marry her. "But," she said, "how the King would marry me, if we are ever to marry, is a question for him to settle with his people."

Later that same afternoon, Wallis told me of the conversation. "Well," I asked after she finished, "what do you think of it?"

"It sounds strange and almost inhuman. Have you had many such marriages in your family?"

"The last one," I answered, "was more than ninety years ago."

Although I am well versed in my family history, this seemed hardly the time for a recital of the complicated circumstances under which some of my ancestors had contracted marriages with commoners. So I shrugged my shoulders, and nothing more was said for a few days.

My first reaction to the morganatic proposal was one of distaste. The term itself repelled me as one of the least graceful that might be applied to the relations between men and women. Yet, deciding after further consideration that as a possible alternative it had its merits, I sent for Esmond Harmsworth.

"With whom did this idea originate?" I asked him.

"With my father, Sir," he answered.

Esmond Harmsworth then asked whether he might lay the plan before the Prime Minister as a possible way out of the existing *impasse*. My earlier misgivings remained. Nevertheless, it must be remembered that at this stage I was ready to welcome any reasonable suggestion that offered hope of allowing me to marry on the throne without precipitating a political struggle. If the constitutional barriers standing in the way could be levelled by my forgoing for Wallis the claims to queenly prerogatives which normally accrued to the King's wife, then a morganatic marriage might indeed prove to be a solution.

It is, I reflected, not the form but the content of things that matters. The lesser status, I was sure, would never prevent Wallis with her American charm and energy from fulfilling with undiminished spirit the many duties devolving upon the King's consort. That side of our combined lives could be discharged without default, even without the formal symbolism of the two gilt thrones side by side which had been an indivisible aspect of the two former reigns. So, though anything but sanguine, I gave Esmond Harmsworth my blessing, and he set off for No. 10 Downing Street.

At this point Walter Monckton, whom I had asked to look into the legal precedents, advised me that even in the unlikely event of the Cabinet's approving a morganatic marriage, special legislation would be required and the prospects of such a Bill's ever passing Parliament were dubious.

A day or two later Esmond Harmsworth returned to the Palace to report on his conversation with Mr. Baldwin, whose reaction he described as surprised, interested, and non-committal. However, the Prime Minister promised to refer the plan to the Cabinet.

"Was that all?" I asked.

"That was all."

Meanwhile, no friendly signal came from No. 10 Downing Street. Within a day or so, I think, I summoned the Prime Minister to another audience. I asked him at once what he thought of the Harmsworth proposal. Slowly and with careful attention to his words, Mr. Baldwin replied that he had not yet considered it.

I must have registered surprise: for after an uncomfortable pause, Mr. Baldwin added that he had not meant to give the impression that the proposition had been ignored, but only that he was not yet ready to render a considered judgment. If, however, I desired a "horseback opinion," he would have to tell me that Parliament would never pass the necessary legislation.

"Are you sure that it wouldn't, Mr. Baldwin?" I asked.

"Sir, would you like me to examine the proposition formally?" he asked.

"Yes; please do so," I answered.

The Prime Minister then reminded me that this meant submitting the morganatic proposal not only to the British Cabinet but to all the Dominion Cabinets as well. "Do you really wish that, Sir?" My answer was that I did. Thereupon the Prime Minister hurried off. As the door closed behind him I realized that with that simple request I had gone a long way towards sealing my own fate. For in asking the Prime Minister to find out the sentiments of the British and Dominion Governments, I had automatically bound myself to submit unquestioningly to their "advice."

At this point, with the issue about to be joined, some explanation is in order concerning my constitutional position *vis-à-vis* the Prime Minister. In theory the Prime Minister had no power to prevent my marriage. He could only proffer "advice" as to what, in the Government's opinion, constituted a proper course for the King. Now the word "advice," like other terms in the constitutional vocabulary, has a special meaning when used in relation to the Sovereign. Whenever the Prime Minister "advises" the King he is using a respectful form of words to express the will and decision of the Government. The King is virtually bound to accept such "advice." Furthermore, he cannot seek "advice" elsewhere. However, if, in the exercise of his undoubted powers, he chooses not to accept the "advice" thus formally tendered, then his Ministers resign, and he must try to form a new Government from the Opposition—a step that may be fraught with the gravest risks, since it would in all probability bring on a General Election.

So far my exchanges with Mr. Baldwin had been entirely informal. At the first meeting, sought by him, he had undertaken only to convey what might be called, for want of a happier phrase, a "friendly warning" that a dangerous situation was in the making. There was no question of his proffering formal advice at that stage. At the second meeting, for which I was the prime mover, I had avowed my intention to marry, but still without seeking the formal advice of the Government. Nevertheless Mr. Baldwin, although he had not yet brought the question formally before the Cabinet, had seen fit, on the strength of his private discussions with his senior Ministers, to advise me not to marry.

Now my situation was further complicated by my special status in relation to the Dominions. Under the Statute of Westminster, passed only five years earlier, the Dominions had in theory become fully independent of the British Government. The Crown survived as the sole legal connecting-link between the mother country and the younger overseas nations of the Commonwealth. The Prime Minister, therefore, was without authority to approach the separate Dominions directly on this question. That prerogative remained the King's alone. In principle, the question should have been broached to each self-governing Dominion through the Governor-General—the King's personal representative in the Dominion. But I was loath to employ this channel. The matter was much too personal, too delicate to be handled by the King himself.

Once I had made up my mind to determine the attitude of the British Cabinet and the Dominion Governments towards the proposal of the morganatic marriage, the only proper course open to me was to instruct the Prime Minister to act as my intermediary, not only with the Home Government but also with the Governments of the British Commonwealth. Many were to argue afterwards that this was a tactical error of the first magnitude on my part. The automatic effect of my action was to deliver the imperial pass-keys into Mr. Baldwin's hands; once inside the door he carefully locked me out.[1] Yet I have never regretted the decision. I am sure it was the only one for me.

The next day Lord Beaverbrook returned from New York. The *Bremen* landed him at Southampton in the forenoon. He motored straight to The Fort, and I was at the door to greet him.

"You have done a fine thing for me," I told him, grasping his hand, "and I shall always remember it."

Luncheon was ready, with special dishes prepared according to Max Beaverbrook's diet. While he ate, I told him what had happened since his departure. The speed with which events had moved during his brief absence plainly astonished him. When I described the last audience with Mr. Baldwin and my request that he should lay the morganatic marriage proposal before the Cabinet, my listener's face darkened. Such an idea, he declared, would appeal neither to the Cabinet nor, in his opinion, to the British people. He was all for a Fabian strategy of delay. He urged me to withdraw at once the Harmsworth proposal, and stave off an undoubted adverse decision until he and others of my friends had had an opportunity of presenting to the public, without cant or prejudice, what he called the "King's Case" for the marriage.

Many brilliant men besides Max Beaverbrook and Duff Cooper were in the next few days to advocate this same Fabian policy. I do not underestimate the cogency of the argument, and I am prepared to concede that such a plan might have succeeded had I acted in time and had my own nature been different. But, in view of the solid alinement of the dominant elements in the political parties that I had reason to believe Mr. Baldwin would be able to achieve, I doubted from the beginning that this strategy could possibly succeed in the foreseeable future. Moreover, I was troubled inwardly by the realization that, however carefully I walked, it would involve me in a long course of seeming dissimulation for which I had neither the talent nor the appetite.

---

[1] It might be noted in point of historical interest that fear was, in fact, expressed in the Cabinet that the Government's action in sending the cables to the Dominions might be criticized in Parliament. Had a question been asked in the House of Commons concerning the precise replies that had been received from the Dominions, the answer would have been, I was informed, that His Majesty's Government was not in a position to divulge this information; the Dominions had communicated directly with the King.

But in any event I was fully aroused to the danger of being pushed into an irrevocable decision before my case had been given a fair hearing. Max Beaverbrook hurried off to London to rally support. Where before I had stood alone, I now had a powerful champion. While I was pondering this new idea, Mr. Baldwin acted. He grasped firmly the nettle he had earlier seemed to shun.

Next morning, Friday, November 27, the Cabinet assembled for a special meeting. Two hours later the Ministers emerged and dispersed, each to return to his own business. No statement concerning the import of the meeting was issued: it was widely assumed that it had to do with some aspect of the ever-mounting international crisis. But I knew from my own reliable sources of information that Mr. Baldwin for the first time had laid before the whole Cabinet the vexatious question of which I was the centre, and had informed them that I had asked him to consult the Dominions on the question of a morganatic marriage.

The following morning I waited anxiously for the arrival of the red box containing the secret minutes of the Cabinet Meeting. I opened it myself with the gold key that had been my father's. But the solitary paper that I found inside, purporting to describe the momentous discussions of that day, was blank except for a perfunctory paragraph relating to the carriage of arms to Spain.

However, before dark that Friday a fragmentary account had reached me of what had been said around the green-baize-covered table over which the Prime Minister presides. Mr. Baldwin had adroitly dismissed the morganatic marriage proposal as impracticable and undesirable. Instead, he narrowed the choices open to me to two: either the Government must accept the King's wife as Queen, or if that status were withheld and the King insisted none the less on marriage in the face of the Government's opposition, abdication was the only alternative.

The Cabinet appears to have concurred with only one dissenting voice. I have been given to understand that Mr. Duff Cooper spoke up eloquently but in vain against precipitate action. He put forward much the same argument that he had earlier used with me, suggesting that the question be dropped for the time being, that I be crowned as planned in May, and the question raised again in a year's time.

Max Beaverbrook had also learned something about this

Cabinet Meeting and hurried to Buckingham Palace in a state of agitation unusual for him. "Sir," he exclaimed, "you have put your head on the execution block. All that Baldwin has to do now is to swing the axe." He looked searchingly at me. "Have you seen the cables to the Dominions?"

"No," I answered.

"Have you any idea what they will say?"

It had not occurred to me to ask nor had Mr. Baldwin deemed it necessary to submit the draft. But now that the question had been raised, I perceived that, with Mr. Baldwin composing the cables, they were hardly likely to be compassionate pleas on behalf of my proposal.

Max Beaverbrook informed me that directly after the Cabinet adjourned a member of the Government, close to Mr. Baldwin, had lunched with him at Stornoway House. From his guest Max learned that not only had the cables gone out to the Governments of Canada, Australia, New Zealand, South Africa, and the Irish Free State, but that they had been framed in much the same rigid terms in which Mr. Baldwin had presented to the Cabinet the case against the marriage. The Dominion Premiers were asked, in effect: "Do you recommend the King's marrying morganatically? Or, if the King insists upon marrying, do you recommend abdication?"

"In any case," Max Beaverbrook insisted, "I would advise you to stop them. I am a Canadian. I know the Dominions. Their answer will be a swift and emphatic No."

But although I conceded the practical wisdom of this counsel, it seemed to me that matters had already progressed much too far for me to wish to reverse the Government machinery. The die was cast; I was impatient for the answer from the Dominions. Besides, my mind was somewhat distracted that day by another unexpected, even sinister development.

During this period both Wallis and I had each received anonymous letters. Having had some experience during my public career of this base and cowardly form of human aberration, I had long before decided that the proper place for such communications is the fire. But they were the first that Wallis had ever received and, not surprisingly, they distressed her. Meanwhile, she had taken a house in Cumberland Terrace, where she was living

347

with her aunt. The house had by now become a point of curiosity, and even shopping had become unpleasant for her. Then a rumour reached me of a plot to blow up the house. Although I dismissed it as ridiculous, I none the less urged Wallis and her aunt to come to The Fort, where no one would bother them.

I called for them myself at Cumberland Terrace. It was the late afternoon of the momentous day the Cabinet rejected the marriage proposal. Under her arm Wallis carried a gay little Cairn terrier, Slipper, which I had given her the year before. Its excited yapping at the prospect of a drive in the motor caused several passers-by to turn and stare as the three of us left the house in the November twilight. We all drove down to Sunningdale. Thus it came to pass that Wallis and I were together when at last the pent-up fury of the storm broke.

At this juncture, the scene shifted momentarily to Stornoway House where Max Beaverbrook, ever since his return from America, had worked feverishly to rally support for me in whatever quarters it might be found. The hour was desperately late and to many his rallying cry, issued through a battery of telephones, must have sounded like a call for volunteers to man a ship patently doomed. Mr. Baldwin was aware of what Max Beaverbrook was up to; and no doubt hoping to check the forces beginning to rally round my cause, he despatched Sir Samuel Hoare on Sunday, the 29th, to explain the attitude of the Government towards the King.

The message which the First Lord of the Admiralty bore was ominous indeed. It was that the Ministers stood with Mr. Baldwin—". . . no breach exists: there is no light or leaning in the King's direction." Then the First Lord fired his second salvo. "The publicity," he said, "is about to break." Many Ministers, he added, were restless and dissatisfied over the failure of the Press to publish the facts of a crisis already the talk of the rest of the world. He stressed Mr. Baldwin's desire that the Press, like the Cabinet, should form an unbroken front against the proposed marriage. It was an undisguised invitation for Max Beaverbrook to change sides. His answer was: "I have taken the King's shilling, I am a King's man."

A bombardment appeared imminent. And because of the intimate association of Mr. Baldwin, the Archbishop of Canterbury, and Mr. Geoffrey Dawson, editor of *The Times*, we had instinctively braced ourselves for an opening salvo from "The Thunderer." In fact, rumour had reached us that *The Times* already had prepared a powerful and unfavourable editorial, and was only awaiting a signal to publish it. However, the shelling, when it did start, came from just about the last place in the world we expected—from the usually sedate and unprovocative Diocesan Conference in Bradford.

On the forenoon of December 1 the Bishop of Bradford, the Right Reverend A. W. F. Blunt, was inspired to address an audience of clergy and laity of his Diocese on the subject of the approaching Coronation service. Ordinarily, this topic would have confined the speaker to a learned discussion of ecclesiastical lore. But for some obscure reason the prelate was moved at this tense moment to express regret that the King had not shown more positive evidence of his awareness of the need for Divine guidance in the discharge of his high office. There was a veiled suggestion of want of sustained habit in my church-going. Until that moment I had never heard of Dr. Blunt, and in the light of the historical consequences of his sudden action it is perhaps worthy of note that I was not to hear of him again until the spring of 1950. On this last occasion I read that he had been attacked in the House of Lords as a leading personality in a strange organization called "The Council of Clergy and Ministers for Common Ownership," which was said to be an instrument for Communist infiltration into the Church. Of such material is history made. What the Bishop of Bradford had to say against me fourteen years ago may to-day appear innocuous to some. Nevertheless, it was criticism of the King, and in that charged atmosphere it proved to be the spark that caused the explosion.

My first intimation of trouble was a telephone call late in the afternoon from Max Beaverbrook. The press agency report on Dr. Blunt's speech had just reached his desk. Max Beaverbrook read out the offending sentences. He then went on to say that the provincial Press, led by the *Yorkshire Post*, would in their morning edition seize upon the Bishop's criticism as a long-awaited excuse for breaking the news of my desire to marry and of my clash with the Government because of it.

"What are the London newspapers going to do?" I asked him.

"They will report Dr. Blunt's speech."

"With editorial comment?"

"No," he answered, "that will be reserved until the results of to-morrow's Cabinet Meeting are available."

By then the answers from the Dominions would in all probability be in Mr. Baldwin's hands.

The immediate effect of the Bradford bombshell was to shatter all my hopes of settling my problem one way or the other by private negotiation with my Ministers. I could no longer afford to wait passively.

And when to-day I survey afresh, for the purpose of this narrative, the swift development of the crisis that was to bring my reign to an end, I am struck by two things. First, by the fantastic acceleration of the march of events and the unbelievable compression of emotions. The whole drama in its public aspects ran its course from haphazard beginning to sudden end in exactly ten days. And next, I am astonished by how much the public furore tended to fall behind the actual decision.

CHAPTER XXII

"ON THE THRONE OR NOT,
I SHALL MARRY"

O N Wednesday morning the provinces all knew what
Dr. Blunt had said. But more than that, they had been
given to understand that the criticism of the King went
deeper than the Bishop's complaint at the irregularity of his
Sovereign's attendance at Divine Service on Sundays. The
Yorkshire Post said, "Dr. Blunt must have had good reason for
so pointed a remark. Most people are by this time aware that
a great deal of rumour has been published of late in the more
sensational American newspapers. . . ." The *Manchester Guardian*
referred explicitly to a "constitutional issue" having arisen
between the King and the Government—a statement which I
felt was still debatable. As with an iceberg, the main burden of
my situation was still hidden from public gaze; yet the menacing
summit was exposed, and I was well aware, as I steeled myself
against the repercussions of Dr. Blunt's outburst, that much of
the country was already seething with speculation.

In London, however, the mass of the population were still in
ignorance of the bombshell that had been let loose in the Diocesan
Conference at Bradford. Although the morning newspapers did
publish the Bishop's speech they did so without comment or
interpretation; and, so far as the ordinary reader could tell, all was
well between the King and his Government. Again, in the morning, while the Cabinet was in session, afternoon newspapers in
their early editions reproduced the speech—prominently, but
without comment and without even mentioning the violent
reverberations that it had produced in the provinces.

But despite Fleet Street's outward calm, there was no mistaking
the sudden tension in the air. Walter Monckton was summoned

to No. 10 Downing Street as the meeting dispersed. Mr. Baldwin advised him of its decision—a decision which, although it came as no surprise, was almost crushing in its impact. The Cabinet would not approve the morganatic marriage. Walter Monckton telephoned the news to me immediately, adding that the Prime Minister himself would come to the Palace in the late afternoon to convey the information.

As I contemplated my prospects, my heart turned heavy. The choice before me was plain. I must either abdicate, or, if I persevered in my intention to marry while on the Throne, the constitutional issue would indeed materialize in all its malignant reality.

While crisis thus enveloped me, my calendar continued to cast up with almost robot-like irrelevance a variety of people totally unconnected with the issue that was claiming my heart and soul. Among the people to whom I gave audience in the early afternoon of that day were the Adjutant-General of the Forces, with samples of a new blue uniform to be worn by the infantry of the line at my Coronation; Mr. Srinivasa Sarma, an Indian journalist, who came to be knighted; Major Alexander Mackenzie, my resident factor at Balmoral, to report on various details connected with the estate; and finally the American Polar explorer, Mr. Lincoln Ellsworth, who evinced some interest in purchasing my ranch in Canada. The conversation with this last caller worked around by chance to his speciality. He had just returned from his flight across the Antarctic, and I was surprised to hear from him, in the course of a description of that region's peculiarities, that it was wholly uninhabited.

"Not even Eskimos?" I asked.

"No one at all, Sir," he answered with the authority of an expert.

"Then, Mr. Ellsworth," I said, "if there are no people, there are no politics."

He looked at me startled. "I am not sure, Sir, that I quite understand."

"Ah!" I went on. "To think of a whole continent with no Prime Minister, no Archbishop, no Chancellor of the Exchequer —not even a King. It must be a paradise."

As matters turned out, Mr. Ellsworth was the last person

except the Prime Minister and members of my household to see King Edward VIII at Buckingham Palace on matters of general business.

Later that afternoon, Max Beaverbrook telephoned the Palace. The news that he related from Fleet Street was disheartening in the extreme. The last vestiges of the "gentleman's agreement" were about to go with a whoop. The Cabinet's decision and the few salient facts of Mr. Baldwin's discussion with me were already common knowledge throughout Fleet Street. All the metropolitan morning newspapers, which wield enormous influence in all walks of national life, were preparing to go to press that night with sensational disclosures of the deadlock between the Government and me. That *The Times*, under the fluent and pitiless pen of Geoffrey Dawson, would lead the attack was a foregone conclusion. I had endeavoured, without success, to obtain assurances that it would at least be temperate. By morning the British people, the whole Empire, and the entire world, would know of my love for Wallis and the crisis that it had brought.

"What do you intend to say in the *Express*, Max?" I asked.

"Sir," he answered, "the *Express* will, with the other newspapers, report the facts. It is our duty to do so."

"I realize that," I said, perhaps bitterly. "I understand why. But will you take up a position in this matter?"

Max exclaimed almost harshly, "Baldwin has seized the initiative. You can be sure that from this moment he will exploit his advantage to the full. The facts about to be revealed to the public will shock and stun. Inevitably its first reaction will be hostile to you and sympathetic to him—the pro-Government Press will see to that. If the flow of adverse opinion is to be halted and reversed, then you must allow your friends to counter hard, and at once."

With this preface, my friend proceeded into a disquisition on the technique of moulding public opinion—a field in which he was a master. He spoke spiritedly and profoundly. The gist of his argument was that if I were to marry and remain on the Throne, I must grapple forthwith with what he called the "essentials of the situation." These, as he enumerated them, were: that Mr. Baldwin was determined to prevent my marriage; that he was resolved to force me off the Throne if I persisted in my intention; that the signal had been given for a concerted attack upon me; that the Prime Minister was prepared to seek to redeem his ebbing political fortunes on this one issue; and that his control of the Party machine, reinforced with his access to the pro-Government Press, not to mention the Established Church, armed him with powerful weapons which would undoubtedly guarantee him victory. Max therefore urged me forcefully to allow his newspapers and those of other friendly groups to strike back vigorously. "Many others hold with me that there is nothing wrong in the King's marrying a woman who has divorced her husband. A strong case can be made."

But I could not see it that way. While it pleased me to hear that many shared this view, "many" was not enough. My whole life—the ordered, sheltered existence that I had known since birth—had blown up and was disintegrating. And in the chaos around me I had three instinctive desires: to dampen the uproar if I could; to avoid the responsibility of splitting the nation and jeopardizing the Monarchy on the issue of my personal happiness; and to protect Wallis from the full blast of sensationalism about to overwhelm us both. These were the keys to my actions in the days that remained to me as King. And so, even as Max Beaverbrook argued on, my subconscious mind was framing what I would say to the Prime Minister at my imminent audience with him. When we rang off, Max's natural belligerence seemed confounded and frustrated by my attitude.

Shortly afterwards the Prime Minister was announced. My first concern was, of course, for the answers he had meanwhile received from the cables to the Dominion Premiers. Before I had even asked the question, I judged from his demeanour that the responses were unfavourable for me.

The inquiries among the Dominions, Mr. Baldwin advised, were still incomplete, but it was already clear to him that the necessary legislation for a morganatic marriage would not be forthcoming.

"What about Parliament?" I asked.

"The answer would, I am sure, be the same."

"But Parliament has not been consulted," I persisted. "The issue has never been presented."

He answered, unruffled, "I have caused inquiries to be set afoot in the usual manner. The response has been such as to convince my colleagues and myself that the people would not approve of Your Majesty's marriage with Mrs. Simpson."

Almost pedantically, he summed up for me the three choices that had faced me from the outset:

(1) I could give up the idea of marriage.
(2) I could marry contrary to the advice of my Ministers.
(3) I could abdicate.

The Prime Minister prayed that I would take the first course. The second course, he continued, watching me closely, was manifestly impossible; if I married in the face of the advice of my Ministers, I could not hope to remain on the Throne. Never taking his eyes off me, he went on to say that if I would not abandon the project there was really no choice for me but to go.

"So, Mr. Baldwin," I said, "you really leave me with only one choice."

With undeniable earnestness, he said, "Believe me, Sir, it is my sincere hope—and the hope of the Cabinet—that you will remain our King."

"Whether on the Throne or not, Mr. Baldwin, " I answered, "I shall marry; and however painful the prospect, I shall, if necessary, abdicate in order to do so."

It was in a sombre mood that I returned to The Fort to tell Wallis what lay in store for both of us. After dinner, not wishing to alarm her aunt, I asked Wallis to come out and walk with me along the flagstone path around the house. The night was appropriate for the story I had to tell—gloomy, cold, and silent. A damp fog had rolled up from across Virginia Water; peering in the direction of London, I could almost feel the vibrations of the Fleet Street presses. "It has been a bad day," I told her. "I have seen Mr. Baldwin: he leaves me no choice. Either I must give you up or abdicate." We walked on. When Wallis spoke, her only thought was what was best for me. Whatever the cost to us personally, she insisted that I should remain on the Throne.

I felt grievously responsible for the trouble and sorrow that my love had brought down upon her head. When I described the fierce attack in preparation by the Press, she fell silent. Then she said that perhaps it would be better if she left England. Dreadful as was the prospect of parting, I realized that she was right. Indeed, I was almost glad that she had made up her mind alone. For I was deeply anxious to move her from the path of the main blow. After all, the great decision was mine, and mine alone: this was something that would have to be thrashed out with my own people.

I suppose that every actor in the Abdication drama has his own idea of where and when the real turning-point occurred. For me, scanning across the years, it came, I am sure, that evening on the flagstones of Fort Belvedere. For in agreeing with Wallis that it would be better for her to leave the country, I must have unconsciously made up my mind that the struggle to save my Throne was hopeless, and that in the end, come what might, I would follow her.

That evening also Walter Monckton called at Stornoway House to inform Max Beaverbrook of the upshot of my audience with the Prime Minister. Knowing this would disappoint Max, I telephoned him myself from The Fort. I told him that the choices put before me seemed to leave only one door open—to retire into private life. "I have not altogether given up hope," I said. "But one thing is certain—no marriage no Coronation."

And because I believed to the end that the innate reasonableness of the British public would prevail, I was determined to hold back from the final and irrevocable step so long as there existed the faintest hope of my being allowed to present my case to them without a disastrous prolongation of public disunity.

It was the spreading disunity that troubled me. I realized as keenly as the next man that public opinion was bound to be distracted and confused. The crisis had come with the violence of a thunderclap. Now everybody's voice would be heard but mine. And the feeling mounted within me that if I could only speak directly to the people, explaining what was in my mind, the confusion would be partly dissipated, the tension relieved, and the atmosphere cleared for the exercise of justice and reason.

It was Wallis, I think, who first had the idea of my going on the air. My father's annual Christmas broadcasts to the Empire, started only four years before, not to mention President Roosevelt's immensely influential "Fireside Chats" to the American people, provided impressive contemporary examples of the unprecedented power of the radio to reach immense audiences with a simple message.

Unfortunately for my case, however, I could not thus reach the people without the Government's "advising" me to do so. And since such a broadcast would in effect be an appeal to the public on an issue to which the Government was already opposed, I realized that the chances of its tendering such "advice" were remote.

Nevertheless, the more I thought about the idea the more a broadcast appealed to me as the only possible way in which I might be able to mobilize the support of the entire Commonwealth. I therefore resolved to raise the question with the Prime Minister.

CHAPTER XXIII

WALLIS DEPARTS FOR FRANCE

PUBLICITY was part of my heritage, and I was never so naïve as to suppose that my romance was a tender shoot to be protected from the prying curiosity of the Press. But what stared at me from the newspapers that were brought to my room on Thursday morning really shocked me. Could this be the King or was I some common felon? The Press creates; the Press destroys. All my life I had been the passive clay which it had enthusiastically worked into the hackneyed image of a Prince Charming. Now it had whirled around, and was bent upon demolishing the natural man who had been there all the time.

The bitter unanimity with which the so-called "quality" newspapers lashed out left little doubt that they reflected the Government's attitude towards me. By that action the Monarchy was brought violently into politics. As the heat of controversy rose, *The Times* particularly struck with a directness that was strangely at variance with the suave discretion that stamped its habitual reference to the King, and even more with its flattering appraisal of my demeanour at the opening of Parliament only a month before.

It was all extremely unpleasant, to say the least. And to the degree that the daily Press reflected British opinion, the Prime Minister had certainly won the opening engagement, as Max Beaverbrook had prophesied he would. Everything had gone Mr. Baldwin's way. No clear and commanding voice had been raised on the King's behalf. The one-sidedness of the situation stirred me to action. If the British people were ever to know what was in my heart and mind, I must speak out without delay. The broadcast which the night before had been a vague and abstract notion became for me a burning necessity.

Pushing the newspapers aside, I started to write. When the draft had progressed far enough, I telephoned Walter Monckton and George Allen in London, and asked them both to come to The Fort at all speed. Just before they arrived, and while I was absorbed in writing, Wallis entered the drawing-room. In her hand she had a London picture newspaper.

"Have you seen this?" she asked.

"Yes," I answered. "It's too bad."

The world can hold few worse shocks for a sensitive woman than to come without warning upon her own grossly magnified countenance upon the front page of a sensational newspaper.

"I had no idea that it would be anything like this," she said.

Nor had I. And trying to reassure her I expressed the hope, but without conviction, that the sensationalism would soon spend itself.

"You do not seem to understand," she said in a troubled voice. "It is not only that they are attacking you personally, or me. They are attacking the King."

To me Wallis has always been a blithe spirit—gay, quick, unconquerable. She has an article of faith which enables her to face the future with untroubled heart—"Don't worry. It never happens." But that morning her face was tragic.

I laid aside the broadcast. We had a long talk. Wallis said something that she had said many times: that it was not too late; I could still draw back. "I wish," she said, "that I had had a clearer understanding of the constitutional questions."

"I must take the blame for that," I answered. "I thought it could be managed."

Then she said, "I cannot stay here another day, with all this going on. I must leave England this afternoon."

But for where? She decided, after some thought, to go to France. Her friends, Katherine and Herman Rogers, she was sure, would welcome her at their villa, Lou Viei, above Cannes.

I put through a call to Cannes. It was dangerous to say too much over the telephone. Nevertheless, the Rogers instantly grasped the meaning of Wallis's guarded inquiries, their invitation was warm and unreserved.

Because of the hue and cry that would be raised by the Press if so much as a hint of Wallis's intention became known, preparations for her departure went forward with the utmost secrecy. It was decided that she should cross the Channel in the night boat from Newhaven to Dieppe, leaving The Fort after dark and motoring to the coast. Once on the Continent, she would drive straight to Cannes. I insisted that my head chauffeur, George Ladbroke, who had been in my service seventeen years, should drive her motor, and that she should be accompanied by a detective from Scotland Yard. I further prevailed upon her to take along a mutual friend, Lord Brownlow, one of my Lords-in-Waiting, and a former Grenadier. Perry—an abbreviation of his baptismal name, Peregrine—was a kinsman of Sir Charles Cust, my father's closest friend. He and his wife, Kitty, had been frequent guests at The Fort and at Bryanston Court. Furthermore, he was on intimate terms with Max Beaverbrook. Thus by temperament, instinct, and association he was uniquely and eminently qualified for this delicate mission—almost too well, I was presently to discover, to my temporary discomfiture.

I telephoned Perry Brownlow in London.

"Perry," I informed him, "Wallis is leaving England to-night. I want you to go with her."

"Sir," was his answer, the Guardsman's unquestioning assent.

"Come to The Fort this afternoon, in your own car. Bring a suitcase and a trunk—you may be away some time. I cannot tell you now where you are going—I will explain everything when you get here. And meanwhile tell no one—not even Kitty."

Perry told me afterwards that Kitty entered his room as he was packing. Noticing the passport in his hand, she inquired gaily, "Perry, have I spoiled a surprise? Are you planning a holiday?" His hastily invented explanation hardly satisfied her.

I left it to my Keeper of the Privy Purse, Major Ulick Alexander, to work out the details of the journey. Throughout that day, whenever I had a free moment to myself, I worked on the broadcast. By this time it was obvious to me that my original idea of merely putting my case before the nation, with a plea for understanding, would no longer suffice. The immediate problem was to contain or divert the avalanche. This I hoped to effect by advancing a novel proposition: specifically, that I should leave my country temporarily, taking up residence in some foreign land, while the nation and the Empire, without the distraction of my presence, made up its mind on the question of my marriage.

With my heart and mind sorely beset, I composed the broadcast. Walter Monckton and George Allen both helped me with it. The result of our combined efforts was a simple statement, never finally polished, never delivered. It was an appeal to the hearth and the home. Its purpose was to present my problem in its true light—not merely as a knotty and abstruse constitutional issue, but as a call of the heart such as countless people of all classes and in all conditions of mankind have experienced in their own lives or witnessed in the lives of their friends, one which men and women will continue to experience so long as men and women cleave to each other. I was sure that were I given the chance to speak in simple human terms to my people, I should not speak in vain. I had nothing to hide. I sought no special privileges. What I desired was something that the fundamental law of the realm allowed my subjects, but which the Prime Minister proposed to deny me. My listeners, I was sure, knew me well enough to realize that I never would enter into a marriage of convenience. I would tell them that it had taken me a long time to find the woman whom I wished to make my wife, and that, having found her, I was determined to marry her. Then came these two paragraphs:

> Neither Mrs. Simpson nor I have ever sought to insist that she should be queen. All we desired was that our married happiness should carry with it a proper title and dignity for her, befitting my wife.
>
> Now that I have at last been able to take you into my confidence, I feel it is best to go away for a while so that you may reflect calmly and quietly, but without undue delay, on what I have said. Nothing is nearer to my heart than that I should return; but whatever may befall, I shall always have a deep affection for my country, for the Empire and for you all.

In short, what I proposed was a brief withdrawal from an overheated atmosphere. I had tentatively fixed upon Belgium, directly across the Channel, as a convenient place to await the verdict. To assure the uninterrupted discharge of the Monarch's constitutional functions during my absence it would have been a simple matter to reconstitute another Council of State, such as had already twice been formed during my father's two serious illnesses.

The broadcast was finished as the afternoon waned. That it contemplated a unique and unprecedented innovation in constitutional procedure I fully realized. And I did not delude myself into imagining that the highly traditionalist Prime Minister would welcome it as a desirable solution to the deadlock between us. Nevertheless, I resolved to take it myself to London that evening, after Wallis had gone, and to ask whether the Government would agree to my making such a broadcast. And since it was an undertaking in which I felt the need of Winston Churchill's wisdom and experience, I further resolved to ask Mr. Baldwin whether I might consult my old friend on this and related matters.

Thus in a fever of work and preparation, the day hurried on to the climax of parting.

There was no time for Wallis to arrange about shutting up her house in Cumberland Terrace. She decided not to attempt to collect any additional clothes, lest her appearance there should excite the curiosity of journalists who presumably had it under surveillance. She even decided, with the utmost reluctance, to leave Slipper behind. Sadly, she consigned him to my safekeeping, saying, "I will let you know when to send him to me. It may be some time." In the bitter days that followed I was to be grateful for his companionship. He followed me around The Fort; he slept by my bed; he was the mute witness of my meetings with the Prime Minister.

Perry arrived from London in his Rolls about dusk. We sat down for tea together—Wallis, her aunt Mrs. Merryman, Ulick Alexander, and Perry Brownlow. But little was eaten, we were all too tense. There was, I recall, a final recapitulation of the arrangements for Wallis's secret departure. Accommodation for her and Perry Brownlow on the Channel steamer had been booked in the name of "Mr. and Mrs. Harris." Wallis's own motor was already aboard the ship. It had been despatched, conspicuously empty, in the direction of London early in the afternoon.

Our last moments together were infinitely sad and forlorn.

The separation was all the harder to contemplate for the reason that there was no way of telling how long it would last. Nothing was said between us as to when or where we would meet again. The parting, I realize now, was much worse for her than I appreciated at the time. Long afterwards she confided to me that only on this last day at The Fort did she begin to comprehend what abdication really involved for me. Until then it had been only a word—a possible remote alternative. That day, however, she had felt for the first time the fierce pressures converging on the King; she had come to fear for me and for what I was. And when in the darkness she left the Fort with Perry Brownlow for France, it was with the hope that she would see me again, but never expecting that she would.

I watched them go. With dimmed lights, and the Scotland Yard man in front, the Rolls took the back drive down towards Virginia Water, and the public road through Windsor Great Park some distance beyond.

Mrs. Merryman was returning to Cumberland Terrace. Before she left, however, I opened my heart to her.

"I feel terribly sorry about all this. I hope you understand."

"In spite of everything, Sir, you are really determined to marry my niece?"

"I am."

"Even if it means giving up the Throne?"

"Yes, even if I have to abdicate. I hope that we shall be able to marry and that I can carry on my work as King. But I am determined in any case to marry her."

"Wallis can make you happy," she said, "if happiness is what you really want."

"It is a great deal, Mrs. Merryman."

"But isn't there perhaps something more? Your country? Are you right in putting your happiness before what your people may regard as your duty?"

"It is not a question merely of happiness," I answered, "I cannot with full heart carry out my duties in the loneliness that surrounds me."

"What you are proposing to do for Wallis," she went on, "is one of the most magnificent compliments that any man has ever paid to a woman. But there is another side to all this."

"What is that, Mrs. Merryman?"

"It is usually said in situations of this sort that it is always the woman who wills the end; that only she can complete the marriage. Wallis will be blamed, perhaps even more than you. She is bewildered. This terrible uproar has frightened her, and not for herself alone. If you had listened to her to-day, she would have told you that you must never think of giving up the Throne. Her reason for going away, I am sure, is to make it easier for you."

"How can separation make things easier?"

"You can always marry someone else," she said. "You can never again be King."

"Believe me, Mrs. Merryman, I know what I am doing. I have thought it all out. I shall not abdicate unless I am forced to do so. But if in the end I have to go, I shall leave the Throne without anger, without recriminations, without even a backward look."

"Then I pray for your sake, and hers, that you will not abdicate."

Mrs. Merryman was the only sister of Wallis's mother. No one else knew her so well. She talked warmly about Wallis's childhood; about her independence and vitality; her sensitiveness and fine instincts, and her love of life. So she appeared to the wise and gentle woman who had raised her from childhood. What a pity, I thought, that those standing in judgment upon us could not have heard what Mrs. Merryman told me about Wallis, the American stranger against whom that night nearly every hand in Britain seemed turned.

Shortly afterwards, probably within the hour, I was myself on the way to London, with the draft of the broadcast, and ahead of me the grim prospect of another meeting with the Prime Minister. On arriving at the Palace, I found Walter Monckton waiting in my room. We had just begun to talk when we heard the crunching approach of the now familiar "black beetle," conveyer of the Prime Minister and symbol of unyielding opposition.

"Wait in the Privy Purse office," I told Walter. "Get hold of George Allen, and I shall see you both as soon as the P.M. leaves."

By this stage the Prime Minister and I had dispensed with all small talk; we were both getting very tired. I thrust at once to the point of the meeting, the project of the broadcast. The idea seemed to startle him and, if I correctly read his thoughts, he seemed to be saying to himself rather irritably, "Damn it; what will this young man be thinking up next?" Whether I actually put into his hands the draft of my broadcast, I am uncertain; he did, at any rate, promise to call a special Cabinet Meeting in the morning to discuss it. But he gave me no reason to believe that he would sponsor my plan. He did, however, agree, unenthusiastically, to my seeing Mr. Winston Churchill.

In response to my summons, my two legal advisers came to my room. I charged them with taking a draft of the broadcast to Stornoway House. On second thoughts I added, "Ask Max Beaverbrook to consult Winston as well. I should like him to see the draft." Before setting out from the Palace they telephoned Max Beaverbrook. Mr. Churchill, they were told, was at that moment about to address a meeting at the Albert Hall and could not be disturbed. However, he sent out word that he would go to Stornoway House afterwards, and would go over the speech.

To add to my tribulations that terrible day, there had been delivered to me that morning at The Fort a short note from my mother. *The reports in the newspapers of that day she had found somewhat upsetting, especially as she had not seen me for ten days. Would I look in sometime during the day?* I suddenly realized how far, since that fateful meeting with the Prime Minister, I had withdrawn into the brooding realm of my private dilemma. It had not been a case of my avoiding her: I had sought only to spare her the crude details of my negotiations with Mr. Baldwin. Yet the request could not be refused, and though the hour was late and my heart heavy, I drove over to Marlborough House.

As simply as I could I explained the reasons for my apparent aloofness. "I have no desire to bring you and the family into all this. This is something I must handle alone." If she had hoped to learn from me that I had changed my mind, she gave no sign. I left Marlborough House sorry that I had had to disappoint her.

The immense forbidding bulk of the Palace loomed up as the motor turned into the Mall. Few windows showed any light.

My presence in London had evidently become known, for as I approached the gates I perceived, gathered around the foot of Queen Victoria's memorial, a small crowd staring at the edifice, thinking of God knows what. At that moment there came over me, like a wave, a powerful resurgence of the intense dislike for the building I had always felt. Did I really belong in there at all? The answer came immediately—certainly not alone.

My two legal advisers were already back from Stornoway House, with adverse news regarding my proposed broadcast. While Mr. Churchill and Max Beaverbrook were both ardently in favour of my carrying the fight to Mr. Baldwin, they doubted that the broadcast as devised was quite the right way to do so. Wholly apart from the possible constitutional impropriety involved in my making the broadcast at all, they deplored the idea of my leaving the country even for a day. Mr. Churchill particularly maintained that the immediate effect of my departure would be to leave Mr. Baldwin in undisputed command of the situation; on that account alone he advised that my plan, if carried out, would almost certainly prove to be a major mistake. These judgments were discouraging, but I was too tired to cope with more that night. Besides, the Cabinet would supply the last word in the morning, and I was anxious to start back to The Fort.

As I rose to go, Walter Monckton asked, almost in alarm:

"But, Sir, you aren't going back to The Fort alone now?"

"I am," I answered.

"But the servants will be in bed," he protested. He did not say so in so many words, but I realized that he did not want me to be quite alone at Sunningdale that night, after all I had been through. However, it is not my character to brood. Laughingly I brushed off his fears by explaining that it had never been my habit to keep the servants at The Fort up at night: I always let myself in with my own latchkey, and was perfectly capable of looking after myself. But Walter Monckton persisted. He sent for his bag, and insisted on going with me.

It was almost 1 a.m. when he and I set out for Sunningdale. Meanwhile the small crowd outside the Palace had grown. As we drove out of the gate a cheer went up.

"Ah," said Walter, rubbing his hands, "that's better."

In this simple, spontaneous demonstration I found consolation for a day of trial. And the episode gave rise to a fleeting and tempting thought—a notion so ephemeral and obviously so impossible that I mention it now merely as an illustration of how a hard-pressed mind will clutch at straws. The people at the gate were for me. Why not turn their undoubted affection to proper account? Manifestly, my Ministers were not going to let me speak to my people. What was there to prevent me from addressing them where they stood. My parents' practice of "showing" themselves on the balcony of Buckingham Palace provided a precedent. The spotlights playing on the façade, the lonely figure of the King pleading his cause—the scene could have been extremely effective. But no sooner had the image formed in my mind than it vanished. For one thing, it smacked of balcony politics, of which there was already too much in the Europe of that era. What was more important, it would have meant driving a wedge into the nation.

The car sped up Constitution Hill, leaving the crowd behind. I never again set foot inside Buckingham Palace as King. That night I made up my mind to withdraw altogether to The Fort, away from the warring pulls and the emotionalism of London in the throes of controversy.

Many have since asked me why I did so. My reasons were compelling. In the first place, I was determined to keep my negotiations with the Government on a high impersonal level. London is a metropolis, subject to the emotions of the hour. I did not want to be accused of seeking to rally support for myself against the Government by encouraging popular movements to which my continued presence at Buckingham Palace might well have given rise; nor did I wish, having been so often in my life the object of friendly demonstrations, to expose myself to the temptations which proximity to such manifestations might have excited. But beyond all that I also wished to be alone with my thoughts at this time of decision, unhampered and undisturbed by associations of the past. At The Fort it had always been my habit to live unattended by private secretaries and equerries. No member of my household ever went there except by appointment or at my invitation to stop there as a guest. It was, therefore, quite normal whenever I lived there for me to detach myself from the Palace secretariat and the other Court officials and to conduct my daily business with them by private telephone and despatch rider.

But there was something else besides. This issue between the Sovereign and the Prime Minister had by now introduced elements totally foreign to the normal transactions between the Palace and No. 10 Downing Street. The King for the first time for many years had come into serious conflict with his Government over a personal issue that had divided public opinion. Courtiers—and I use that much-abused word with deference and without malice—are by the nature of their jobs hypersensitive to public opinion where the interests of the Monarch and his Court are concerned. By instinct they are guardians of the *status quo*; their fealty is to precedent; all too often with them allegiance to mere form overrides the elementary human considerations. I therefore could not look in that direction for understanding, sympathy, or support. What I needed at this crucial stage was unbiased professional minds, steeped in the Law and versed in the technique of corporate negotiations.

The Fort was in darkness when, at two o'clock in the morning, I let Walter Monckton and myself in.

So ended a tremendous day. While I was undressing, Walter came into my room. He had in his hand a small box from which he took two white pills.

"What are those?" I asked.

"Sleeping-pills, Sir, and very mild." Handing them to me, he explained that while dining at his Club he had yielded to a sudden impulse and had telephoned the famous London surgeon, Sir Lancelot Barrington-Ward. "I told him that an important friend of mine had been through a hell of a day, and that I wanted to make sure that he slept to-night. Could he prescribe something mild but effective. You may be grateful for these to-night."

Now I have seldom taken a sleeping-pill in my life, and have an instinctive abhorrence of even the mildest form of narcotic. I thanked my friend for his thoughtfulness and took the box. However, observing his tired face, I was prompted to suggest, "You know, Walter, I believe you need two of these pills as much as I do. I insist that you take them."

Walter smiled. "Sir, I believe that you are right." He popped the pills into his mouth, disappeared into his room. We both slept well, although my pills remained untouched. Lancelot Barrington-Ward was an older brother of Robert Barrington-Ward, who was Assistant Editor of *The Times*. I went to bed reflecting upon the perverse compensations of a civilized society.

CHAPTER XXIV

ANSWER FROM THE DOMINIONS

WHEN I awoke on Friday morning I stepped out for a moment upon the terrace. Wallis was gone. Except for Slipper, the living bonds between us had momentarily parted. A sense of acute loneliness filled me. I stood there enveloped in my own thoughts. The morning sky was cloudless and the sun imparted a golden radiance to the mist over Virginia Water. In that brief moment of meditation—one of the few allowed me during those last grinding days—I was thankful for the happiness and pleasure that I had found at The Fort. With its row of cannon, its vine-covered ramparts, its tall tower, and all around the birch and Scotch fir-trees, it put me in mind of a picture in a child's book, a most appropriate place for a King making his last stand.

And the sense of being in a state of siege was more than an illusion. The Press, British and international, had descended meanwhile *en masse* upon the village of Sunningdale. They established themselves in the local inn, the Station Hotel. They posted watches at the two main gates, noting the cars that came and went. The photographers, always more daring and less inhibited than the reporters, refused to be restrained by the high fence surrounding the property. Armed with long-range lenses, they closed about The Fort with the stealthy resolve of Commandos. Whenever I observed a convulsive movement in the undergrowth or the unnatural bending of the branch of a tree, I had good reason to suspect the presence of a journalistic sleuth. One evening as we were all sitting down for dinner the sounds of a scuffle were heard outside the house. A photographer had managed to creep unnoticed to the battlements. There his shadow, flitting among the ancient cannon, betrayed his presence to the police and he was hustled away.

I was virtually a prisoner inside my house. Part of the joys of The Fort were the many lovely walks through the glades and clearings of the one-hundred-acre property. It would have done much to relieve the strain of that last week had I been allowed to escape now and then from Mr. Baldwin, the telephone, my advisers, and the red boxes long enough to stride down the paths to Virginia Water. And the need for exercise upon which I relied perhaps more than most men had to be satisfied with occasional descents to the steam bath in the cellar.

I now summoned to The Fort three men who, I thought, would serve me best in this crisis. Only one was a member of my household—Major Ulick Alexander. Having been appointed Keeper of the Privy Purse less than five months before, he was a newcomer at Court, and had not been entangled in the subtle alliances that bind together the self-contained, highly inbred hierarchy. In an atmosphere embroiled with prejudice and darkened by suspicion, he retained a detached, impersonal outlook towards my affairs. He provided under my direction the link with the Palace. Until I actually ceased to be King the "boxes" containing State papers continued to arrive at The Fort by motor-cycle from London. And throughout my personal struggle with the Government I dealt with all the innumerable documents demanding the King's attention and the Royal signature.

The other two men were lawyers. Walter Monckton gave up his practice and moved to The Fort. From this point on he became the direct channel of communication between the Prime Minister and me. He also, at the end, collaborated in the drafting of the constitutional documents by means of which the change in the Succession was effected. To assist him, and at the same time to advise me personally, I also enlisted the services of my solicitor, Mr. George Allen. He and Walter Monckton were old friends: they had served together in the trenches in France. Moreover, George Allen was already familiar with many aspects of the questions at issue. Several years older than I, a gallant and much-decorated officer of the First World War, he had a fine reputation in the legal world, where his law firm ranked among the foremost. Like Walter Monckton, he put aside his other business to be with me. To describe George as a man of few words would be an overstatement. Long experience in the Law had taught him that words, whether spoken or written, were perilous and irresponsible expedients to be employed only after extreme deliberation and in the briefest possible form. Nature had further endowed him with a poker face that provided a formidable frame for his sage counsel. During our worst hours together he stood like a stone wall, and a remark that was subsequently cherished by all those who stood with me at the end was George Allen's calm pronouncement, at a time of extreme tension, "I won't be stampeded." Nor was he ever.

With Walter shuttling almost continuously between Sunningdale and No. 10 Downing Street, the other two evidently had a private understanding that I should never be left alone; for whenever I called for anything, whatever the hour, one or the other would instantly respond. If I were restless, they tried to distract me; if I wanted to be left alone with my thoughts, they did not intrude. And however they may have felt privately about the right or wrong of my determined course, they never attempted to divert me from it. My instructions were carried out promptly and with resolution. Never was a Monarch better served.

Now to this list of those who stood with me to the end must be added the name of a man of whom the public was quite unaware —William Bateman, my personal telephone operator at Buckingham Palace. William had served me for many years in the same capacity at York House. When I had the extra switchboard installed at Buckingham Palace, I put him in charge. Now that the private telephone line to The Fort was loaded with top-secret calls to Downing Street, and later on with confidential conversations with Wallis at Cannes, in the control of careless or unfriendly hands that switchboard could have been the most vulnerable point in my defences. But so determined was William that there should be no possible leak that he refused to relinquish it even for a few hours at night while he slept. Instead, he moved a cot alongside the switchboard and took cat naps when he could. For ten days he almost never left this room.

While I thus cleared the decks, so to speak, for the final struggle, a remarkable change in the atmosphere occurred on this same Friday morning. There came a sudden and strongly buoyant upsurge in public sentiment towards me that was encouraging.

When I entered Walter Monckton's room after breakfast the newspapers were spread all over the floor. "They make better reading this morning," he said. "Beaverbrook and Rothermere have opened fire."

They had indeed. "No Government," cried the *Daily Express*, "can stand in the King's way if he is resolved to walk that way. . . . Let the King give his decision to the people and let him give the reasons for it, too." And the *Daily Mail* declared, "Abdication is out of the question because its possibilities of mischief are endless. The effect on the Empire would be calamitous."

Nor were these the only voices raised in my favour. The *Western Morning News* argued for the marriage. Sir Walter Layton, now Lord Layton, wheeled the Liberal *News Chronicle* to my support with a powerful article advocating the morganatic marriage.

The *Mail* and *Express* both spoke for a public deeply imbued with the Royal tradition. Their position could hardly have surprised Mr. Baldwin. But the attitude of the *News Chronicle* must have seemed to him ominous. This newspaper spoke for the Liberal tradition, which was Nonconformist in outlook and regulated by strict and uncompromising moral judgments. Yet it advocated the morganatic marriage. Clearly, the solid Press front desired by Mr. Baldwin had been shattered.[1] The break widened rapidly. Among the intellectual weeklies the *New Statesman and Nation* spoke up sympathetically for the marriage. While the Catholic *Tablet* held that the question of marriage was one for the King to decide for himself and was not in any case constitutional cause for abdication.

Equally heartening was the news brought back from London

---

[1] Out of curiosity I recently endeavoured to assess the weight of the journalistic opinion for and against me. When the abdication question arose the aggregate circulations of the various newspapers that took a position in the matter was approximately 21,000,000. Of these, newspapers with a total circulation of 8,500,000 supported the Government and 12,500,000—or 60 per cent.—were for me. Now I grant that these figures were not necessarily a true reflection of the state of public opinion. Realistically, it can be argued only that in the final taking of sides the proprietors of the newspapers with the largest total circulations and with the strongest appeal to the masses were on my side. All the same, the statistics give force to a fact that prejudice and controversy have combined to obscure. It is that the powerful Press support ranged on my side represented a tremendous potential leverage on public opinion—a leverage that out of consideration for my constitutional obligations I declined to employ.

by Walter Monckton of the attitude of the crowds outside
Buckingham Palace, in St. James's Park, and in Downing Street
before the Prime Minister's residence. The crowds were not
large or particularly demonstrative, but their sympathies were
unmistakably for the King. They sang "God Save the King"
and "For He's a Jolly Good Fellow." They were pathetically un-
organized, but there was no mistaking the spontaneity of the
emotions that had brought them together; they were inarticulate,
humble people who seemed to be waiting for some word from
the King. When I heard of this, Chesterton's prophetic lines
came irresistibly to mind:

> "Smile at us, pay us, pass us; but do not quite forget;
> For we are the people of England, that never have spoken yet."

Something, I realized, was stirring in the hearts of these people
—a side of national character that the Prime Minister, in his
practised homilies on national virtues, had neglected to
enumerate: a saving capacity for second thought, a deep-rooted
sense of fair play. Was he also sensible of those deep stirrings on
this same day? He gave no sign. But that day he struck twice—
and struck hard, in a manner that I shall presently describe.

However, the impact of the Prime Minister's moves was
reserved for the afternoon. In the meantime the morning
produced its own full measure of difficulties.

Walter Monckton left for London directly after breakfast for
a round of meetings with various Government officials, beginning with the Prime Minister himself. The special Cabinet
Meeting summoned by Mr. Baldwin to consider my proposed
broadcast met at 10.30. While still waiting word of its decision,
I received bad news.

A Fleet Street friend, Mr. Bernard Rickatson-Hatt, then chief
editor of Reuters, telephoned to warn me that Wallis's presence
in France had been discovered, and that while she had subsequently managed to give the world Press the slip, her destina-
tion, Cannes, had been shrewdly surmised, and scores of reporters
were in hot pursuit. That was the only information that he was
able to give me then. Afterwards I was able to string together the
story of that extraordinary journey from the bits and pieces that
Wallis and Perry Brownlow supplied.

The departure from The Fort was negotiated without mishap. Without being discovered by the watching Press at the top gate, they had managed to gain the main road through Windsor Great Park. However, on the way to Newhaven, while driving fast through the town of Mitcham, Perry's Rolls was "gonged" by a police car, and obliged to pull up to the side of the road. Fortunately, the presence of the detective in the front seat saved them from embarrassing questioning and possible delay. A glimpse of the police warrant that the detective carried caused the local police officers to retire with apologies, and Wallis and Perry continued, shaken but in good order, to the coast. In the dark they went aboard the ferry unrecognized. Several hours later, preparing to disembark on the French side of the Channel, they were in the process of congratulating themselves upon the successful management of their journey when, through the miscarriage of a small and insignificant detail, their identities were suddenly exposed. In the rush of getting off, the fact had been overlooked that the papers for Wallis's motor were in her own name. The discrepancy was instantly noted by the French *douaniers*. There was a flurry of recognition, followed at once by an admirable demonstration of *la politesse* in which the French authorities have no peers. Relieved and grateful, Wallis and Perry hurried on to Rouen, intending to pause there for a few hours' sleep before resuming the long motor journey to the Côte d'Azur. But their secret was out. Next morning at Rouen, as they were leaving the hotel, Wallis was recognized in the lobby by a French woman; an actress, so the story goes, from the Comédie Française. She followed them out of the hotel, and her cry "Voilà la dame!" electrified the early morning passers-by. To escape the gathering crowd, Perry Brownlow hustled Wallis into the motor, and, slamming the door shut, he ordered Ladbroke to drive off, taking the back road out of Rouen.

It was shortly after noon that William, from his switchboard at Buckingham Palace, notified me that Wallis, having identified herself by a code name previously arranged, was trying to reach me from Evreux, and that I might find it hard to understand her because of the bad connexion.

It was not the telephone that worried me—it was Evreux.

The only Evreux that I knew about was in Normandy, well off the route that she had planned to take. In some alarm I waited for her voice, but the connexion proved almost hopeless. However, I finally gathered that because of some mishap they were taking a circuitous route—hence Evreux. She also seemed to be urging upon me some point that I could not understand. But so unintelligible were the words, that in my frustration I nearly threw the receiver against the wall.

Many months were to pass before I found out what Wallis had tried to tell me from Evreux, and but for the chance that directed a mutual friend, Mr. Harold Nicolson, to the same hotel where she and Perry had stopped for lunch and to telephone, I might never have known the facts.

The proprietor of the Hôtellerie du Grand Cerf, a charming old inn obliterated eight years later during the fighting in Normandy, knew Mr. Nicolson as a distinguished man of letters. And feeling no doubt that he was uniquely privileged to supply a missing footnote to a famous historical episode, the Frenchman described how Mrs. Simpson had stopped there to telephone the King. She was, the patron recalled, plainly in profound distress: the conversation, owing to the execrable connexion, had obviously only increased her agitation, for, hurrying off, she had left beside the telephone a slip of paper of some importance. This piece of paper he produced, insisting that Mr. Nicolson should have it. Mr. Nicolson sent it on to Wallis—she has it now. It consisted, in part, of the code that we had arranged before she left. Max Beaverbrook was *Tornado*; Mr. Baldwin was *Crutch*; Mr. Churchill was *W.S.C.*, from his initials; and I was simply *Mr. James*, after St. James's Palace. With it were a series of notes that she had jotted down to guide her in her conversation with me. One idea was foremost in her mind: *under no circumstances was Mr. James to step down*— i.e. from the Throne. I was afterwards to contemplate that note with profound emotion. Yet even had I grasped what Wallis had tried to tell me from Evreux, her pleas would never have diverted me from my determined course. Nevertheless, the note reveals the depth of her emotion. Although several more agonizing days would pass before I understood what was in her mind, the truth is that in the desperate hope of staying my abdication, she had decided to leave me. In putting the English Channel behind her, she intended also to put behind her Britain and what I had in my love planned for her. She had made up her mind to stop only a moment with the Rogers at Cannes, and then to hurry on, perhaps to the United States, or even to China, where she had lived for a while thirteen years before.

Well did I know that part of France over which she and Perry Brownlow were traversing. Its little old towns, its shuttered houses and quiet squares, and the remembered roads that as a Prince I had explored with a *Guide Michelin*, returned to my mind. The change in route would, I foresaw, add many kilometres to an already exhausting journey. All the rest of that day my mind, or the subconscious part of it anyhow, followed her harried car, doubling and twisting as it travelled south along the tree-lined roads throughout the length of France.

By early afternoon I learned from Walter Monckton that the proposed broadcast was lost. The Cabinet had considered it, only to reject it. To let me address my people would involve risks that Mr. Baldwin and his colleagues were apparently unwilling to take. With its rejection disappeared my only possible means of rallying the whole nation. Thus Mr. Baldwin dealt the first crushing blow.

A few hours later, in the House of Commons, he struck again. So far he had made no public acknowledgment of the conflict between us. Mr. Churchill's question the previous day—"Will my Right Honourable friend give us an assurance that no irrevocable step will be taken before a formal statement is made to Parliament?"—had been allowed to pass unanswered; and because Mr. Baldwin's political genius frequently took the form of an almost Oriental inaction in the face of crisis, the preponderant opinion of my advisers was that if he moved at all he would move slowly.

Now he manœuvred with a swiftness and directness that astonished even his colleagues. Possibly his hand was forced by the various manifestations of loyalty on my behalf. Possibly he was disturbed by the speed with which the idea of the morganatic marriage appeared to be gaining ground. Or perhaps he simply decided that it was now or never for him.

Whatever the reason, he undertook in a few shrewdly chosen words to demolish for Parliament's benefit the case for the middle way—the morganatic marriage. Concerning the general question of my right to marry, he maintained:

> The King himself requires no consent from any other authority to make his marriage legal. But, as I have said, the lady whom he marries, by the fact of her marriage to the King, necessarily becomes Queen. She herself therefore enjoys all the status, rights and privileges which both by positive law and custom attach to that position, and with which we are familiar in the cases of her late Majesty Queen Alexandra and Her Majesty Queen Mary; and her children will be in the direct succession to the Throne.

Having established this point, the Prime Minister went on to say that the Government would not sponsor legislation to alter the traditional status of the King's wife. Furthermore, he argued that public discussion over the morganatic marriage had ceased to be of practical importance inasmuch as he had satisfied himself ("from inquiries I have made") that the Dominion Governments would never approve such an accommodation.

In other words, there was to be no conciliation, no palliation, no marriage. It was abdication for me or resignation for him.

I was to receive Mr. Baldwin that evening to hear from his own lips the Cabinet's decision concerning the broadcast—news that was no longer news. In the meantime Mr. Rickatson-Hatt had sent me from London, at my request, the Reuter despatches from the Dominion capitals reporting their reactions to my proposed marriage. I read them swiftly.

Canberra, Ottawa, Wellington, Capetown—everywhere the story was the same. There had been no attempt to assess popular opinion, which to the small degree that it had been sounded at all appeared to be divided. But official opinion was solidly behind Mr. Baldwin. The Prime Minister, I thought to myself, had framed his cables well.

It was a somewhat brisker Prime Minister who appeared at The Fort that evening. Wasting no words, he announced in the usual formal idiom that "my" Ministers could not "advise" me to broadcast in the manner that I had suggested. And as if to reassure me that the Cabinet had given my proposal full and generous consideration he presented me with a précis, prepared by Sir John Simon, setting forth the bases for its adverse opinion.

I scanned the précis swiftly. The arguments it advanced came as no surprise: the Sovereign could make no public statement except on the advice of his Ministers. The King is bound to accept their advice; they had already tendered advice in the matter at issue; and for me to broadcast my views would, in effect, be an attempt on my part to reach and possibly divide the people over the heads of my constitional advisers.

But the learned opinions expressed therein struck me, on second thoughts, as being less than adequate explanation of why my proposal had not been accepted. Mr. Baldwin may have prided himself on his knowledge and understanding of what the British people thought and felt. But it was now abundantly clear that he wanted no test of their sentiments at this critical moment. He and his colleagues were therefore guarding themselves at every vulnerable point. Events had begun to take charge of them, as they had also begun to take charge of me.

Thinking that the audience was at an end, I started to rise, but Mr. Baldwin checked me with a gesture. The continued uncertainty, he began, if allowed to persist, was certain to create a dangerous constitutional situation not only in this country but throughout the Empire. Could I give the Government my decision without further delay, if possible during the week-end? Better still, could I supply it before he started back for London?

I answered, steadily, that he knew my views and that I had not altered them. "You will not have to wait much longer, Mr. Baldwin."

Moving to the edge of the chair, he looked at me fixedly. "There is still time for you to change your mind, Sir. That is indeed the prayer of your Majesty's servants."

I studied the Prime Minister some time before answering. Why should he now address to me so urgent an appeal to remain on the Throne. For me to do what he asked would have meant my abandoning, in the full view of the watching world, the woman whom I had asked to marry me. If it were indeed Mr. Baldwin's prayer that I should save my crown by so base a surrender, that noble ornament would have been laid upon a head for ever bent in shame.

"Mr. Baldwin," I finally said, "I will let you know as soon as possible."

CHAPTER XXV

THE KING'S PARTY

B Y the time night descended, The Fort had become like a
battle headquarters, with telephones ringing continuously,
and despatch riders on motor-cycles bringing State papers
from London.

Where, before, every voice had seemed to be raised against me,
now many seemed anxious that I should stand firm. I was
beginning to get letters of advice, counsel, and sympathy. There
were heartening messages from all parts of the United Kingdom
and from the Dominions. An Irish baronet of ancient lineage
and antique gallantry offered to place his sword at my service at
this menacing hour.

So the day had not been all debits as far as I was concerned.
From Stornoway House Max Beaverbrook, sensing the favourable
upsurge in public opinion, had steadily hammered away on
the theme of delay. I must not allow myself, he urged, to be
harried and hurried into precipitous action. He had seen Sir
Samuel Hoare again, and in conversation with him had formed
the impression that many Ministers were troubled by the turn
the crisis had taken, and would welcome a withdrawal of my
request for advice on the morganatic marriage proposal.

But I was wearied to the point of exhaustion. Mr. Baldwin's
statement in the House of Commons had touched off an
avalanche, and in the vast ensuing concussions I could hear all
my hopes and the results of my years of public service crashing
down in thundering ruin. The friendly voices struggling to
make themselves heard came to me but faintly through the
din. And even if they had helped to mitigate to some extent
the sense of loneliness and isolation that had oppressed me
from the beginning, I could not bring myself to believe

that they constituted a mandate that I should challenge the Government.

It was all very well for my supporters to argue that the mass of the people were for me, and to point to the Press and the friendly crowds as proof that a signal from me would instantly rally a vast majority around me. But when I lost the opportunity to broadcast, I lost at the same time the chance to give that signal in the only way open to me, short of open defiance of the Cabinet. The more I pondered the situation, the more I became convinced that immediate abdication was now the only decision left to me, if the dignity of the Throne was to be preserved and the unity of the Empire maintained.

Accordingly, I notified Max Beaverbrook through an intermediary that I would temporarily cease all communication with him. The question of Abdication was no longer the issue. I was preparing now to discuss terms with the Prime Minister. However, lest my old friend should mistake the abrupt closing of the door for a turning of my back, I hastened to explain that since I had decided to come to terms with Mr. Baldwin, I could not very well go on seeing him without seeming to be trying to ride two horses at the same time.

Thus I had already passed, so to speak, the point of no-return when, about eight o'clock in the evening, after a day of great emotional strain, I entered the octagonal drawing-room to greet Mr. Winston Churchill, who had motored from London to dine with me.

It is no doubt somewhat difficult for many of us, whose impression of recent history is so dominated by the immeasurable greatness and prestige of this man, to remember, let alone believe, that in 1936 his position in British life, and even more in his own Party, was regarded as anything but immortal. Throughout the period when the events that are the subject of this narrative were unfolding he was, in fact, a virtual outcast of the Conservative Party, respected and even feared for his undoubted intellectual brilliance and audacity, but distrusted by the Party leaders, who denied him a place in the Government.

We were five for dinner—Mr. Churchill, Walter Monckton, Ulick Alexander, George Allen, and myself. Our famous guest did not address himself to the personal aspects of my situation:

the personal issue, in his view, lay wholly outside the argument. He was entirely taken up with the threat to the Constitution—with the fact that the Executive had forced a constitutional issue for political reasons, and had taken steps against me without warrant in Law.

Believing this, he was determined to call for "time and patience"—a phrase that supplied the theme of the powerful statement which he issued the next day.

Although I had long admired Mr. Churchill, I saw him that evening in his true stature. When Mr. Baldwin had talked to me about the Monarchy, it had seemed a dry and lifeless thing. But when Mr. Churchill spoke it lived, it grew, it became suffused with light. His argument was simple and convincing. No constitutional issue had arisen between me and my Cabinet, and none could arise until Wallis's decree nisi became absolute in April, then nearly five months off. Mr. Baldwin was therefore without authority to confront me with the choice of Abdication on an issue not yet of immediate urgency. Such an action demanded the most serious Parliamentary processes. If I had for-mally asked the Government to enact legislation that would make it possible for me to marry on the Throne, and if the Government was unwilling to do so, then, in the proper order of things, the obligation to resign devolved not upon the Sovereign but upon his Ministers. And Mr. Churchill was particularly outraged by Mr. Baldwin's action in securing from the leaders of the Opposi-tion parties, namely Mr. Clement Attlee of the Labour Party and Sir Archibald Sinclair of the Liberals, a promise not to participate in the formation of a new Government were he to resign and were I to ask them to form another in its place. The practical effect of this *modus vivendi*, he insisted, was to confront the Sovereign with an ultimatum.

Whatever else might happen, he argued, the hereditary principle must not be left to the mercy of politicians trimming their doctrines "to the varying hour."

As is usual with Mr. Churchill, there was a practical plan behind the fine words. If the Prime Minister persisted with his importunities he suggested that I should claim a respite from strain, adding half whimsically that I should retire to Windsor Castle and close the gates, stationing at one my father's old doctor, Lord

Dawson of Penn, and at the other my recently appointed Physician-in-Ordinary, Lord Horder.

Mr. Churchill informed us of his own intentions. First, he proposed to despatch on the morrow a private letter to the Prime Minister warning him and his Cabinet colleagues of the disaster that would ensue if they persisted in hurrying the King. At the same time, he would issue a statement to the Press bringing forward all the compelling arguments for delay. His parting words, as he left us well after midnight, were: "Sir, it is a time for reflection. You must allow time for the battalions to march." Then he set off for London, to Max Beaverbrook.

During the dark watches of that night, after Mr. Churchill had gone, I weighed in the scales of my mind the various propositions being urged upon me.

From the onset of the crisis my actions at all times had been regulated by the desire to dampen controversy, prevent the spread of schism and disunity, and hold the Crown above the clamour. This desire, as already stated, underlay my resolve not to return to London so long as the conflict with the Government continued. After all, I had been raised under the great imperative that the Crown must remain above politics. If adherence to this doctrine should cost me the Crown, I had no choice but to subscribe. That was the price of being the Monarch in a constitutional system.

At the same time I dreaded lest Wallis should become the shuttlecock of violent party conflict. Max Beaverbrook was particularly anxious to present her attitude and her position in a fair and true light, but I opposed him. To have her innermost feelings explained and defended in print could only have exposed her to a martyrdom that was contrary to her nature and which I could not wish for anybody I held dear. By reason of the brake which I applied, Max insisted that his newspapers were ineffective during the critical first days.

Yet in spite of everything, support for me had gathered and was to continue to gather. And there were influential men who were ready and willing to organize that support into something formidable were I to give my consent. Indeed, a curious thing had already happened. Out of the hot, crackling splutter of discussion there had shot up a rocket, not a very big rocket, but for a moment it hung brilliantly in the sky. It was something the newspapers had begun to call the "King's Party."

The swift rise of the King's Party, its even swifter fall, constitute a unique incident in British history; the more so, perhaps, because its intended beneficiary was dubious of its motives and apprehensive of its consequences.

Nobody seemed to know how it started; nobody appeared to have organized it. It had no visible leader. No one had thrust himself through the gates of The Fort, exclaiming, "I demand an audience with His Majesty. I am the leader of the 'King's Party'." In fact, it was no party at all in the usual meaning of the term. All that it ever consisted of, so far as I was able to tell, were scattered groups of people in cars who toured the streets of London and other cities with home-made signs and loud speakers; of crowds outside Buckingham Palace and in Whitehall who shouted "God Save the King—from Stanley Baldwin"; and of slogans like "Stand by the King" that were chalked up on blank walls; and of a cheer for Walter Monckton as he drove up to No. 10 in the King's motor.

Even the Archbishop of Canterbury appears to have felt the change in the weather. It is recorded in his recent biography that about this time he discussed the state of public opinion in what he personally termed "The King's Matter" with two influential ecclesiastical officials: the Moderator and Secretary of the Federal Council of Evangelical Free Churches. While confirming the Archbishop's belief that the British people would in the main support the Government, they nevertheless warned him that "a large proportion" had a "strong sympathy" for the King. This dissident factor was, in these churchmen's opinion, recruited largely from the younger generation, who seemed to see the issue in simple terms: "He is doing the right thing. He wants to marry the woman he loves. Why shouldn't he?"

It is gratifying to discover after so many years that the Archbishop had been made aware by such reputable witnesses of the existence among the youth of the country of a viewpoint other than his own. At that time, I had supposed that such support as had mobilized for me issued chiefly from my own contemporaries—the middle generation of men and women that came of age in the First World War. And further, it had seemed reasonable to expect that among people of all classes there still persisted, unimpaired by controversy, a residue of good will accruing from my services to the Empire. However, something else may have been at work—sportsmanship.

Let us grant that the so-called King's Party was only an idea in people's heads—a simple idea that their King should have justice and that they should have their King, and that I, isolated at the Fort from the street clamour, was barely sensible of its demonstrations; nevertheless, it may well be that Mr. Baldwin was startled by the phenomenon; hence his abrupt moves. For no doubt there had by this time emerged, in an inchoate form, many elements conducive to a popular movement in my favour.

Had I made a move to encourage the growth of this movement, it might have grown. If I had made an appeal to the public I might have persuaded a majority, and a large majority at that. I shall go further and say that had I remained passive while my friends acted, the result might well have been the same. For there is no want of evidence that a multitude of the plain people stood waiting to be rallied to my side.

It was a night of soul-searching. While I paced my bedroom floor my mind retraced the myriad paths of my life. In the end, the decision I reached was the one which had been implicit throughout the course of my action—to put out of mind all thought of challenging the Prime Minister. Actually there was no third way open. Even though I might have been able to recruit a commanding majority, I could not have persuaded the entire nation and all the Dominions. My friends would have had to carry the issue into every hamlet of the Commonwealth. By making a stand for myself, I should have left the scars of a civil war. A civil war is the worst of all wars. Its passions soar highest, its hatreds last longest. And a civil war is not less a war when it is fought in words and not in blood. The price of my marriage under such circumstances would have been the infliction of a grievous wound on the social unity of my native land and on that wider unity that is the Empire. The British Crown is the living symbol of Imperial unity and voluntary allegiance. It inspires unity. But it would no longer inspire unity if the man who wore it reigned over a community riven and divided. True, I should still be King. But I should no longer be King by the free and common consent of all. The Crown would have lost, in consequence, much of its aura of beneficent usefulness. The cherished conception of the Monarchy above politics would have been shattered, and the party system might have suffered a fatal hurt. Could Wallis and I have hoped to find happiness under that condition? This was the question I answered in my soul that night. The answer was No.

I felt I had come to the limit of a man's power to shape events and fend off catastrophe. Were I to wait longer I might indeed reap the whirlwind. And so, in faith and calmness, not unmixed with sorrow, I resolved to end the constitutional crisis forthwith. I decided to abdicate. I would close my reign with dignity, clear the Succession for my brother with the least possible embarrassment and avoid all appearance of faction.

These being the circumstances that guided my decision, I reject the notion put forward by some that, faced with a choice between love and duty, I chose love. I certainly married because I chose the path of love. But I abdicated because I chose the path of duty. I did not value the Crown so lightly that I gave it away hastily. I valued it so deeply that I surrendered it, rather than risk any impairment of its prestige.

It is for this reason that I treasure a letter that was sent to me only three days after I left England, when emotions were still running high. It came from an old friend, an official in the House of Lords, killed in action in Tunisia during World War Two. I include the following excerpts with some diffidence. Composed in friendship, they may perhaps overstate the case:

> . . . When the history of this episode comes to be written it will be realized that your nobility in refusing even to test your popularity was a sign of true greatness, and probably saved the very existence of the Empire. . . . I must humbly express my intense admiration for your obvious and inflexible determination not to encourage a "King's Party." It was within your power to create Civil War and chaos. You had only to lift a finger or even to come to London and show yourself, to arouse millions of your subjects to your support. . . .

Finally morning came and after breakfast I called Walter Monckton to my room to tell him of my decision. "I want you to go to London immediately and warn the Prime Minister that when he comes to The Fort this afternoon I shall notify him formally that I have decided to abdicate."

Until that moment I had not inquired into the constitutional procedure which would be set in motion by my action. Since the sovereign powers reside with the people, I had assumed that an Act of Parliament of some sort would be required. Walter now outlined how the constitutional machinery would come into play. On finishing, he asked whether I had given thought to the situation that would confront me personally as soon as I had taken this step. The truth is that I had not. Walter then reminded me that within a few days I should be a private citizen in a foreign land, subjected to the inconveniences that beset anyone caught in so sensational an incident. Yet because it would be obviously unwise for Wallis and me to meet anywhere until her decree was made absolute, I would therefore face the lonely prospect, after I ceased to be King, of a prolonged separation that would impose a monstrous strain upon two people who had already been through the fire.

He therefore suggested a possible solution for this distressing situation. It was that I should authorize him to ask the Government, when it submitted to Parliament an Abdication Bill, to present simultaneously a second Bill that would make Wallis's divorce absolute forthwith, and thus avoid the legal delay of six months which the law required. If that were done, I should then be able to join her directly, and our marriage need not be delayed. There already existed a growing opinion that this interval was too long. (It has since been reduced to six weeks.) In any case, Walter argued, since I should now ease the pressure upon the Prime Minister and the Cabinet by giving them the speedy answer which they wanted, they might in the name of humanity show me equal consideration in the one matter that most affected me.

Gratefully, I grasped Walter's proposal—it was a lifeline thrown across a crevasse.

Walter set off for London on his mission. I returned to my study, to meditate briefly upon the lack of logic governing the fate of constitutional monarchs. Kingship is perhaps the last remaining occupation from which it is impossible to resign in good grace, with the confidence that one's motives will be understood. Chairmen of boards can resign, and high officials may retire, but the hereditary principle allows no easy release from birth to death.

Well, for me the golden thread of my inheritance had snapped. I asked George Allen to despatch to Switzerland at once a trusted agent who would inquire discreetly into suitable hotel accommodation near Zürich. If nothing came of Walter Monckton's proposed two Bills, I would repair there to wait.

CHAPTER XXVI

THE FATE OF THE TWO BILLS

THUS, on Saturday, December 5, over lunch at the Windham Club in St. James's Square, Walter Monckton and George Allen broached the subject of the proposed Divorce Bill to two of Mr. Baldwin's closer associates. They were Sir Horace Wilson and Major Thomas Dugdale, M.P. The latter was the Prime Minister's Parliamentary Private Secretary. The former, a spare, austere civil servant with pale blue eyes and stooped shoulders, wielded a good deal more power behind the scenes than his actual title—Chief Industrial Adviser to H.M. Government, "seconded to the Treasury for service for the Prime Minister"—might suggest. He was an adroit and able counsellor close to the Prime Minister, whose words carried great weight in the day-to-day evolution of high Government policy. His speciality had been labour relations.

My two legal advisers returned to The Fort well pleased with the initial response to the Divorce Bill. To Walter Monckton's surprise and satisfaction, both Sir Horace Wilson and Major Dugdale conceded the essential justice of the proposed arrangement, and the former undertook to present it to the Prime Minister, who agreed to the idea. The drafting of the two Bills—the first giving effect to my abdication, the other relating to Wallis's divorce—was at once begun.

"I believe," said Walter hopefully, "that now we shall be able to tidy everything up."

I thought with relief, tinged with sadness, that the spiral of crisis had finally reached its climax, and that I could begin to wind up my affairs in comparative calm. But it was not to be so.

Mr. Churchill at this point despatched to the Prime Minister for the Cabinet's consideration a communication the burden of which was a trenchant criticism of its policy towards me. The contents of that letter have never been revealed; however, I have been given to understand that it paralleled, in important respects, a public statement of his own views on the crisis that he issued to the Press that evening. This was a masterly and objective exposition. And because it stated the case with power and dignity I have included it here, as a proper part of the narrative:

I plead for time and patience. The nation must realize the character of the constitutional issue. There is no question of any conflict between the King and Parliament. Parliament has not been consulted in any way, nor allowed to express any opinion.

The question is whether the King is to abdicate upon the advice of the Ministry of the day. No such advice has ever before been tendered to a Sovereign in Parliamentary times. . . .

In this case we are in presence of a wish expressed by the Sovereign to perform an act which in no circumstances can be accomplished for nearly five months, and may conceivably, for various reasons, never be accomplished at all.

That, on such a hypothetical supposititious basis the supreme sacrifice of abdication and potential exile of the Sovereign should be demanded, finds no support whatever in the British constitution. No Ministry has the authority to advise the abdication of the Sovereign. Only the most serious Parliamentary processes could even raise the issue in a decisive form. . . .

If the King refuses to take the advice of his Ministers they are, of course, free to resign. They have no right whatever to put pressure upon him to accept their advice by soliciting beforehand assurances from the Leader of the Opposition that he will not form an alternative Administration in the event of their resignation, and thus confronting the King with an ultimatum. Again, there is cause for time and patience. . . .

Howsoever this matter may turn, it is pregnant with calamity and inseparable from inconvenience. But all the evil aspects will be aggravated beyond measure if the utmost chivalry and compassion are not shown, both by Ministers and by the British nation, towards a gifted and beloved King torn between private and public obligations of love and duty.

The Churches stand for charity. They believe in the efficacy of prayer. Surely their influence must not oppose a period of reflection. I plead, I pray, that time and tolerance will not be denied.

The King has no means of personal access to his Parliament or his people. Between him and them stand in their office the Ministers of the Crown. If they thought it their duty to engage all their power and influence against him, still he must remain silent.

All the more must they be careful not to be the judge in their own case, and to show a loyal and Christian patience even at some political embarrassment to themselves. . . .

Under different circumstances the effect of Mr. Churchill's magnificent plea on my behalf would almost certainly have been profound. It might well have reversed the situation. But through no fault of Mr. Churchill's it came too late. There could be no turning back for me now. By nightfall Mr. Baldwin was himself at The Fort, to discuss the two Bills.

Mr. Baldwin was understandably concerned over the propriety of raising with me the question of the special Divorce Bill. Although he had agreed to it in principle, he had not discussed it with his colleagues; and he said he could not sponsor it himself. Walter Monckton was quick to answer that it would be equally impossible for the King to raise the question. As a means of resolving the impasse, he asked that he be allowed to raise the question of the two Bills himself, when the Prime Minister came to The Fort that afternoon.

When Mr. Baldwin arrived at The Fort, I escorted him into the drawing-room, as usual. The door closed behind us. The Prime Minister and I talked for a while. Presently there came a knock on the door. Walter Monckton entered, "May I have leave to speak, Sir?" he asked. He rapidly sketched out the plan that Mr. Baldwin and I by then knew so well.

The Prime Minister listened gravely. He assured me that it was a just accommodation. However, on further consideration of the project he had decided that opposition must be expected from certain members of the Cabinet—especially from some of the senior ones most closely affiliated with Church affairs. Hoping to disarm this opposition he had summoned to a special meeting at No. 10 Downing Street on the next morning, Sunday, almost a dozen colleagues from whom he expected the most resistance.

"Sir," he assured me, "I shall resign if the Cabinet refuses you the second Bill."

Mr. Baldwin was a cautious man, and I never understood what persuaded him to make this handsome but rash promise. But it was made, I am sure, in good heart, although I do recall exchanging a wondering glance with Walter Monckton.

Directly after the Prime Minister left, Walter Monckton and George Allen hastened back to London for another conference with Whitehall officials. Copies of the two Bills were then ready for them to read. The proposed drafts satisfied my lawyers and appeared to satisfy the Attorney-General, Sir Donald Somervell. Sir John Simon, the Secretary of State for Home Affairs, offered no criticism. I retired that night greatly encouraged to learn of this progress. But the Prime Minister's Sunday morning meeting with his Ministers produced a sorry aftermath.

Walter Monckton was an uncomfortable witness of the death of his project. On arriving at No. 10 Downing Street he was shown into a small office adjoining that of Sir Horace Wilson. Mr. Baldwin emerged from the Cabinet Room to greet Walter pleasantly and to announce that he would shortly be able to inform him of his colleagues' decision. He went back into the room, the door closed behind him and did not open for a long time. Sir Horace Wilson brooded over a large pile of papers and Walter anxiously studied the blank door. It was nearly two hours before the door eventually reopened and the Prime Minister emerged. "Come in, Monckton," he said. Entering the room, Walter found himself facing the concentrated gaze of the Ministers ranged round the famous green-baize table.

The atmosphere was strained. Walter sensed at once that the idea of the Divorce Bill had not prospered. As he settled into an empty chair beside Mr. Baldwin, the Prime Minister said many of his colleagues felt that the bracketing of the two Bills would smack of a bargain where there ought to be none, and therefore they could not support it. He was of the opinion that the second Bill would affront the moral sense of the nation and might be interpreted as an abandonment of the moral position the Cabinet had taken up.

Walter remained silent. A Minister asked what would be the King's reaction to the decision.

Walter answered that he did not know. "His Majesty," he said, "had hoped that the two Bills which the Prime Minister had looked upon with favour would be acceptable. This decision will greatly disappoint him. In light of the present circumstances, he will undoubtedly ask for additional time for further thought."

Mr. Ramsay MacDonald, the Lord President of the Council, asked gravely, "How much time will the King ask for? How many days?"

"Hardly days," answered Walter. "I anticipate that he will require weeks."

Mr. Baldwin, who had been silent, now said, "This matter must be finished before Christmas." Other Ministers interrupted to say that Christmas would be too long to wait: the King should make up his mind immediately. Someone murmured that the continued uncertainty had already hurt the Christmas trade.

According to Walter Monckton's recollection the last observation emanated from Mr. Chamberlain. When Walter came to describe this part of the proceedings to me, his voice reflected his personal feelings. I was more philosophical, although it did seem to me that the Chancellor of the Exchequer was being a trifle more mercenary than his office demanded.

Still, there is no denying that my disappointment was profound. It drove home to me the onesidedness of my struggle with the Government. Mr. Baldwin's supporters at the time rejected indignantly the "abominable and malignant insinuations that pressure had been brought to bear upon the King by his Ministers." And to the extent that no active force was ever applied, the statement was technically correct. But pressure of a kind was certainly applied—the static yet implacable grip of a vice which, having fastened about an object, never relaxes. First the idea of the morganatic marriage, then the proposed broadcast, and finally the two Bills that would have given my intended wife and myself a measure of security—each in turn had been refused. Clear to the end, Mr. Baldwin in his exchanges with me followed with scrupulous exactitude the constitutional rhetoric which preserves the fiction of kingly authority. It was always *my* Ministers who would not let me do what I wished. It was always with *his humble duty* that he did what *he* wished. The Prime Minister controlled all the levers of power. He could bargain with the Opposition. He could canvass Members of

393

Parliament. He could exert Party pressure for the support of the newspapers. He could even consult the Dominion premiers in his own terms. He could do all this and more. Such was the discipline of the Party machine under Mr. Baldwin's control that influential friends upon whom I might otherwise have counted never dared to step forward—perhaps not wishing to risk loss of Party favour. I had to stand silent. How lonely is a Monarch in a struggle with a shrewd Prime Minister backed by all the apparatus of the modern State!

Walter related how the crowd outside No. 10 Downing Street, recognizing the King's motor, cheered as he drove away. That was probably the last audible demonstration of the "King's Party." By Monday it was a corpse. It died swiftly but not painlessly. Over the week-end, word went out through the lobbies and beyond into the cities and the provinces that the fight was over— if indeed it had ever begun.

Although my advisers and I realised that there was nothing more to be gained by prolonging the unequal contest, Mr. Churchill at this late hour still insisted that more remained to be said. Having from the outset taken his stand on the lofty constitutional principle that the Government had no right to force the King to abdicate without consulting Parliament, he strode into the House of Commons on the Monday afternoon undaunted, and quite alone, to launch his attack. Hardly was he on his feet before the hostility smote him like a great wave. The memorable scene of Mr. Churchill being howled down has often been described.

I have always regretted that incident, and would give much for the power to erase it from the records of that ancient assembly that owes him so much. Yet I am proud, also, that of all Englishmen it was Mr. Churchill who spoke up to the last for the King, his friend.

CHAPTER XXVII

THE "CONSPIRACY" THAT FAILED

NOTHING more remained to be decided between the Prime Minister and myself. It was only a matter of going through the mechanical formalities of Abdication; of passing on to my brother Bertie the Succession to the Throne; and of settling various family matters. Yet even as I began to apply myself to these last preparations, the whole structure of my decision, formed in mental anguish and under the relentless pressure of conflicting forces, was menaced by an unexpected development which for a short but terrifying interval threatened me with the loss of the marriage for which I had already in spirit relinquished my Throne.

Much of what went on at this time still remains obscure. It involved something which, without anger and rather for want of a better word, I call the "Conspiracy." Mr. Baldwin, Lord Beaverbrook, Sir Horace Wilson, Perry Brownlow, even the solicitor who handled Wallis's divorce petition, Mr. Theodore Goddard, were briefly involved in it.

I shall begin with an account of Max Beaverbrook's part, based upon the facts as I was subsequently able to piece them together, and from his own wry reminiscences.

First, a word as to his motives. Max Beaverbrook is a subtle and highly political animal. No doubt friendship for me, perhaps even a romantic desire to encourage the course of true love in the face of a Prime Minister's opposition, had all been impelling considerations. And an additional impulse was furnished by his longstanding enmity for Mr. Baldwin. Yet there was something more. I had tramped the outer marches of the Empire he had loved. He truly believed, I think, that its interests would best be served by my remaining King. All other arguments and pulls having failed, he was inspired, at this stage, to try to plant in Wallis's mind the idea of renouncing the marriage. It was not his intention to destroy my happiness. Max has since put down on paper what he hoped to achieve in what he conceived to be my best interests: "We wanted only a postponement of the great decision. If Mrs. Simpson renounced the marriage, Mr. Baldwin's crisis would die on his hands. Public excitement would sink. The great aim of delay for second thought and calm consideration would have been achieved. Then, later, the question of marriage could have been re-opened at the time of the King's choosing."

The plot was hatched at Stornoway House the night before Wallis left England. There, with several friends, Perry Brownlow, George Allen, and Walter Monckton (the presence of the last two perhaps needs a word of explanation. While they were completely loyal to me in spirit and in deed, that very excess of loyalty prompted them to leave no avenue unexplored, however unpromising its turnings, that held out the remotest prospect of keeping me on the Throne), Max Beaverbrook reviewed the situation as it had then developed. The immediate practical difficulty that had to be resolved was to open, unknown to me, a line of communication with Wallis.

Earlier on the preceding day Max had tried to reach her with a stratagem of his own. He had prepared an editorial which he thought would be pleasing to her, and had telephoned The Fort, hoping that I would allow him to show it to her. But instinct warned me not to allow this step, and I asked him to read it first to me. My instinct was borne out. The article was designed to induce her to make a declaration of renunciation. Wallis never saw it because I would not permit Max to show it to her. It was never published. Max now produced a more subtle idea. Since Perry Brownlow was a friend of Wallis's as well as of mine, Max saw in him a possible means of access to her. The plan was roughly as follows: as I was still conducting business in my office at Buckingham Palace every morning, Perry was deputed to ascertain my movements and to take advantage of one of these daily absences in London to make his way into The Fort and approach Wallis, whom Max, with his remarkable intuition, had sensed must be desperately casting about for some means of ending the crisis. Thus when, by a remarkable coincidence, I asked Perry Brownlow next morning to accompany Wallis to Cannes, I chose in all innocence Max's agent.

An advocate charged with so delicate a task could hardly have asked for a more favourable opportunity to present his case. Perry Brownlow was alone with Wallis throughout the long drive across France from Dieppe to Cannes, where they arrived shortly after midnight on Saturday, December 4. Whether he ever actually broached the idea of her withdrawing from the marriage Wallis herself does not remember, and the point, in any case, is not important. She needed no persuading. Not knowing how far matters had progressed in London, she devised, with the help of Perry Brownlow and Herman Rogers, the following public statement which was released to the Press from Cannes the Monday evening following her arrival :

> Mrs. Simpson, throughout the last few weeks, has invariably wished to avoid any action or proposal which would hurt or damage His Majesty or the Throne.
>
> To-day her attitude is unchanged, and she is willing, if such action would solve the problem, to withdraw forthwith from a situation that has been rendered both unhappy and untenable.

Wallis read the statement to me over the telephone. I readily consented to its release; it set forth her attitude in a proper and dignified manner. My hope was that it would silence those who imputed to her an indifference to the tremendous things at stake for me. But it never occurred to me that she was actually asking to be released from the claims of my love. Yet that was what she meant. And others read into her statement the same meaning.

At this juncture a plot developed within the plot. Several days after Max Beaverbrook had had his sudden inspiration Sir Horace Wilson appears to have entertained a remarkably similar one of his own. He summoned Mr. Goddard, Wallis's solicitor, to Whitehall for an interview. The circumstances that brought about the reappearance of this gentleman into our affairs remain obscure. It may have been that Sir Horace was himself moment-arily attracted by the possibility of breaking the abdication impasse with a sudden and overpowering appeal to Wallis.

Whatever the reasons, Mr. Goddard in any event suddenly appeared at The Fort this same Monday afternoon, with a vague plan for going to Cannes to talk to her. My recollection, which is none too certain regarding this particular meeting, is that I expressly forbade him to go. I do remember helping the visitor on with his coat and escorting him to the door. My new motor was standing outside; Mr. Goddard admired it, and was so impressed by its appearance that he announced his intention of purchasing one himself. But I was presently to discover, somewhat ruefully, that Mr. Goddard's curiosity about American motors was not quite as intense as I had assumed.

On leaving me, Mr. Goddard, it appears, hastened back to London, where Sir Horace Wilson was waiting at the Travellers' Club to learn the results of his talk with me. Almost immediately Sir Horace exhibited a sheet of paper on which was written what Mr. Goddard afterwards described as an "epitome" of Wallis's statement from Cannes. Sir Horace asked whether, in the solicitor's opinion, it represented a sincere desire on the part of Wallis to renounce the marriage. The latter answered that from what he knew of the lady it was undoubtedly her intention.

Sir Horace Wilson suddenly excused himself. Presumably he telephoned No. 10 Downing Street. Returning, he informed Mr. Goddard that the Prime Minister wished to see him at once. It was now well past the dinner hour. Mr. Baldwin was alone in his office. He handed the solicitor a sheet of paper that he had been studying on his desk. It was a copy of the "epitome" that Sir Horace Wilson had just shown him.

"What does this mean?" the Prime Minister asked.

"I have only just seen it," Mr. Goddard answered.

However, he repeated in substance what he had already told Sir Horace Wilson; namely, that from what he knew of Mrs. Simpson the facts were undoubtedly as set forth.

The Prime Minister listened thoughtfully. "I want you to go to Cannes and find out what is really behind this," he said.

"When?" asked the solicitor.

"Immediately—to-night."

"If you ask me to go, I shall of course do so."

Mr. Baldwin summoned Sir Horace Wilson into the office.

"Mr. Goddard is flying to Cannes to-night. Make the necessary arrangements."

By Mr. Baldwin's order the special aeroplane used for Prime Ministerial business was made available for the journey. It was to be Mr. Goddard's first flight, and as he had a heart condition that might be adversely affected by altitude, his doctor insisted upon accompanying him. The two travellers hastened to Croydon, intending to take off by 2 a.m. in the hope of reaching the South of France by the early morning. But the weather was unfavourable, and the start was delayed until daylight. In the air they were immediately beset by storms and engine trouble which obliged them to make several emergency descents *en route*.

Having been warned by George Allen of what was afoot, I telephoned Wallis in Cannes, warning her of Mr. Goddard's imminent arrival, on an errand apparently undertaken with the Prime Minister's knowledge and approval. Perhaps in my wrath I was rather imperious. "You must not listen to this man," I insisted. "Do not be influenced by anything he says."

Wallis has a mind of her own. After some hesitation, she answered that she would of course have to receive him. After all, he was coming a long way, at some risk to himself, and courtesy required that she should listen to what he had to say. But she promised to do nothing without consulting me. Her answer was reassuring. Little did I realize that she was then on the verge of slipping out of my life. Deprived of my moral support, she was no longer so sure of herself, and the violence of the storm raging about us both terrified her.

During the rest of that day, while Mr. Goddard was beating his way south through cloud and storm, I turned wearily to deal with my personal affairs. My time, I realized, was fast running out, and I therefore asked my brother Bertie to come to The Fort to discuss the disposition of family property, heirlooms and so forth, for, in the process of stepping down from the Throne, I should also abdicate, for legal purposes, the position of head of the House of Windsor.

In a manner of speaking, this was the first time since the onset of the crisis that I had reopened the door of The Fort to my family. With brotherly affection George had tried again and again to see me, but although I missed his companionship during those lonely

days, I held fast to my original policy of self-imposed isolation. However, after he learned that I had sent for Bertie,
nothing could keep him away. Uninvited and unannounced,
he showed up at The Fort during the afternoon. Surprised, I
asked:

"What the dickens are you doing here?"

"Whether you want to see me or not, I have come," he said.

Thus, what had started out as a family business discussion
became a brotherly reunion which, later that afternoon, was
interrupted by the unexpected arrival of the Prime Minister.

Walter Monckton flashed a warning from London that the
Prime Minister was anxious to see me for a last talk.

"But why could he possibly wish to see me again?" I asked.
"Hasn't everything been said that needs to be said?"

Walter answered that the Prime Minister apparently wished
to reassure himself that he had exhausted all possible solutions,
and to see whether anything more could be done.

In the light of the rebuffs that I had already suffered at the
hands of my Prime Minister, this sudden solicitude struck me as
a trifle odd, if not gratuitous. However, it would have been
ungracious not to receive him, so I said he could come.

Walter Monckton was with the Prime Minister when he
arrived at The Fort about 5.30. So was "Tommy" Dugdale.
The trip from London, judging from Walter's account, must have
been a harrowing experience. It was made in the familiar undersized motor; all three passengers, as well as the driver, were fairly
bulky; when they had all squeezed themselves into the cramped
interior Walter felt as if he were caged. As the chauffeur was
obviously under strict orders to remain well within the Prime
Ministerial speed limit of twenty-five miles an hour, their
deliberate progress towards the waiting Monarch was something
of a road hazard to overtaking drivers who, unaware of the motor-
car's exalted occupant, set up a furious honking in their wake.
Mr. Baldwin himself seemed utterly oblivious of the mounting
pandemonium behind. Apparently lost in thought, he hummed
intermittently to himself, cracked and snapped his fingers in his
peculiar fashion, and puffed contentedly at his pipe until the
packed motor-car became so full of smoke that the other
occupants gasped for air.

As I greeted the party in the hall, I noticed Tommy Dugdale in the act of depositing near the door what was undoubtedly a suitcase.

"Good God," I swore softly to myself. "Surely S.B. doesn't intend to spend the night."

Taking the Prime Minister into the drawing-room, where I left him with Bertie, I hurriedly excused myself. Sir Edward Peacock was outside.

"E.R.P.," I said in a low voice, "did you see that thing in the hall?"

"You mean Mr. Baldwin's suitcase?" He asked, though it was obvious that he knew to what I was referring.

"Correct. Why did he bring it?"

Sir Edward smiled wearily. "I believe that he expects to spend the night here."

That suitcase was just too much. Mr. Baldwin, I suspected, was already at work on the speech in which he would describe his negotiations with me, and perhaps he calculated that his story would sound much better if he were able to tell the country that he had spent a last night with the King in a humble and sincere effort to talk him out of his project. But I had already had quite enough of Mr. Baldwin; his part in my life was over, and I did not propose to have him on my hands that night, snapping his fingers, storing up little homely touches for his report to Parliament.

"E.R.P.," I said, "will you do something for me? Please take the Prime Minister aside and explain to him that while I do not wish to seem inhospitable, I am worn out. Tell him that he is, of course, welcome at my table for dinner, but with so little time left and so much to be done . . . tell him anything. But please see that he doesn't stay."

In a minute or two, Sir Edward Peacock returned. "S.B. quite understands. I shall take him away myself."

The Prime Minister and I had a last fruitless talk. We got no further and our repetitions are not worth going over again.

When dinner was announced I joined the company in the dining-room. We were nine: Mr. Baldwin on my right, Sir Edward Peacock on my left; my brothers, Bertie and George, Tommy Dugdale, Walter Monckton, George Allen, and Ulick

Alexander made up the rest of the party, disposed around the table as follows:

The King

Mr. Baldwin		Sir Edward Peacock
Duke of York		Duke of Kent
Mr. Monckton		Major Thomas Dugdale
		Mr. George Allen

Major Ulick Alexander

Conversation never flagged. But I saw to it that the topic that was responsible for bringing us together was never once mentioned.

The Prime Minister took his leave about half-past nine. Towards the end of dinner, under the candlelight, his heavy face seemed pasty and lifeless; the strain, I realized, had also taken a heavy toll of him. Although I never saw Mr. Baldwin again, I believe that he took from The Fort, that evening, the recollection of an unbowed, unresentful if somewhat whimsical Sovereign.

In any case, describing the dinner at a Cabinet Meeting the following day, he remarked, more puzzled than disapproving, that "the King appeared happy and gay, as if he were looking forward to his honeymoon."

I woke up believing that the worst was now over; that no more painful surprises could possibly assail me. I was soon to learn otherwise. Some 600 miles from The Fort, while I was still sound asleep, Mr. Goddard had been forced to land at Marseilles. Without a pause he continued by car on to Cannes. Wallis received him at Lou Viei after breakfast. They talked together in front of an open fire. Mr. Goddard discovered that her desire to keep the King on the Throne was, if anything, more intense than that of the Ministers in Whitehall. Together they discussed a way by which she might confront me with an impassable barrier: the withdrawal, at the sacrifice of her freedom, of her still incomplete divorce action.

In Mr. Goddard's presence Wallis telephoned to say that since I would not renounce her she would perform the act of renunciation herself, and that she intended to leave France for another country. "But it's too late," I pleaded. "The Abdication documents are being drawn up. The Cabinet is meeting this very moment to act upon them. Of course you can do whatever you wish. You can go wherever you want—to China, Labrador, or the South Seas. But wherever you go, I will follow you."

In the face of my determination Mr. Goddard finally conceded defeat. Presently he telephoned George Allen to say that but for the King's iron resolve he would have succeeded in his mission. "Mrs. Simpson," he said in effect, "is willing to agree to anything; but other decisions have been made, and I am powerless." His fleeting but critical part in the drama finished, Mr. Goddard withdrew from the stage, and I assumed with relief that the plan to break down Wallis's resistance had been scotched.

That day in London the Cabinet met twice. At the morning session the Prime Minister apparently gave his colleagues formal notice of a situation that could hardly have brought surprise; namely, that the King, denied the right to marry on the Throne, was determined to abdicate immediately. As the Ministers dispersed, cables went out to the Dominion Premiers and the Viceroy of India, telling of my decision; and the Prime Minister composed two letters which were rushed to The Fort.

One might be described as a formality—reiteration by the Cabinet of its prayer that my decision was not irrevocable and that I would reconsider it.

The answer to this communication presented no difficulty. It was one with which I had lived for weeks. With the help of Walter Monckton, I addressed to Mr. Baldwin in my own hand the formal declaration of my intention to abdicate—the last remaining action required to start the constitutional machinery turning in high gear:

> The King has received the Prime Minister's letter of the 9th December, 1936, informing him of the view of the Cabinet.
> His Majesty has given the matter his further consideration, but regrets that he is unable to alter his decision.

The other letter is interesting only because it reminded me of the curious unprecedented and constitutional quirk which the passing of the succession from a living monarch would entail. Since no higher authority existed, I should be obliged as King to provide Parliament with my own Royal Assent to my own Act of Abdication.

Walter immediately started back to London with my formal declaration. A dense fog had meanwhile descended over the Thames Valley; I was afraid that he might be delayed on the road, and in consequence keep the Cabinet waiting. Thus at the end even Nature seemed to conspire to retard the resolution of a situation that all concerned were anxious to end.

For me it was all over. My mother was the first to know that my business with Mr. Baldwin was finished. Notwithstanding the weather, she drove out that afternoon to see me. She must have passed Walter Monckton on the Great West Road on his way to London with the fateful document. I should have preferred to receive her at The Fort, but because it was still under siege by the Press I decided that it would be easier for her if we met under my brother Bertie's roof at Royal Lodge, three miles away, in Windsor Great Park.

Taking the grassy road along the banks of Virginia Water, I joined her there briefly about three o'clock. She was already waiting in the drawing-room when I arrived. I gave her a full account of all that had passed between Mr. Baldwin and myself during the six days since our last meeting on the Thursday before. She still disapproved of and was bewildered by my action, but now that it was all over, her heart went out to her hard-pressed son, prompting her to say with tenderness: "And to me, the worst thing is that you won't be able to see her for so long."

Through the french windows, I noticed that the fog had thickened; I could hardly see into my brother's garden. I therefore urged my mother, for her own safety, to start back for London before dark. I watched her go, and returned to The Fort to find George Allen in what was for him a state of extreme agitation.

During my brief absence at Royal Lodge there had been another urgent telephone call from Cannes. Esmond Harmsworth, George Allen told me with concern, had unexpectedly turned up on the Côte d'Azur, taking up Max Beaverbrook's torch, and was urging Wallis to withdraw.

"Do you mean," I asked George, "that I have to go through all that again?"

"I am afraid, Sir," said George, "that Mrs. Simpson is determined."

Now perversely occurred a final moment of agony for me. When I called up Wallis on the telephone, she returned to the despairing entreaties of the morning. "Anything," she insisted, "would be better than abdication." She was distraught; so was I. With the last exits of my reign closing one by one, I found myself facing a void.

Finally, I summoned George Allen into the room while she talked. "What can I say to make myself clear? How can I convince her that what she suggests is utterly impossible?" George Allen took a piece of paper off the desk, and wrote upon it a single sentence: "The only conditions on which I can stay here are if I renounce you for all time." I read it to Wallis first, and then handing the telephone to Mr. Allen, I asked him to repeat it. Her answer to me was worthy of the occasion. The void between us disappeared. The truth, of course, is that she tried throughout to make me turn back, and she would have succeeded had I not loved her so desperately and therefore been so determined.

In the meantime Walter had returned from London with his report on the four o'clock Cabinet Meeting, and was off again on his third round trip between The Fort and Whitehall since breakfast.

Government draftsmen were already at work on the Instrument of Abdication by means of which I would pass the Succession to my brother. It was Mr. Baldwin's desire to have the document signed by me and witnessed by my three brothers the next morning, submitted to Parliament in the afternoon, and given my formal assent on Friday, when I would cease by law to be King.

Since Bertie would have to be proclaimed the new King at an Accession Council on the Saturday, I resolved to leave Britain the night before.

In London the tall, stooping figure of Sir John Simon joined Mr. Baldwin and Walter Monckton in scrutinizing the drafts of the Instrument of Abdication and the Royal Message which were passed back and forth until the fastidious requirements of Whitehall wording had been satisfied. It was a worn and somewhat rumpled barrister who finally materialized out of the fog some-time after midnight, bearing the decisive papers.

Late as was the hour, and tired though we both were, never-theless we studied them afresh. The Instrument of Abdication was the important one.

> I, Edward the Eighth, of Great Britain, Ireland, and the British Dominions beyond the Seas, King, Emperor of India, do hereby declare My irrevocable determination to renounce the Throne for Myself and for My descendants, and My desire that effect should be given to this Instrument of Abdication immediately.
>
> In token whereof I have hereunto set My hand this tenth day of December, nineteen hundred and thirty six, in the presence of the witnesses whose signatures are subscribed.

"Tell them," I finally said, "that I approve and will sign it in the morning."

Walter went to the telephone in the little hall off the drawing-room. A minute later I heard him telling Tommy Dugdale at No. 10 Downing Street that the King had approved the draft, and would sign it in the presence of his brothers in the morning.

CHAPTER XXVIII

"GOD SAVE THE KING"

B<small>Y</small> breakfast time next morning the official copies of the Instrument of Abdication and the companion Royal Message, locked up in the familiar red despatch box, were already on my desk. My three brothers arrived at the Fort about ten o'clock. With Sir Edward Peacock, Walter Monckton, Ulick Alexander, and George Allen in attendance, we assembled immediately in the octagonal drawing-room. And as if in harmony with the lifting of the almost intolerable pressure of the last few weeks, the fog which for some days had added to the gloom had also lifted.

Sitting at the desk, with my three brothers watching, I began to sign the documents. There were seven copies of one, and eight of the other—just why there should be this discrepancy I never knew. Separate copies were required for the Prime Minister, the House of Lords, the House of Commons, the Governors-General of the Dominions, the President of the Executive Council of the Irish Free State, the Secretary of State for India.

It was all quite informal. The room was filled with a dignified dull murmur. When I had signed the last document I yielded the chair to my brothers, who in turn appended their signatures as witnesses in their order of precedence. The occasion moved me. Like a swimmer surfacing from a great depth, I left the room and stepped outside, inhaling the fresh morning air.

Walter Monckton followed me outside. Apologizing for intruding, he said that he was anxious to tell me something before he took the documents back to London. The Prime Minister had asked him to ascertain whether there were any particular points concerning our negotiations that I might wish him to mention in his report to Parliament that afternoon. Quite surprised, I answered, "That's nice of S.B. I appreciate his thoughtfulness." After a moment's reflection I decided there were two points of some importance to me personally that he might introduce. I wrote two brief notes on separate pieces of paper, which I handed to Walter Monckton. I kept no copies. The first had to do with my brother Bertie, for whose future I felt a special responsibility. I am able to quote this one because Mr. Baldwin included it in his speech. It read:

> The Duke of York. He and the King have always been on the best of terms as brothers, and the King is confident that the Duke deserves and will receive the support of the whole Empire.

The other note dealt with Wallis's rôle in the historical episode then drawing to a close. I wanted the Prime Minister to tell the nation that "the other person most intimately concerned" had steadily tried to the last to dissuade the King from the decision he had taken. Such a statement should not have been difficult for the Prime Minister to make: it was reasonable to suppose that Mr. Goddard had reported as much upon his return from Cannes. But this second note, I regret to say, cannot be quoted; Mr. Baldwin, for reasons he never divulged, elected to leave it out of his speech.

Then the fateful documents were locked up in the same official red box in which they had been brought to The Fort, and Walter Monckton carried it back to London. My negotiations with the Government having terminated, his rôle as liaison officer with the Prime Minister had come to an end. Instead of proceeding directly to No. 10 Downing Street he drove to Buckingham Palace, where he delivered the box to my private secretary, Alec Hardinge. And thus it fell to him to carry to the Prime Minister the papers in which the King had signed away his Throne. A few hours later, Mr. Baldwin rose in the House of Commons with the Instrument of Abdication and my message in his hand.

I had meanwhile notified the Prime Minister that I proposed to make a farewell broadcast before I left the country the next night. Since by then I should no longer be King, the Government would have no authority to seal my lips. However, I instructed Walter Monckton to inform Mr. Baldwin that I would, out of courtesy, let the Cabinet see in advance what I intended to say.

Hence, on my last morning in Great Britain I was up early, striving to finish the broadcast upon which I had worked well into the night. Some in the Government looked coldly upon the idea of my supplying an epilogue to a drama upon which the curtain had already descended. And even my mother tried to dissuade me. But I was determined to speak. I did not propose to leave my country like a fugitive in the night.

It has become part of the Abdication legend that the broadcast was actually written by Mr. Churchill. The truth is that, as he had often done before with other speeches, he generously supplied the final brush-strokes. Wanting to say good-bye to my old friend, I invited him to lunch with me that last day at The Fort. Before he left I asked him to read my modest effort. He made several admirable suggestions which a practised student of Churchilliana could spot at a glance: "bred in the constitutional tradition by my Father"; "one matchless blessing, enjoyed by so many of you and not bestowed on me—a happy home with his wife and children."

While we were thus at table, I ceased to be King. As I saw Mr. Churchill off, there were tears in his eyes. I can still see him standing at the door; hat in one hand, stick in the other. Something must have stirred in his mind; tapping out the solemn measure with his walking-stick, he began to recite, as if to himself:

> "He nothing common did or mean
> Upon that memorable scene."

His resonant voice seemed to give an especial poignancy to these lines from the ode by Andrew Marvell, on the beheading of Charles I.

Bertie came into my room alone that evening for a last talk. I was in the midst of packing my most personal possessions. I closed the door, and pushed aside the things on the sofa to make a place for him to sit down.

Shy and retiring by nature, he shrank instinctively from the gregarious life I had lived with some zest. Yet he possessed admirable qualities—qualities that may not have been so marked in me. He would make a fine King; I was confident of that.

During these last days we had spoken to each other with a frankness recalling the untroubled companionship of our youth.

The situation seemed to cry mutely for a symbolical laying on of hands, a passing of the torch. But there is not much that a former Monarch can tell his successor.

"You are not going to find this a difficult job at all," I assured him. "You know all the ropes, and you have almost overcome that slight hesitation in your speech which used to make public speaking so hard for you."

Words do not come easily to Bertie on occasions of great emotion; without his having to tell me so, I knew that he felt my going keenly. At the same time he can be extremely practical.

"By the way, David," he asked me, "have you given any thought as to what you are going to be called now?"

This question took me aback. "Why no, as a matter of fact, I haven't."

At that late hour the question of another title seemed of little consequence to a man who had been King. Immediate reflection told me that, as the son of the Sovereign, I was in my case by right of birth a prince—His Royal Highness the Prince Edward. But Bertie had evidently pondered the question and no doubt judging it only proper that I should bear a title at least equal to that of my younger brothers, Harry Duke of Gloucester and George Duke of Kent, he said thoughtfully: "I shall create you a Duke. How about the family name of Windsor?"

"Duke of Windsor," I said, half to myself. Liking the sound of it, I nodded in agreement.

"It shall be the first act of my reign. I shall announce it at my Accession Council to-morrow morning."

Walter Monckton returned before dinner with the draft of the broadcast which, out of courtesy, I had wanted the Government to see. The Prime Minister had dropped a hint that he would be gratified if I would stress that he had at all times shown me every possible form of consideration. "That's a good one," I said, remembering how he had ignored my simple request the day before that he should do justice in his speech to Wallis. His omission was all the harder to understand because of the apparent benevolence that pervaded his own speech—an autobiographical triumph disguised as a homily on the errors of a King. However, determined not to be petty at the last moment, I incorporated into my broadcast that little item that Mr. Baldwin had valued.

Perhaps the rendering of these simple courtesies falls more easily upon kings than upon politicians; after all, we do not have to run for office.

I had arranged to dine with my family at Royal Lodge before making the broadcast from Windsor Castle at ten o'clock. Before leaving The Fort I telephoned Wallis at Cannes to tell her that I was on my way and should not be able to talk to her again until sometime on the Sunday.

"Where are you going?" she asked.

"To Zürich."

Surprised, she asked, "But why Zürich?"

"Oh, one of my household informs me that there is an hotel just outside the city where I shall be comfortable."

"But you can't go to an hotel. You will have no privacy; you will be hounded to death."

Until then, in my overwrought state, I had given little thought to where I would go; and so long as I could not be with Wallis until April, the question of where I should stay had seemed to me of no importance.

She now made a suggestion. Our friends the Rothschilds had invited her to spend Christmas with them at their country home at Enzesfeld, near Vienna. Although she had been looking forward to the change, she urged me to go in her place.

"I will telephone them right now," Wallis said. "I am sure they will be glad to have you."

The moment had come to leave The Fort for good. My bags were packed. In the act of bidding farewell to the small group of personal retainers gathered in the hall, I discovered Slipper at my heels. In the commotion of packing, he was obviously worried that he would be left behind. Patting the little dog to reassure him, I said, "Of course you are coming away with me, Slipper. But you can't come to this family dinner-party." And turning to Walter Monckton, I said, "Be sure to bring Slipper with you in the car when you come to fetch me for the broadcast."

As I drove off down the hill towards Virginia Water, I turned for a last look at the place I loved so much. The Fort was in sight for only a few seconds—a mere *augenblick*—before the motor turned out of the gates and it disappeared. In that moment I realized how heavy was the price I had paid: for,

411

along with all the other things I should have to give up The Fort, probably for ever. The thought brought me great sadness. The Fort had been more than a home; it had been a way of life for me. I had created The Fort just as my grandfather had created Sandringham; I loved it in the same way; it was there that I had passed the happiest days of my life.

A few minutes later I joined my family at Royal Lodge. My mother and Mary had come from London; my three brothers were with them in the drawing-room. Dinner passed pleasantly enough under the circumstances. I hope I was a good guest, but I rather doubt it.

While we were still at dinner, the butler announced that Walter Monckton had arrived to take me to the Castle. When I stepped into the car I found Slipper on the seat, no doubt be-wildered by the sudden excursion into the night, but cheerfully wagging his tail. Driving down the Long Walk, Walter Monck-ton told me that Wallis had telephoned to say that the Rothschilds would be glad to have me. The knowledge that I now had a place where I should be left undisturbed to wait out the months before our marriage helped to soften the bitter prospect of a long separa-tion.

The great quadrangle was dark and deserted as we entered. Only at the Sovereign's Entrance was there light and activity. A few of the officials of the Castle, among them my father's old Private Secretary, Lord Wigram, in his dual capacity of Deputy Constable and Lieutenant-Governor of the Castle, received me at the doors. I mounted the Gothic staircase to my old rooms in the Augusta Tower, where I found Sir John Reith, Director of the British Broadcasting Corporation. At my request he had come from London to supervise the broadcast, bringing with him equipment and technicians. Although I was hardly a novice, he suggested that I should run through the usual practice routine. So that I might test my voice he handed me a newspaper from which to read aloud. The paragraph I picked at random had an unexpected relevance. It was the report of a speech by Sam Hoare at a tennis gathering, to whose attention he hopefully commended the fact that the new King was an ardent tennis player. This information I read aloud with the utmost gravity. The time signal came. In a deep voice Sir John announced into the microphone—"This is Windsor Castle. His Royal Highness, Prince Edward." With those words my senses became utterly absorbed with the job in hand. Sensing that I might wish to be left alone with Walter Monckton, Sir John slipped out of the room. I do not myself remember the sound that mystified millions of listeners—the slamming of a door. The noise, I believe, was actually caused by my banging my shoe against the table leg as I shifted my position to read. This is what I said:

> At long last I am able to say a few words of my own.
>
> I have never wanted to withhold anything, but until now it has been not constitutionally possible for me to speak.
>
> A few hours ago I discharged my last duty as King and Emperor, and now that I have been succeeded by my brother, the Duke of York, my first words must be to declare my allegiance to him. This I do with all my heart.
>
> You all know the reasons which have impelled me to renounce the Throne. But I want you to understand that in making up my mind I did not forget the country or the Empire which as Prince of Wales, and lately as King, I have for twenty-five years tried to serve. But you must believe me when I tell you that I have found it impossible to carry the heavy burden of responsibility and to discharge my duties as King as I would wish to do without the help and support of the woman I love.
>
> And I want you to know that the decision I have made has been mine and mine alone. This was a thing I had to judge entirely for myself. The other person most nearly concerned has tried up to the last to persuade me to take a different course. I have made this, the most serious decision of my life, upon a single thought of what would in the end be best for all.
>
> This decision has been made less difficult to me by the sure knowledge that my Brother, with his long training in the public affairs of this country and with his fine qualities, will be able to take my place forthwith, without interruption or injury to the life and progress of the Empire. And he has one matchless blessing, enjoyed by so many of you and not bestowed on me—a happy home with his wife and children.
>
> During these hard days I have been comforted by my Mother and by my Family. The Ministers of the Crown, and in particular Mr. Baldwin, the Prime Minister, have always treated me with full consideration. There has never been any constitutional difference between me and them and between me and Parliament.

Bred in the constitutional tradition by my Father, I should never have allowed any such issue to arise.

Ever since I was Prince of Wales, and later on when I occupied the Throne, I have been treated with the greatest kindness by all classes, wherever I have lived or journeyed throughout the Empire. For that I am very grateful.

I now quit altogether public affairs, and I lay down my burden. It may be some time before I return to my native land, but I shall always follow the fortunes of the British race and Empire with profound interest, and if at any time in the future I can be found of service to His Majesty in a private station I shall not fail.

And now we all have a new King. I wish him, and you, his people, happiness and prosperity with all my heart. God bless you all. God Save the King.

At Royal Lodge, my family had listened to the broadcast, and when I returned to them I had the feeling that what I had said had to some extent eased the tension between us. It was getting late for my mother, and she left first, with Mary. I stayed on until midnight with my brothers, and Walter Monckton joined us all in a farewell drink before he and I took the road to Portsmouth. My brothers walked with me to the door exactly as they would have done were I leaving for Balmoral, Sandringham, or some other familiar place. On this leave-taking, however, it was I who, as the subject to the King, bowed to Bertie, and George, watching, shook his head and cried almost fiercely, "It isn't possible! It isn't happening!"

But it had happened. It was all over.

The Admiralty had a destroyer, the *Fury*, waiting at Portsmouth, to take me across the Channel.

It was a clear winter night; we were lucky not to strike fog. During the hour's drive to Portsmouth, Walter Monckton and I talked about many things. The details of the crisis fell behind. Our association had begun at Oxford, before the First World War, and as the car sped along across the Hartford Bridge Flats, we were simultaneously reminded of a two-day field exercise in which we had jointly taken part as members of the O.T.C. in the summer of 1914—he as a young cavalryman, I as a still younger corporal in the infantry. But I wondered whether Walter really remembered that hot, dusty plain exactly as I did

—not merely because he had in comparative comfort ridden a horse while I marched on my flat feet carrying rifle and equipment, but rather because his place among men was taken for granted, while I was secretly obsessed with the desire to be found worthy and to share in the risks and struggles of men. And I meditated how strange it was that chance should have taken me through this obscure part of England on this particular night, for it was here that I had begun to fit myself for life in the real world—the world which by my own free will I had chosen.

Reaching Portsmouth, we entered the Navy Yard by the wrong gate, and found ourselves on a dark and deserted quay from which I made out against the night the shadowy outlines of the *Victory*. It was not long before we were located by an officer whom the Commander-in-Chief had sent to search for us. He quickly guided us to the berth where the destroyer was made fast. There at the dock we found Piers Legh, Ulick Alexander, and Godfrey Thomas waiting with Admiral Sir William Fisher and a few of his staff. The farewells were brief. The captain of the destroyer, Commander C. L. Howe, met me on board as I crossed the gangway with Slipper under my arm. He asked for leave to sail. I told him to carry on and followed him up to the bridge. A moment later I heard him give the order to cast off the hawsers; the engine-room telegraph clanged; the deck began to throb to the pulse of the engines. As these familiar sounds entered my consciousness, I thought how often I had put to sea in the same manner.

And so it came to pass that at two o'clock on the morning of December 12, 1936, H.M.S. *Fury* slid silently and unescorted out of Portsmouth Harbour. Watching the shore of England recede, I was swept by many emotions. If it had been hard to give up the Throne, it had been even harder to give up my country. I knew now that I was irretrievably on my own. The drawbridges were going up behind me. But of one thing I was certain: so far as I was concerned love had triumphed over the exigencies of politics.

Though it has proved my fate to sacrifice my cherished British heritage along with all the years in its service, I to-day draw comfort from the knowledge that time has long since sanctified a true and faithful union.

MY JOURNEYS

1898
Sept. Copenhagen

1912

Apr.		May		June	
1	Dover	26–27	Arles	19–21	Paris
	Calais	27–28	Avignon	21	Dover
1–20	Paris	28–29	Valence	27	Calais
22	Chantilly	29–30	Grenoble	27–	
May		30–		July	
5	Chartres	June		4	Paris
	Reims	2	Annecy	5–6	Rouen
6	Fontainebleau	2–4	Reyrieux	6–31	Chevreuse
21	Toulon	3	Lyon	31	Paris
21–25	Aboard French battleship	4–6	Le Creusot	31–	
	Danton	6–7	Bourges	Aug.	
22	Hyères ,,	7–13	Paris	1	Amiens
23	Golfe de Juan ,,	13–15	Blois		Calais
25	Villefranche ,,	15–17	Tours		Dover
25–26	Marseilles	17–18	Saint Patrice		
26	Nîmes	18–19	Orléans		

1913

Mar.		Apr.		July	
17	Dover	17	Calais	28–29	Hamburg
	Calais		Dover	29–30	Berlin
18–19	Cologne	July		30–	
19–20	Coblenz	1	Calais	Aug.	
20–22	Wiesbaden	2–4	Munich	9	Neustrelitz
22–24	Darmstadt	4–5	Salzburg	10–17	Gotha
24–26	Heidelberg	5–6	Munich	17–18	Berlin
26–27	Karlsruhe	6–7	Ratisbon	18–30	Neustrelitz
27–30	Stuttgart	7–8	Nuremberg	30–	
30	Ulm	8–9	Marienbad	Sept.	
30–		9–10	Prague	1	Berlin
Apr.		10–14	Dresden	2–3	Friedrichshafen
1	Friedrichshafen	14–15	Leipzig	3–4	Sigmaringen
	Liechtenstein	15–18	Berlin	5	Calais
1–15	Stuttgart	18–23	Neustrelitz		Dover
16–17	Paris	24–28	Eckernförde, Kiel		

1914

Mar.		Mar.		Apr.	
16	Dover	21–25	Voksenkollen	2–6	Christiania
	Calais	25–27	Christiania	7	Copenhagen
17–18	Copenhagen	28–			Hamburg
18	Elsinore	Apr.		8	Calais
	Hälsingborg	1	Finse		Dover
19–21	Christiania (Oslo)		Bergen		

On active service: First World War

Nov. 16 *G.H.Q. British Expeditionary Force*
St. Omer

1915

Jan.		Jan.			*H.Q. Guards Division*
13–14	Compiègne	21–22	Amiens	Sept.	
14–15	Chalons sur Marne	22	St. Omer	1	Nœux-les-Mines for the
15–17	Belfort		*H.Q. I Army Corps*		Battle of Loos
17–19	Nancy	May			Laventie
19–20	Chalons sur Marne	2	Béthune		
20–21	Compiègne				

MY JOURNEYS

1916

Mar.
10–12 Marseilles
12–15 At sea H.M.S. *Liverpool*
15–16 Alexandria
16–17 Cairo
17–31 G.H.Q. *Mediterranean Expeditionary Force*
Ismalia
31–
Apr.
3 At sea R.I.M.S. *Dufferin*
3 Port Sudan „
Atbara „
4–6 Khartoum

Apr.
7 Abu Hamed
Wadi Halfa
7–11 On the Nile aboard S.S. *Ibis*
8 Abul Simbel „
9 Shellal, Aswan Dam „
Kom Ombo „
10–11 Karnak „
12–23 Ismalia
23–25 In Suez Canal aboard S.S. *Nitocris*
23 Kabrit
23–25 Suez
24 El Kubri

Apr.
25–
May
1 Ismalia
1 Port Said
1–4 At sea H.M.S. *Weymouth*
4 Spezzia
5–9 Udine
10 Boulogne
22 *H.Q. XIV Army Corps*
Poperinghe
July
30 Albert for the Battle of the Somme

1917

June
11 Elverdinghe for the Battle of Passchendaele

Nov.
6 Il Montello, Piave River

1918

Mar.
Asiago Plateau
H.Q. Canadian Army Corps
Oct.
14 Douai

Nov.
11 Mons Area
H.Q. Australian Army Corps
Dec.
18 Charleroi

1919

H.Q. Royal Air Force
Jan.
8–9 Spa

Canadian Corps
9–10 Bonn

H.Q. Third American Army
10–12 Coblenz

Guards Division
Jan.
12–16 Cologne

H.Q. New Zealand Division
Jan.
16–19 Cologne
19–
Feb.
16 Visits to various British Army Units in FRANCE and BELGIUM

G.H.Q. American Expeditionary Force
16–17 Chaumont

1919

Aug.
5 Portsmouth
5–11 At sea H.M.S. *Renown*
11 Topsail, Conception Bay
12 At sea H.M.S. *Dragon*
12–13 St. John's
13–15 At sea H.M.S. *Dragon*
15 St. John's
16–17 At sea H.M.S. *Dragon*
17–18 Halifax
18–19 At sea H.M.S. *Dragon*
19 Charlottetown
19–21 At sea H.M.S. *Renown*
21–24 Quebec
Three Rivers
Berthieville
25–27 Toronto
28–
Sept.
1 Ottawa
2 Montreal
3 North Bay
Sudbury
4 Algoma
Sault Ste. Marie

Sept.
5–8 Orient Bay, Nipigon River
Port Arthur
Fort William
9–10 Winnipeg
11 Saskatoon
12–13 Edmonton
14–17 Calgary
17–18 Banff
18–19 Lake Louise
19 Field
20 Golden
Revelstoke
21 Kamloops
22–23 Vancouver
23 At sea S.S. *Princess Alice*
23–28 Victoria, Vancouver Is.
28–29 At sea S.S. *Princess Alice*
29 Vancouver
New Westminster
Mission
Penticton
30 Okanagan
Penticton

Oct.
1 Nelson
Kootenay Lake
2 Macleod
Lethbridge
3 Medicine Hat
4 Moose Jaw
4–6 Regina
6–9 Edenwald Camp
10 Brandon
Portage la Prairie
10–14 Winnipeg
16 Cobalt
Timmins
17–18 Hamilton
18–20 Niagara Falls
Brantford
21 Guelph
Stratford
22 Woodstock
Chatham
22–23 London
23–24 Windsor
Galt
25–26 Kingston

Oct.		Nov.		Nov.	
27–		11–14	Washington	21	Oyster Bay, L.I.
Nov.		14	Annapolis (Maryland)	22–24	At sea H.M.S. *Renown*
2	Montreal	15–17	White Sulphur (West Vir-	24–25	Halifax
	St. Annes		ginia)	25–	
3–4	Toronto	18	Philadelphia	Dec.	
5–10	Ottawa	18–22	New York	1	At sea H.M.S. *Renown*
10	Rouses Point (Maine)	20	West Point	1	Portsmouth

1920

Mar.		May		July	
16	Portsmouth	20	Invercargill	12–16	Adelaide
16–25	At sea H.M.S. *Renown*	21	Christchurch	16	Hindmarsh
25–27	Bridgetown		Lyttelton	16–19	At sea H.M.S. *Renown*
27–30	At sea H.M.S. *Renown*	22–26	At sea H.M.S. *Renown*	19–20	Hobart
30–		26–		21–22	Launceston
Apr.		June		22	Campbell Town
1	Panama Canal	13	Melbourne		Ross
1–7	At sea H.M.S. *Renown*	May			Parattali
7–8	San Diego (California)	28	Malvern		Brighton
8–13	At sea H.M.S. *Renown*	29	Essendon		Hobart
13	Honolulu	30	Sassafras	23–25	At sea H.M.S. *Renown*
14–20	At sea H.M.S. *Renown*	June		25	Sydney
20	Suva	1	Geelong		West Maitland
22–24	At sea H.M.S. *Renown*		Winchelsea		Singleton
24–27	Auckland, North Island, N.Z.		Colac		Muswellbrook
27–29	Rotorua		Camperdown		Marrundi
28	Ohinemutu	2	Terang	26	Wallangarra (Queensland)
	Whakarewarewa		Cressy		Amiens
30–			Ballarat		Warwick
May		4	Kyneton		Hendon
2	Auckland		Castlemaine		Clifton
	Frankton Junction		Bendigo	27–31	Brisbane
	Te Kuiti	5	Brighton	31	Ipswich
	Taumarunui	13–14	At sea H.M.S. *Renown*		Harrisville
3	New Plymouth	14–15	Jervis Bay (N.S.W.)	31–	
	Stratford	15	At sea H.M.S. *Renown*	Aug.	
	Hawera	16	Sydney	2	Boonah
	Patea	21	Queenbeyan	3	Maryborough
	Wanganui		Canberra		Tiaro
4	Marton		Goulburn		Gympie
	Feilding		Moss Vale		Cooroy
	Palmerston North	21–24	Sydney		Nambour
4–5	Napier	24	Parramatta		Landsborough
5	Hastings		Windsor		Berburrum
	Waipawa		Sackville Reach		Caboolture
	Waipukurau		Hawkesbury River Station	3–4	Brisbane
	Dannevirke	24–25	Toronto	4	Rosewood
	Woodville	25	Newcastle		Laidley
	Masterton		Gosford		Gatton
	Carterton		Sydney		Helidon
	Featherston	25–30	At sea H.M.S *Renown*		Toowoomba
5–9	Wellington	30	Albany	5	Stanthorpe
9–10	At sea H.M.S. *Renown*		Cranbrook		Tenterfield (N.S.W.)
10	Picton, South Island		Mt. Barker		Glen Innes
	Blenheim	July			Ben Lomond
	Havelock	1–4	Perth		Guyha
10–11	Nelson	2	Freemantle		Armidale
11	Glenhope		Keane's Point		Tamworth
	Reefton	5	Pemberton	6	Valley Heights
	Murchison		Jarnadup		Lawson
12	Westport		Bridgetown		Kelso
	Reefton	6	Bunbury		Bathurst
12–13	Hokitika	6–8	Perth	7	Coonamble
13	Greymouth	8	Northam		Wingadee
	Otira	9	Coolgardie	9	Coonamble
13–17	Christchurch		Kalgoorlie		Gular
17	Ashburton		Boulder		Gilgandra
	Temuka	10	Nullarbor Plain	10	Miowera
	Timaru		Cook		Nyngan
	Oamaru	11	Port Augusta	11–13	Canonbar
	Palmerston		Quorn	13	Narromine
17–20	Dunedin		Petersborough		Dubbo
18	Port Chalmers		Terowie		Wellington
20	Milton	12	Gawler		Orange
	Balclutha		Smithfield		Blayney

Aug.
13 Bathurst
   Tarana
   Wallerawang (Queensland)
14-19 Sydney
19-23 At sea H.M.S. *Renown*
23 Suva
24 At sea H.M.S. *Renown*
25 Apia
25-30 At sea H.M.S. *Renown*
30-
Sept.
1 Honolulu

Sept.
1-9 At sea H.M.S. *Renown*
9 Acapulco
10-13 At sea H.M.S. *Renown*
13-14 Panama Canal
14-17 At sea H.M.S. *Renown*
17-18 Port of Spain
18 St. Joseph
19-20 At sea H.M.S. *Calcutta*
20-22 Georgetown
22-23 At sea H.M.S. *Calcutta*
23-24 Port of Spain
24 At sea H.M.S. *Renown*
24-25 St. George's ,,

Sept.
   At sea H.M.S. *Renown*
25-26 Castries ,,
26 Roseau ,,
27-28 Plymouth ,,
28 St. John ,,
28-
Oct.
1 At sea H.M.S. *Renown*
1-3 Hamilton ,,
3 St. George's ,,
3-10 At sea H.M.S. *Renown*
10 Portsmouth

1921

Oct.
26 Portsmouth
26-29 At sea H.M.S. *Renown*
29 Gibraltar
29-
Nov.
1 At sea H.M.S. *Renown*
1-3 Valetta
3-5 At sea H.M.S. *Renown*
5-6 Port Said ,,
6-7 Suez Canal ,,
7-8 Suez ,,
8-12 At sea H.M.S. *Renown*
12 Aden ,,

Nov.
12-17 At sea H.M.S. *Renown*
17-18 Bombay
19 Poona
20-22 Bombay
23-24 Baroda
24 Rutlam
25-27 Udaipur
28 Ajmer
29-
Dec.
1 Jodhpur
2-3 Bikaner
3-6 Gujner

Dec.
5 Bikaner
7-8 Bharatpur
9-11 Lucknow
12 Allahabad
13 Benares
14-21 Bhikna Thori
22-23 Patna
24-30 Calcutta
30-31 At sea R.I.M.S. *Dufferin*

1922

Jan.
1-2 At sea R.I.M.S. *Dufferin*
2-4 Rangoon
5-7 Mandalay
8-10 Rangoon
10-13 At sea R.I.M.S. *Dufferin*
13-17 Madras
18 Bangalore
18-21 Mysore
21-23 Karapur
23 Mysore
25-28 Hyderabad
26 Secunderabad
30-31 Nagpur
Feb.
1-3 Indore
3 Mhow
4-5 Bhopal
5-7 Kachnaria
7 Bhopal
8-12 Gwalior
13 Fatehpur Sikri
13-14 Agra
14-21 Delhi
22-24 Patiala
25 Jullundur
25-
Mar.
1 Lahore
2-3 Jammu
3 Sialkot
   Jhelum
4-7 Peshawar
5 Khyber Pass
   Shahgai
   Landi Kotal
   Mardan
   Durgai
   Malakand
   Chakdara

Mar.
8-9 Risalpur
9 Nowshera
   Campbellpur
9-11 Rawalpindi
12 Kapurthala
13 Dehra Dun
   Hardwar
   Sharpur Bachraon
13-15 Gajroula, Meerut Kadir
17 Karachi
17-21 At sea H.M.S. *Renown*
21-23 Colombo
23-24 Kandy
24-25 Colombo
25-28 At sea H.M.S. *Renown*
28 Port Swettenham
28-30 Kuala Lumpur
30 Port Swettenham
30-31 At sea H.M.S. *Renown*
31-
Apr.
2 Singapore
2-6 At sea H.M.S. *Renown*
6-8 Hong Kong
8 Kowloon
8-12 At sea H.M.S. *Renown*
12 Yokohama
12-19 Tokyo
19-21 Nikko
21-22 Tokyo
22-23 Yokohama
23-26 Yumoto, Hakone
25 Miyanoshita
26 Nagao Pass
27-
May
4 Kyoto
Apr.
28 Lake Biwa

Apr.
28 Gifu
May
4-5 Nara
5 Osaka
   Kobe
5-8 On inland Sea aboard S.S. *Keifuku Maru*
7-8 Miyajima
8 Etajima
   Kure
8-9 At sea H.M.S. *Renown*
9 Kagoshima
9-13 At sea H.M.S. *Renown*
13-15 Manila
15 Cavite
15-17 At sea H.M.S. *Renown*
17-18 Victoria, Labuan Is.
18 Jesselton
19 Brunei
19-22 At sea H.M.S. *Renown*
23 Penang
23-27 At sea H.M.S. *Renown*
27-28 Trincomalee
28-29 Colombo
30 Trincomalee
30-
June
5 At sea H.M.S. *Renown*
   Great Hamish Is., Red Sea
5-9 At sea H.M.S. *Renown*
9 Suez
9-11 Cairo
12 Port Said
12-17 At sea H.M.S. *Renown*
17 Gibraltar
17-20 At sea H.M.S. *Renown*
20 Plymouth

1923

Sept.
5 Southampton
5-12 At sea S.S. *Empress of France*
12-13 Quebec
13 Ottawa
15 Winnipeg
16 Calgary
High River
16-21 E.P. Ranch

Sept.
21 High River
Calgary
21-25 Banff
25 Calgary
High River
25-30 E.P. Ranch
30-
Oct.
2 Calgary

Oct.
3-4 Winnipeg
6-10 Ottawa
10-13 Montreal
13 Quebec
13-20 At sea S.S. *Empress of France*
20 Southampton

1924

Aug.
23 Southampton
23-29 At sea S.S. *Berengaria*
29 New York
29-30 Washington
30-
Sept.
21 Syosset, L.I.
22 Ottawa
24 Winnipeg
25 Calgary
25-26 High River

Sept.
26-
Oct.
1 E.P. Ranch
2 Jasper
3-5 Vancouver
5 At sea S.S. *Princess Louise*
5-7 Victoria, Vancouver Is.
7 At sea S.S. *Princess Louise*
7-8 Vancouver
9 Calgary
10-12 Winnipeg

Oct.
12 Duluth
13-14 Chicago
14 Detroit
15-16 Toronto
16-19 Ottawa
19-22 Montreal
23-24 Lowell
24-25 New York City
25-31 At sea S.S. *Olympic*
31 Southampton

1925

Mar.
28 Portsmouth
28-
Apr.
4 At sea H.M.S. *Repulse*
Bathurst   „
Cape St. Mary
4-6 At sea H.M.S *Repulse*
6-7 Freetown
7-9 At sea H.M.S. *Repulse*
9 Takoradi
Sekondi
10 Kumasi
11 Nmawmaw
Nsawam
11-14 Accra
14-15 At sea H.M.S. *Repulse*
15 Iddo
16 Offa
Ilorin
Jebba
17-19 Kano
19 Kaduna
Minna
Zungeru
20 Ibadan
Aro
Ebute Metta
20-22 Lagos
22-30 At sea H.M.S. *Repulse*
30-
May
4 Cape Town
2 Simonstown
Wynberg
4 Somerset West
Stellenbosch
Paarl
Robertson
Ashton
Swellendam
5 Worcester
6 Heidelberg
Mossel Bay
Great Brak River
6-8 George

May
7 Knysna
8 Oudtshoorn
Cango Caves
9 Graaff-Reinet
Middleburg
Rosmead
9-12 Colesberg
13 Cradock
Cookhouse
Alicedale
13-14 Port Elizabeth
14 Uitenhage
Addo
Sundays River Valley
15 Grahamstown
15-18 Port Alfred
18 Grahamstown
19 Bedford
Adelaide
Fort Beaufort
Alice
19-20 King William's Town
20-21 East London
21 Cambridge
Koomka
22 Umtata
Butterworth
Idutywa
23 Cathcart
Imvani
Queenstown
Sterkstroom
Monteno
Stromberg
Burghersdorp
24 Philippolis Road
Jagersfontein
25 Springfontein
Edenberg
25-26 Bloemfontein
27 Winberg
Theunissen
Virginia
Wonderkop
Steynsrust

May
27 Lindley Road
28 Ficksburg
28 Ladybrand
28-30 Maseru
30-31 Westminster
June
1 Bethlehem
Harrismith
2 Ladysmith
Helpmakaar Ridge
Spion Kop
Colenso
3-5 Durban
5 Verulam
Stanger
Gingindhlove
5-6 Eshowe
6-10 Durban
10-11 Pietermaritzburg
11 Mooi River
Estcourt
Glencoe
12 Newcastle
Dannhauser
Dundee
Talana Hill
Zuinguin
13-14 Ermelo
14-15 Mbabane
15 Carolina
Machadodorp
Waterval Boven
16 Barberton
Komatipoort
17 Tzaneen
Mokeetsi
Guidplaats
Zoekmakaar
17-18 Pietersburg
18 Potgietersrust
Naboomspruit
Mylstroom
Warmbads
19-21 Pretoria
22 Potchefstroom

June
22 Randfontein
22-25 Johannesburg
23 Brakpan
Benoni
Boksburg
Germiston
25 Krugersdorp
Florida Lake
Gillwell
Crown Mine
26 Zeerust
Ottoshoop
Mafeking
Pitsani
Lobatsi
Sebele
27-28 Palapye Road
27 Serowe
29-
July
1 Bulawayo
2 Victoria
Chatsworth
Umvuma
2-5 Camp in Central Estates
5 Enkeldoorn
Range
5-6 Umvuma
6 Gwelo
Que Que
7-10 Salisbury
10 Gatooma
Umswezwe
Que Que
Gwelo
Daisyville
Bulawayo
11-13 Livingstone
12 Victoria Falls
13 Kamujoma
14-15 Kafue
15 Broken Hill

July
15 Boma
Mulunguishidam
16 Livingstone
17 Bulawayo
18 Mahalapye
Gaberones
19 Vryburg
Tigerskloof
Pudimoe
Taungs
Pokwani
Border
Warrenton
Bloemhof
20-22 Johannesburg
23-24 Kimberley
Beaconsfield
24 Paardeberg
Magersfontein
Modder River
Belmont
Grasspan
Enslin
25 De Aar
Meriman
Hutchinson
Nelspoort
Beaufort West
26 Worcester
26-29 Capetown
28 Table Mountain
29 Simonstown
29-
Aug.
3 At sea H.M.S. *Repulse*
3-5 Jamestown   „
4 Longwood
5-14 At sea H.M.S. *Repulse*
14-16 Montevideo
16-17 At sea H.M.S. *Curlew*
17-23 Buenos Aires
19 La Plata

Aug.
20 Devoto
Hurlingham
24-25 Huetel
25-30 Buenos Aires
30 Zárate
Ibicuy
Holt
31 Mercedes
Sept.
1 Parada Liebigs
1-2 On the Uruguay River aboard *Ciudad de Buenos Aires*
2 Buenos Aires
3-5 San Patricio
5 Laboulaye
Mackenna
Justo Daract
6 Mendoza
Las Cuevas
Los Andes
6-10 Santiago
10-14 Viña del Mar
15 Juneal
15-16 Los Andes
16-19 Viña del Mar
17 Valparaiso
20 Los Andes
Caracoles
Mendoza
21 Junín
21-23 Buenos Aires
23 Maipo
23-26 Chapadmalal
26 Mar del Plata
27-
Oct.
8 At sea H.M.S. *Repulse*
8 St. Vincent   „
9-16 At sea H.M.S. *Repulse*
16 Portsmouth

1927

Apr.
13 Folkestone
Boulogne
13-19 Paris
20-21 Biarritz
22-23 Madrid
23 El Escorial
24-
May
1 Seville
1-3 Granada
3 Cordoba
4-5 Madrid
5 Aranjuez
6-11 Paris
11 Folkestone
July
23 Southampton
23-30 At sea S.S. *Empress of Australia*
30-31 Quebec
31-
Aug.
2 Montreal
2-5 Ottawa
5 Brockville
Thousand Islands
Gananoque
Kingston
6-8 Toronto

Aug.
7 Niagara Falls
Fort Erie
Buffalo
Queenston
On Lake Ontario aboard S.S. *Cayuga*
7-8 Toronto
8 Sudbury
Schreiber
9 Kenora
Winnipeg
Brandon
Broadview
Moose Jaw
10 Calgary
High River
10-12 E.P. Ranch
High River
13 Edmonton
14 High River
14-15 E.P. Ranch
High River
15-16 Calgary
16-17 Banff
17 Lake Louise
Revelstoke
18-19 Vancouver
19 At sea S.S. *Princess Adelaide*

Aug.
19-23 Victoria
23 Vancouver
At sea S.S. *Princess Alice*
Penticton
24 Tadanac
Nelson
24 Proctor
Kootenay Landing
Bonington
25 Kimberley
Cronbrook
Fernie
Crowsnest
Lethbridge
26 Regina
27-28 Winnipeg
28 Fort William
Port Arthur
29-31 Toronto
31-
Sept.
1 Ottawa
1-7 Montreal
7 Quebec
7-14 At sea S.S. *Empress of Scotland*
14 Southampton

1928

Sept.		Oct.		Nov.	
6	Dover	18	Hoima	14-15	Kajiado
	Calais		Masindi	15-16	Camp at Longido
7-8	Marseilles	18-19	Butiaba on Lake Albert aboard S.S. *Baker*	16-17	Arusha
8-11	At sea S.S. *Kaisar-I-Hind*			17-18	Camp at Babati
11-13	Alexandria	19-20	Murchison Falls ,,	18	Kwakuchinga
13-14	Cairo	20	Ndandumure ,,	18-22	Camp at Pinnear's Heights
14	Ismalia		Malisa ,,	22-23	Dodoma
14-17	At sea S.S. *Malda*	20-24	Camp at Kigoya ,,	23-24	Kondoa-Irangi
17	Port Sudan	24	Ndandumure on Lake Albert aboard S.S. *Baker*	24-26	Camp near Nderaida
17-20	At sea S.S. *Malda*			26-27	Camp at Ufiomi
20	Aden	24-25	Ntoroko ,,	27	Kondoa-Irangi
20-28	At sea S.S. *Malda*	25-26	Bushed	27-28	Dodoma
28-30	Mombasa	26	Fort Portal	28-	
Oct.		26-29	Entebbe	Dec.	
1	Simba	29	Jinja	2	Dar-es-Salaam
	Kiu		Tororo	2-5	At sea H.M.S. *Enterprise*
1-7	Nairobi	30	Kitale	5	Aden
7-12	Elmenteita	31-		5-7	At sea H.M.S. *Enterprise*
8	Lake Nakuru	Nov.		7	Suez
9	Gilgil	2	Eldoret	8	Cairo
12-13	Nairobi	2	Rongai		Port Said
14	Kisumu	3-4	Nakuru	8-10	At sea H.M.S. *Enterprise*
14-15	On Lake Victoria aboard S.S. *Clement Hill*	5-6	Nairobi	10	Brindisi
		7-8	Naro Moru	11	Basle
15-18	Entebbe	8	Nyeri		Boulogne
16	Kampala	9-14	Nairobi		Folkestone

1930

Jan.		Mar.		Mar.	
3	Southampton	10	Jinja	30-	
3-7	At sea S.S. *Kenilworth Castle*	10-12	Entebbe	Apr.	
7	Funchal	12-13	Masindi	1	Juba on White Nile aboard S.S. *Omdurman*
7-20	At sea S.S. *Kenilworth Castle*	13	Butiaba on Lake Albert aboard S.S. *Lugard*	Mar.	
20-30	Capetown			31	Kanga ,,
31	De Aar	13-14	Packwatch on White Nile aboard S.S. *Lugard*	Apr.	
	Kimberley	14	Ajai	1	Wanimoke ,,
Feb.		14-16	Camp on Tangri River	1-2	Camp at Lotti ,,
1	Johannesburg	16-17	Packwatch on White Nile aboard S.S. *Lugard*	2	Opari ,,
3	Bulawayo			2-3	Camp at Gambiri ,,
4	Salisbury	17	Asswa River ,,	3-4	Juba ,,
	Umtali	17-18	Wadelai ,,	4-5	Mongulla ,,
5	Beira	18	Orme River ,,	5	Nalek ,,
5-8	At sea S.S. *Modassa*		Mutir ,,	5-6	Bor ,,
8-9	Dar-es-Salaam ,,	18-19	Rhino Camp ,,	7	Shambe ,,
9	Zanzibar ,,	19	Liri ,,	9-10	Bahr el Chazal ,,
10	Tanga ,,	19-20	Laropi ,,	10	Kanga ,,
11	Mombasa ,,	20	Soka Forest ,,	10-11	Lake No ,,
12	Maungu	20-21	Rhino Camp ,,	11-12	Bahr el Zeraf ,,
12-13	Kasigua	21-22	Arua	12-13	Malakal ,,
14-17	Maktaw	22-23	Watsa	13	Kosti
18	Voi	23-24	Camp at Mando	13-15	Khartoum
19-21	Kasigua	24	Majubenque	15	Omdurman
21	Maungu	24-25	Membo	16	Wadi Halfa
22-25	Nairobi	25-27	Camp at Ne Musa	16-17	Aswan
25-28	Camp in Masai Reserve near Kajiado	27	Mgao	17-20	Cairo
		27-28	Okondongue	20	Port Said
28	Kiu	28	Dungu	21-25	At sea S.S. *Rawalpindi*
Mar.		28-29	Wando	25	Marseilles
1	Voi	29	Farage		Lyons
2-9	Nairobi	29-30	Aba		Paris
10	Tororo	30	Yei		Windsor Great Park
			Loka		

1931

Jan.		Jan.		Feb.	
16	London	19-28	At sea S.S. *Oropesa*	4-6	At sea S.S. *Oropesa*
16-17	Paris	28	Hamilton	6	Panama Canal ,,
18	Hendaye	Feb.		7-9	At sea S.S. *Oropesa*
	Santander	1	At sea S.S. *Oropesa*	9	Talara ,,
18-19	At sea S.S. *Oropesa*		Havana ,,		Lobitos ,,
19	Coruna ,,	1-3	At sea S.S. *Oropesa*	10-11	At sea S.S. *Oropesa*
	Vigo ,,	3-4	Jamaica ,,	11	Callao ,,

Feb.
11-15 Lima
15 Arequipa
16 La Raya
16-17 Cuzco
17 Sacsayhuman Fortress
  Chuquibambilla
  Juliaca
  Puno
18-19 On Lake Titicaca aboard S.S. *Inca*
19 Guaqui
  Tiahuanaca
  La Paz
  Calacota
20 Oruro
  Calama
21 Portuzuelo, Antofagasta
  Copiago
21-23 Santiago de Chile
23-27 Viña del Mar
27 Valparaiso
  Santiago de Chile
28 Temuco

Feb.
28 Orsorno
  Puerto Varas
28–
Mar.
1 La Sentinella Is., Lago Llanguihue
1 Ensenada
  Petrohue, Lago Todos los Santos
  Puella
  Lago Aguas Frias
  Puerto Blest, Lago Nahuel Huagi
1-3 Huemul, Bariloche
4 San Antonio
  Puerto Belgrano (Bahia Blanca, B.A.)
4-5 Mar del Plata
5-8 Buenos Aires
9-13 Mar del Plata
13-15 Buenos Aires
15-16 Marion
16-18 Cordoba

Mar.
18-21 Buenos Aires
21 Montevideo
21-25 At sea S.S. *Alcantara*
24 Santos „
25-27 Rio de Janeiro
28-30 São Paulo (by train)
31 Cambara
31–
Apr.
1 Cornelio Pocopio
2 Paulo Souzra
3 São Paulo
4 Belo Horizonte
5-12 Rio de Janeiro
12-25 At sea S.S. *Arlanza*
14 Bahia „
16 Pernambuco „
25 Lisbon „
25-27 At sea H.M.S. *Kent*
27 Bordeaux „
27-29 Paris
  Windsor Great Park

1932

Aug.
11 London
  Paris
12-13 Lido Venice
13 Brindisi
13-16 Corfu
16-18 At sea H.M.S. *Queen Elizabeth*
18-20 Malta
20-22 At sea H.M.S. *Shropshire*
22-24 Cannes
24–
Sept.
13 Biarritz

Sept.
14 Paris
  Windsor Great Park
22 London
22-27 Copenhagen
27 Roskilde
27-28 Bjergbygaard
28-30 Wedellsborg, Fÿn Is.
30 Waldemar Slot, Thun Is.
  Copenhagen
Oct.
1-8 Stockholm
5 Gefle
8 Upsala

Oct.
8-9 Frötuna
9-11 Stockholm
11 Göteborg
12 Malmö
  Falsterbo
12-13 Hamburg
13 Amsterdam
13-14 Le Hague
14 Hook of Holland
14-15 At sea
15 Harwich

1934

Aug.
1 Windsor Great Park
  Paris
2-30 Biarritz
30 St. Jean de Luz
30–
Sept.
1 At sea S.Y. *Rosaura*
1-2 La Coruna „
2 Santiago della Compostella
  Vigo
2-3 Oporto

Sept.
3 Leixoes
3-6 At sea S.Y. *Rosaura*
4 Arenas Gordas Huelva „
5 Cabo de Gato Almeria „
6 Palma „
6-9 Formentor „
9-10 At sea „
10 Ajaccio „
10-11 Calvi „
11-16 Cannes „
15 St. Tropez „

Sept.
16-17 At sea S.Y. *Rosaura*
17 Genoa „
  Milan
17-23 Como „
23 Arona
  Lausanne
  Vallorbe
24-25 Paris
  Windsor Great Park

1935

Feb.
4 London
  Calais
5-17 Kitzbuhl
18-20 Vienna
20-24 Budapest
25 Vienna
  Munich
26-28 Paris
  Windsor Great Park

Aug.
5 Paris
Sept.
9 Cannes
10 Geneva
11-16 Budapest
16-20 Vienna
20 St. Polten
  Linz

Sept.
20 Gmunden
20-24 St. Wolfgang
24 Salzburg
  Herren Chiemsee
24-25 Munich
26–
Oct.
2 Paris
  Windsor Great Park

1936

Aug.
8 Windsor Great Park
  Calais
9 Salzburg

Aug.
10 Sibernik
  Aboard S.Y. *Nahlin*
10-11 Port Tajer „

Aug.
11-12 Rab S.Y. *Nahlin*
12-13 Planeski „
13-14 Brgulje Bay „

MY JOURNEYS

Aug.
14–15 Trogir   S.Y. *Nahlin*
15–16 Stari Grad   ,,
16–17 Korcula   ,,
17–19 Dubrovnik   ,,
19   Kotor   ,,
20–22 Corfu   ,,
22–24 Cephalonia Is.   ,,
24–25 Itea   ,,
25   Corinth Canal   ,,
25–29 Piraeus, Athens   ,,
29–30 At sea   ,,
30–31 Karistos Bay, Ubea   ,,

Aug.
31–
Sept.
1   Graltra Bay   S.Y. *Nahlin*
1–2   Skiathos   ,,
2–4   At sea   ,,
3   Gallipoli Peninsula   ,,
    Cape Hellas   ,,
    Anzac Cove   ,,
    Dardanelles   ,,
4   Sea of Marmara   ,,
4–6   Istanbul   ,,
5   Bosporus   ,,

Sept.
6   Prinkipo Is.   S.Y. *Nahlin*
7   Sofia
    Belgrade
8   Budapest
8–13   Vienna
14   Zurich
    Paris
    Windsor Great Park

INDEX

Throughout this Index all references to the DUKE apply to the Duke of Windsor

INDEX

436

his marriage, 258; wedding of Duke of Gloucester, 258; death of Princess Victoria, 259; resignation of Sir Samuel Hoare, 259; fails to broach problem to King George V, 259–60; hears of King George V's failing health, 261; realizes King George's life is ending, 262; reports to Baldwin, 262; in Council of State, 263; at King George's deathbed, 264; is proclaimed King Edward VIII, 264–5
King Edward VIII
Arranges funeral of King George V, 265–6; accompanies his father's body to London, 266–7; impressed by a bad omen, 267; receives foreign dignitaries, 268; joins officers on guard at King George V's lying in state, 269; at funeral, 269; first days as King, 270–1; his welcome as King, 271–2; gives audience to Dr. Lang, 272–3; first intimation of conflict, 274; his new obligations, 275; his time wasted on formalities, 276; his conservative outlook, 277; his desire for success, 278; on the monarchy in modern society, 278–81; his innovations, 281; first signs of disapproval, 281–3; changes annual routine, 283–4; his first broadcast as King, 284–5; his reaction to Hitler's reoccupation of Rhineland, 286–7; his daily routine, 287; his "field work," 288–9; responsibility for Royal Establishment, 289; on operation of Civil List, 291–2; his retrenchment at Sandringham, 292–3; attempts to break a tradition, 293–4; and resignation of J. H. Thomas, 295; refuses to receive Haile Selassie, 296; disagrees with treatment of Mussolini, 297; and "The Dastardly Attempt," 297–9; holds a garden party, 300–1; appoints new members of Royal Household, 302–4; inaugurates monument at Vimy Ridge, 305; plans cruise in Adriatic, 305; is advised to avoid Italy, 306; is pursued by American journalist, 307; cruises along Balkan coast, 307–8; returns via Bulgaria, Yugoslavia and Austria, 308–10; presents York House to Duke of Gloucester, 312; his first house-party at Balmoral, 312–13; resides at Buckingham Palace, 313–14; his marriage to Mrs. Simpson predicted by American Press, 314; enlists aid of Beaverbrook and Harmsworth, 315; receives Baldwin, 316–18; seeks advice of Walter Monckton, 318–19, 328–9; receives news of Mrs. Simpson's decree nisi, 320; re-

ceives Ribbentrop, 321–2; at State Opening of Parliament, 322–5; visits Home Fleet, 325; is warned of coming clash over Mrs. Simpson, 326–7; acquaints Mrs. Simpson with problem, 329; appeals to Beaverbrook, 330; informs Baldwin of his intention to marry Mrs. Simpson, 330–2; informs Queen Mary and the Princess Royal of his intentions, 333–4; informs his brothers, 335; visits South Wales coalfields, 336–8; seeks political advice, 339–40; hears suggestion of morganatic marriage, 341; pursues possibility of morganatic marriage, 342; requests Baldwin to submit morganatic proposition to Dominions, 343–4; receives advice from Beaverbrook, 345; hears Cabinet decision, 346; warned by Beaverbrook of Dominions reaction, 347; takes Mrs. Simpson to The Fort, 348; and Bishop of Bradford's public criticism, 349–50; sees provincial Press reports, 351; informed of Cabinet decision, 352; advised by Beaverbrook to permit attack on decision, 353–4; informed by Baldwin of choice to be made, 355; approves Mrs. Simpson's leaving England, 356; decides to propose broadcast to nation, 356–7; shocked by Press attacks, 358; arranges Mrs. Simpson's departure, 359–60, 362–3; composes broadcast speech, 361; discusses his decision with Mrs. Simpson's aunt, 363–4; proposes broadcast to Baldwin, 365; sends draft of speech to Churchill, 365; visits Queen Mary, 365; receives adverse advice on speech, 366; withdraws from London to The Fort, 367; besieged by Press, 370; his helpers throughout crisis, 371–2; support from Press and public, 373–4; telephoned by Mrs. Simpson, 376; rejection of broadcast proposal, 377; receives dispatches from Dominions, 378; is pressed by Baldwin for decision, 379; receives heartening messages, 380; receives Churchill, 381; is informed of Churchill's support and intentions, 382–3; his desire to prevent disunity, 383; and the "King's Party," 384–6; decides to abdicate, 387; his position after abdication, 387; his proposed Divorce Bill accepted by Baldwin, 389; his case stated by Churchill, 390–1; discusses Divorce Bill with Baldwin, 391; his Divorce Bill rejected by Ministers, 393; supported by Churchill in the House, 394; his marriage threatened by "con-